ELIZABETH AND
LEICESTER

Elizabeth Jenkins was educated at St Christopher School, Letchworth, and Newnham College, Cambridge. A distinguished novelist, historian and biographer she was awarded the Femina Vie Heureuse Prize in 1934 for her novel *Harriet*, and she received the OBE in 1981.

Also by Elizabeth Jenkins

The Winters
Lady Caroline Lamb
Harriet
The Phoenix's Nest
Jane Austen
Robert and Helen
Young Enthusiasts
Henry Fielding
Six Criminal Women
The Tortoise and the Hare
Ten Fascinating Women
The Princes in the Tower (Phoenix Press)
Brightness
Honey
Dr Gully
The Mystery of King Arthur
Elizabeth the Great (Phoenix Press)
The Shadow and the Light
A Silent Joy

ELIZABETH AND LEICESTER

Elizabeth Jenkins

PHOENIX
PRESS

5 UPPER SAINT MARTIN'S LANE
LONDON
WC2H 9EA

A PHOENIX PRESS PAPERBACK

First published in Great Britain
by Victor Gollancz in 1961
This paperback edition published in 2002
by Phoenix Press,
a division of The Orion Publishing Group Ltd,
Orion House, 5 Upper St Martin's Lane,
London WC2H 9EA

Phoenix Press
Sterling Publishing Co Inc
387 Park Avenue South
New York
NY 10016-8810
USA

Printed and bound in Great Britain by
Butler and Tanner Ltd, Frome and London

ISBN 1 84212 560 5

PREFACE

THIS BOOK IS not a definitive biography of Lord Leicester. A great deal of material about him is in print, but so much of it is fragmentary and diffused that in the interests of coherent narrative I thought it best to depict only the most interesting aspect of his life and character. This, in my view, is the hold he maintained over the affections of Queen Elizabeth. I have therefore used, broadly speaking, only the material which illustrates his personality and the Queen's and the history of their relationship. Some of Leicester's activities, of much interest in themselves, such as his trading ventures and the schemes for mining and for the production of copper ore in which he engaged with Lord Burleigh and Sir Thomas Smith, since they have no bearing on this theme, have been omitted. On the same principle I have reduced to a minimum the account of his military operations in the Netherlands.

The work covers much of the same period as my book *Elizabeth the Great*, and though most of it treats of matters not included in the latter, to make the present book an independent whole it has sometimes been necessary to repeat what any reader of the previous one will have read before. The period is so fully documented, however, that I have in most cases been able to choose fresh details to illustrate facts already set out.

I would mention here that though the date of Lord Leicester's birth was said by Camden to be that of Queen Elizabeth's, which was September 7th, 1533, it is sometimes given by modern writers as June 24th, 1532. This date is derived from George Adlard, who, ignoring Camden, says (*Amy Robsart and the Earl of Leicester*, London, 1870): "Robert Dudley was born on the 24th of June, 1532 [*sic*]. The date of his birth is not given by any historian. I discovered it in one of his letters to Queen Elizabeth in which he says, 'This is my birthday'." Adlard does not give the year in which this letter was written, nor does he say where he found it. Until someone else should find it, it seems allowable to retain Camden's date as the correct one.

In making acknowledgments I must first record the debt I owe to

Dr. A. L. Rowse, not only for his directing me to sources of unparalleled importance, including the *Letters of Thomas Wood* in the Special Supplement No. 5 of the Bulletin of Historical Research, but for the privilege of his conversation on the subject of Lord Leicester, some brief spells of which were packed with such information and charged with such encouragement and inspiration as only a master could convey.

My especial thanks are due: to Miss Enid Welsford of Newnham College, who first assured me that material for this book existed, and directed me to Professor C. E. Mounts' valuable paper, "*Spenser and the Countess of Leicester*"; to Miss Joan Bulman, who brought to my attention Fridolf Ödberg's *Om Princessan Cecilia Wasa* and translated a passage of it for me; and to Miss N. McN. O'Farrell for her sympathetic co-operation in transcribing documents in the Public Record Office and the MSS. Department of the British Museum.

Finally I must thank Mr. and Mrs. Watney of Cornbury Park, Oxfordshire, for their delightful hospitality and their kindness in showing me the room where Lord Leicester died.

E. J.

NOTE ON REFERENCES

References indicated in the text by numerals will be found on page 374.

I

T HE DUDLEY FAMILY produced, in three successive generations, three men whose careers, end to end, almost equalled the span of the dynasty of the Tudors, the great reigning house from whose fortunes they quarried their own.

The foundation of the Dudleys' enterprise was laid by Edmund Dudley, financial minister to Henry VII. This King had succeeded to the Crown in 1485 at the end of a long and hideous civil war. He founded that ruling family which produced three of the most able sovereigns who ever sat upon the English throne, of which he himself was the first. Henry showed his insight into the conditions of the modern world by his grasp of the principle that Money is Power. The amassing of money was doubly desirable in his eyes, since getting it both strengthened the Crown and weakened the crew of powerful and dangerous subjects from whom he extorted it. As a monarch whose aim was first to restore order and then to keep it, Henry VII believed that, provided he could do this, the bulk of the nation, sickened beyond bearing by thirty years of fighting between the Houses of Lancaster and York, would not criticize him too sharply for the way in which it was done. He had good grounds for thinking so, and in the end he was proved right, but the inventive genius of his financial ministers very nearly overset this calculation.

Edmund Dudley came of a professional family connected with the barony of Dudley. He was a member of Gray's Inn, and, in a very small society where the qualities of each person were easily recognized, his uncommon ability attracted the notice of Henry VII, who took over his entire services. He was associated with another very able lawyer, Richard Empson, and the pair of them were told that the King required the transfer of the greatest possible quantity of private wealth to the Crown. How this was to be done was left to them. The two commissioners thereupon began a system of extortion which, in its devilish ingenuity and its merciless rapacity, was like nothing known in England before or since. Bacon said they turned justice into wormwood rapine, Holinshed called them two ravening wolves. Though their gains were made for a master whom they dared not cheat, they had ample chances to enrich themselves, and the hatred they aroused was heightened by the knowledge that, of the great heaps of money that passed through their hands, no mean quantity stuck to their fingers.

On the death of Henry VII, public fury demanded vengeance on them. The young Henry VIII, who had inherited the comfortable sum of four and half million pounds in money of the time owing to the commissioners' exertions, made a popular gesture by sacrificing them, and they were both indicted on the capital charge of treason. This was possible because when Henry VII was dying the commissioners, fearing that mob violence would break out against them when their master should be dead, had collected armour in their houses and urged some of their friends to do the same. This was paraphrased as a conspiracy to over-awe the City of London.

The three Dudleys who became eminent, Edmund Dudley, his son, John Dudley, Duke of Northumberland, and his grandson, Robert Dudley, Earl of Leicester, had these traits in common: they combined a degree of ruthless self-interest, rare even for the times in which they lived, with a strong turn for edifying other people. Strangely as it might come from their lips, moral conversation was almost their hobby. While Edmund Dudley sat in the Tower awaiting execution, he composed a treatise which he called *The Tree of Commonwealth*. In it he discussed the evils inherent in the body politic, especially those of greed and corruption, into which his professional experience had allowed him to gain unusual insight. "Not," he wrote in his opening pages, "that I am of ability in any condition to counsel or advise any living creature, mine own life hath been so wicked and so openly known." He went on to do it, none the less. The treatise defended the claims of absolute government, centred in the person of the King, and showed that failure to exercise a just authority caused demoralization in every walk of life. Dudley's reforming eye surveyed domestic as well as social and political abuses, and his wholesome strictures on spoilt children did the heart good to read. Here, it seemed, was an enlightened and practical moralist whose views, if attended to, would make the world a better place. *The Tree of Commonwealth* was a characteristic production in that it was an admirable piece of work. It showed a remarkable penetration and power of constructive criticism. The remarks made on corruption were true, and the man who made them knew that they were true; they could not be called hypocritical, yet unexpected they certainly were. Though in the last resort Henry VII himself was responsible for Dudley's acts, since the King gave his orders and shut his eyes to the way they were performed, Dudley's fitness for the task, the resource he brought to bear on it and the relish with which he carried it out made him rightly the victim of public hatred, and, though the means taken to remove him and his partner were unjust, their execution in the first year of the new reign was the only imaginable retribution for a career of enthusiastic villainy.

At the time of his father's taking-off, John Dudley was a boy of eight. He was given in ward to Sir Edward Guildford, who was very kind to him, whose daughter Jane he afterwards married, and whose surname he gave as a Christian name to one of his children. The consummate ability he showed gained him the favour and confidence of Henry VIII, and a career of continuous advancement as soldier, sailor, administrator and statesman. His father's attainder was cancelled, and he was allowed to take the title of Lord Lisle, which was in his mother's family. He served as Deputy-Governor of Calais, that last fragment of the conquests of Henry V remaining in English hands; he was Warden of the Scots Marches; he was appointed Master of the Horse to the luckless Anne of Cleves on her arrival in England in 1540. In 1542 he was made Great Admiral, in 1543 Privy Councillor and Knight of the Garter. In this next year he led the assault which Henry made on Boulogne, and when the port fell temporarily into English hands Dudley was made its Governor. His professional abilities were widely recognized, his reputation as a soldier long outlived him. He had, however, none of the brusqueness that sometimes goes with a martial character. Dudley had an unusual perception of other people's feelings, and it seemed to delight him, as a subtle exercise of power, to please and soothe and gain golden opinions for himself. Hypocrisy was too crude a word for his playing on the emotions he so acutely estimated.

The well-bred, well-spoken man had one consuming passion: the advancement of himself and his children. Of thirteen born to him, seven survived adolescence; five sons, John, Henry, Ambrose, Guildford and Robert, and two daughters, Mary and Katherine. He loved them, they admired and loved him in their turn; and the warmth and tenderness between the surviving brothers and their sisters was a sign of that strong family feeling which existed inside the enclave of the Dudley household, a self-contained world created by Dudley and his wife for their children and themselves, inside which all the domestic virtues were cherished, while the world outside it was treated as the haunt of a savage beast foraging for its young.

On the death of Henry VIII in 1547, the accession of a small boy, the nine-year-old Edward VI, placed the chief powers in the hands of the little King's uncle, Edward Seymour, who was left as Lord Protector of the Realm. Seymour made the King create him Duke of Somerset, and at the same time the Earldom of Warwick, which had lapsed for sixty years, was re-created for John Dudley. The cognizance of the Nevilles, who had last held the title, was the Bear and Ragged Staff, and when John Dudley obtained the Warwick earldom he adopted the cognizance as his own. For the next forty years it was one of the most famous devices in England.

The being who was to raise the fortunes of the Dudley family to their highest point, was not yet recognized as its lodestar. In July, 1549, the Princess Elizabeth was within two months of her seventeenth birthday. From the great King, her admired and dreaded father, she had received an upbringing which combined the intensive education due to a very clever child with the rigorous social training of a Princess. Her intellect and her personal magnetism, her learning and acquirements had come to her from King Henry VIII; at his hands also she had received a nervous injury so deep-seated and severe that it had left her with a life-long incapacity to submit herself to a normal sexual relationship.

When she was two years and eight months old her mother Ann Boleyn was beheaded on a five-fold charge of adultery. Just before her arrest, the Queen was seen in the courtyard of Greenwich Palace holding up her little girl in her arms, in a despairing attempt to win a smile from the angry King as he stood frowning in a window above them. Three days later she was committed to the Tower, where her head was cut off on May 19th, three years to the very month after the spectacular triumph of her coronation.

This was the first of a series of domestic events assuring Elizabeth, before her mind could defend itself by reason, that sexual intercourse was the bringer-on of some terrifying form of death. When she was four years old the King's third wife, Jane Seymour, achieved, at the expense of her own life, the feat of bearing him a living son. The association of her brother's birth with the death, after prolonged agonies, of his mother was one but too familiar in many households, but it was followed four years later by a third event, dreadful in itself and to Elizabeth an unspeakable calamity, for it repeated the horror of her mother's death at a time when she herself, no longer protected by infancy, had her faculties wide awake. When she was eight years and five months old the King's fifth wife, Katherine Howard, her mother's cousin, her young, enchanting step-mother, was suddenly brought to book as Ann Boleyn had been. When confined to her rooms in Hampton Court during an investigation, Katherine escaped from her guards and tried to reach the King in the chapel where he was at Mass. She was caught before she had reached the end of the gallery, and dragged back, uttering such screams that the spot is said to be haunted still. Accused, convicted of adultery, the young Queen was brought to the block early in the morning of a day in February. Her head and headless body, wrapped in a sheet, were carried into the chapel on Tower Green and buried under the flags where Elizabeth's mother was already lying. Within this year, while she was still called eight years old, Elizabeth said, "I will never marry".

She said it to another child of eight years old, Dudley's fifth son, Robert Dudley. The boy to whom she said it did not believe her, the men to whom in later years she repeated it did not believe her, but she had said it, and time was to show the implacable force of her determination.

When she reached years of discretion she preserved, with very few exceptions, a death-like silence over her mother's name; but she would seem to have thought much about this passionate, reckless woman, whose death lay like a pit in the road of her own young life. She gave signs in her later years that the memory of which she did not speak was living in her; she was strongly drawn to her mother's relatives and the descendants of her mother's friends, and the crowned falcon stamped on the bindings of Queen Elizabeth's books was a cognizance of Ann Boleyn's.

In the portrait at Windsor Castle, painted when Elizabeth was not more than fourteen, for it is listed in the inventory of the King's pictures made for Edward VI in the first year of his reign, many aspects of the Princess's childhood have been conveyed. She is shown as a young lady much given to her books; she holds one in her right hand, with the fingers of her left within its leaves, while a much larger volume is propped, open, on a stand at her elbow. The physical traits familiar in the portraits of Elizabeth as Queen are recognizable in the child's portrait: the long, oval outline of cheek and chin that was her mother's, the acquiline nose and the arched, delicately pencilled eyebrows that had been such incongruous features in her father's fleshy and brutal face; the hands with fingers of exotic length and slenderness; and, shining out against the sombre background, the Tudor colouring of white skin, gold-brown eyes and reddish-golden hair. The softness of the childish features is strangely at variance with the unnatural wariness of the eyes. The leading qualities of Elizabeth's temperament were, indeed, those bestowed by remarkable intelligence, but a strain of hysteria was markedly present among them. Her passionate weeping, her raging anger, have caused the word hysterical to be applied to her, but the ascription proves much truer than is usually the case in a casual use of medical terms. Modern clinical descriptions of hysteria go very far to explain the effect upon her of her circumstances and to illuminate some of the most debated actions and tendencies of her life. Hysterical subjects, it is said, are almost always found to be suffering from some form of sexual inadequacy; they have frequently been deprived of affection in early childhood, a condition which has bred in them an insatiable demand for attention; above all, they develop a capacity for preventing the right hand from knowing what the left hand is doing. When she had passed beyond the restraints and limitations of childhood, Elizabeth showed all three of these symptoms most strongly.

The first fourteen years of Elizabeth's life had been an era of severe training, of exacting routine, impressed with the consciousness of her father's overbearing majesty and his supernatural importance; in the sphere where family love and the security derived from it should have been, there was a blank. Yet some objects of affection were within her view, and to these the child clung with a tenacious, demanding, passionate emotion. The first was her governess, Katherine Ashley, who had been with her since she was four and fulfilled at least two of the functions of a mother, by wholly loving and admiring her, and by being always there. The second was her brother Edward. The latter's importance, first as King Henry's longed-for son, and then, at nine years old, as King himself, added a lustre to the attractiveness he had for Elizabeth as her small brother. That her feeling for him was genuine, however, was obvious to everyone who saw them, and also that her brother returned it. Shortly before their father's death their two households had been under one roof in the Palace of Hatfield. When they were separated by arbitrary decree sent through the Privy Council, and Elizabeth wrote lamenting their departure from this favourite place, Edward's reply, written in Latin, began: "Change of place, my dearest sister, did not vex me so much as your going from me." After Edward's accession, the time spent by the brother and sister in each other's company was very brief; the intimacy was maintained by Elizabeth's own letters, in which she never failed to assure him of her fondness: "I, who have ever been your Majesty's most loving sister."

Such expressions came from her pen in every letter; but the third object of her affection was one for whom she could not publicly avow her feelings. They transpired in spite of herself.

Lord Thomas Seymour, the younger of Edward's uncles, was furiously resentful that the office of Protector had been bestowed on his brother instead of being divided between his brother and himself. He planned and began rapidly to execute a scheme of political brigandage which was meant to wrest the power from Somerset, but which within two years brought Seymour himself to the block.

The Will of Henry VIII, confirmed by Parliament as the Act of Succession, left the Crown first to his own children in the order of Edward, Mary and Elizabeth. Should none of these leave an heir, it was to go to the descendants of his younger sister Mary, who had first been obliged to marry the old King Louis XII of France and on his death had become the wife of the man she loved, Charles Brandon, Duke of Suffolk. The heiress of this family was her daughter, Frances Brandon, now the wife of Lord Henry Grey, Marquess of Dorset. This lady, however, was passed over by the treason-brokers. Already married, so that the bestowal of her hand could form no part of a conspiracy, she had furthermore lost her male children, and her family now consisted of three daughters. By and large, it was clear that no wide support could be expected for a rebellion to put the Marchioness of Dorset on the throne. But this woman's heiress and eldest daughter, the Lady Jane Grey, was a very different proposition. She would marry and bear sons. Like her cousins Edward and Elizabeth, she was remarkable for the ease with which she learned Greek and Latin, and for the unchildlike seriousness of her cast of mind; like them, also, she had a quality of her own, not immediately recognized, which in her case was to prove disastrous to the criminals who exploited her. This child, eleven years old at the time of King Henry's death, formed with Edward and Elizabeth the trio which it was essential to Seymour's purposes to win over to himself. The Princess Mary he had already discounted: he had tried to ingratiate himself by offering her the services of a man to mend her musical instruments, but the mature Princess, reserved, clear-sighted and disapproving, had civilly but decidedly rebuffed his overtures. With Edward, Elizabeth and Jane, nine, fourteen and eleven years old respectively, he was sanguine of success. Tall and handsome, with red hair and beard, jovial and high-spirited, Seymour, for all that he possessed the total selfishness of the criminal, was extremely attractive to many people, notably to women, children and servants. Among the little to his credit was the strong faithfulness he inspired in the members of his household.

As soon as Henry VIII was dead, Seymour approached the Council to know if he might marry the Princess Elizabeth. Receiving a blunt refusal, he thereupon proposed to and was accepted by the King's widow, Katherine Parr. The Queen Dowager was thirty-four, a pretty, attractive woman who had once refused Seymour in favour of the King and now surrendered completely to an infatuation for him. She married Seymour secretly. Her passion was soon crowned with the delight of a first pregnancy, and it seemed that Katherine Parr had entered on a radiant Indian summer.

But an unsuspected danger revealed itself. She had always been very kind to Elizabeth, and on the King's death the Council, knowing nothing of her marriage plans, allowed her to have the Princess to live with her, Elizabeth's household forming a separate unit in that of her step-mother. Under the same roof with this pale, enigmatic child who had been schooled to a reserve and discretion beyond her years, Seymour now set himself to gain her affections. One day the Queen Dowager came unexpectedly into the room, and found her husband with Elizabeth in his arms.

The situation was appalling. Katherine had to contend not only with an abominable shock but with a state of actual danger, for she was responsible to the Council for the safe-keeping of the King's young sister. She arranged for Elizabeth's household to be moved at once to Cheshunt in Hertfordshire, to the house of Sir Anthony Denny. Elizabeth's departure was made at Whitsun, and she went in a state of agitation that was the preliminary to a long-drawn-out nervous collapse. Into the Maytime scenery of Hertfordshire, of green fields and dazzling may-bushes on the banks of winding streams, she carried shame, remorse, compunction towards her kind step-mother, the agony of an abrupt severance from Seymour, and the warring of passion with those deep-buried instincts which told her that the wages of sin is death. The crisis occurred in May, and Mrs. Ashley said afterwards in evidence: "She was first sick about mid-summer", and that she was so generally ailing that for a whole year Mrs. Ashley herself never went above a mile from the house.

In this state Elizabeth had one sheet anchor. The year before her young tutor, William Grindal, had died of the plague, and after a period of consultation Roger Ascham had been appointed in his place. The Queen Dowager had suggested Mr. Goldsmith, but Mr. Ascham had already made an impression on the Princess, and

Elizabeth's wishes were allowed to prevail. In February, 1548, Ascham took up the appointment. It was not perhaps without significance that Ascham's wife was a connection of Mrs. Ashley's husband, and that the Ashleys were distantly related to the Boleyns; but whatever mingling of motives had guided her, Elizabeth's choice was an early instance of her unerring selection of men. Ascham was the educational genius of the century. Not only was he a brilliant teacher, but his cast of mind was enlightened to a degree never yet surpassed. He expressed his loathing of the brutal severity commonly used by masters. The schoolhouse, said Ascham, was in general a place of torment, but it should be "a refuge against fear". This inspiring idea he embodied in his teaching of his most famous pupil. He not only calmed her nerves by leading her on to work at which she would excel, but he chose passages from the poets and historians for her to study which he thought would teach her about the trials which must be encountered in this world, and how to arm the mind against them. That by modern standards he worked her much too hard will scarcely be gainsaid, and the racking headaches with which she was visited during the next few years must partly no doubt be laid at his door; but he imparted a sense of stability to her desperate existence, and she seized upon the support he gave with a passionate tenacity.

Three months after sending Elizabeth away, the Queen Dowager was brought to bed of a daughter. In the delirium of puerperal fever, the words of a piteous hallucination came from her moaning lips; she said that those to whom she wished most good stood about her, laughing at her harms. Within a week of the confinement she was dead, and Seymour was free to embark upon his plans.

In the custom of the time, by which the children of noblemen spent some years in the household of their parents' friends, Jane Grey was living in the Queen Dowager's family at the time of Katherine's death. Though an inmate of the same household as Elizabeth until the latter's sudden departure in May, 1548, no record remains of any intercourse between the young ladies. The size of the combined households made it possible for the various members to avoid each other if they so wished, and Jane Grey's intensely moral outlook, combined with a complete outspokenness about her views, may have made her an uncongenial companion to a repressed but high-spirited and haughty cousin, three years older than herself.

On the death of the lady of the house, though Seymour's old mother was there to act as chaperone, Dorset said his daughter must come home. This was natural enough, but the father's letter revealed the disagreeable attitude of his wife and himself towards their child, and confirms the account of the situation which Jane Grey afterwards gave to Ascham. The independent and moral nature of the daughter had exasperated, indeed outraged both her parents, and from the evidence of the girl herself, who was both courageous and innately truthful, it was clear that their behaviour could not be ascribed merely to the strictness of the times, but that they perpetually revenged themselves on her by a morbid and pathological severity. Jane Grey once told Ascham that her love of reading sprang from the fact that her parents treated her with such unkindness, while her tutor, John Aylmer, was gentle and sympathetic to her. Whatever she did in her parents' presence, they watched it for the slightest imperfection, and made it the occasion for tauntings, cruel threats and physical violence which, she said, "I will not name for the honour I bear them". The result was that she fled to her kind tutor and his instruction with such eagerness, the hours of her lessons went all too fast, and when they were done she shrank and wept at the prospect of facing her savage tormentors again.

With this domestic background a child of Jane Grey's age, even of Jane Grey's temperament, might well feel drawn to Lord Thomas Seymour, especially as Seymour's plans for her disposal did not involve a romantic approach by himself, which would have startled her. Indeed, his scheme for her was altogether different. He restored her to her parents the month after Katherine Parr's death, but at the end of that September he summoned the father and mother to London for a highly confidential interview. He assured the Dorsets: "If I may once get the King at liberty, I dare warrant you that his Majesty shall marry none other than Jane." The Dorsets were agog at the idea, and the fatal ambition that their daughter should wear the crown, thus planted, never left them. It outlived its originator, and four years later it killed its victim.

Meanwhile, Seymour's plans, including as they did the kidnapping of the King and bearing him off to Holt Castle, and the suborning of the Master of the Bristol Mint to strike bucketsful of money for raising fifteen thousand men at arms, were so incompetently and rashly handled that the Council had a long indictment of his offences all ready drawn up when he precipitated his own arrest. Late at night, Edward's spaniel gave the alarm, and the guard found Seymour attempting to enter the King's bedchamber. He was arrested, and in the early hours of January 18, 1549, he was taken to the Tower.

The King and Jane Grey were not personally implicated in the attainder of Seymour for high treason, but on his third victim, Elizabeth, the result of his arrest fell with crushing injury. One of the most serious of the many offences charged against him was that he had attempted, without the Council's permission, to marry one of the heiresses to the throne. This constituted high treason on his part, and if it could be proved that the Princess had accepted a clandestine proposal then she too was guilty of high treason, for which, in an extremity, she might be either beheaded or burned alive, whichever the sovereign should decree. Elizabeth was able to prove, what was confirmed by the independent testimony of Mrs. Ashley and of Parry, her treasurer, that, whatever Seymour's plans for secretly marrying her might have been, he had not discussed them with either her or her servants. So far as they were concerned, the matter was always spoken of as contingent on the Council's permission. The lethal danger was thus avoided, but the depositions of Mrs. Ashley and Parry went into all the details of Seymour's familiarities, his love-making under his wife's roof, and Elizabeth's being sent away to Cheshunt.

The making public of these experiences, and the foreseeing of Seymour's inevitable fate, were the culmination of a train of terrors and griefs; the child of fifteen-and-a-half was attacked by spells of nervous prostration, when she was too weak to leave her bed.

But one resource remained to her, one lenitive, one refuge, the refuge Ascham had prepared for her. She clung to it with despair. She could not bring herself to resign his help, his guidance, the mental distraction he provided, for even the shortest time. In July, his friend William Ireland had written inviting him to come to Cambridge to put up at St. John's College and be present at a meeting of the Senate. Ascham would have enjoyed the small expedition very much, and Cambridge and Cheshunt were not far distant, but he found it could not be. The accomplished young lady was holding him with the grasp of a terrified child. He wrote in Latin to Ireland from Cheshunt on July 8th, 1549: "I would willingly have come to see you all . . . had not my illustrious mistress prevented me . . . she never lets me go away anywhere."

Ascham's appointment to Elizabeth, which he held from 1548–1551, was the most rewarding experience of his professional career, but he had several interesting pupils. He had taught Edward VI to write, and he had taught Latin to Robert Dudley; he may therefore have taught all the Dudley children. It is often asserted that Robert Dudley shared Elizabeth's lessons with Ascham; there is no evidence that they were taught together, only that Ascham taught both of them. Their bents were not the same. Robert Dudley could have become a good Latin scholar, but he disappointed Ascham by preferring mathematics. Elizabeth had an excellent head for figures, but her passion was history; she would study the same period in as many different books as she could find, and she liked to spend two or three hours a day on this subject. What Ascham, however, found most remarkable in her was her capacity for learning languages. At seventeen she read and wrote Greek, Latin, French, Italian, Spanish and Flemish with ease, and she spoke all of them fluently except Greek. Ascham could not reconcile himself to Robert Dudley's preferring to give his time to mathematics rather than to the study of the classics. He told his pupil later: "You did yourself injury in exchanging Tully's wisdom for Euclid's pricks and lines." John Dudley saw to it that all his boys were well educated— Ascham paid him this tribute—but he was particularly careful to see that Ambrose and Robert, especially, were given a social training as well. They were kept in close attendance on the young King, and though it attracted no comment, or none that survived, Robert kept up an intimate childish and then youthful friendship with the Princess Elizabeth.

Robert Dudley did not at first seem the brother out of the five destined for particular advancement; the hierarchical character of family life tended to diminish the importance of sons from the heir downwards. But the personal factor, as always, counteracted all others, and of the two who were to survive to a later reign it was not the elder brother, the honest, amiable Ambrose, but Robert, who showed himself to have inherited the complex character of the father and, on a lesser scale, his many-sided, suspect abilities.

A much worse man than Somerset, but infinitely more capable, John Dudley saw that a ruthless course of undermining could not fail to bring Somerset down, and that when he was down he himself was the only successor. Fate enabled him, in the next three years, to take gigantic strides to power. An expedition against Scotland failed of its object, to force the Scots to agree to the betrothal of the six-year-old Mary, Queen of Scots, to Edward VI, but it left Scotland, as far as Edinburgh, devastated by slaughter and fire. Somerset was officially in command of the expedition, but the success had been Dudley's, and the latter returned with a reputation formidably increased. 1549 marked another stage in the development of his engulfing might. The enclosure of lands for sheep-farming, with the consequent decay of agriculture, culminated in outbreaks of rebellion in the West, and in a more serious, organized form in Norwich under Robert Kett. A force was despatched to Norwich under Lord Northampton, a man without martial ability or force of character. He entered Norwich but was thrown out of it again, and it was clear that the disciplined force under Kett would soon have a very dangerous ascendancy. Dudley was again marching on Scotland, but a message from the Council halted him, ordering him to return and take command of the action at Norwich. Dudley did so, and *en route* he wrote a letter to the Council addressed to the Secretary, William Cecil. All he had to say was that he was moving at his best speed to give all the help in his power, but that he did not want the titular command at the expense of Lord Northampton. A mere honest soldier would have felt no need to explain his motives, he would have assumed that they must be plain as day; but Dudley luxuriated in the sensation of showing how tactful, how considerate, how modest a great general could be when dealing even with such a noodle as Lord Northampton. "My Lord Northampton," he wrote, "by misfortune hath received discouragement enough; haply this might give him occasion to think himself utterly discredited, and so forever discourage him. I shall be as glad for my part to join with him, yea with all my heart to serve under him, as I would be to have the whole authority myself." On and on he went, with exultant generosity and tenderness: "I would wish that no man, for one mischance or evil hap, to which all be subject, should be utterly abject."[1] This delicately minded approach was followed by an exhibition of military genius that overpowered the rebellion and left it permanently extinguished. Dudley in three days completed the subjugation of Kett's forces, and with the grasp of a great soldier refrained his men from unnecessary killing; riding alone into the rebel ranks, he promised mercy to all who submitted. It was not his fault that these promises were afterwards dishonoured.

Without overt signs of triumph, with unruffled courtesy towards Lord Northampton, Dudley now prepared to advance upon the seat of power. Dissensions between Somerset and the Council had meanwhile reached such a pitch that the Protector hurried the young King away in the night to Hampton Court, and there announced to a gathering crowd that if the Lords intended his death the King should die before him. His enemies themselves could not make him out more unfit for the office of Protector than he showed himself. Within a week he was a prisoner in the Tower, and Dudley's assumption of the chief powers of the realm was unchallenged. His offices included those of Lord Great Master of the Household, President of the Council, Lord Warden General of the North, Earl Marshal of England.

In February, 1550, Somerset was released and, though deprived of office, was given a seat on the Council. The ambassador to Charles V, Sir Richard Moryson, said of Dudley: "He had such a head that he seldom went about anything but he conceived three or four purposes beforehand"; and in June of this year he made a family alliance with Somerset, when his eldest son, John Lord Lisle, was married to Somerset's daughter, Lady Ann Seymour. The alliance must have seemed to Dudley an insurance against some contingency: Somerset had held supreme power, he might have had it in him to rise again. The wedding, whatever its object, was celebrated on June 3rd, 1550, at Somerset's palace of Sheen. On the following day the palace was the scene of another wedding in the Dudley family. This was much less distinguished in its connections than that with Somerset's daughter, but destined to be of very much greater consequence. On June 4th Lord Robert Dudley, then seventeen years old, was married to Amy, daughter and heiress of Sir John Robsart, of Syderstone in Norfolk. The bride's mother had inherited among her properties that of Stanfield in the parish of Wymondham. When Dudley had ridden against Kett the previous year, his sons Ambrose and Robert had accompanied him, and the party had stayed in Wymondham on their journey. This may have been the origin of the acquaintance.* Many years afterwards the marriage was said to have been a love-match, but, by the standards which John Dudley at that time exacted, the girl was sufficiently well-dowered to make her eligible in his view. At present his conditions for the marriages of his children were no more exigent than those of other noblemen: a certain degree of influence or a compensating quantity of money. Lord Ambrose Dudley was twice married by his father, each time to an heiress; Lord Henry was married to the daughter of Henry VIII's Chancellor, Lord Rich. Their sister Mary was married to Sir Henry Sidney, of slender fortune but Gentleman of the Bedchamber to Edward VI and on terms of great affection with the young King. Lord Robert's match was not markedly inferior to those of the rest.

The unspoiled shore of Thames in the month of June was a paradisial scene for the marriage of a young pair enamoured of each other. It was gaily celebrated; the young King was there; so was the Princess Elizabeth. "Begun in passion, ended in mourning", was William Cecil's comment on the wedding, ten years later.

Dudley's influence with the King was steadily increasing; he was a kind father to his own children, and he knew how to please, encourage

* H. T. Bartle Frere, *Amy Robsart of Wymondham.*

and amuse the reserved, clear-headed boy, as Somerset had neither known nor cared to know. On October 11th, 1550, Edward created him Duke of Northumberland, while the Dukedom of Suffolk, vacant through the death of two of Lady Dorset's half-brothers, was bestowed on her husband. Jane Grey's parents were now, therefore, Duke and Duchess of Suffolk.

The open advancement of his enemies had driven Somerset to a reckless attempt to regain his ascendancy. Northumberland, seizing his opportunity, suborned Sir Thomas Palmer and Sir John Gates to bear false witness that Somerset was planning to murder him. This criminal conspiracy was successful, and on October 16th Somerset was again lodged in the Tower, from which he emerged only to his execution the following January.

With Somerset in the Tower, and the King more and more under his influence, Northumberland's authority was supreme. But the need of money to carry on the government was dire. Under a show of fanatical Protestant zeal he revived a religious persecution which Somerset, to do him justice, had put down, and began a furious pillaging of the churches, in which the reformers were entertained by the smashing of stained glass and defacing of monuments, and under cover of which Northumberland's men swept up gold and silver altar plate, and vestments valuable for their gold and silver thread.

The pace at which Northumberland now advanced his personal and material ascendancy gave a supernatural character to his tyranny. In the month of Somerset's arrest two Yeomen of the Guard were examined on a declaration they had made, the result of a hysterical delusion. They thought they had seen a coin of the realm stamped with the Bear and Ragged Staff.* Such a hallucination was scarcely surprising. When the King made a progress in the summer of 1552 Northumberland, for reasons of his own convenience, did not accompany him. The great Duke's absence was at once remarked, and two men at least spoke their opinion that it meant he was out of favour: in September, John Kyston was put in gaol for reporting that "the Duke of Northumberland was commanded to be absent from the Court", and John Burroughs was "committed to the Fleet for the like matter".†
In the spring of 1553, Northumberland's ambition developed its last and most desperate phase. By April of that year Edward had had two eruptive illnesses; from these he had made a surprisingly good recovery, but his latent tuberculosis now showed itself; with fearful rapidity he became a victim to galloping consumption. It was almost certain he

* Pollard, *Political History of England.*   † Strype, *Memorials*, II, 2.

would not live out the year, and his immediate heirs, by his father's Will, were Mary and Elizabeth. The all-important question now was not, how did England stand affected by this prospect, but what was to happen to the Duke of Northumberland and his family?

The Princess Mary Northumberland wrote off immediately; her accession would terminate his ascendancy, for she would not be in any way amenable to a man who had showed himself a merciless persecutor of the Catholic Church. So much was obvious. But his decision with regard to the second heiress was more subtle. For one who had committed himself to the Reformation, Elizabeth was the obvious choice, with the additional advantage that she stood next in her father's Will and had been the favourite sister of her brother. But in 1551, when she was eighteen years old, the Princess had been allowed to visit her brother's court. Her plainness of dress, her unadorned hair, the quietness of her manner had struck everybody and particularly delighted the young King, who had not seen her since the scandal and calamity caused by Lord Seymour, two years before. The general impression she made was eminently favourable; but her visit had given Northumberland an opportunity of scanning narrowly this reserved young lady. His observation told him that in her he would find no instrument of his will. When she left the Court he never allowed her to see the King again; he withheld the letters she wrote to her brother in his last illness, and sent a company to stop her on the road, as she was coming to his bedside, with a pretended message from Edward telling her to go home.

The two daughters of Henry VIII were thus put on one side as unsuitable to Northumberland's purpose, but there remained a third possibility: the Lady Jane Grey, fifteen years old, modest, studious, and kept in excellent order by her parents. Northumberland had at home two unmarried children; his fourth son, Guildford, aged nineteen, and the younger of his two daughters, Katherine. The marriages he planned for these showed how high a pitch his resolution soared. Lord Thomas Seymour had once promised Jane Grey's parents to place a crown on her head by marrying her to Edward VI; another plan was now put before them, in a nimbus of glory. To carry it out, Northumberland's services were necessary; to obtain them, Jane must be married to one of his sons. The only one available was Lord Guildford Dudley.

The young man, like his brother Robert, was tall; he was said to be good looking and good natured. There is no evidence that up to this point Jane Grey either liked or disliked him. Her vehement protests against being married to him might have arisen from personal dislike or from the fierce reluctance of a bookish girl scarcely out of childhood towards going to bed with a young man. Whatever her motives, they could not be permitted to obstruct the Duke of Northumberland's plans and those of her parents for their joint advancement by means of her body. Her mother poured abuse on her, her father thrashed her, and between them they reduced her to acquiescence. The wedding was celebrated in Whit Week at Durham House on the Strand.

This was not the only wedding of the day. The eighteen-year-old Lord Henry Hastings, eldest son of the Earl of Huntingdon, was the great-great-grandson of George Duke of Clarence, who had died in the Tower, drowned, it was said, in a butt of Malmsey wine. Henry Hastings, therefore, through his mother, derived his Plantagenet descent from the man who was own brother to King Edward IV and King Richard III. To the reflective mind, the sight of this young man's family tree was alarming. There was one Plantagenet with a yet nearer claim; Henry Hastings claimed through Edward IV's brother, but young Edward Courtenay claimed through Edward IV's daughter, the Princess Katherine Plantagenet. Henry VIII had seen in a trice to what complications such a heredity might lead, and Edward Courtenay had long been living a life of retirement within the Tower. Henry Hastings was, for some reason, still at large, and in one morning Northumberland swept into his gripe the third Tudor claimant whom he meant should supplant the other two, and the last available descendant of the Plantagenets who was outside prison walls. The marriage of Lord Guildford Dudley to Lady Jane Grey was followed by that of Lord Henry Hastings to Lady Katherine Dudley. A third marriage of altogether inferior importance, though useful in its way, was celebrated at the same time; Jane Grey's younger sister Katherine was married to Lord Henry Herbert, son of the rough and brutish Earl of Pembroke who, after Northumberland himself, was counted the most capable soldier of the day. As the six young people were all members of the innermost circle of the Court, it was strange to hold such a three-fold festival when the King lay too ill to come out of his palace.

The King's illness, however, was the very cause of the indecorous haste. By June, Edward was horribly, desperately ill. To the racking cough which brought up fragments of his lungs was added a disease of the circulation which caused the top joints of his fingers and toes to fall off. His mind was not clouded, but every conviction he had held in his short life he now held with a hundredfold intensity. Three beliefs possessed him with maniacal fervour: the belief that it was his duty to God to secure a Protestant succession, the belief that he could provide for this by the exercise of his arbitrary power, and the belief that Northumberland deserved all his confidence.

On these three beliefs Northumberland staked everything. He persuaded Edward that Henry VIII's Act of Succession must be set aside. Mary was a Catholic, Elizabeth might marry one; the only way to safeguard the Protestant religion was to devise the crown to Jane Grey, a Protestant and already married to a Protestant husband. Edward with his own hand wrote the document which he called "My Devise for the Crown". In its first form it devised the crown to "the Lady Jane's heirs male". A few weeks later Edward himself realized that he would not live to see the birth of his cousin's children, and he altered the words to: "The Lady Jane and her heirs male." Against time, Northumberland now had to get this document accepted by the Council and given, so far as might be without consent of Parliament, the force of law. The Lord Chief Justice, with the Attorney General, the Solicitor General and a deputation of Judges of the King's Bench, was summoned to Greenwich Palace to receive the King's instructions and draw the letters patent. They saw at once, and explained, that this was not feasible. Anyone who attempted to alter the succession while the Act of Succession was still unrepealed would be guilty of high treason. Told that the King insisted on their compliance, they asked for time to consider. Two days later they returned to Greenwich, saying the thing could not be done except through Parliament. Northumberland was not in the Council Chamber when they arrived, but word was brought to him that the judges had announced their refusal. He had been in close attendance at the King's bedside. Edward's dreadful condition, his sleeplessness, his inability to eat, his weakness animated only by a feverish determination, were all before Northumberland's eyes: he needed no doctor to tell him that the King's expectation of life was a matter of weeks. It might be of hours, even. He could scarcely leave the bedchamber where the ghastly little figure sat or lay, worn, hectic, racked with coughing, covered with sores, the hands and feet shockingly disfigured, the fair hair piteously fallen out, without fearing that when he returned to it the fatal change might have set in. In this crisis of affairs he heard that the judges had refused to draw the letters patent.

He entered the Council Chamber, a sight that no one who saw it ever forgot. The well-known suavity of the Duke's manners had totally disappeared. He was trembling with rage. He swore that he would "fight in his shirt" with any man that refused his demands.

The judges said afterwards they thought he meant to knock them down where they stood. An audience of the dying King, in which, exhausted but with desperate haughtiness, he asked them how they dared hesitate to obey his will, finally drove them to do what their professional training had made them declare impossible. First conditioning for a pardon for themselves should they be afterwards indicted of high treason, they withdrew to prepare the letters patent, devising the crown to Jane Grey and her heirs male, which were afterwards, the King promised, to be given force of law by a Parliament assembled for the purpose. Meantime, Northumberland tried to safeguard himself by securing the signatures of as many influential persons as he might; bishops, peers, law officers, knights and sheriffs. William Cecil signed the document, but as a witness only, he afterwards said. His account of the matter has an ominous ring: "I did refuse to subscribe . . . when none of the Council did refuse . . . in what peril I refer it to be considered by them that know the Duke."*

The public image of Northumberland up till this time was of a man eminently courteous, sympathetic even. Though backed by force, he did not ostensibly impose his will by harsh and brutal means. But to those near enough to be his personal victims he was very frightening. Jane Grey was a courageous girl, but she was afraid of Northumberland. She had begged that immediately after her marriage, instead of remaining in her husband's family, she might go back to her parents. This arrangement was often made where the married pair were very young, and the request was granted in her case. She had been very urgent in it; bad as her parents were, at least they were not the Duke and Duchess of Northumberland. But the promise was broken immediately, and when she attempted to go home she was ordered by her mother-in-law to stay where she was.

The Duchess of Suffolk, whose claims had been set aside in favour of her daughter's, had no mind to see this valuable being, to whom a talismanic importance now attached, pass entirely into the Northumberlands' hands. A high-pitched scene ensued between the mothers-in-law, but in the end a compromise was reached. As in Jane Grey's view any situation must be better than Durham House with the Duke and Duchess of Northumberland in residence, she got leave to transfer herself to the riverside palace of Chelsea. This had lately been the Dower House of Katherine Parr, and by a kind of inevitable process the property had now become that of Northumberland, who had already taken to himself the palaces of Sheen and Sion. At Chelsea

* Tytler, *England under the Reigns of Edward VI and Mary*

she was allowed to remain, alone except for her servants. She developed a rash and found that her hair was falling out, from which the oppressed and frightened girl concluded that someone was trying to poison her.

On the evening of July 6th a fearful tempest swept London; lightning and thunder racked the sky, torrential rain drowned the streets, at 6 o'clock the summer evening was dark as night. At that hour, King Edward died in the arms of Sir Henry Sidney. The final act of Northumberland's drama was at hand.

For three days he concealed the fact that the King was dead, and sent in his name messengers asking Edward's sisters to come to him. On July 9th he sent his daughter, Mary Sidney, to fetch Jane Grey. Of a charming, affectionate nature, little older than her sister-in-law, if anyone could reassure Lady Jane it was the young Lady Mary Sidney. Her father sent her in a barge quite alone except for her attendants, with instructions to bring Lady Jane to Sion House. The two girls entered the barge at the garden stairs of Chelsea Palace, and the oars-men, rowing upstream, brought them in two hours to Sion.

The great hall was empty when they entered it, but in a few minutes four members of the Council appeared who made Lady Jane a deep obeisance; they were followed by her mother-in-law and her mother, who, to her rising dismay, paid her the same homage. Last of all came in Northumberland, who told her that the King was dead, that he had felt it his duty to disinherit his two sisters, and that she was now Queen.

Jane Grey burst into tears and exclaimed it could not be true! But then she saw Northumberland and the Councillors going down on their knees before her, heard them promising to maintain her rights with their hearts' blood, and fell down in a dead faint. When they had brought her to, she got up as far as her knees, and prayed aloud that if the throne were hers, God would help her to govern to His glory. Set on her feet, she then entered upon her brief reign.

The announcements of her accession which Northumberland caused to be made in London were received with cold silence. The writer of an open letter, signing himself Poor Pratte, gave some indication of how Northumberland was now regarded in the London streets; he was "the ragged Bear most rank, the cruel bear with whom is neither mercy, pity, nor compassion . . . The world is dangerous. The great devil Dudley ruleth."[1]

The next day Jane Grey was brought in state to the Tower, her mother carrying her train and her husband walking at her side, cap in hand and bowing to the ground. On this occasion, Guildford Dudley was content to play a secondary role; but his father had engineered the whole of this monstrous plot, not, in the last resort, that Suffolk's daughter might be queen, but that his own son should be king. And now a totally unexpected reverse awaited him. Jane Grey had not wanted to think herself Queen, but when Northumberland had finally overcome her reluctance and disbelief this modest, retiring, self-contained girl took him aback by behaving as the Queen he had convinced her that she was. Like the Sorcerer's Apprentice, he found he had summoned up a power he could not control. On the evening of July 10th, Lord Winchester came to her carrying a crown which he wanted to put on her head to see if it fitted her; he observed casually that another should be prepared for her husband.

Jane Grey had submitted to the assurances that she must ascend the throne because she thought it was the way devised to safeguard the Protestant religion. As Lord Winchester stood before her with the circlet which she would not allow him to put on her head, she would seem to have realized for the first time what Northumberland's scheme really meant. As soon as Guildford joined her she spoke to him plainly. She said that, as Queen, it was in her power to make him a duke, and she would do this; but he could be made King only by Act of Parliament and he must wait till this should be passed. A double coronation was out of the question.

The good-natured young man was transformed by an outburst of furious anger and disappointment. Unable to make any impression on his wife, he went off to fetch his mother. The Duchess of Northumberland could at first scarcely believe her ears; she poured out commands and revilings with a degree of ire that would have cowed many people. Jane Grey was under five feet high, and she was altogether diminutive, but she was not the great-niece of Henry VIII for nothing. She knew what the Duchess either did not know or had decided to ignore, that the only way for a person outside the succession to be made King was by Act of Parliament. She said so, and her manner indicated that thenceforward the matter was not open to discussion.

The Duchess, beside herself with rage, told her son to come away with her. They would go to Sion House, and he should no longer share the bed of a disobedient and ungrateful wife. Jane Grey would not prolong the interview by attempting to argue with her mother-in-law; but as soon as the Duchess and her son had left her presence she sent Lord Arundel and Lord Pembroke after her husband. He was not to go to Sion House, she said. He was to stay where he was and behave himself to her in a friendly fashion. Her commands were obeyed.

Northumberland's scheme for getting the Princesses into his power had failed. Elizabeth, warned, it was assumed, by William Cecil, secretary to the Council, never set out for London; Mary was warned in mid-journey, at Broxbourne in Hertfordshire, where, wheeling round, she made off for Suffolk. Northumberland despatched two of his sons, Lord Warwick and Lord Robert Dudley, with a troop of horse, in pursuit of her; but when they came up with the Princess's troop the Dudleys' men went over to her. The brothers had to flee, and only the speed of their horses saved them.

Meanwhile support was rallying to Mary, who had raised her standard at Framlingham Castle and announced her accession. Having failed to entice her into the snare, Northumberland was obliged to lead an army against her. He was unwilling to leave London, for he more than suspected that as Mary's forces were increasing every day the Council would not long remain faithful to him behind his back; but the only alternative commander was the Duke of Suffolk. In all the scenes which had been enacted since Jane Grey became his daughter-in-law, Northumberland had remained in the background; the aggressors had been the Duchess and Guildford Dudley. Jane's version was not: "I was deluded by the Duke and the Council," but "I was maltreated by my husband and his mother." Northumberland himself had treated her with that silken courtesy which, coming from a man of great ability and power, is apt to produce uneasiness rather than confidence; it had never concealed from her which of the Dudley family was the really formidable member. At the suggestion that her father, who was at least her nominal protector, should ride away and leave her in the Tower at Northumberland's mercy, she asserted herself with all the energy at her command, demanding that her father should remain with her. Though at this crisis Northumberland might have been prepared to overrule her, it was clear that the military situation demanded the best man available. He decided that the lesser danger lay in leaving London to put down the resistance, which he hoped to do by trained troops against volunteers and with the monopoly of the cannon which were kept in the Tower. On July 15th he rode out of London for Cambridgeshire, the rendezvous of his forces, accompanied by Lord Ambrose and Lord Robert. Before he went, among somewhat bitter exhortations to the Council to stand firm, for they were all in the same boat, he made one of those utterances, sincere, yet so oddly at variance with his conduct. He charged them to take care of Lady Jane Grey, "who by your and our enticement is rather of force placed therein than of her own seeking or request".

As his cavalcade left the city, he noted the ominous fact that, though plenty of people stood to watch them pass, none cried "God speed ye!" By the time they had reached Bury St. Edmunds large-scale desertions made him fall back on Cambridge itself. Lord Ambrose remained with him, but Lord Robert had pushed on to King's Lynn, where he proclaimed the Lady Jane Queen in the market place. Northumberland now heard that behind his back the Council had proclaimed Mary. His suppleness was equal to the reverse. He said that all this while he had been acting in obedience to the Council; he would do so still, and he proclaimed Mary Queen at the market cross, throwing up his cap and scattering money to the crowd.

This was the last public action of his career. A force despatched from London arrested and brought him and Lord Ambrose back to the Tower. As Lord Ambrose rode beside his father to the gateway which they had last entered in triumph, it was seen that tears were pouring down the young man's face. He was separated from his father and taken to the first floor of the Beauchamp Tower, a great stone-walled, stone-floored chamber where his brothers John, Henry and Guildford were lodged already. On July 26th Lord Robert was brought in. He, at first, was not put with his brothers, but shut up by himself on the floor below. In their harrowing state of anxiety and vacancy, the brothers in the room above spent some of their time in cutting on the stone wall an elaborate trophy. A lion and a bear supporting a ragged staff formed its apex; under it was cut the name of the eldest son, John Dudle [sic]. The others were represented by emblems: roses for Ambrose, honeysuckle for Henry, gilliflowers for Guildford, and oak leaves, from the Latin robur, for Robert. Three complete lines and a part of one make a verse: You that these beasts do well behold and see, May deem with ease wherefor here made they be, With borders wherein— (and here the second half of the line should probably end with "found") —Four brothers' names, who list to search the ground. While his brothers commemorated his name with theirs, Robert, solitary in the room beneath, cut his own on the wall by the door: ROBART DUDLEY.

Mary's government was now firmly established. On August 18th Northumberland was brought to trial in Westminster Hall, and condemned on a charge of high treason. His eldest son was arraigned with him. Young Lord Warwick displayed the family feeling of the Dudleys. On hearing sentence pronounced upon him, he said with simple dignity that he had followed his father and was content to share his father's fate. He asked only that, though his goods were forfeit to the Crown, his debts might be paid out of them.

Northumberland's own conduct was surprising. Instead of facing death like the brave man he was, he grovelled for mercy to the Queen he had so outrageously injured. He implored Arundel to plead his case. "Alas," he wrote, "is my crime so heinous as no redemption but my blood can wash away the spot thereof? . . . How little profit my dead and dismembered body can bring her, but how great and glorious an honour it will be in all posterity, when the report shall be that so gracious and mighty a queen had granted life to so miserable and penitent an object!"[1]

His political recantation was accompanied by another even more complete. Northumberland had brought up his children as Protestants; he had attacked and pillaged without mercy the Catholic Church in England; by his monstrous treason he had brought the country to the verge of civil war, all, ostensibly, because he believed in the Protestant religion, and thought that any action was to be condoned that helped to establish it. It now turned out, according to himself, that in his heart he had been a Catholic all the time. If this were true it was, of course, right to say so, and in the infinite complexities of the human mind there was no doubt room for such a truth. That by this confession he might soften the Queen's heart and gain a reprieve from death was an obvious motive, and yet possibly not the whole; but whatever the reasons for it might be, one person at least felt nothing but bitter scorn and indignation on hearing of Northumberland's confession. Lady Jane not only was a devoted Protestant; under colour of protecting the Protestant succession she had been forced to submit to a situation which she had at first repudiated, then suffered with dismay, and which had brought her, at the age of sixteen, to imprisonment, awaiting trial for the capital offence of high treason. All this had been drawn on her by the man who now declared that secretly he had always been a member of the Catholic Church. She had been separated from her husband, and was living under arrest in the house of the Lieutenant of the Tower. Here, the writer of the *Chronicle of Queen Jane and Queen Mary* dined in her presence on August 27th, five days after Northumberland's execution. He heard her exclaim in bitter astonishment at the Duke's reversion to the Catholic faith.

"'Perchance,' the guest suggested, 'he hoped thereby to have had his pardon?'"

"'Pardon!' quoth she. 'Woe worth him! He hath brought me and our stock in most miserable calamity!'" As for pardon, she said, it was scarcely credible that he should have even hoped it. "'What man is there, I pray you, though he had been innocent, that would hope of life in that case? Being in the field against the Queen in person as a general?'" No sovereign could pardon such an act. She was not Queen, but this young creature of the Tudor blood understood more of the science of royalty than all the Dudley family put together.

Despite the formal passing of the death sentence, upon her and her husband, her existence as a state prisoner might have lasted indefinitely; it might even, at long last, have ended in liberation. Mary had generously pardoned the Suffolks; their daughter who had actually been declared queen, she was obliged to keep under restraint for the time being, but she had already told the Imperial Ambassador Renard when he urged Jane's execution, that her cousin, a girl of sixteen, was in no way responsible for her position. Young Lord Warwick, condemned with his father, had been reprieved and sent back to his brothers in prison, and the Queen had shown no wish to punish any of Northumberland's family.

Jane's fate was sealed by the conduct of her father. In January a rising under Sir Thomas Wyatt, in protest against the Queen's determination to marry the Prince Philip of Spain, bore at first an alarming appearance. Wyatt was marching on London, and if the Queen were to surmount this peril those who had been disloyal to her in the crisis could expect no mercy. With a treachery and ingratitude equalled only by his incompetence, Suffolk made a last throw; he attempted to bring a force to Wyatt's assistance. He failed of his object and was ignominiously arrested. That this act signed his own death warrant was a matter of course. It also made inevitable the carrying out of sentence on his daughter and her husband.

Jane faced the prospect of death with steady courage. Her husband had begged for a farewell interview, and the Queen had granted it but it was refused by Jane herself. She sent the wretched young man a message, saying that the sight of her would weaken rather than strengthen him. Let them put off their meeting till they should greet each other in the next world. There they would meet, she promised him.

Guildford Dudley was executed outside the Tower walls, on Tower Hill, and the cart containing his body wrapped in a bloody sheet at one end of it and at the other his head, was driven back into the Tower precincts and across Tower Green to the Chapel of St. Peter and Vincula. By a fearful mischance Jane stood at the window of the Lieutenant's house, looking on Tower Green where her scaffold was being made ready, and as the cart was driven over the Green, she looked down into it. That she was not brought out to execution until an hour after the appointed time was perhaps due to this incident. Beside her on the scaffold, stood Dr. Feckenham, the Abbot of Westminster, a man of exceptional kindness, who had spent many hours with her trying, at the Queen's behest, to make her recant her heresy.

Though she had steadily repudiated all his efforts to influence her, she turned to him with childlike confidence and said: "Shall I say this psalm?" It was psalm lvii. She repeated it in English, by heart: "Be merciful unto me, O God, be merciful unto me, for my soul trusteth in thee; and under the shadow of thy wings shall be my refuge, till this tyranny be overpassed." When she had finished she said: "God will abundantly requite you, Sir, for your kindness to me", and kissed him.

The executioner then asked her to step forward on to the straw and for the first time she saw the block. She said: "I pray you, despatch me quickly. Will you take it off before I lay me down?" The headsman said: "No, madam." She knelt and they gave her a handkerchief which she tied over her eyes; but then she groped with her outstretched hands, exclaiming: "Where is it? What shall I do?" They guided her to the block and she laid down her head on it, saying: "Lord, into Thy hands I commend my spirit." One blow severed the childish neck, and the gush of blood was so frightful the onlookers were astounded that so much should come from so small a girl.

So died the Duke of Northumberland's victim, sixteen years and four months old, on February 12th, 1554. As the torrents of her blood poured out and soaked the straw, it seemed that the far-ranging plans to bring the Crown of England into the Dudley family had foundered and expired. But there remained, among Northumberland's surviving sons, one who had inherited the ambition of the father, and there remained another Princess of the House of Tudor. Though John Dudley had failed to achieve the family's ambition through Jane, it was yet to be seen whether Robert Dudley would succeed in it through Elizabeth.

II

SIR WILLIAM CECIL said that the marriage of Robert Dudley and Amy Robsart was one of desire, begun in joy, ended in mourning. At least, it began in bliss. The young pair lived in Norfolk, but from their first year some separation obtained. Northumberland had placed his youngest son at the Court of Edward VI, who was thirteen years old when he noted Robert Dudley's wedding in his journal. In 1551, the year after the wedding, Northumberland had Lord Robert made one of the Gentlemen of the King's Privy Chamber. This appointment in itself implied that Robert Dudley spent a good deal of his time at Court; not to do so would be to throw away the high advantage it conferred. It was said that, in a foreign country, a courtier gave the Prince a yearly rent, for the sole privilege of being allowed, every day, in open audience, to come and whisper "good morning" in the Prince's ear. The impression of confidence and secret favour which this created made the man so influential that he gained the amount he paid the Prince over and over again in the trafficking this reputation brought him.[1] Robert's careful father had not procured such an appointment to have its uses neglected. At the same time the young husband was taking his part in the Norfolk neighbourhood. In this year he was made joint steward of the Manor of Castle Rising and Constable of the castle. For the next two years his energies seemed fairly divided between the two spheres. In January, 1552, he took part in two tournaments at Court; in May he was appointed joint commissioner for the Lord Lieutenant of Norfolk. In September his father secured for him another Court appointment, that of Master of the Buckhounds. In 1553 he was returned as Member of Parliament for Norfolk. In June this year Northumberland settled some land of his own on the pair: Hemsby Manor near Yarmouth was bestowed on "Robert Dudley, Lord Dudley my son and the Lady Amy his wife"; while in the next month a grant for Robert Dudley was obtained from the dying King of Rockingham in Northamptonshire and Eston in Leicestershire.

In all his visits at Court, there is no evidence that his wife ever came with him On the other hand, there is some to show that she lived an active life, and that she was very fond of her husband.

In August, 1553, Northumberland had been beheaded on Tower Green, just outside the precincts where his five sons were imprisoned. The head of a traitor was usually stuck on a pole over the Bankside Gate of London Bridge, but the Lancaster Herald, who had been a retainer of Northumberland's, went upstream to Richmond Palace, where, in an audience with Queen Mary, he begged to be allowed to take his master's head and give it decent burial. "Take the body as well," said the Queen. The corpse were therefore taken down to the parish church of Warwick and buried in the Beauchamp Chapel. This exquisite place had been built by Warwick the King-Maker to house the remains of his father-in-law, Richard Beauchamp fifth Earl of Warwick. The late fifteenth century tracery of pale stone encloses stained glass windows whose upper lights carry, all round the chapel, scrolls of music. Behind these are seen an uninterrupted procession of angels who are playing on musical instruments, walking barefoot on an indigo sky powdered with gold stars. On the stone floor, far below, his sons Ambrose and Robert, many years later, raised a funeral monument to the High and Mighty Prince, John, Duke of Northumberland.

Mary had acted with unusual clemency in putting to death only their father. His sons and his hapless daughter-in-law had to await indefinitely the next manifestation of her will. However, in September of this year the Privy Council gave permission to "the Lady Robert Dudley and other ladies to visit their husbands imprisoned in the Tower". Lady John, Lady Henry, Lady Ambrose, Lady Robert Dudley, all bringing with them affection, presents, news of the outside world, must have lightened considerably the darkness of the Beauchamp Tower, and made the prisoners feel that fortune would, before long, turn her wheel.

The Queen's coronation took place in October, and, though the sovereign was the magnet to the public gaze, another figure attracted great attention. In the procession immediately following the Queen's litter came an open carriage containing two ladies. Seated with her back to the horses was King Henry VIII's luckless, comical, good-natured erstwhile wife, Anne of Cleves. Facing her, in a white dress figured with silver, was the twenty-year-old Princess Elizabeth. The pale face and reddish golden hair were unmistakable. The Princess's head bore a heavy coronet. For several years she had suffered a good deal of ill-health, including severe attacks of migraine.

Inside the Abbey the French Ambassador, de Noailles, placed himself so near to her that they could exchange whispered conversation, and his own statement was that at one point during the lengthy cere- monial the Princess had complained to him of the weight of her circlet. He had replied by indicating the Crown worn by the Queen herself, and whispering to the Princess that when that one was on her head she would not find it too heavy.[1] Meanwhile Mary dedicated herself to the service of God and her people. The altar cloth made for this coronation was of white satin embroidered with a profusion of roses, from which a silver dove flew up, surrounded by silver rays, towards the words embroidered in silver: Veritas Temporis Filia. Its radiant beauty matched the Queen's aspirations, her eagerness and hope, her long-awaited opportunity to restore the authority of the Catholic Church.

Mary announced her proposed Spanish match before Christmas, and the rebellion raised by Thomas Wyatt in January, 1554, was an answer to it. This abortive rising, which brought about the destruc- tion of Jane Grey and her husband, might well have destroyed Robert Dudley. John, Henry, Ambrose and Guildford Dudley were already under sentence of death;[2] and in this fresh outbreak, in the face of what had been singular mercy from the Queen, it was thought proper to sentence the one brother who, though fully implicated with his father, had so far escaped trial. On January 22nd Lord Robert Dudley was tried under the name of "the late Lord Robert Dudley", for Northumberland's execution for high treason meant that his children were de-nobled. Robert Dudley was sentenced to death, but, though the death sentence on Guildford was carried out, the Queen forbore to inflict the penalty on the four remaining brothers, who still waited in the Beauchamp Tower to know their fate.

Wyatt's rebellion was crushed, but it had seriously implicated the Princess Elizabeth, since its announced object had been to turn Mary off the throne and replace her by her sister, whom the conspirators meant to marry to Edward Courtenay, the Plantagenet descendant whom Mary herself had released from the Tower immediately upon her accession. The Emperor Charles V's ambassador, Renard, and Mary's chancellor, Gardiner Bishop of Winchester, both urged her not to neglect this heaven-sent opportunity to cut off her sister's head. The Princess was obnoxious to both of them as a heretic, and especi- ally so to Renard, since he had noted her attraction for the people, which he thought might menace the prospects of his master's son, the Prince of Spain, when he should be married to the English Queen. He warned the Emperor: "The Princess Elizabeth is very dangerous; she has a spirit full of incantation."[1]

But Mary said that her sister could not be put to death unless proof were forthcoming that she knew beforehand of Wyatt's plans. She could, however, be placed under arrest and interrogated. The Princess was taken down the river to the Tower, on the rainy morning of Palm Sunday, 1554, because it was thought unsafe to convey her through the streets for fear of an attempted rescue. She protested vehemently at being landed at the Traitors' Gate as the arch yawned above her, filled with the gloom of a rainy morning, and the tide covered the topmost stair so that she "stepped over the shoes in water" in landing. The resistance she made to going in was ended by the sight of her gentleman-usher, who broke down and wept. Elizabeth realized that she must take charge of her servants. She rated him; truth was what mattered, she said, nor misfortune, and none of her friends should ever have cause to weep for her. So saying, she allowed herself to be led inside the gateway and to the left, in the direction of the Bell Tower. That it had been wise not to take her through the streets was confirmed even here; a posse of yeomen-warders broke rank, and, kneeling down, called out: "God save your Grace!"

The Bell Tower stands at a corner of the curtain wall enclosing the great fortress. The next tower along the wall is the Beauchamp Tower. Inside the wall between the two towers is the King's house built by Henry VIII, and the house belonging to the Yeoman Gaoler, where Jane Grey had been lodged, both looking upon Tower Green. Locked into the great stone-walled chamber on the first floor of the Bell Tower with six of her faithful ladies, Elizabeth was separated from the Dudley brothers by the walk on the leads, running along the top of the curtain wall. The distance was but seventy feet or so, but the separation was absolute. The young men were state prisoners under sentence of death, the young lady was not under sentence of death but her importance as a state prisoner was infinitely greater than theirs. She had come to the Tower barely recovered from illness, and after some weeks of confinement, during which, she afterwards said, she was in such despair that she thought only of asking the Queen to have her beheaded by the sword as her mother had been, a method swifter and more certain than the axe, she became so enfeebled that her condition was reported to the Council. It was then decided that she should be allowed to walk upon the

leads, in the narrow trough between the battlements on one side
and the gables of the King's House and the Yeoman Gaoler's house
on the other. Here, however, she had the illimitable skies overhead,
and through the crenellations she could see far away over the Essex
marshes. At the end of the walk was the little door leading into the
Beauchamp Tower, but she was not allowed to walk even here
without two guards in front of her and two behind;* therefore
whether she approached the door or retreated from it made no odds;
the prisoners behind it remained invisible, but their nearness, in her
terrible situation, could but strengthen the hold of one of them on
her imagination.

The Prince of Spain was expected to arrive in London in the early
summer, and so much did Renard fear another popular rising against
the unwelcome bridegroom in the Princess's favour that it was
decided to send Elizabeth out of the capital. Sir Henry Bedingfield
was appointed to take her to Woodstock in Oxfordshire and keep
her there till further orders. On May 19th, 1554, the Princess left
the Tower for another form of imprisonment, but, seeing her barge
moving upstream, the gunners in the Steelyard thought she had been
set at liberty and fired a thunderous salute. The noise of firing that
signalized Elizabeth's departure must have echoed and re-echoed in
the ears of the inmates of the Beauchamp Tower. For three months
longer they remained there. Philip of Spain arrived in August, and
the Queen's wedding was celebrated at Winchester in floods of
English summer rain. The Duchess of Northumberland had died
some months earlier, but before her death she had been ceaselessly
active on her sons' behalf, suing the Spanish ladies at Court. The
interest she had created now brought Philip to the Dudleys' aid, and
in October, 1554, the brothers were pardoned and released after
fourteen months of wearing and harassing confinement. Within a
few days of his release, young Lord Warwick died.

Philip had a war with France on his hands; his father, the Emperor
Charles V, numbered among his vast possessions the kingdom of
Naples, and Pope Paul IV, a Neapolitan by birth, who was thoroughly inimical to the Spaniards, called upon the French to turn
them out of his native state. The struggle thus joined involved a
campaign on the soil of France, and Northumberland's three surviving sons took service with Philip's army. In 1557, at the Battle
of St. Quentin, Lord Robert Dudley was made Master of the
Ordinance, and showed a courage and administrative skill that

* Oral tradition of the Tower of London.

pleased Philip greatly. Lord Henry was killed in the fighting, and henceforward Ambrose and Robert were the only male representatives of their once large family.

On March 17th, 1557, Philip sent Robert Dudley home with despatches. "The Lord Robert Dudley having been beyond the sea with King Philip came riding unto the Queen at Court at Greenwich with letters." As a recognition of his services at St. Quentin, he and his brother and sisters were "restored in blood", and once more could claim the rank of duke's children. The Queen granted him again the manor of Hemsby, the property his father had once given him, that had escheated to the Crown.

Lord Robert was in England for the last eighteen months of Mary's catastrophic reign. The Princess Elizabeth had been released from imprisonment at Woodstock, and was at Court in a position of semi-official favour. The abdication of the Emperor Charles V had made Philip King of Spain and King of Naples, but he was not King of England, for Parliament had not granted him the Crown Matrimonial. His hold upon the country was precarious, and in the event of his wife's death, which in 1558 was clearly not far distant, it would very possibly disappear. Philip therefore ordered the Queen to maintain friendly relations with her sister. Should Mary die without children, as she was almost certain to do, the heir to the throne in Catholic eyes was Mary Queen of Scots the granddaughter of Henry VIII's elder sister Margaret, who had married James IV of Scotland. Henry VIII had, it is true, excluded Mary Stuart from the succession by omitting from his Will all mention of his sister's line, and Parliament had given this Will the force of law by turning it into the Act of Succession. But Catholics had two arguments against its validity: they denied that an Act of Parliament could supersede the claims of primogeniture; and they declared Elizabeth to be illegitimate because a marriage contracted with her mother during the lifetime of the King's wife, Catherine of Aragon, for which no Papal sanction had been given, was *ipso facto* invalid. With both these arguments Philip concurred as heartily as anyone. But Mary Queen of Scots was now betrothed to the Dauphin of France. If the next King and Queen of France were to be also King and Queen of England, the balance of power in Europe would tell heavily against Spain. To keep England out of French clutches, the claim of the bastard and heretic Elizabeth must be supported. That Philip confessed in his late years that he had conceived a passion for his pale, strange sister-in-law added a certain sinister interest to the affair.

The wretched Queen, disappointed in her hopes of a baby, and aware that her Spanish marriage, and her enforcing of the burning alive of those who denied the truth of the Catholic faith, had created a widespread detestation of herself, did nevertheless maintain a semblance of sisterly relationship with Elizabeth. For the last two years of the reign the latter was living at Hatfield under the surveillance of Sir Thomas Pope, who admired and liked her, enjoyed long, learned conversations with her, and did what he could for her amusement. Ascham was allowed to visit her and read with her. He had gone abroad with Sir Richard Moryson, the ambassador to the Imperial Court, and from Augsberg he had written a letter describing the dinner of the Emperor's sister. She had dined on "bacon and chickens almost covered with sodden onions, that all the chamber smelled of it". This would not have done for "my Lady Elizabeth", the sensitiveness of whose nose, either to bad smells or even to a scent that was too strong, was proverbial.

In May, 1557, Giovanni Michele included in his despatch to the Venetian Senate a description of Elizabeth and her circumstances. "My Lady Elizabeth," he wrote, "is a lady of great elegance both of mind and body. She has fine eyes and above all a beautiful hand which she takes care to display." He speaks of the Princess's fluency in foreign languages and of her liking to show off her knowledge of Italian. "She prides herself," he said, "on her father and glories in him; everybody says she resembles him more than the Queen does." He then went on to say that though careful and economical she was always in debt, and would be still more so if she did not steadily refuse to take into her household all the gentlemen and pages who were anxious to enter her service. He said everyone knew how narrow her means were compared to the state she was expected to keep, and it aroused much sympathy for her.

This statement is very interesting in view of the often told story, repeated, it was said, even by Elizabeth herself but without any details, that Robert Dudley had a strong claim on her gratitude, because during her sister's reign, when she was in straits for money, he sold some of his lands and gave her the proceeds. The authority for saying that Elizabeth herself had told this story was Hubert Languet, whose reliability has been denied; but of the contemporary prevalence of the story there is evidence in the statement of the jeweller Dymock, who was visiting the Swedish Court in 1562. The Swedish King asked Dymock the cause of Lord Robert's great favour with the Queen, and Dymock said: "When she was but Lady

Elizabeth . . . in her trouble he did sell away a good piece of his
land to aid her, which divers supposed to be the cause the Queen so
favoured him."[1]

The domestic life of Lord Robert and Lady Dudley from 1558 to
1559 is reflected in the account books of the former's secretary, Mr.
Chancey. Lord Robert was on very familiar terms with his servants,
and the chief of these was his Treasurer of the Household, Antony
Forster. In 1558 Chancey opened his accounts by saying he had
received £300 from Antony Forster. In July, 1558, Lord Robert
had made enquiries about an estate at Fitcham, saying that Syderstone was not well appointed. It seems clear that, by the time these
accounts were started, the Dudleys' had ceased to live at Syderstone
and were sharing a house with Antony Forster's brother-in-law, Mr.
Hyde, at Denchurch, near Abingdon in Berkshire. Chancey notes
"charges for my Lady", and these show that Lady Dudley lived a
free, active life, waited upon as became a young woman of her
position. Money was given "to Gower for his riding into Lincolnshire with my Lady", "for hire of hackneys for my Lady", to John
Forrest "riding to Mr. Hyde's to my Lady", for "Mr. Blount's
horse-hire when he rode to my Lady in the Christmas", for "hire of
horses when my Lady came from Mr. Hyde's to London", to
Langham "for two days board wages attending upon my Lady at
Christchurch, your Lordship being at Windsor". Chancey himself
put in a claim "for my boat hire to London about the despatch of
my Lady". There were expenses for her properties and clothes, "for
a trunk, saddle and appurtenances for carrying my Lady's apparel.
To buy a hood for my Lady. For six dozen gold buttons of the Spanish
pattern and a little chain delivered to Mr. Forrest for my Lady's use.
For two ells of fine holland to make my Lady's ruffs, two and a half
ells of russet taffeta to make my Lady a gown", and "a sum delivered
for my Lady's charge, riding into Suffolk, with 46 pistoles to Hogan
to put in her Ladyship's purse". The pistole was a gold coin worth
about sixteen shillings.[2]

Wherever she went, however, and whatever she did, there was no
word about her being in London with her husband, going to Court,
or being pregnant by him. The events of November, 1558, made any
such companionship the more unlikely. Before daybreak on November 17th Mary Tudor died, and three days later the young Queen held
her first Council Meeting in the hall of Hatfield Palace, the red brick
Gothic building with its arched wooden roof, set in a park lovely
even in November with its dark leafless boughs, low sun and rising

mists. In the intense excitement of the hour, the event of greatest importance was the confirmation of the appointment of William Cecil as Secretary of State, and the most piercing words those the Queen spoke to him upon it: "I give you this charge, that you shall be of my Privy Council and content yourself to take pains for me and my realm. This judgment I have of you, that you will not be corrupted by any manner of gift . . . and that without respect to my private will, you will give me that council which you think best." She added a promise, most difficult for a woman to keep: "If you shall know of anything necessary to be declared to me of secrecy, you shall show it to myself only, and assure yourself I will not fail to keep taciturnity therein." Forty arduous, exhausting, inspiring years were to prove the soundness of the judgment and the sincerity of the promise.

Among the numerous lesser appointments were those to posts about her person, all given to friends. Kat Ashley was named First Lady of the Bedchamber, her husband, Mr. Ashley, Keeper of the Queen's Jewels. For one friend a post of especial suitability was reserved. Lord Robert Dudley was made "Master of the Queen's Horse". He had presented himself at the Court at Hatfield without loss of time. "Immediately after Queen Mary's death, this young nobleman mounted a snow-white horse and went to the Princess Elizabeth at Hatfield, being well skilled at riding a managed horse." His horsemanship was of course a recommendation, since the office required him to attend the Queen when she appeared on horseback on public occasions, but it was also an administrative one of considerable importance. It entailed the buying, stabling, physicking, training, breeding and making available at all times of the large body of horses required by the Queen and her household—the Queen's riding horses and those of her attendants as well as the pack-horses and mules for her baggage trains when she moved from place to place. Dudley threw himself into the work with all his energy and intelligence. He was fond of horses and considered an exceptionally good rider even in an age in which riding was a universal accomplishment, and he had made a study of the "manège" and "dressage" of a mount, which was essential in pageants and tournaments. His presence of mind, his *savoir vivre*, his training as a courtier and the self-confidence of a man who is tall, powerful, active and handsome, all fitted him exactly for the post the Queen bestowed on him. So much did he appreciate the opportunities it gave that in spite of numerous other appointments, and an income out of which he could well have spared the salary of 100 marks a year, he would never relinquish it, but thirty years later died in the possession of it. Its bestowal in 1558 meant that he could not have much time to spend on a domestic existence in the country.

The Queen left Hatfield on November 23rd with her retinue and made her way to London, where she stayed five days at the Charterhouse. This was the town house of Lord North, whose son Roger, succeeding his father as 2nd Baron in 1564, was a lifelong friend of Lord Robert Dudley. From this house on November 28th, she made the first of her famous processions through London, to take possession of the Tower. She rode in a chariot as far as Cripplegate, then she mounted. The Lord Mayor rode in front of her carrying the sceptre, Garter King-at-Arms beside him. Then came Lord Pembroke bearing the sword of state, then the Sergeants-at-Arms surrounding the Queen.

Elizabeth, whose horsemanship was as celebrated as Lord Robert's, appeared to great advantage when mounted. So many women rode pillion behind a man that it struck the French ambassador as noteworthy that "the Queen always rides alone"*. On this occasion she rode a white horse; her habit was of violet velvet. Her skin was "candidus",† of glowing whiteness; her reddish hair and her aquiline features, as well as her air and manner, made the onlookers say how like she was to her father. Behind her, on a black horse, rode Lord Robert Dudley. On this, the first public occasion of the reign, he was once for all established in the public eye.

* De Maisse, *Journal*, ed. Harrison.
† Robert Johnston, *Historia Britannicarum*.

III

THAT ROBERT DUDLEY was greatly in the Queen's confidence was already clear. It was confirmed by his being entrusted with a peculiar errand. Dr. Dee, a remarkable man who had many academic distinctions, was also an astrologer and a setter-up of horoscopes. Elizabeth was very much interested in the occult. During Mary's reign Dee had been up before the Privy Council for casting the Princess's horoscope, which, in the hands of a competent practitioner, must inevitably have foretold the Queen's death at no long-distant date. The new Queen now wished that he should choose an auspicious date for her coronation. Lord Robert Dudley was sent to him on this mission, and Dee advised January 15th, 1559. Meantime, the Court was established at Whitehall, one of the two London palaces, of which St. James was the other. The grounds of Whitehall Palace, which lay between Charing Cross and Westminster, covered twenty-four acres, and it was the largest as well as the most splendid of all the Royal dwellings. Upon the accession of Elizabeth, a young woman unmarried and therefore able to bring the English alliance to whomsoever she gave her hand, this Court became a target for intense speculation in every capital in Europe.

In the dead time of the year, the Coronation day dawned. On January 12th the Queen went to the Tower, that she might from there make her recognition procession through the streets of London. The procession took place on the afternoon of January 14th; in its long, stately course it bore the Queen, in a robe of gold tissue and a gold mantle lined with ermine, through crowded streets, halting with her at agreed points on the route where symbolical trophies had been raised, twined with the red and white roses of Lancaster and York, and allegorical figures recited welcomes, and stopping too at her own command when she saw some old person labouring towards her or some poor woman eagerly offering flowers. When she had gained Whitehall after going at a foot-pace over nearly three crowded miles, and had disappeared from the people's gaze, the winter twilight, deepening into night, was illuminated, starred, gemmed with a dazzling display of fireworks along the Thames. The contemporary French print: "Représentation des feux de joie qui furent faits sur l'eau dans Londres à l'honneur de la reine la nuit du jour de son entrée", gives a picture of the Thames facing upstream: from the Tower, a line of buildings and steeples on the right-hand bank ends in St. Paul's Cathedral; an enormous sailing ship fills the foreground, two more are seen in the distance, while rowing boats bob on the waves; from the decks of all of them, from the turrets of the White Tower, the church steeples, and St. Paul's roof, fireworks are being discharged while cannon belch smoke and flame from Tower Wharf.

The next day was that of the Coronation itself. The Queen's clothes for this ceremony had been prepared by the Wardrobe office. The Wardrobe itself was a long, low building, standing in Black Friars behind Baynard's Castle; here were kept a vast store of robes, gowns, lengths of material and all the haberdashery needed for making up— hooks and eyes, laces, tassles, linings. The Wardrobe listed the three sets of robes which the Queen wore at the ceremony, each consisting of a kirtle or underdress and a mantle of the same material, lined with ermine. The first were the mantle and robe of gold and silver tissue "with miniver powderings and furrings of the same", which she had already worn in the recognition procession. The powderings were the sprink-ling of black tails on the white fur. The second was the "Parliament robes of crimson velvet, a fur of powdered ermines for the same". This robe could be produced from material remaining in store. "If her Majesty do make a new robe, then must be had 13 yards." As the officials then list thirteen yards of crimson velvet for a kirtle, a surcoat and a mantle, the Queen must have decided that what was there would not do. The third set were of purple velvet, a kirtle, a surcoat and a mantle with a long train, and a fur of powdered ermine. The Wardrobe produced seventy-two pairs of silver-gilt hooks and eyes, a pair of shoes of gold and silver tissue lined with crimson satin, a pair of gloves "knit with fine white thread", also a crimson velvet cloak-bag in which the robes were carried. The properties for the various cere-monies were supplied by them: "a tabard of white sarcenet to be put on the Queen's gown when she is annointed", and "cotton wool to dry up the oil after the Queen is annointed".[1] When Elizabeth retired into a side chapel to change the crimson robes for the golden ones, she complained to the ladies re-robing her that the oil stank.

The Wardrobe issued to the Stables, to cover the Queen's litter, yellow cloth of gold, a material woven of yellow silk one way and gold thread the other, and white damask for a quilt to cover her inside it, yellow cloth of gold for cushions, and cloth of gold to caparison the Horse of Estate who was led after the litter as the Sovereign was not riding. They also issued material for the occasion to the Master of the Horse, who rode in the procession; this was two lengths of cloth of silk and gold to make a gown, one carnation-gold, the other purple-gold, and purple-gold to caparison his horse.

By three o'clock the Coronation was over and the Queen in her violet velvet was sitting down to the banquet prepared in West-minster Hall, at the dais under the lofty window. Four tables ran the length of the hall, seating two hundred people each; they were waited on by servants all in red. The Earl of Arundel in silver and the Duke of Norfolk in gold rode their horses into the hall to announce the cere-monial entrance of each course, and when they had done so trumpets sounded. On one side of the Queen stood her great-uncle Lord William Howard, and on the other the man who throughout his life was to be one of her most staunch and chivalrous defenders, Thomas Radcliffe, third Earl of Sussex. They carved everything she ate and poured out what she drank. This indeed was but little. Exhaustion and the oncoming of a severe cold had made her almost speechless. At one point, however, she did speak. She thanked all the lords for their trouble about her coronation; she drank to them. As she raised the cup to her lips all the peers took off their coronets and the high roof echoed to a fanfare of trumpets. The scene was not over till one in the morning. The Queen, having got to bed so late, was too tired to attend a joust which had been arranged for that day, in which Lord Robert Dudley was to have taken part, and her cold was so severe that the opening of Parliament had to be postponed from January 23rd to the 25th.

The tasks before the Queen and the Privy Council, of whom the most important member was Sir William Cecil, were urgent. They included a religious settlement which, while it could satisfy neither the ardent Catholics nor the Calvinists who were coming back to England after their flight from the persecutions of Mary Tudor, should be tolerable to as many as possible of the Queen's subjects. Another was the immediate reform of the Crown's derelict financial position. Elizabeth, in the first six months of her reign, reduced the Crown's expenditure from £267,000, which it had been in the last half-year of her sister's reign, to £108,000. The great financier, Thomas Gresham, was sent to the Low Countries to negotiate transactions which should ultimately repair English credit, and at home the thorny project was grasped of calling in the coinage, so debased as seriously to interfere with trade, and facing boldly the inconvenience and expense of re-issuing it in reliable form. A major problem was that of foreign policy. The English were still fighting in France to support the quarrel of Philip II. They had already lost Calais as a result of this intervention, but this was as nothing compared to the threat to English peace and independence that Europe now presented. England was regarded as the legitimate prey of either Spain or France. Henri II had here one advantage over Philip; Mary Stuart was the undoubted Queen of Scotland, and, though this country was not in itself of great value to the French, as a sphere from which to organize a successful invasion of England its importance was pivotal. The one bulwark on which the English could rely on this northern frontier was the strong Protestant element among the Scots, who detested French interference in their country and abhorred the Mass as indivisible from it. If this element could be protected and strengthened, it would prove invaluable to English safety.

Such being the situation at home and abroad, the marriage of Queen Elizabeth was considered an overriding necessity. A powerful alliance from it would be very welcome, but it was even more desired as a means of producing from her body a child whose existence would shut out the likelihood of civil war upon her death. The Wars of the Roses, when the houses of York and Lancaster had fought a bloody war for thirty years to decide which family should wear the Crown, had ended in the settled domination of Henry VII and Henry VIII. The disturbed reign of Edward VI and the disastrous one of Mary had inspired the nation with a desperate determination that they would slip no further down the slope that led back to the reign of chaos and old night. The rate of mortality in every walk of life was high; the Queen might die from one of a dozen causes, and, if she did, then the people must be able to point to a child of hers and say, this is her undoubted heir, whom we acclaim as our lawful sovereign. Only so could the hideous spectre be exorcised of a war, fought by French and Spanish armies on English soil, to decide whose candidate should occupy the vacant throne. With this prospect impending, the Queen's marriage was a topic of such engrossing importance that it filled the foreground of all discussion.

Suitors declared themselves in a bevy. The Count de Feria, the Spanish Ambassador, was instructed by Philip to explain to Elizabeth that if he married her, as he had half made up his mind to do, certain conditions must be observed. She must return to the Catholic Church, and she must understand that he could spend very little time with her;

when his affairs called him away, he must leave her "whether pregnant or not". It was soon plain that the Queen was going to decline this splendid alliance, and substitutes in the Spanish interest were immediately put forward. Philip's nephews, the sons of the Emperor Maximilian, the Archdukes Ferdinand and Charles, were introduced upon the scene. The Prince of Savoy, a connection of the Hapsburgs, to whom Philip had attempted to marry Elizabeth during her sister's reign, was encouraged to make another attack. Prince Eric of Sweden, whose father King Gustav was about to die, so that Eric was proposing virtually as King of Sweden, sent his brother, Duke John of Finland, to treat for him, and when Duke John failed as a proxy for his brother he began to urge his own suit.

The lady, the object of so much speculation, was something more mysterious than a sought-after young woman who had not made up her mind. Portraits of Elizabeth in her youth are rare, and the one painted by Streetes of the Queen in her gold Coronation robe is particularly valuable. It shows not only the smoothness and the rounded slenderness of youth, the hair limp and flowing before she took to crimping it, but also the effect of years of intermittent illness and of near escapes from death. The face is transparent, the temples hollow, and the crown poised on the head, though de Noailles was right in prophesying that she would not find it too heavy, does weigh it down so that the face is pushed forward, in a pose markedly different from that of the high-held head of the later portraits. Fragile and strange, she has a supernatural look.

The descriptions of her in youth agree, whether collected from hearsay or given from personal knowledge. Sir Richard Baker said "she was of stature indifferent tall, slender and straight". Puttenham, who knew her and composed verses upon her which he introduced into his *Art of Poetry*, wrote "Her body, shaped as straight as shaft". Of her hands, which were frequently celebrated ("the fingers of unusual length", "whiter than whitest snow", "the delightful hands of her Majesty"), Puttenham said: *Her hand as white as whale-bone, Each finger tipped with calcedone*—a happy image, for calcedone is a variant of cornelian. In the long oval of her face, as is usual with the faces of the highly intelligent, the most striking feature was the eyes. The brows were very delicate and light. Baker said: her eyes were "lively and sweet but short-sighted". Judging by portraits, they were a golden yellow; it was probably the enlarged pupils of short sight which caused them to be called black.

Her eyes, God wot what stuff they are,
I durst be sworn each is a star
As clear and bright as wont to guide
The pilot in his winter tide.

The versifier's description is confirmed by the historian. "She had a piercing eye," said Fuller, "by which she was used to touch what metal strangers were made of that came into her presence."

The eyes and the agile frame were in harmony with the impression she gave of very great intelligence. Ascham and Cecil had assessed this quality long since; in February, 1559, Lord William Paget wrote to Cecil of "that goodly wit; that goodly knowledge and that great and special grace of understanding and judgment of things that God hath given her". With this went an air and manner that struck everybody. Feria told Philip a month after her accession: "She is incomparably more feared than her sister was. She gives her orders and has her own way as absolutely as her father did."[1]

Now that the long restraints and suppressions of her girlhood were over, Elizabeth did not let go her native caution, her vigilance, her sleepless apprehension, but she showed freely a keen love of pleasure. The Venetian Ambassador said: "The Queen's daily amusements are musical performances and other entertainments and she takes marvellous pleasure in seeing people dance." She loved to dance herself; in February, 1559, he said: "Last evening at the Court . . . at the dance the Queen performed her part, the Duke of Norfolk being her partner, in superb array." It soon became clear that one of her favourite diversions was amorous conversation. This extended itself to a great enjoyment of receiving proposals of marriage. There was, of course, very great diplomatic advantage in such proposals; a marriage negotiation was an even stronger diplomatic bond than a marriage, just as man and wife may fall out, but a man will do everything he can not to offend a woman whom he is courting. It was an extraordinary element in Elizabeth's composition that whatever she personally enjoyed contributed something to her life's passion, the government of her country. Stranger still, everything important that ever happened to her contributed, through its effect on her personality, to the supreme end of her existence.

The long-drawn out negotiations for marriage with the House of Valois were of vital importance during fifteen years of her reign, and they could not have been entertained had she not carried conviction while she was about them. Such an arid wilderness of deceptions would have proved tedious beyond endurance—had not the Queen enjoyed every moment of them. Any woman likes to hear that she is beloved, that she is desired; but in Elizabeth the liking outwent the normal bounds of vanity: it was mania; she could never hear it too often, or too strongly urged. Such was the abnormal condition set up by a fearful past. Her mother had aroused her father's passionate desire; while this lasted she was a queen, worshipped and secure; when she could no longer charm the King, he cut her head off. Only so long as men adored you and yearned for you were you safe, and Elizabeth demanded the perpetual assurance of their passionate devotion. The nervous injury had had an even deeper consequence. The terror of being possessed had settled into an implacable resistance, so fierce that, secret though it was, it dominated every phase of life; but it was secret, and the exaggerated love of flattery, of flirtation, of a romantic element in friendship, naturally gave rise to rumours, surmises, scandals which could not be put down. These sprang up suddenly from nowhere and reached gale force in April, 1559.

On April 18th, de Feria wrote to the King of Spain: "During the last few days Lord Robert has come so much into favour, that he does what he likes with affairs and it is even said that her Majesty visits him in his chamber day and night. People talk of this so freely that they go so far as to say that his wife has a malady in one of her breasts and the Queen is only waiting for her to die, to marry Lord Robert." If this rumour were well founded, de Feria thought that the English alliance might be secured by adopting Lord Robert, who had already served the King of Spain abroad, as Philip's protégé. "I have been brought to consider whether it would not be well to approach Lord Robert on your Majesty's behalf, promising your help and favour and coming to terms with him."

Lord Robert Dudley said of the Queen: " I have known her better than any man alive since she was eight years old",* but even so it might be wondered how well he knew her. Nevertheless, it was over-whelmingly clear that Elizabeth delighted in his company. She had stood at his wedding, hearing him say to another woman: "With my body I thee worship, with this ring I thee wed"; but he had at another time shown her ardent generosity and kindness, and there was no doubt that, however attractive he might have found her before, in her new lustre he was dazzled by her. He himself was admitted, even by people who disliked him, to be very attractive to women; he had the great charm of combining a splendid physique and high vitality with

* De la Forêt, Dépêches, quoted by Von Raumer, *Elizabeth and Mary Stuart*.

"a stately carriage" and "a grave look". Though there was nothing unsuitable in his occupying a place among junior councillors, for he had a sound head, a quick wit and a power of learning by experience, the greatness of his position was explained by that which, in itself cannot be explained; explanations convey nothing, to see him walk into a room would be to understand everything. Occasionally a glimpse is caught, as at a distance, of his spell in operation. "He was an excellent dancer", said Bohun, and the Queen loved to watch people dancing and to dance herself. In the midst of her gaieties, and the enchanting music of strings, tall as he was, and obliged to look down upon the woman to whom he spoke, "he would sometimes ask her if she did not think she had some subjects of her own . . . able to make an heir for the kingdom of England?"*

Whether Elizabeth's passion for him had developed before, or whether it burst suddenly into flower in the intoxication of power and energy of the opening of her reign, at least by April it was there for all to see. On April 23rd, St. George's Day, the ceremony of the Garter was held in the hall of Windsor Castle. "The Queen went about the Hall and all the Knights of the Garter, singing in procession. The same day in the afternoon four Knights of the Garter were created. The Duke of Norfolk, the Marquis of Northampton, the Earl of Rutland and the Lord Robert Dudley." The Venetian Ambassador at Brussels described the ceremony on hearsay from England, and said that Lord Robert was "a very handsome young man towards whom in various ways the Queen evinces such affection and inclination that many persons believe that if his wife, who has been ailing some time, were perchance to die, the Queen might easily take him for her husband".

On April 25th, St. Mark's Day, the Queen supped at Lord Pembroke's town house; this was Baynard's Castle, standing on the Thames between Blackfriars and London Bridge. Lord Pembroke had been an ally of the Duke of Northumberland, and his son Lord Henry Herbert was an intimate friend of Lord Robert Dudley. After supper the Queen took boat and became, in the April dusk, the centre of a glittering water-spectacle. "Hundreds of boats and barges rowing about her and thousands of people thronging at the water-side. Trumpets blew, drums beat, flutes played, guns were discharged, fireworks rose into the air", as the Queen was rowed up and down the river. April was the loveliest month for taking pleasure on the Thames; between Baynard's Castle and Bridewell, it was true, the Fleet ditch, an open sewer, discharged its filth into the main stream, but the great

* Francis Osborne, *Traditional Memoirs.*

river, tidal as far as Richmond, carried off the horrible contents. The lovely serpentine curves that it took from the Tower to Greenwich, and through the downs to the open sea, wound through continuous water-meadows; its strand was gravel, and it was famous for the clearness of its water and its sailing fleets of swans. The pestilent air of the City of London, a small area densely populated, with rudimentary sanitation, was made more endurable because immediately outside the City walls were open country, fields, lanes, trees, and the loveliest of river shores.

Every festivity of the Queen's, every private engagement, every conversation, even, attracted some ambassador's scrutinizing eye and was reported by his pen. On April 29th de Feria informed the King: "Sometimes she speaks like a woman who will only accept a great prince, and then they say she is in love with Lord Robert and will never let him leave her." He added: "For a certain reason they have recently given me, I understand she will not bear children." The symptom he spoke of, which was also repeated to the Scottish ambassador, Sir James Melville, was probably that the Queen had very few monthly periods, a condition impossible to keep entirely secret in a very large household in which waiting women and launderesses were surrounded by people who would pay them for any interesting information. This condition is often the result of severe shock, and Thomas Seymour's perilous association with her, and his execution when Elizabeth was fifteen, may have been the cause of this derangement. The doctors did not, apparently regard it as a sign of infertility; twice, a committee of them gave it as their view that the Queen could expect children; at all events, it seemed to have righted itself later on. Whatever could be collected in the way of gossip, it made no difference to the avidity with which Elizabeth's hand was sought, and this situation threw into prominence the figure of Lord Robert Dudley. On May 10th, the Venetian Ambassador wrote: "My Lord Robert Dudley is in very great favour and very intimate with her Majesty. In this subject I ought to report the opinion of many, but I doubt whether my letter may not miscarry . . . wherefor it is better to keep silence than to speak ill."

Onlookers might assume that only Lord Robert's wife stood between him and the Crown. He himself would not have agreed. In May there came over from the continent Sir William Pickering, who had been employed in secret service, and possessed height, good looks and a way of recommending himself. No preoccupation ever made Elizabeth indifferent to new attractions. She took advantage of Lord

Robert's being at Windsor on a hunting expedition, and had several very long and private conversations with Pickering. When Lord Robert returned to Whitehall it was to find Pickering occupying rooms in the palace and giving himself considerable airs: dining alone while minstrels played to him, and insisting on attending services in the private chapel that was reserved for the Queen and the Privy Council. Pickering did not long remain on the crest of the wave; but before he disappeared into obscurity he made a significant remark. The slow-witted Baron Ravenstein, the plenipotentiary of the Archduke Charles, was out of his depth and was being steered by the new Spanish Ambassador, de Quadra, Bishop of Aquila. Pickering roared with laughter at the pair, saying the Archduke was wasting his time and so was everyone on a like errand; he, Pickering, knew that the Queen meant to die a maid.

This opinion, which he had formed as a result of his long, mysterious interviews, was by no means generally held. But de Quadra, who was much sharper-witted than de Feria, in narrating to his King the favours Lord Robert received, and that it was said the Queen had just given him £12,000 "as an aid towards his expenses", nevertheless, in his attempt to sum up the situation between the two, said: "I am not sure about her, for I do not understand her."

In this month of June, Lord Robert had become the patron of a company of players; he was one of the first noblemen to have a company known by his name. The Privy Council had recently issued a proclamation, saying that plays must not deal with any matter of religion or of state, and that none was to be performed without permission of the Mayor of a town, or the Lord Lieutenant of the shire, or two justices of the peace for the locality. The great Earl of Shrewsbury, whose family was connected with the Beauchamp ancestors of the Dudleys, was President of the North. Lord Robert was on very good terms with the older man, whose friendship he cultivated throughout his life. He wrote to Lord Shrewsbury now, asking for a licence for the company to play in Yorkshire, and he guaranteed their "being honest men and such as shall play none other matters, I trust, but tolerable and convenient".

Meanwhile he was very closely concerned with political matters. If the Stuarts were put aside, the ruling family in Scotland would be the Hamiltons, Earls of Arran. The young Earl of Arran was offered as a husband to Elizabeth by the Scots, who wanted to oust the French connection altogether. Cecil was strongly inclined towards this marriage, for the young man's mental weakness, which afterwards

became insanity, had not yet shown itself strongly enough to dis-
qualify him. Lord Robert was much alarmed by this prospect. To
deflect the scheme, he gave his own support to the Archduke Charles's
suit. From the informed English point of view, it was almost certain
this could never succeed; many of the Emperor's subject states were
Protestant, so the match did not appear an out-and-out Catholic
alliance, but Philip II would never support his nephew's suit except on
such terms as the Protestant interest in England would not accept. So
early was Lord Robert recognized as an intriguer against the Queen's
marriages.

Deeply engaged as he was with affairs at Court, Lord Robert still
had some existence in common with his wife. The accounts for this
year say: "To Smith the mercer for 6 yards of velvet at 43/- a yard,
four yards to the Spanish tailor for your Lordship's doublet, 2 yards for
guarding my Lady's cloak." They also show Lord Robert's presence
at Mr. Hyde's establishment. "To Mr. Hyde, money which he lent
your Lordship at play at his own house, delivered to your Lordship
at Mr. Hyde's house at sundry times."[1] In August, of which year she
did not say, Lady Dudley wrote a letter from Hayes Court near Chisle-
hurst. She was apparently staying there, and her husband had been
there with her. The previous year she had been at Mr. Hyde's, the
following year she was living at another place; if her writing from
Hayes Court meant that she was living there, the letter presumably
refers to the August of 1559. It is written to her half-sister's husband,
Flowerdew, who was obviously acting as a steward for him. Lady
Dudley tells him to make haste in selling some wool off the sheeps'
backs, even if it must be done at a loss, for her husband is anxious to
discharge a debt. Flowerdew had suggested this wool should be sold,
but she had forgotten to tell her husband. "I forgot to move my Lord
thereof before his departing, he being sore troubled with weighty
affairs, and I not being altogether in quiet for his sudden departing."
Now she begs Flowerdew to make the sale as soon as he can, "though
you sell it for six shillings the stone, or as you would sell it for yourself;
for my Lord so earnestly desired me at his departing to see those poor
men satisfied as though it had been a matter depending upon life;
wherefor I force not to sustain a little loss thereby, to satisfy my Lord's
desires, and so to send that money to Grise's house to London by
Bridewell, to whom my Lord hath given order for the payment
thereof." The end of the letter is written to the brother-in-law rather
than the steward: "And thus I end, always troubling you, wishing that
occasion serve me to requite you: until that time I must pay you with

thanks. And so to God I leave you, from Hayes this 7 of August, your assured during life—Amye Dudley."[1]

There was in fact, in this August, good reason for Lord Robert to show himself troubled with weighty affairs, to leave his home suddenly. Arran had been in France, and, word getting about of his suit to the English Queen, the French had tried to lock him up. He had escaped, and had arrived in England at the end of July. Here he made for Sir William Cecil, and was concealed in Cecil's town house, in Canon Row, Westminster. At this house Elizabeth had a private interview with the poor young man. It came to nothing and he went on to Scotland, but this was the match Lord Robert feared, for, apart from Arran's mental state, which had not yet collapsed, there was no drawback to the match on which a strenuous opposition could be founded.

The match with the Archduke was a protection against any other, and to bring it on again Lord Robert made use of his sister, Lady Mary Sidney. Lord Ambrose Dudley, Lord Robert and Lady Mary were all three on intimate terms with the Queen. Ambrose and Mary were both charming and sincere; their great devotion to their brother Robert, whom, for his personal brilliance and his position with the Queen, they regarded as the great man of the family, did not mean that their own natures were like his. The Queen would probably have liked them for themselves; she was thoroughly attached to them as the loving brother and sister of Lord Robert. Lady Sidney, therefore, was an apt instrument, and it appeared afterwards that she thought her brother was employing her in all good faith and really wanted to see the Queen accept the Archduke.

De Quadra used to send his despatches for the Spanish King via Brussels, where Philip II's sister was Regent of the Netherlands. On September 7th, 1559, he wrote: "A sister of Lord Robert's called Lady Sidney, said this was the time to speak to the Queen about the Archduke . . . She said I must not mind what the Queen said, it was not the custom here for ladies to give their consent till they were teased into it." De Quadra thought he must have this confirmed by Lord Robert. The latter spoke most openly. "He said, in this as in all things, he was at the disposal of my King, to whom he owed his life." At the end of the conversation he assured the Ambassador that the Queen would take the Archduke; she must do so; the marriage was necessary to her. Thinking he was now on safe ground, de Quadra opened the matter with the Queen. He was taken aback because "when I pressed her much, she seemed frightened and protested, over and over again, that she was not to be bound". Judging merely from her behaviour he would have thought he had been mistaken, "but," he said, "I do not believe that Lady Sidney and Lord Robert could be mistaken, and the latter says he never thought the Queen would go so far". He had a good deal of conversation with Lady Mary. Apropos the rumours about Lord Robert and herself, the Queen had said to him, as a kind of feint, that she feared the Archduke might have heard something to her discredit, to which he made a soothing reply.

At the beginning of October, Lord Robert was appointed to welcome another suitor. Duke John of Finland, called the Prince of Sweden, arrived at Harwich to treat for his brother, Prince Eric, and was met at Colchester by the Earl of Oxford and Lord Robert Dudley, who brought him and his train to London, which they entered by Aldgate. By November 2nd Bishop Jewel was writing to a friend at Zurich: "The Swede and Charles the son of the Emperor are courting at a most marvellous rate. But the Swede is the most in earnest, for he promises mountains of money in case of success. The lady, however, is probably thinking of an alliance nearer home." Jewel was a thorough admirer of Elizabeth; he had been present at her first Council meeting, and had written down the charge she had given to the judges to administer justice to those seeking it: "See to them, see to them, for they are my people", saying he had heard her say the words with his own ears. If he really thought the Queen was considering a marriage with Lord Robert Dudley, he must have assumed that a divorce would make way for it; but de Quadra wrote to Philip on November 13th: "I have heard . . . veracious news that Lord Robert has sent to poison his wife." The Swedish and Spanish overtures, he said, were only being entertained to keep the country engaged "until this wicked deed is consummated".

The Duke of Norfolk, the only Duke in England at the time, and the head of the ancient nobility, had very soon conceived a fierce hostility to Lord Robert Dudley. De Quadra reported him as having said that if Lord Robert did not abandon his present pretentions, "he would not die in his bed". "I think," said de Quadra, "this hatred of the Lord Robert will continue as the Duke and the rest of them cannot put up with his being King." On November 18th he continued in the same strain: "He has been warned there is a plot to kill him, which I quite believe, for not a man in the realm can suffer the idea of his being king." De Quadra had not perceived that there was a woman in the realm who could not suffer it either.

The turn of events had shocked Lady Mary Sidney; for once she was angry with her brother. She saw that he had employed her in a scheme without being candid with her. If de Quadra is to be believed, she spoke very angrily to him, declaring that speak she would about what was going on, if she went to the Tower for it, and saying that her worst enemy was her brother. The last words sound unconvincing as they stand; perhaps de Quadra had condensed and crystallized into them a temporary mood of more mildly expressed annoyance and disapproval. There was, however, a piece of confirmatory gossip in one of his letters in December. He said Lord Robert had recently been on very bad terms with his brother-in-law, Sir Henry Sidney. As Sir Henry, like Lord Ambrose, was in the usual way devoted to Lord Robert, this bad feeling on Sir Henry's part may have been owing to the fact that he shared his wife's anger at her having been exploited and deceived. Whatever the cause, the anger did not last long.

The close of the year saw no abating of the scandals about the Queen. Baron Brenner, who was a representative of the Emperor Ferdinand, the father of the Archduke, had naturally a duty to transmit to his court any well-founded rumours about the Queen, but what he said was remarkably sympathetic. The previous August, he said he had been told that Kat Ashley had warned the Queen seriously as to the gossip about her and Lord Robert Dudley. The Queen had replied: "She hoped she had given no one just cause to associate her name with that of her equerry or of any other man. But, she said, in this world, she had had so much sorrow and so little joy! If she showed herself gracious to her Master of the Horse, he deserved it, for his honourable nature and dealing." In December he wrote again on the subject: "The Queen has more than once been addressed and entreated by various persons to exercise more prudence and not give people cause to suspect her in connection with this man." The kind German added: "I rather incline to believe it is but the innocent love which subsists at times between young men and young maidens though it be unseemly for such a Princess."*

* Von Klarwill, *Queen Elizabeth and some Foreigners.*

IV

In JANUARY, 1560, the boys at Eton gave the Queen a New Year's gift. It was a little volume, written on vellum and illuminated, to which forty-four of them had contributed Latin verses, exhorting and beseeching her to marry.* In the same month de Quadra informed the Count de Feria, who was in Brussels, that the English were already considering alternatives to Queen Elizabeth, among whom, however, they did not include Mary Queen of Scots. In mentioning possible substitutes, he thought their choice rested between two claimants. The first was Catherine Grey, a sister of the late Lady Jane, a vain, touchy, silly girl, eagerly responsive to attention and very ready to feel herself slighted. Elizabeth was temperamentally averse from this young woman, nor could she forget the fact that Jane Grey, however unwillingly, had been proclaimed Queen, in defiance of the rights of the Tudors. As Lady Catherine had a great awareness of her position as one of the heiresses presumptive to the throne, but not a grain of common sense to accompany it, she was bound to fall a victim to whatever party, hostile to the Queen, wanted to exploit her. De Quadra now spoke of Elizabeth as "making much of Lady Catherine to keep her quiet". He next spoke of Lord Henry Hastings, whose Plantagenet blood had caused the Duke of Northumberland to acquire the young man as a husband for his daughter Katherine. The gossip-mongers had told de Quadra that "Hastings would succeed".

So long as the Queen remained unmarried there was bound to be conversation about all the persons with any claim to succeed her, but that de Quadra should think the nation as a whole was contemplating the exchange of Queen Elizabeth for either Catherine Grey or Henry Hastings, or indeed for anyone at all, showed how very little he was in touch with national feeling. The government of Elizabeth had made an excellent beginning. In April, 1559, a peace with France had been concluded, and the English were no longer fighting an expensive and unpopular war. The reform of the coinage was a measure of which the benefit was felt in every walk of life. The Religious Settlement had

* Maxwell Lyte, *History of Eton College.*

begun with a policy of such moderation that, after the persecution of Catholics by Northumberland and of Protestants at the hands of Mary, the bulk of the nation of either creed, who were neither persecutors nor fanatics, were for the time being ready to acquiesce in the Settlement even if they did not approve of it. In the very first meeting of Parliament Sir Nicholas Bacon, Lord Keeper of the Great Seal, had spoken of their good fortune in "a princess to whom nothing—what, nothing? no, no worldly thing—was so dear as the hearty love and good will of her subjects", and Camden commented on that "correspondence between the Queen and her subjects" which had showed itself by the end of the first year, "the Commonwealth seeming to take life and strength, to the common joy of all".

Meanwhile, Lord Robert Dudley's domestic and public lives were kept entirely separate. He was now in a better position to buy a country place than he had been when he considered buying Fitcham: the Queen had already given him land in Yorkshire and the manor of Kew, made him Lieutenant of the Castle and Forest of Windsor, and granted him one of the most valuable of all the gifts she ever made him, a licence to export woollen cloth free of duty; yet he did not buy an estate. Instead, he made an arrangement for his wife which was, to say the least, barely appropriate.

Mr. Hyde being already settled in the neighbourhood of Abingdon, his brother-in-law Antony Forster, at some time before the opening of 1560, took a lease of a property in the same neighbourhood; this was Cumnor Place in North Berkshire, near the Oxfordshire border. The house, which had been a monastic building before the Reformation, was not large. It consisted of four wings, each having one floor above the ground floor, built round a courtyard. The property belonged to the family of the late Dr. Owen, who had been physician to Henry VIII, Edward VI and Mary. Forster rented it from them, and one of the family, Mrs. Owen, continued to live in a part of it. Forster lived in another part, and yet another section of the building was made over to Lady Dudley, her household servants and her confidential maid, Mrs. Pinto. If she had had the whole house, it would have been suitable enough; or if she had had this third of it as a country residence and lived part of her time in her husband's manor house at Kew, the arrangement would have been tolerable; as it was, there could be no doubt that she was neglected by her husband. She not only stood in his light, as he supposed; since as long ago as April, 1559, she was said to be suffering from "a malady in one of her breasts". From Lord Robert's own point of view, there was every reason for seeing as little of her as possible.

By March, 1560, de Quadra's reliance on Lord Robert's help with the Archduke's suit was exhausted; so was his patience. "Lord Robert," he declared, "is the worst and most procrastinating young man I ever saw and not at all courageous or spirited." This was an interesting comment, made very early in his career, on Robert Dudley's sinuous and quiet behaviour, which, though contrasting strangely with some of his other traits, is mentioned so frequently in descriptions of his character. He knew, it was said, how "to put his passion in his pocket". "He was the most reserved man of that age, that saw all and was invisible." David Lloyd said of him: "He carried a depth not to be fathomed, but by the Searcher of Hearts. Many fell in his time who saw not the hand that pulled them down and many died that knew not their own disease."*

His plans seemed to de Quadra to be going on apace, and de Quadra had no doubt as to what they were. He reported that Lord Robert had been heard to say, "if he live another year, he will be in a very different position from now". On March 28th de Quadra wrote: "He is laying in a good stock of arms and every day is assuming a more masterful part in affairs. They say that he thinks of divorcing his wife."

In this same month, in the bills presented to Lord Robert Dudley's steward, were the last items concerning Lady Dudley in her lifetime. They ran: "Delivered, a velvet hat, embroidered for my Lady. A pair of velvet shoes for my Lady."[1]

At the beginning of this year, the English government achieved a success of the greatest importance. Mary of Guise, the mother of Mary Queen of Scots and Queen Regent of Scotland, had come to open conflict with her Protestant nobles, who called themselves the Lords of the Congregation. After harrowing indecisions and misgivings, Elizabeth, strongly urged by Cecil and the Council, had consented to send assistance to the Scots Protestants. Admiral Winter, sent north in January, destroyed French shipping and supplies in the Firth of Forth. An English army crossed the border in March, and, though it was at first defeated by the French outside Leith, its presence turned the scale; the Queen Regent was dying and the French government, occupied by insurrection at home, could send no further help to Scotland. In May, Cecil went north to negotiate the Treaty of Edinburgh, which, though in the interests of the Scots Reformers, gained three points of inestimable value to the English: Mary Queen of Scots and her husband

* *State Worthies.*

were to relinquish the use of the English Royal Arms—which Mary
had quartered with her own at the time of her marriage to the Dauphin
two years before; they were to recognize Elizabeth's title as Queen of
England; and the French army was to leave Scotland at once. The
Treaty was concluded in July, and at the end of July Cecil began his
journey back to England.

Robert Dudley, in the absence of the one man whose influence with
Elizabeth was never rivalled, made the most of having the field to
himself. Cecil's position with Elizabeth was unique—Dudley said so on
a later occasion—but Dudley himself had many rivals. None of them
superseded him but, throughout his career, he was merely the most
successful of a numerous band. The Queen had many lovers, but her
passion was for her kingdom, and no one of her ability could be in
doubt for one instant as to whether Cecil or Dudley were the more
valuable for what he could contribute to her great aim. She frequently
fell out with Cecil—on this very question of sending an army to
Scotland, he had said: "I have had such a torment herein with the
Queen's Majesty as an ague hath not in five fits so much abated"; but
the underlying mutual confidence was complete, for each wanted,
more than anything in the world, to make a success of governing the
country, and neither could succeed without the other.

Robert Dudley's ambition was in a different category. Towards the
end of thirty years of tireless self-seeking, some alteration of his views
did become perceptible; he came at last to adopt something of the
attitude of the two people from whom, during those years, he had
been inseparable; but the change was slow. In 1560 he had but one
idea: to stimulate Elizabeth's passion and overcome her resistance, so
that, by becoming her husband, he could become King of England.

During Cecil's absence, it was noticed what a long time the Queen
spent without "coming abroad"; it was said Lord Robert kept her
shut up with him, and that her health was suffering. For the first and
only time, it was said during these weeks that Elizabeth could not be
got to attend to matters of state; but the conduct of either was in fact
far from "light": he was engaged in promoting, and she in repressing,
a consuming ambition. Meanwhile he discharged the duties of his
office. He was never accused of laziness, or of treating any appointment as a sinecure; the office of the Master of the Queen's Horses was
always under his personal supervision.

The accounts submitted to him for the first two years of the reign
give an insight into the Queen's stud, though they deal only with those
horses which were ill or needed attention. The accounts were sent in

by Martin Almayne, claiming "allowance for dressing the Queen's coursers", and ran from Christmas 1559 for two years following. They mentioned treatment "for Bay Bell, foundered in his fore-feet", for "Bay Star, dressed under the belly", for "dressing Bay Gentle in his fore-feet", for "dressing one of the carriage mules' sore foot", for "dressing Bay Killigrew's hinder leg", for "dressing Gray Jennet on the shoulder", for "dressing fifteen colts on their legs", for "dressing Dun Arundel on his fore-legs", Several horses suffered from glanders, an infectious disease producing boils inside the nose; it was called the farcy, and Gray Sparrow was dressed for it. Great Savoy was bathed when he came from the mares. Some of the horses had no names and were identified by description as: "For dressing the bay jennet with the great cod, for the hurt in one of his hips". "For dressing Bay Prince of his sore eye", the account continued[1]. "A drink for the pied colt, a drink to jennet Ringrave, a drink to Bay Altabelle, for dressing of Bay Minion upon the hinder legs. For malt and other medicines, for brimstone, for venerick, for dressing Bay Sudbery of the stranglion." It is interesting to see how many horses were called after members of the Court: Arundel, Killigrew, Hastings, Hunsdon. Others had charming fanciful names, such as Speedwell, Delicate, Bellaface and Gentle. Later in the year Lord Robert wrote to Lord Sussex, then Lord Deputy of Ireland, saying the Queen wanted some Irish horses sent over "for her own saddle, especially for strong, good gallopers, which are better than her geldings, which she spareth not to try as fast as they can go. And I fear them much," he wrote, "but she will prove them."

In these weeks of high summer, while Dudley engrossed the Queen entirely and she was scarcely seen, on July 17th there was had up before the justices Ann Dowe of Brentwood, sixty-eight years old, known as Mother Dowe, who spent most of her time on the road. Five weeks before, at Rochford, in a house on the green beyond the parsonage, where she went to mend a fan (for which she was paid ninepence), the wife of that house said in her hearing that Dudley had given the Queen a new petticoat that cost twenty nobles. To this, Mother Dowe had said, the Queen had no need of the coat for she was able to buy one herself. Three days later in a broomfield in the same parish she met one Mr. Coke riding on a horse. "What news, Mother Dowe?" he said. She repeated the story of Dudley's giving the Queen a petticoat that cost twenty nobles. Coke said: "Thinkst thou it was a petticoat? No, no, he gave her a child, I warrant thee." And, having a bottle of wine at his saddle-bow, gave her a drink from the said bottle and so they parted. On July 16th she came to Donbery. It was eight in the morning, and the tailor John King was already at his work when Mother Dowe came into his shop. She began by saying that there was things nowadays that she might say nothing of, and then she said that Dudley and the Queen played legerdemain together. "That is not so!" exclaimed King. "Is," said Mother Dowe, "for he hath given her a child." When King said: "Why, she hath no child yet!", "No," said Mother Dowe, "if she hath not, he hath put one to the making." She said Dudley had given the Queen a petticoat that he and she should rue. King thought, early as it was, she must be drunk. She went off and kept walking till she was run in by the sheriff living in the town of Donbery.*

Lady Dudley cannot but have heard the talk about her husband and the Queen, for she was surrounded by people connected with the small inner circle of those who were devoted to Elizabeth. They would not speak either with Mother Dowe's broadness or with her total inaccuracy, but what they could say, and what their servants could repeat to hers, would be equally dreadful to her, allied with her husband's total neglect, and the consciousness of mortal disease which she had had for eighteen months at least. Her woman, Pinto, said she had often heard her mistress "pray to God to deliver her from desperation".

On Sunday evening, September 8th, she was discovered at the foot of the stone staircase, dead. The detail that seized the public imagination was that, though her neck was broken, the hood upon her head was not disarranged.

Coming at it did after eighteen months of rumour, not only as to Dudley's relations with the Queen, but as to his intentions of getting rid of his wife, either by waiting for her death from disease, or by divorce, or by poison, the news of the discovery produced an effect that was appalling. The degree, if any, of Lord Robert's responsibility was a most serious matter; but the burning question was whether the Queen were implicated. Was the death a murder, to which the Queen had been accessory before the fact?

The evidence for saying so consists in a despatch written by de Quadra for the King of Spain but sent to the Queen Regent at Brussels for more rapid transmission to Madrid. The despatch is dated September 11th, and in it he says: "I came to Windsor where the Queen is, five days ago." He arrived, that is, on September 6. This was a Friday. He goes on to say that Cecil, who had now returned from Scotland, had had a most confidential conversation with him. "After exacting many pledges of strict secrecy, he said . . . he clearly foresaw the ruin of the state through Robert's intimacy with the Queen, who surrendered all affairs to him and meant to marry him." Cecil himself meant to retire, though he supposed they would put him in the Tower if he said so. "He ended by begging me in God's name to point out to the Queen the effect of her misconduct." To this de Quadra, according to himself, replied that he had always begged the Queen to live quietly and to marry; he would try his persuasions once more. Cecil ended, he wrote, by saying: "Robert was thinking of killing his wife, who was publicly announced to be ill, though she was quite well and would take good care they did not poison her." De Quadra then says: "The next day the Queen told me as she returned from hunting that Robert's wife was dead or nearly so, and asked me not to say anything about it. Certainly this business is most shameful and scandalous, and withal I am not sure whether she will marry the man at once, or even if she will marry at all, as I do not think she has her mind sufficiently fixed. Since writing the above, I hear the Queen has published the death of Robert's wife and said in Italian: *Si ha rotto il collo*. She must have fallen down a staircase."

The death occurred on Sunday the 8th, the news reached Windsor on Monday 9th. De Quadra does not give either of these dates himself, but, assuming them to be generally known, the impression given by the despatch is that the Queen announced the death before the news of it arrived—before, indeed, it had occurred. He does not actually say so, and a striking feature of his version is that, in spite of their importance, he gives no dates at all except that he arrived at Windsor on September 6th and is writing on the 11th.[1] Writers who wish to convey the idea that Elizabeth was accessory to the murder, and had it so much on her mind that she said the death had occurred not only before official news of it had been received but before it had even happened, argue—as indeed they are bound to do if they are to make out their case—that de Quadra's conversation with Cecil must have taken place on the day of his arrival, Friday 6th. The "next day" of the Queen's communication would be Saturday 7th. This is pure assumption, and nothing in the letter gives it any support whatever. He begins by relating a very important discussion he had with the Queen about the French, who, she said, did not lack the will, only the power, to injure her, and who had not yet, in spite of the Treaty of Edinburgh, begun to withdraw their troops from Scotland. He does not give the date even of this interview. Then he says, "*after this* I had an opportunity of talking to Cecil"; thus the interview with Cecil is undated also. "*The next day*" the Queen told him Lord Robert's wife was dead or nearly so. "*Since writing the above*" he hears she has published the news of the death. There is, therefore, nothing in what he actually says to disprove the fact that the Queen told him of the death on Monday 9th or Tuesday 10th. The reasonable deduction is that she did: for if he had gained news of this importance by Saturday 7th, why did he delay to write of it till Wednesday 11th? As to why he should have allowed his words to carry this implication, Throckmorton, the ambassador at Paris, said that de Quadra was in the pay of the Guises, and was doing what he could so to discredit Elizabeth in the eyes of Philip that the latter would cease to support her. In any case, Spanish hostility to Elizabeth was so pronounced that, had de Quadra been able to bring home to her this fatally damaging accusation by stating categorically: "The death of Lady Dudley occurred on September 8th, but on September 7th the Queen told me it had already happened", it cannot be supposed that he would have failed to do it; an impartial or even a friendly writer could not have omitted such an extraordinary fact.

The accusation of guilty foreknowledge of a murder is not brought home by de Quadra's letter; and the suggestion that Elizabeth, with her exceptional acuteness and talent for intrigue, would have behaved with a stupidity that a woman of even average capacity would have been expected to avoid can hardly be taken seriously. The words in which she announced the death to de Quadra, supposing him to have reported them accurately, give a strong impression that she was startled, even horrified by the news: "She told me Lord Robert's wife was dead, or nearly so, and asked me not to say anything about it". She tried to delay the impact of this terrifying truth—"dead, or nearly so"—and to postpone as long as she might the publication of this shocking scandal.

The question, inseparable from that of the Queen's complicity, is that of the death itself. An ordinary fall downstairs, even down a stone staircase, would not produce a broken neck, unless the person had fallen from top to bottom, and the undisturbed state of Amy Dudley's headdress showed she had not done this. The fall, therefore, cannot have been the result of suicide. On the other hand, if she had first been murdered, and an attempt was made to suggest that the death was the result of an accident, the device of a fall downstairs could hardly have been chosen; it carries no conviction. And yet, perhaps, the poor young woman did die from a fall downstairs, and the verdict of death by misadventure, which has been scouted for four hundred years as an impudent farce, may have been the true one after all.

Professor Ian Aird★ has put forward a theory of fascinating interest, which for the first time covers all the facts, and which, as he explains, could not have been advanced before since it depends on medical research whose results have only very recently been known. Professor Aird says that in fifty per cent of fatal cases of cancer of the breast "secondary deposits" are present in the bones, and of these six per cent are found in the spine. The effect of these deposits in the spine is to make it very brittle. The bones may collapse from the slight strain imposed on them by walking. "If that part of the spine which lies in the neck suffers in this way, the affected person gets spontaneously a broken neck. Such a fracture is more likely to occur in stepping downstairs than in walking on the level." Professor Aird says that what attracted his attention to the case, as a possible instance of this theory, was the satirical statement that the dead woman's fall, though violent enough to kill her, was not violent enough to disturb "the hood that stood upon her head", which fact was printed for the first time in 1584.[1] Ironically, the instantaneous snapping of the brittle neck-bones would be attended with just this result. He also points out that Cecil's remark to de Quadra that Lady Dudley was quite well and was taking care not to be poisoned was consistent with a cancer of the breast, which would not be noticeable when the woman was dressed; but that such a condition would give a terrible significance to her being found often on her knees, praying to God to deliver her from desperation.

Elizabeth's undeniable guilt was that she encouraged Robert Dudley to be with her all the time, knowing that this must mean his desertion of an affectionate and faithful young wife.

On Monday, September 9th, Lord Robert had sent his kinsman Thomas Blount on an errand to Cumnor. After Blount had left, a servant arrived with news of the tragedy, and in all haste Lord Robert sent a letter on Blount's heels. In it he made no conventional expression of grief; he merely stated the fact and his consciousness of the alarming suspicions that must attach to himself. "Immediately upon your departing from me there came to me Bowes by whom I understand that my wife is dead, as he saith by a fall from a pair of stairs; little other understanding can I have of him. The greatness and suddenness of the misfortune doth so perplex me, until I do hear from you how the matter stands or how this evil doth light upon me, considering what the malicious world will bruit, as I can take no rest." He knew,

★ *English Historical Review*, 1956.

he said, his only means of combating "the malicious talk that I know the wicked world will use" was to make everything open. "Therefore, I do pray you, as you have loved me, and do tender me and my quietness, and as now my special trust is in you, that you will use all devices and means you possibly can, for learning of the truth, wherein, have no respect to any living person." As to the jury, he told Blount to call upon the coroner, "and charge him to the uttermost from me to have good regard to make choice of no light nor slight persons, but the most discreet and substantial men for the jurors, such as for their knowledge may be able to search honourably and duly, by all manner of exertion, the bottom of the matter, and that the body be viewed and searched accordingly by them, and in every respect to proceed by order and law. In the meantime, Cousin Blount, let me be advertized from you, by this bearer, with all speed, how the matter doth stand; for, as the cause and manner thereof doth marvellously trouble me, considering my case many ways, so I shall not be at rest till I may be ascertained thereof." The absence of grief, tenderness, remorse, or any feeling whatever except anxiety, "considering my case many ways", is at least an argument for the letter's honesty. "As I have ever loved you," he urged, "do not dissemble with me . . . but send me your true conceit and opinion of the matter, whether it happened by evil chance or villainy: and fail not to let me hear continually from you. And thus fare you well in much haste. Your loving friend and kinsman much perplexed, Robert Dudley." A postscript added that he had sent for his wife's half-brother, Appleyard, "and other of her friends also, to be there, that they may be privy and see how all things do proceed".[1]

Blount's reply was written from Cumnor on September 11th. "The present advertizement I can give to your Lordship at this time is, too true it is that my Lady is dead and, as it seemeth, with a fall, but yet, how or which way I cannot learn." He now related his doings since Monday. He had learned the news before it reached Lord Robert, for he had crossed Bowes, riding with it to Windsor. Thus informed of the matter, and realizing its horrifying implications, he had not gone at once to Cumnor but, to test public opinion, had stopped at an inn in Abingdon, and there asked the landlord what news was stirring. The landlord said: "There was a great misfortune within three or four miles of the town; my Lord Robert Dudley's wife was dead." How was that? Blount asked. "He said, by a misfortune, as he heard; by a fall from a pair of stairs." Blount then asked the significant question, what did the neighbours think of this? The landlord answered that though some said well, some evil, most of them, including himself, thought that no foul play could have happened in Mr. Antony Forster's house.

Blount said, surely Lady Dudley's servants must have had something to say about her death? Very little, said the landlord. Then he gave the curious piece of information that on the Sunday she had almost driven her servants out of the house, to the fair which was being held at Abingdon. Bowes had also told Blount this, and when the latter arrived at Cumnor the servants confirmed it, and Mrs. Odingsell, Forster's sister-in-law, said that she had told Lady Dudley she herself would not go to the fair on a Sunday; it was no day for a gentlewoman to go; she would go on Monday. Lady Dudley said she might please herself as to that, but all the Dudley servants should go, and she would have Mrs. Owen in to keep her company at dinner. This strange, impatient banishing of the servants presumably included the waiting woman, Pinto. It looked to Blount not inconsistent with an impression about Lady Dudley which he had gathered from Pinto herself, who, he said, "doth dearly love her". "Certainly, my Lord," he wrote, "as little while as I have been here, I have heard divers tales that maketh me to judge her a strange woman of mind." He asked Pinto outright if in her view the cause of death were mischance, murder or suicide? She said, mischance. She did not entertain the possibility of murder, and as to suicide, her mistress was too good a woman to commit that mortal sin. She prayed daily on her knees—and then Pinto uttered the ominous words, that she had heard her "divers times, pray to God to deliver her from desperation". Then, said Blount, she might have had some dark design? "No, good Mr. Blount," cried the woman, "do not so judge of my words; if you should so gather I am sorry I said as much." On the spot as he was, and able to question the household, Blount could get no further. "My Lord, it is most strange that this chance should fall upon you, as it passeth the judgment of any man to say how it is." Her sending away her servants was the only piece of evidence to suggest the cause of death, and this appeared to be strengthened by the poor young woman's state of mind. Blount repeated: "The tales I do hear of her make me think she had a strange mind as I will tell you at my coming." A strange mind she may well have had, lonely and ill, while it was being rumoured over Europe that her husband was waiting for her to die that he might marry the Queen.

Blount finished his letter with a word about the jury. They had been chosen already and some of them were in the house. He assured Lord Robert they were as able men of their kind as were to be found anywhere. He thought it a guarantee of their integrity that some of them entertained a distinct prejudice against Antony Forster. He promised to send word constantly. He added in a postscript: "Your Lordship hath done very well in sending for Mr. Appleyard."[1]

At Windsor, the Queen had ordered Lord Robert to retire from Court while the enquiries were pending, for no one under suspicion of a serious crime was allowed in the sovereign's presence until he had cleared himself, or, failing to do so, had received a pardon. Lord Robert went to his house at Kew. His agitation was increased by this inevitable banishment; to be unable to enter Elizabeth's presence was a severe disadvantage to him, for his influence was entirely that of a personal relationship. All his life he intrigued to get others posted away from Court while remaining there himself, and in this crisis his own enforced absence heightened his anxiety and alarm. "In haste, at Kew this 12 of September," he wrote. "Cousin Blount, until I hear from you again how the matter falleth out, in very truth I cannot be in quiet, and yet you do satisfy me with the discreet jury you say are chosen already." Nevertheless, he wanted a word of exhortation given to them, "so to find it, as they shall see it fall out. And if it so fall out a chance or misfortune, so to find, and if it appear villainy (as God forbid so mischievous or wicked a person should live), then to find it so, and God willing I shall never fear the day of prosecution accordingly, what person soever it may appear any way to touch, so well for the just punishment of the act as to mine own true justification." From this is appears that he was facing in his own mind the possibility of someone being brought to trial if the coroner's jury returned a verdict of murder.[2]

Meanwhile, Sir William Cecil had visited the exile at Kew. Since Cecil's great hope was to see the Queen make a marriage which would produce children but also secure a valuable alliance, his objections to Lord Robert as a consort were both strong and well-founded. The present catastrophe, which, though removing the physical bar to such a marriage, erected the strongest possible moral one against it, could not but go some way to re-assuring him. When he came back from Edinburgh, he had found Lord Robert in a phase of close intimacy with the Queen, who appeared to be quite engrossed by his society. The position of a few weeks before was now entirely reversed. When he visited the dismayed young man, his company was eagerly welcomed as the favour which it was. In Lord Robert's isolation, contact with the Secretary of State was a boon indeed. When Cecil left, Lord Robert wrote after him: "Sir, I thank you much for your being here, and the great friendship you have shown towards me I shall not forget. I am very loath to wish you here again, but would be very glad to be with you there. I pray you, let me hear from you what you think best for me to do." The suddenness with which the reverse had overtaken him had left him with the typical symptom of shock: "Methinks, I am here all this while as it were in a dream, and too far, too far from the place where I am bound to be." Not only that; he felt that his enforced retirement at Kew prevented him from discharging the affairs of his office. Surely the Queen could be made to understand this? "Methinks also this long, idle time cannot excuse me for the duty I have to discharge elsewhere. I pray you, help him that sues to be at liberty, out of so great bondage."[1] This at least makes it clear that he had been ordered to keep himself at Kew till further notice, and that he could not have gone down to Cumnor even had he wished. While he remained at Kew, his tailor's servant came there to measure him for his mourning clothes. A payment was made: "To Jennings, Mr. Whittle's servant, for his boat hire and pains in coming to Kew to take measure of your Lordship."[2]

The jury returned a verdict of accidental death, and the foreman wrote to tell Lord Robert so. By the time the latter wrote to Blount again, he had been recalled to Court. He said: "I have received a letter from one Smith that seemeth to be the foreman of the jury . . . and for anything I hear that by any search or examination they can make in the world hitherto it doth plainly appear, he saith, a very misfortune, which for mine own part, Counsin Blount, doth very much satisfy and quiet me." But with his father's turn for making a good impression several times over, he said, "for his own thorough quietness", and "though it be never so plainly found", he would like "another substantial company of honest men" to try the matter again. No lengths would be too far to go to hammer home a verdict on which so much depended. "I have also required Sir Richard Blount who is a perfect honest gentleman to help the furtherance thereof . . . I trust he be with you . . . Appleyard I hear hath been there as I appointed and Arthur Robsart, her brothers; if any more of her friends had been to be had, I would also have caused them to have seen and been privy to all the dealings there."[3]

On September 17th the news of the death reached Leicestershire, and when it arrived at Ashby-de-la-Zouche, the country house of Lord and Lady Hastings, Lord Hastings had a letter to his brother-in-law already half-written. "My very good Lord," it ran, "I am sure you are not without plenty of red deer," but still he was sending him six venison pies, "of a stag bred in the little garden of Ashby-de-la-Zouche". He would be glad to hear, he wrote, "how the baking doth like you, for I am in some doubt how my cook hath done his part". Into the middle of this came the news that his brother-in-law was now a widower. Lord Hastings wrote some conventional expressions of piety and resignation, that the hour must be considered a happy one that brings man from sorrow to joy, from mortality to immortality, from care and trouble to rest and quietness. Then he said he would cease his rude postscript for he was sure his brother-in-law understood all this much better than he himself could tell it him. It did not appear to him necessary to cancel the first part of the letter about venison pies, to say one word about Lord Robert's suffering a personal grief, or to include a message from the latter's sister, Katherine. Few things could illustrate more plainly than this letter the attitude which Lord Robert's family had long adopted towards his marriage.[1]

On Friday, September 20th, Lady Dudley's coffin was brought to Oxford and laid in Worcester College. On September 22nd an elaborate funeral cortège bore it to St. Mary's Church. A story went that the funeral oration was pronounced by Lord Robert's Chaplain, Dr. Babington, afterwards Vice-Chancellor of Oxford, and that in the course of it the Chaplain, meaning to speak of "the lady so pitifully dead", made a slip and said "so pitifully slain". This, however, was not heard till twenty-four years after the funeral and fifteen years after the death of Dr. Babington. It is possible that he never made the oration at all, for, on much sounder evidence, one was made by Edmund Campion,* then twenty years old, a fellow of St. John's, already distinguished for his scholarship and grace. But whether or not such a contretemps occurred, it would have been in keeping with the gloom and uneasiness of the occasion. The husband was not present, but this was according to the usage of the day.

The accounts of the steward, Richard Ellis, give full particulars of expenses incurred for the funeral. First came the amount paid for the chief item: "To Jasper the Joiner, £11.10.6." The grave-clothes were sent for to London. "For apparel for my Lady and for charges of her man Higgins lying in London for the same. £3.0.6." At the same time, Mr. Whittle the tailor was paid £25 "for redeeming a diamond of my Ladys". The Church of St. Mary was draped in black at Lord Robert's expense, and the cost of "mailing cord for cloth that was sent to Oxford" was entered, also the fee "unto carriers that carried the said packs to Oxford". "The exchange of one hundred pounds of white

---

* Bede Camm, *Lives of the English Martyrs*, *Edmund Campion*.

money into gold, which was sent to Oxford for the charges of the burial", cost 16/8. Fees to the heralds who attended the corpse were £56.6.8. Finally was entered "for Ellis the steward, a pair of black velvet hose to mourn in, £1.2.0, and for Mr. Browshill the same".[1]

By October, the scandal had burst upon Europe. Sir Nicholas Throckmorton was ambassador at Paris, where the boy Francis II and his nineteen-year-old wife Mary Queen of Scots were now King and Queen, but where the power was wielded by Mary's uncles, the Cardinal and the Duke of Guise. On October 10th Throckmorton wrote three letters. One, to Lord Robert, condoled with him on the death of "my Lady, his late bedfellow". He thanked Lord Robert for sending him a nag and would thank him yet more, he said, if Lord Robert could get him recalled, to hawk and hunt in England, which it were meeter for him to do, than to be Ambassador here, *as things had fallen out*. Much plainer he dared not speak to a man who might become King Consort. But to Lord North he wrote that he wished he were dead, or away, for people were not hesitating "to speak, of the Queen *and some others*, that which every hair on my head standeth at, and my ears glow to hear". Catholics asked him triumphantly: "What religion is this, that a subject shall kill his wife and the Prince not only bear withal but marry him?" While to Cecil he wrote: "I pray God this cruel and hard hap be not the messenger of a further disaster towards, in our country! You can consider the rest." He would not even write down the hideous possibility of a marriage between the Queen and Lord Robert Dudley.[2]

The only man who was prepared to consider it without loathing was, remarkably, one between whom and Lord Robert there was a life-long enmity. Lord Sussex had the lowest opinion of Lord Robert; there were times when he quarrelled furiously with him at the Council table, and when even the Queen's presence could not prevent them from going for each other like fighting dogs; but in this month he wrote a characteristic letter to Cecil. He said they were all agreed that what they most wanted to see was a child of the Queen's body. "Therefore, let her choose after her own affection; let her take the man at sight of whom all her senses are aroused by desire." That was the surest way to bring them a blessed Prince, and he declared: "Whomsoever she will choose, him will I love and honour, and serve to the uttermost." But if he could have brought round all the Council to his way of thinking, there would still have been one person he could not have persuaded to this marriage.

But till time should show, the sayings that Dudley had had his wife murdered with the Queen's connivance, and that the pair were about to marry, grew louder and louder until Throckmorton was driven almost wild with dismay. In November he sent his confidential secretary, Jones, to London to tell the Queen and Council by word of mouth the damaging nature of the situation in Paris.

The Court was at Greenwich when Jones arrived on the night of Monday the 25th. On Tuesday he saw Mr. Secretary Cecil. He gave Cecil Throckmorton's opinions on various matters of policy, and Cecil made him write these down. He then, by word of mouth only, made Cecil acquainted with a remark the Queen of Scots had uttered in the lightness of her heart, which was to attain a disastrous celebrity. Mary, who regarded the English crown as her own and Elizabeth as unlawfully keeping it from her, had listened to the scandal with vivid enthusiasm, and had exlaimed: "The Queen of England is going to marry the Master of her Horses, who has killed his wife to make room for her!"

Jones had had as yet no audience of Elizabeth. That day he dined in the Scottish Ambassador's lodging and Lord Robert Dudley was of the party. Halfway through dinner, Lord Robert got up and said he was returning to the Court. On his way, he sent back a message to Jones, asking him to follow him. Jones did so. When he was in Lord Robert's presence, the latter asked him point blank whether the Queen of France had said those words? Jones, alone with a man whose reputation was already somewhat sinister, and who might, if evil befel, prove to be his Queen's husband, denied being the source of the story. Lord Robert at once told him that he had seen a written statement of the matter, and that Mr. Secretary had told him that Jones was the source of the anecdote. So cornered, Jones could no longer refuse to admit that he was. This was all Lord Robert wanted to hear. He left Jones, but with this parting injunction, that he should in no case tell Mr. Secretary of their conversation. Jones gave the required promise and, as he told Throckmorton, he could see well enough why it had been demanded. The statement about the Queen of Scots had not been written down at all. Jones judged "that Mr. Secretary did declare it only to the Queen, at whose hands My Lord Robert had it". His feelings of apprehension were increased when he gave Sir Henry Killigrew a despatch from Throckmorton. Killigrew took it, saying with a sad look: "I think verily that my Lord Robert will run away with the hare and have the Queen."

Jones had his first interview with the Queen at 6 o'clock on Wednesday evening. She had spent the day at Eltham, dining and hunting "with divers of my Lords", and had now come back to Greenwich to spend the night. He noticed a change in her since he had seen her last. She looked frail, and as if she were under a nervous strain. Though telling him it had been unnecessary for him to come at all, she listened to him, he said, very patiently. Jones first related various matters with which Throckmorton had charged him; then he came to the quick. At once the Queen said: "I have heard of this before, and he needed not to have sent you withal." Jones pleaded Throckmorton's vigilance and care, his grasp of affairs and strong sense of the Queen's danger. Once launched, he threw discretion to the winds, and spoke straightforwardly of the injuries Lord Robert Dudley was working on her name and dignity. The Queen writhed in her chair and put her fingers over her face, but then she laughed. Jones reminded her that Dudley came of an injurious race, that Northumberland had been her enemy even more than her sister's. At this the Queen laughed again; but she then gave Jones a plain statement of facts. She told him there had been an inquest on Lady Dudley's death in the county where it took place, and the jury's verdict gave the lie to the rumours of Lord Robert's complicity. He was at Court when the death occurred, and none of his people were "at the attempt at his wife's house". These words, if accurately reported, sound as if Elizabeth thought a murder had been committed by somebody; but, she went on, the results of the investigation had cleared "both Lord Robert's honesty and her own honour".*

Jones heard the Queen speak; even more to the purpose, he saw how she looked; and the effect of the audience was to lessen his alarm. Commenting on Elizabeth's sickly air, he said: "Sureley the matter of my Lord Robert doth greatly perplex her and is never like to take place." His confidence was confirmed by an anecdote some courtiers had told him. The Queen had considered bestowing on Lord Robert the Earldom of Leicester. She had gone so far as to have the letters patent drawn up; but when they were brought for her signature who knows what memories, what insight, what caution checked her? Instead of her pen she took the penknife and cut the document in pieces, saying: the Dudleys had been traitors for three generations.[1] Was this said of a man she meant to marry? Lord Robert, ambitious at any time, and particularly anxious now for such a solid sign of favour as the bestowal of an earldom, having, too, so nearly gained it, was as angry as he dared to be. He had failed of this promotion: that was bad enough, but the Court had known he was to have it, and now they knew he was not to have it. The Dudley family did not bear a loss of

* Hardwicke State Papers.

face easily. Lord Robert's father had put men in gaol for commenting on his mere absence from the King's progress. He reproached the Queen bitterly with the injury which her unkindness was doing him, but it did not move her; she was in tormenting mood. Patting his cheeks, she exclaimed: "No, no! The bear and the ragged staff are not so easily overthrown!" His followers attempted to press his suit upon her, but she pouted and said she could not marry a subject. But, urged his well-wishers, she could make him a King? "No," the Queen said.*

Five years later, when Sir Henry Sidney was Lord Deputy of Ireland, the Queen wrote to him about the need for caution in dealing with the descendants of those who had been traitors. Her letter said: "A strength to harm is perilous in the hand of an ambitious head . . . Believe not, though they swear, that they can be full sound, whose parents sought the rule that they full fain would have. I warrant you, they will never be accused of bastardy." The letter was written about the Lords of Desmond and Ormonde, but it was capable of application much nearer home.

Nevertheless, the rumours abroad continued in full force. On December 31st Throckmorton wrote to Cecil almost frantically. A marriage to Lord Robert in the circumstances would so extinguish the Queen's reputation, she would cease to carry any weight in European diplomacy. (Such an outcome as he feared for Elizabeth was the fate, seven years later, of Mary Queen of Scots, as a result of her marriage to Bothwell.) If, said Throckmorton, the Queen should "so foully forget herself . . . never think to bring anything to pass, here or elsewhere". Cecil, however, had convinced himself that for the time being at least there was no danger, and he wanted to hear less of these croakings. His letter crossed Throckmorton's on December 31st, saying: "Whatsoever reports and opinions be, I know surely that my Lord Robert himself hath more fear than hope, and so doth the Queen give him cause." In January he added a postscript to one of his letters, warning the Ambassador "not to be too busy about the matters between the Queen's Majesty and my Lord Robert".[1]

The jeweller Dymock, who had been to the Swedish Court "with jewels and patterns of jewels drawn on parchment", was in London early in 1561, and here he heard the Swedish envoy Walwicke say: "The Queen would have Lord Robert." As the suit of Prince Eric of Sweden was still being made, Dymock thought he must remove this impression if he could, so being an acquaintance of Mrs. Ashley he went to Whitehall Palace and was received by her in her chamber.

* Conway MSS., quoted by Mumby, *Elizabeth and Mary Stuart.*

Kat Ashley told him "solemnly" that the Queen was not entangled with any man living, that she would *not* have Lord Robert; and, as the matter was serious, told Dymock to come next day, when her husband could talk to him. The Ashleys knew Elizabeth more thoroughly and intimately than any living creatures. Katherin Champernowne had been her adoring governess since she was four years old. When Elizabeth was twelve the governess had married John Ashley, a distant connection of the Boleyns, and it was Ashley's sympathetic observation which first gave warning that the fourteen-year-old Princess was becoming dangerously attached to Lord Thomas Seymour; Ashley had noticed that she blushed when Seymour was spoken of. Their candid opinion of her nature and her state of mind was more worth having than that of anybody. Ashley being Keeper of the Queen's Jewels, a conversation between him and Dymock could be held without arousing comment. In the course of this one, Ashley said to him that the Queen would rather not marry. As for the rumour about Lord Robert, it was no such thing. After Twelfth Night, Ashley asked Dymock to come again, as he had something more to tell him. This was, that Lord Robert had given the Queen "a notable New Year's gift", and it was expected that she would have given him at least £4,000 and made him a duke; whereas she had bestowed no title and given him only £400 of land, and not of the very best land, either. So, whatever the Swedish Ambassador himself might have written to his Court, Dymock might certify the contrary.*

* C.S.P. Foreign.

V

THOSE WHO WERE in a position to know best might decide that Lord Robert had no chance of gaining the Queen's hand but he himself had determined that he had; he did not relax his pursuit for a moment; at the same time, like his father who always had three or four purposes in his head at once, he entertained other possibilities in case his main prize eluded him.

Prince Eric of Sweden whose presents of ermine furs and gold and silver money had invested his courtship of Elizabeth with a glamorous air, was shortly to succeed his father, King Gustavus Vasa. This forthright, irascible old gentleman, in his kingdom under the northern lights, had beside his sons five daughters, who, with their yards of fair hair and their yellow velvet skirts bordered with pearl, sounded like the Princesses of a fairy tale. One night in 1560, during the wedding festivities of the Princess Catalina, the bridegroom's brother was found undressed in the bedchamber of the Princess Cecilia. This was awkward. Old King Gustavus called for an inventory of Cecilia's jewels, which he scanned with ominous concentration. Observing "We have spent enough money on her magnificence which does not seem to have produced much return in honour", he ordered the Princess's diamond cross to be taken away and given to one of her sisters.

But the Crown Prince Eric took his sister's part nobly; he had a medal struck, on one side of which was engraved a picture of that abused, chaste heroine of old time, Susannah, on the other a likeness of her modern counterpart, Cecilia. The medal was for general distribution, but a copy of it in gold, rimmed with rubies, diamonds and pearls, was given to the Princess herself as a token of her brother's affection and confidence.[1]

In 1561, old Gustavus died and Eric was King of Sweden. He continued his courtship of the English Queen, who, though she did not accept his proposals, did not convince him that they would never be accepted. When Dymock returned to Sweden with more jewels to sell, in the course of conversation over his glittering store he made an interesting suggestion. In the Council, he said, the Lords Shrewsbury,

Derby, Cumberland and Westmorland were already urging the King of Sweden's suit on the Queen. Dymock, as a result of his visit to England, was now in a position to offer the aid of a more influential supporter. Lord Robert Dudley, he said, would give the project his voice, if it were made worth his while—if he were to be rewarded with the hand of the Princess Cecilia and a suitable fortune. Nothing came of the proposal, but this was not the last time Lord Robert considered the alliance.[1]

The constant, relentless pressure on Elizabeth to marry and produce an heir showed itself on every hand. Archbishop Parker, with the Bishops of London and Ely, wrote a joint letter, pointing out that it was her duty, as the only means of safeguarding the Protestant succession, to submit herself to marriage and childbearing. Sir Thomas Smith made a more oblique attack. He composed a series of addresses put into the mouths of various characters who adopted different points of view about the Queen's marrying or not marrying, and whether her husband should be a foreigner or an Englishman. The perils of childbirth were urged by Wedspite, but scouted by Philoxenes, who declared that an active life and a simple medical treatment were sure preservatives, "To bear children is painful, I do not deny," said Philoxenes generously, but, he urged stoutly: "For a little pain in birth, peradventure of an hour or two, or at most one day (for the extremity of the pain cannot lightly be longer), would you counsel us to run away like cowards, and leave all this so rich and so precious treasure ungotten and unlaboured for, for the travail of one hour?"[2] No, no one counselled that. The reluctance was of a deeper, deadlier nature.

The matter was put forward in more general terms in a play acted at Court in the New Year of 1561. Sir Thomas Sackville, a relative of the Queen on her mother's side, whom she had from the beginning of her reign, in his own words, "promoted to a continual private attendance upon her", was a member of the Inner Temple, and he had written a tragedy, the first English play ever to be penned in blank verse. It was called *Ferrex and Porrex*, which were the names of the two sons of Gorboduc, King of Britain. The Queen, hearing of her cousin's play, suggested that the gentlemen of the Inner Temple should put it on for their customary New Year festivity. On January 18th, therefore, in the great hall of Whitehall Palace, the Queen and Court sat through that five-act drama whose unique historical and literary interest is equalled only by its tediousness and gloom. In *Ferrox and Porrex*, what is not tiresome. is ghastly. The brothers quarrel over the succession, and the younger slays the elder. Their mother, who loved the elder most, kills the younger in revenge. The people rise up and kill both King and Queen. The nobility fall upon the insurgents, and the "argument" of the printed version says: "For want of issue of the Prince, whereby the succession of the Crown became uncertain, they fell to civil war", so that the land was "almost desolate and miserably wasted". The action is developed through long and lifeless speeches, but there are gleams here and there of imaginative vision and dramatic effect. Whether the audience enjoyed this play or not, they could not fail to understand the lesson it conveyed:

> Each change of course, unjoints the whole estate
> And yields it thrall to ruin by debate.

Its dark and bloody mimicry gained a force outside itself, for it called up the awful spectre of the Wars of the Roses.

In 1561, the Queen had not seen enough plays to give her an exacting standard of theatrical entertainment, and she had, by nature as well as cultivation, a talent for listening attentively to anything produced for her benefit. She was as tireless in presenting herself to her ever-present audience as the players were eager in presenting themselves to her. The amazing development of national genius that was fostered by her reign could hardly be more vividly shown than by the fact that in January 1561 she sat through *Ferrex and Porrex*, and in January 1601, in the same hall, she saw the first performance of *Twelfth Night*.

Lord Robert Dudley's wife had died in September, 1560. For a short time his position had looked distinctly dangerous. It had righted itself when the coroner's jury returned their verdict; he was recalled to Court, and it was found that Elizabeth's affection for him was still intact. More than this; he was now free to marry, and though he was, as all his life, generally unpopular, anxiety to see the Queen married was so intense that, if she would make up her mind to take him for her husband, a certain number of influential people would give the marriage their support.

His first task was to secure Elizabeth's consent, and the difficulties of this were the greater for being hidden and not understood. He was in no doubt that he commanded her affection, her jealous affection, and though their intimacy stopped short of complete possession it went very far indeed; yet she did not say the words that everyone was either hoping, expecting or dreading to hear that she had said. The puzzle which obviously defeated Lord Robert was her refusing to marry him, but showing an eager, enthralled, enchanted pleasure in talking about marrying him. The contradiction was resolved by the fact that the panic of fear aroused by the idea of capture by a man was counter-balanced by abnormal fondness for all those delights and amusements of love which are ordinarily a prelude to self-surrender. For years Lord Robert, expert as he was with women, did not understand this; he was like a man trying to find his way through a yew maze by moon-light; the light is there, but it makes the shadows deeper.

Within five months of his wife's death, he made his first strong attack. His sister Mary's husband, Sir Henry Sidney, who had served in Ireland with Lord Sussex and was now Lord President of Wales, was an honest, high-minded man. That he should have lent himself to the plan now hatched by Lord Robert showed the influence which the latter exerted over all his connections; and also that Sir Henry Sidney, like a great number of Protestants, had Catholic affiliations and therefore Catholic sympathies, that he saw no harm in Catholic-ism's being restored as the state religion, even if this meant a restoration of Papal authority, and that he assumed the power of Spain to be so great that English subjection to it was inevitable and might as well be voluntary. Such being Sir Henry Sidney's view, Lord Robert con-vinced him that he had Elizabeth's consent to his schemes, and per-suaded Sidney to speak to de Quadra about it. The plan was merely this. The King of Spain was to be asked to give the whole weight of his support to the marriage of Lord Robert with the Queen, including, naturally, armed force if the marriage provoked a rebellion. In return for this the Queen would restore Catholicism as the state religion, put down heresy, and regard Philip as the arbiter of her policy at home and abroad. De Quadra, recounting Sir Henry's promises on Lord Robert's behalf, said that when Lord Robert had attained the crown matrimonial "he would thereafter serve and obey your Majesty as one of your own vassals".

In the face of these astonishing proposals, de Quadra answered cautiously. Such wild stories were abroad about the Queen and Lord Robert, he said, he had hardly ventured to write to the King about them. Sidney said bluntly, if de Quadra were satisfied that Lord Robert had no hand in his wife's death, he could see no other objection to the match. The Queen and Lord Robert were lovers, but since their object was marriage, what did this matter? He had made searching enquiries into Lady Dudley's death himself, and could find nothing to contradict the jury's verdict. He was convinced it was a case of accidental death, though he admitted the public thought differently. He finished by promising that, once the marriage was accomplished, Lord Robert would help the Queen to put down the heretics.

The bishop replied with great dignity. He said the religious policy of the Queen and Lord Robert was a matter for their own consciences; the King of Spain could not make it a bargaining point.

When he wrote to the King, however, he took a much stronger line. He said: "I have no doubt that if there is any way to cure the bad spirit of the Queen, both as regards religion and your Majesty's interests, it is by means of this marriage, at least while her desire for it lasts." Then he said: "The general opinion, confirmed by certain physicians, is that this woman is unhealthy, and it is believed she will not have children, although there is no lack of people who say she has already had some, but of this I have seen no trace and do not believe it. This being so, perhaps some step may be taken in your Majesty's interests towards declaring, as the Queen's successor after her death, whoever may be most desirable for your Majesty."

In February the Ambassador had an audience of the Queen, in which, as he had promised to do, he praised Lord Robert and said how much affection the King of Spain had always had for him. The Queen first indulged "in much circumlocution". Then she said she wanted to make the Bishop her confessor, and to tell him a secret under the seal of confession. The Bishop was all attention. She said, she was no angel. This he can hardly have regarded as a revelation. She continued, however, that she did not deny that she had some affection for Lord Robert, for the many good qualities he possessed, but she certainly had never decided to marry him or anybody else. However, she saw more and more clearly every day that she would have to marry somebody, and she thought the people would prefer her to choose an Englishman. Well, said de Quadra, the King of Spain would be pleased to hear of her marriage, to whomever it might be, and would be especially pleased to hear of the aggrandizement of Lord Robert, of whom he had always been very fond. "She seemed," he said, "as pleased by this as her position allowed her to be." It was often noticed that it gave Elizabeth great pleasure to hear Lord Robert kindly spoken of.

The next day Lord Robert besieged de Quadra again, thanking him and entreating him to further efforts. He knew, he declared, it was only timidity that withheld the Queen from deciding to marry him. Urging de Quadra to use his influence, "he assured me," the Bishop wrote, "that everything should be placed in your Majesty's hands".

The extraordinary feature of this affair was not that Elizabeth should have deceived Lord Robert, but that he was capable of being so deceived. Though he did not occupy a position comparable with Cecil's, he had been, since the beginning of the reign, at the centre of affairs and on a footing of the closest personal intimacy. Yet he not only did not know how deceitful she was; he had not, apparently, grasped even the outline of her ambition and her achievement. The Religious Settlement of 1559 was a most determined attempt at religious toleration. It declared that supreme power over the national church was vested in the Crown, but the oath of supremacy was administered only to those in office; refusal to take it meant loss of office, but it was not to be put to old and venerable men. People who wrote or spoke against the supremacy were liable to the death penalty, but only on the third conviction. Elizabeth had not only assented to these regulations; she had been a member of the Committee that drew them up. She had refused the hand of the King of Spain with what was great courage and appeared to be insane recklessness. Finally, she possessed, and showed that she possessed, a genius for creating a *rapport* with her people, whose love and support were her passion. With all this known to him, as it must have been, Lord Robert was so blinded by greed that he imagined she would throw over the Religious Settlement, submit to Spain in the most abject and grovelling terms, and invite the Spanish King to send an army into her kingdom to massacre her people if they objected to Lord Robert Dudley's taking the place that his family had once intended for Lord Guildford Dudley.

By March 25th de Quadra was reporting: "Robert is very much aggrieved and dissatisfied that the Queen should defer placing matters in your Majesty's hands." Cecil had now entered the affair, and suggested cordially that de Quadra should ask the King for a letter recommending Lord Robert's suit, which could be laid before Parliament—a plan that would ensure Parliament's rejection of the proposal even if nothing else did. Lord Robert's well-wishers, Lord Pembroke and Sir Henry Sidney, were advising him to take a manly course; let him, they said, ask the Queen to marry him before Easter, or else let him go to the wars in the King of Spain's service; but they themselves had neither Lord Robert's flexibility nor his ravening ambition.

It was clear, now, that when Lord Robert had said he had the Queen's consent, and needed only the King of Spain's assistance, he was either exaggerating or else had been deceived. The plan of handing over the Kingdom to Spain melted into thin air. To create the illusion of a Spanish-Catholic conspiracy, Cecil caused the arrest of several Catholics whose doings would otherwise have been ignored; and when de Quadra asked Lord Robert to use his influence on their behalf he found that the latter would not even attempt do anything for them.

Defeated in his great object for the time being, Lord Robert none the less filled the place of Queen's favourite, with very great influence and power. Sir Thomas Sackville's Inn, the Inner Temple, was engaged in a controversy with the Middle Temple as to which body should have control of one of the smaller Inns. Lord Robert's influence secured the victory for the Inner Temple. As a result, the Inner Temple laid down that none of their members should ever act in a suit again Lord Robert Dudley or his heirs, and they hung his arms up in their hall.

On June 30th, Midsummer Day, Lord Robert gave a water-party for the Queen, and she invited the Spanish Ambassador to attend it. In the afternoon the three were sitting on the poop of a barge, looking at games being played on the water. Lord Robert and the Queen began talking nonsense, de Quadra said, and Lord Robert proposed that, as the Bishop was on the spot, they should be married then and there. The Queen made a characteristic feint: she said she doubted if the Bishop knew enough English? De Quadra seized the opportunity to speak seriously. Let the Queen get rid of the heretics, he said, who were oppressing her and the realm; if she and Lord Robert were to restore religion and good order, then they could marry when they liked, and de Quadra added with gracious kindness that he would be very glad to be the priest who performed the ceremony.

What a vision this conjured up before Lord Robert Dudley! To take the Queen's left hand in his, and slide his ring on to the fourth finger—but the coronation ring was there. "I am married already to a husband, which is the people of England", she had said to a deputation from her first parliament when they asked her to decide upon a marriage. On the same day that he described the water-party to Philip, de Quadra wrote to Cardinal Granvella at Brussels: "You will see by my letter to the King how we are going on. She on her part knows that it is to her interest to keep well with me, because with this love affair of hers she would be a lost woman if the King our master so pleased."

In July the Queen's summer progress began; this year it was into Suffolk. Elizabeth was in irritable spirits and very pale. So pale, it was said, "she looked like one lately come out of childbed". The pressure on her to marry had been increased, because the Queen of Scots, now widowed at nineteen, had seen that there were no prospects for her in France, where her inimical mother-in-law, Catherine de Medici, ruled for the boy Charles IX, and had decided to return, *faute de mieux*, to her despised Scottish kingdom. What Cecil called "her appetite to the

Crown", the English Crown, made her much more formidable in Scotland than she had been in France. Scotland was the recognized base from which to launch an attack on England; and all Protestants, indeed everyone who shrank from the prospect of civil war, were increasingly eager to see Elizabeth married and a mother. The demand was reasonable, it was urgent. The Queen could not bring herself to meet it, but if she convinced the world at large that she would never do so, the invaluable diplomatic weapon would drop from her hand. However much she enjoyed the game of receiving courtship and amorous homage, the task of satisfying the nation without giving herself to a marriage was one that kept her nerves overstrung.

This summer she told Archbishop Parker she disapproved of married clergy and wished she had not appointed any. When Dr. Parker pointed out to her that a celibate clergy was a Catholic, not a Protestant, institution, the Queen's self-control gave way. "She took occasion to speak in that bitterness of the holy estate of matrimony," Parker told Cecil, "that I was in a horror to hear her."[1] The Queen's agitation of mind was reflected in the weather; it was a year of apocalyptic storms. After one in June that had destroyed the spire of St. Paul's by lightning, the evening of July 30th, between 8 and 9, saw "as great thunder and lightning as any man had ever heard, till past 10. After that, great rain till midnight, insomuch that people thought the world was at an end and the day of doom was come, it was so terrible."[2]

In this frame of mind the Queen arrived with her train at Ipswich. Sir William Cecil as First Secretary was indispensably present; Lord Robert Dudley was, of course, in charge of the horse transport. Among the ladies-in-waiting was one with whom he had little personal connection, but who was in fact loosely to be termed his sister-in-law; she was Lady Catherine Grey, the sister of his brother Guildford's wife. Lady Catherine's marriage to Lord Herbert, the Earl of Pembroke's son, had been performed on the day of Lady Jane's to Lord Guildford Dudley. On the fall of Northumberland and the extinction of Lady Jane's importance, Lord Pembroke had brusquely severed his connection with the Dudley family; he had his son's marriage annulled, and the fourteen-year-old bride was sent home to her mother. Mary Tudor had been very kind to Catherine and her younger sister Mary, and had made them Ladies of the Privy Chamber. Elizabeth, upon her accession, had demoted them to Ladies of the Presence Chamber. Lady Catherine had resented this, and had showed that she resented the Queen's treatment of her altogether. She felt that, since she and her sister had been nominated in the Will of Henry VIII as the successors of his own children in default of the latter's heirs, she should have been accorded official status as heiress-presumptive to the throne. Her conduct had been inconsistent to the point of idiocy. She resented her undistinguished treatment on the ground that she was of royal blood; then she had done the thing that in those of royal blood was regarded as high treason—she had made a clandestine marriage. Her partner was the young Earl of Hertford, the eldest son of the Protector Somerset. Very shortly after their secret wedding, Hertford had been ordered abroad. Before leaving, he had given his bride a deed of jointure, which, since the clergyman who had married them was not forthcoming and the single witness was dead, was the only proof that the marriage had taken place. This document Lady Catherine had lost; such was the capacity of the would-be successor to Queen Elizabeth. The unhappy young woman was now many months gone with child. In this plight she came with the Court to Ipswich.

She realized that her pregnancy had already been noticed by some members of the Court; very soon it would be obvious to all. She was impelled to tell her troubles to someone. She approached Lady Seintlow, afterwards known to fame as Bess of Hardwicke, and told her of her desperate situation. If Lady Catherine had not yet fully understood the seriousness of her conduct, she did so now. Lady Seintlow called down curses on the wretched girl for making her party to so dangerous a secret. This was on Saturday. On Sunday night Lady Catherine made another attempt, and bestowed her confidence where it was even more unwelcome. The lack of intimacy between her and Lord Robert Dudley, and his close attendance on the Queen, made a private interview with him unattainable while everyone was up and about. But that night she made her way to his bedchamber and, rousing him from sleep, "she declared the same unto my Lord Robert by his bed's side requesting him to be a mean to the Queen's Highness for her".* Pitiable as her circumstances were, her action in coming to his bedchamber at night, when Elizabeth might hear of it, ruined any chance she might have had of enlisting his help and protection. He got rid of her as quickly as he could, and next morning told her story to the Queen.

The offence, that of a member of the royal line contracting a marriage without the consent of the Queen and the Privy Council, was, of course, to be visited by imprisonment; and that Monday saw the first stage of Lady Catherine's journey towards the Tower. But worse than her marriage was the fact of her pregnancy. The Queen was evading marriage, and therefore avoiding the bearing of a child,

* MSS. British Museum: Harleian 6286.

"the blessed Prince" for whom the country yearned, to save them from the horrors of civil war. Now it looked as though Lady Catherine Grey might bear him.

Lord Robert pressed on with his schemes. As he had been prepared to hand over the country to the Papists, he now made a démarche in the opposite direction. The heir-presumptive of the Valois was the Huguenot Henry of Navarre, the head of the Protestant faction which was already waging a religious war with the French Catholics, and which might possibly prove victorious. The Huguenots, Lord Robert felt, might welcome an offer to bring the forces of the English crown wholly over to their side. In the autumn he sent an emissary of his own to treat with them, promising them English support in their struggle if they would forward his marriage with the Queen. The Huguenot leaders replied in friendly fashion, but their own difficulties made it impossible for them to guarantee him any aid. All that resulted from this attempt was the fury of the English Ambassador, Sir Nicholas Throckmorton; he thoroughly disapproved of Lord Robert, and this treating with a French faction over his head was an aggravation of his dislike.

Altogether the year had not been one of outstanding success for Lord Robert, but it did not close without some good fortune to his family. On December 27th, 1561, he wrote to Lord Shrewsbury, in order, he said, "having reposed a special confidence in your Lordship's friendship and good will towards my brother Ambrose and me, to participate with your Lordship these comfortable news, which are, that it hath pleased the Queen Majesty of her great bounty and goodness to restore to our house the name of Warwick and yesterday hath created my brother the Earl thereof."

As it was said of the two brothers by David Lloyd: "Lord Ambrose was heir to the estate, he to the wisdom of that family." †

* Lodge, *Illustrations of British History*, Vol. I.   † *State Worthies*.

VI

In the following year, 1562, there came into the hands of the chronicler, John Stow, the manuscript of *The Tree of Commonwealth* that Lord Robert's grandfather had written in the Tower. Stow kept the original for himself, but he made "a fair copy" and gave it to Lord Robert. It was at the latter's "request and earnest persuasion", Stow said, that "I then first collected my summary of the chronicles of England". This was one of the earliest instances of Lord Robert's interest in literature of all kinds, and his kindly, personal encouragement of writers, for which he became famous.

His intellectual interests were genuine and constant; his religious views, like those of his father, varied with the times. The previous year he had been doing his level best to ensure that England should be handed over to the dominion of Spain and the Catholic Church. In the autumn he had approached the French Protestants with offers of whole-hearted support. In January, 1562, he assured the Spanish Ambassador once again that he was eager as ever for Spanish assistance with the conditions it entailed, but on May 8th, 1562, he wrote to Throckmorton at Paris on the question of the Queen's sending some aid to the Huguenots. The Queen had said the matter required great discretion, for open aid to the Huguenots might be tantamount to declaring war on the King of France. However, Lord Robert said: "Thanks be to God, she doth not so much measure common policy as she doth weigh the prosperity of *true religion*, as well for the world as for conscience' sake."*

In June, de Quadra met with a sudden calamity. His confidential secretary, Borghese, betrayed him to Cecil, who thus gained an insight into his secret dealings with disaffected English Catholics. The most serious of these intrigues was the one he had undertaken for Lady Lennox, by sending to the Low Countries to discover what support might be forthcoming from English exiles there, for forwarding her ambitions to see her son Lord Darnley, who was first cousin to Mary Queen of Scots, ascend the English throne. Moreover, he caused great

* C.S.P. Foreign.

annoyance and indignation to the Queen and the Council by the things he wrote to his master about her behaviour; in particular, the Council told him, by having informed the King that the Queen was secretly married to Lord Robert Dudley. The Bishop replied to this that what he had told the King was merely what the Queen herself had told him, that *people were saying* the wedding had taken place. She had said that when she came back one afternoon from a visit to Lord Pembroke's house, and entered the Privy Chamber accompanied by Lord Robert, her own ladies in waiting had asked whether they were to kiss his hand as well as hers? She had told them, no, and they must not believe everything they heard. "In addition to this," said de Quadra, "Robert told me two or three days after that the Queen had promised to marry him, only not this year. She had told me also, with an oath, that if she had to marry an Englishman, it should only be Robert." He added: "I do not think, considering what others say of the Queen, that I should be doing her any injury in writing to his Majesty that she was married, which, in fact," he said, "I never have written, and I am sorry I cannot do so with truth."

A promise to marry—only not this year; *if* she had to marry an Englishman, it should be he. It was assumed, and has been frequently said, that the Queen was passionately eager to marry Lord Robert; what she herself actually said does not bear out that impression. But Lord Robert did not understand her shimmering words as meaning that she would marry nobody; he was still apprehensive that he might lose her to another man, and he went to extraordinary lengths to prevent the possibility. In July, 1562, Robert Keyle, the attaché to the Swedish embassy, arrived in London to renew the King of Sweden's suit. He informed the Swedish Court: "Lord Robert at my coming made a great search for me to some of his friends, that he might speak with me ere I dealt with the Queen and Council. But when he saw he might not, he wrought marvellously to have me in prison; but he troubled himself in vain, wherefor he is very angry." His anger, it appears, took a horrible and savage turn, for Keyle says: "His cutters look as though they would do some hurt and I have been warned to take heed."

This conduct must have reached the Queen's ear. It was not only disgraceful towards the emissary of a foreign Court, it was also a brazen attempt to interfere with her diplomacy. Whether for this or for some other reason, Elizabeth was furious with Lord Robert. On July 27th Keyle was able to report: "Lord Robert had plain answer from the Queen's mouth in the Chamber of Presence (all the nobility being there) that she would never marry him, nor none so mean as he, with a great rage and great checks and taunts to such as travailled for him, seeing they went about to dishonour her." This public humiliation was more than Lord Robert could endure. He asked permission to leave the country and go overseas. "This," said Keyle, "was easily granted to!" But of course he had not gone; removing himself from Court was the last thing he would do, unless he heard that the King of Sweden was coming in person.*

This summer Elizabeth had promised to meet the Queen of Scots at York. Mary Stuart was burningly eager for the conference. With a natural confidence in her powers of attraction, she always demanded and longed for personal interviews: she thought that, face to face with rival, opponent or anyone who disliked her, she must triumph. The Council dissuaded the Queen strongly from the meeting: the northern shires were predominantly Catholic; the great landowners living in them still exercised almost feudal powers; the Queen of Scots had refused to ratify the Treaty of Edinburgh and therefore still called herself Queen of England. Elizabeth really wanted to go very much. She argued with the Council, and, accustomed though they were to hearing her, they were struck with the way she expressed herself, "with such fineness of wit and excellency of utterance as for the same with great admiration she was commended",† but they voted unanimously against her going. Mary Stuart's chief aim with regard to the meeting was to persuade Elizabeth to agree that she should succeed her if Elizabeth died without heirs. There was only one person at the English Court, it was said, who supported this demand. Lord Robert Dudley thought that, if the Queen of Scots were officially recognized as heiress presumptive, the English Protestants would be so terrified at the prospect of her accession they would wish to see him marry Elizabeth and get her with child as soon as possible.

It was decisively settled that Elizabeth could not after all meet the Queen of Scots when the Duke of Guise began a heavy onslaught on the Huguenots in July. It was impossible for the Queen of a Protestant people to hold a ceremonious and widely reported meeting with a member of the House of Guise while its head was preparing to exterminate the Protestants in France. On receiving a letter from Elizabeth, courteously explaining this, the Queen of Scots in a passion of disappointment took to her bed and remained there for the rest of the day.

The English believed that, if Guise were able to massacre the Huguenots and consolidate his position, England would be the next

* R. Simpson, *The School of Shakespeare.*   † Conway MSS., quoted by Froude.

victim of Catholic attack. Some help, it was felt, must be given to the Protestants who were opposing him. By the Treaty of Hampton Court, Elizabeth agreed, with less reluctance than she was ever to show again, to intervene on foreign soil. The English were to put a garrison into Havre to hold it for the Huguenots, and to provide three thousand soldiers to help Condé in the defence of Dieppe and Rouen. The force to hold Havre was entrusted to Ambrose Dudley, Earl of Warwick.

Elizabeth was at Hampton Court in October, and she began to feel unwell. On October 10th she took a bath, thinking it would refresh her, and went out after it. Her uneasiness increased. A week later she was so violently ill, the doctors told Cecil they did not expect her to live. The moment, long dreaded, had, it seemed, arrived: the Queen was about to die, leaving no undisputed heir. A meeting of the Council, hurriedly convened, discussed the various claimants; some were for Lady Catherine Grey, some for Lord Hastings, who had succeeded his father the year before and was now Lord Huntingdon. Meanwhile, the Queen was the centre of all the medical care that could be devised. The lady in charge of the arrangements for nursing her was Lord Robert's sister, the charming Lady Mary Sidney. Elizabeth had been lying in a stupor, but presently she recovered consciousness and the Council grouped themselves about her bed. Thinking herself on the point of death, she spoke with utter directness. She asked them to make Lord Robert Dudley Protector of the Realm, to give him a title and an income of £20,000 a year. She said that, though she had always loved him dearly, as God was her witness nothing improper had ever passed between them. But she then asked also that his body servant Tamworth, who slept in his bedchamber, should be given £500 a year for life. She commended her cousin, her mother's relative, Lord Hunsdon, and all the members of her household to the Council's kindness. To soothe her in this extremity, her hearers promised everything she asked.*

They were not, fortunately, called upon to break these promises. The German doctor, Burcot, hurriedly sent for, wrapped the Queen in a bolt of red cloth and laid her on a mattress before the fire, at the same time giving her something to drink which she found "very comfortable". As she lay there she noticed spots coming on one of her hands and began to bewail herself, but the doctor asked her impatiently if it were better to have the spots, or to die?† The treatment succeeded, and in less than a month Elizabeth was up and about and

* C.S.P. Spanish.   † Halliday, *History Today*, August, 1955.

her spots disappeared without damage to her face; but the nightmarish disfigurement she had so much dreaded was visited on Lady Mary Sidney, who caught the disease from her. Lady Mary never liked to show herself in public again. When at Court, she kept to her own chamber as much as possible. The chief of her time she spent at her husband's house, Penshurst, in Kent, or at Ludlow Castle, his seat as Lord President of Wales, taking care of her children. The eldest, Philip, was now eight, Ambrosia two, Mary one. Next year was born her son Robert.

On November 26th the Queen gave proof that she was fully recovered. Lord Robert Dudley and Lord Windsor were having a shooting match in Windsor Park. Elizabeth wanted to watch. Her young cousin, Kate Carey, and two other ladies came out to do so, and the Queen came behind them, dressed as a maid. They stationed themselves very near the rivals "within the pales", and presently an onlooker saw the Queen glide up to Lord Robert and heard her say he should be beholden to her, she had passed the pikes for his sake.*

It was clear, from the words she had uttered on her bed, that she had never allowed Lord Robert to possess her; and this impression was confirmed by their relationship all their joint lives, for never at any point did Elizabeth show the entire devotion to him, the willing subservience to his wishes, which, for however short a time, would have been the normal outcome of a completed sexual intercourse. Elizabeth did not want to give herself to men; she wanted them to want her, and to want no other woman. In this desire she allowed intimacies which, since they were normally the prelude to sexual intercourse, caused her all her life to be abused and condemned as unchaste. Nor indeed without reason: a woman who tries deliberately to arouse men's desire cannot be called chaste merely because she does not mean to satisfy it. This side of her nature was suggested by Osborne when he said she was "apter to raise flames than to quench them", and is borne out both by her solemn statement that nothing wrong had passed between Lord Robert and herself, and by the lavish pension she wanted to be given to the confidential servant who slept in his bedchamber. Lord Robert, conscious of great virility, strength, handsomeness, all those qualities to which Elizabeth was highly susceptible, and having, moreover, gained not only such a hold on her affections but a footing of such personal intimacy with her that in all but one respect he was her accepted lover, was not to blame because it took him so long to learn that no one, not even he, was going to capture the citadel.

* Conway MSS., quoted by Froude.

The last New Year's day Sir Thomas Heneage, a great friend of Elizabeth, and one of the men who thought her personally attractive, had given her "an hour glass, garnished with gold, with glass sand, in a black velvet case". The pretty present marked the passage of the hours with its softly shining fall of powdered glass; the minutes ran away in time to the dropping of the luminous atoms, silent and bright. It told only the passing of the hours, not what would come from them.

VII

THE YEAR 1563 began with another exhortation to the Queen. The opening of parliament was preceded by a service at 11 a.m. in Westminster Abbey, at which the Queen was present in her crimson parliament robes. The Dean of Westminster, Dr. Nowell, preached the sermon and addressed her as she sat before him. "As the marriage of Queen Mary was a terrible plague to all England," he said, "so now the want of *your* marriage and issue is like to prove as great a plague. . . . If your parents had been of your mind, where had you been then? Or what had become of us now?"

The Queen had so much on her mind that she might be forgiven for not going into that question. Beyond Hadrian's Wall was a menace, half-declared as yet, the more alarming because it was unpredictable. Across the Channel the English forces were besieged in Havre. Lord Robert kept in close touch with his brother. On January 23rd, Lord Warwick wrote to thank him for sending him so fine a horse, saying when he was upon that horse, with the token the Queen had sent him about his neck, he thought he should do wonders. In exchange, he sent Lord Robert the best setter in France, with a paper bearing a list of all its qualities, written in French and English.[1]

Lady Catherine Grey had given birth to a son and was still in the Tower. Lord Hertford had been recalled from France, and was imprisoned also in another part of the fortress. It was of the greatest importance that their marriage should be either proved or disproved, so that it could be decided whether this baby were illegitimate or in the line of succession to the throne. Elizabeth naturally wished that the marriage should not be found capable of proof. The commission presided over by the Archbishop of Canterbury could scarcely have found otherwise, whatever the Queen's wishes had been. Each partner, separately examined, told a story consistent with the other's, but of tangible proof there was no trace. Neither of them knew the name of the clergyman or where he was to be found; their sole witness, Lady Jane Seymour, was dead; and the one document that could have been put in as evidence, the deed of jointure which Hertford had given

Catherine as his wife, she had lost so completely that "she never knew afterwards where it was become". Dr. Parker therefore pronounced that no legal marriage had been proved, and the pair remained in prison during the Queen's pleasure. Their gaolers, however, had connived at their meeting, and in February, 1563, Lady Catherine bore a second son. Lord Hertford was fined by the Council 15,000 marks for seducing a virgin of the royal blood, and the young pair continued shut up, though the steadfast refusal of the Queen to marry and conceive, and the unabated alarm which this situation inspired, began to turn some minds in the direction of Lady Catherine, who was not only in the succession by Henry VIII's Will, but was the mother of two little sons.

Mary Queen of Scots, the other young woman who was prepared to ascend Queen Elizabeth's throne, was now, with her ministers, considering what marriage alliance would best help her to gain this object. She refused to consider the Archduke Charles, observing candidly that he was too poor and too weak to help her assert her rights to the English crown. There was the possibility that she might marry once again into the French royal house, but her mother-in-law, Catherine de Medici, having once got her out of France, would not see her back again if she could help it. Nor was this Mary's own wish; her favourite project was that she should be united to the King of Spain's son, Don Carlos, a criminal lunatic, it was true, but one who would bring with him the enormous prestige and power of the greatest Catholic ruler on earth. Either a French or a Spanish marriage for the Queen of Scots would be excessively dangerous for the English, since the marriage in either case would be entered upon, not to make the bridegroom King of Scotland, but to give him the chance of becoming King of England.

Elizabeth told Mary plainly that if she made a marriage menacing to England Elizabeth must regard her as an enemy. The English Queen, however, could not continue to disapprove of matches for her cousin unless she were prepared to suggest one that she would herself approve. In March, 1563, the ablest of Mary's ministers, Maitland of Lethington, was in London to discuss with the English Queen and her Council the matter of Mary's marriage and the other matter which was inseparable from it, of whether Elizabeth could be persuaded to recognize Mary Stuart as heiress presumptive to her Crown.

On March 23rd Elizabeth, in the course of a conversation with Lethington, proposed as a husband for the Queen of Scots—Lord Robert Dudley.

Capable and astute as he was, Lethington was utterly taken aback.
The Queen went on to praise Lord Robert, saying he was one "in
whom nature had implanted so many graces, that if she wished to
marry, she would prefer him to all the Princes in the world". Lethington, having regained breath, answered in a sly, Scots vein of humour;
he said it was a great proof of love to his Queen that her Majesty was
prepared to give her a thing so dearly prized by herself, but he did not
think the Queen of Scots would deprive her of the joy and solace of
his companionship. Elizabeth said she wished to God Lord Warwick
had the grace and good looks of Lord Robert, and then each could have
one of the brothers. This interview was reported by de Quadra, to
whom Lethington had confided the details of it. Lethington told
de Quadra that at this point he was so staggered he could not fetch
his tongue to a reply. Ignoring his speechlessness, the Queen went on to
say that the Earl of Warwick was not ugly, either, nor was he ungrace-
ful, but his manner was rather rough, and he was not so gentle as Lord
Robert.

The proposal that Lord Robert Dudley should be the Queen of
Scots' husband was in the circumstances so amazing that it baffled
conjecture, even, let alone understanding. From Elizabeth's point of
view such a marriage would have had one undeniable advantage; it
would have kept out the menace of a Frenchman or a Spaniard, and
ensured a friend to England at the Scottish Court. This at the time was
recognized as so powerful an inducement that the Scots envoy, Sir
James Melville, wrote it down in his Memoirs as the Queen's genuine
reason for making the suggestion. The proposal was bound to offend
the Queen of Scots, first because Dudley was not of royal blood, and
secondly because he was widely spoken of as Elizabeth's lover; and
Mary at first regarded it as a deliberate insult. It is sometimes affirmed
that this was what Elizabeth intended it to be, but political genius does
not behave like this. When, later, it was suggested to Mary that if she
accepted Lord Robert the match might bring with it her recognition
as heiress to the English Crown, she retracted what she had said in his
disparagement; she could not imagine, she declared, who could have
said that she thought meanly of him.

It has always remained an enigma whether, if the matter had come
to the push, Elizabeth would have brought herself to consent to the
match. If Mary had been willing to accept Lord Robert, and if this
had seemed the only way to avoid the fearful danger of seeing Don
Carlos or one of the Valois enter Scotland as a bridegroom, it seems
arguable that Elizabeth would have made the sacrifice; in the last

resort she cared for nothing so much as the security and prosperity of the kingdom with which she had completely identified herself.

For once, however, it was not a question of what the Queen wished or intended. Lord Robert had no intention whatever of exiling himself to Scotland, even as King Consort. He had never seen the Queen of Scots, but her mere reputation, as one of the loveliest women in the world, might have been expected to inspire him with a determination to have her for himself; but strange as it was he had, it seemed, no wish to embrace this spectacular fortune. He allowed his name to be put forward, but he appeared to do everything he could to counteract the effect of it. He apologized to Sir James Melville for the presumption of which he had unavoidably seemed guilty, and said it was all the fault of Cecil, who hoped by this means to make him incur the anger of both ladies. According to a statement made by Mary herself, he privately informed her that as far as he was concerned the proposal was a mere fetch;[1] and when Randolph, the English Ambassador at Holyrood, thought he had persuaded the Queen of Scots to accept the English candidate, Lord Robert drove him nearly wild by his lack of interest and attention, so that Randolph exclaimed: "Now I have got this Queen's good will to marry where I would have her, I cannot get the man to take her for whom I was a suitor."

How much personal devotion to Elizabeth played in this determination not to marry her rival is not easily assessed; it was not the deciding factor—the English crown was that—but it may well have played some part in Lord Robert's unwillingness to court Mary Stuart. Whatever his motives, the sum of them led him to fix his hopes and ambitions on the English Queen, and when he wooed Elizabeth as an ardent lover his words were inspired at least by a whole-hearted wish to marry her.

Lord Warwick, conducting the defence of Havre with great bravery and constancy, found difficulties piling up against him. English intervention had done what nothing else had been able to do; it had united the factions of Catholic and Huguenot in a determination to drive out the foreigners. It became impossible for the small English garrison to hold the beleaguered city, and in the summer of 1563 their fate was decided by an outbreak of plague among them. At the beginning of July Elizabeth ordered the withdrawal of the English troops, but she dictated a letter to Warwick praising their conduct, and saying that despite the failure of the enterprise the English Crown had been once more vindicated in the fields of France by their bravery. This letter was signed formally, Elizabeth R, but with it was sent a small note written by the Queen herself, not in her beautiful Italianate script but her rapidly written private hand. "My dear Warwick, ... I will rather drink in an ashen cup than that you or yours should not be succoured by sea and land. Yea, and that with all speed possible, and let this my scribbling hand witness it to them all." This was signed: "Yours, as my own, E. R."

Lord Warwick replied: "My most dear Queen and gracious Mistress. I have received your letter by which I, with the rest of us, have well perceived that great care your Majesty hath of us all, and that in respect of our lives and safeties, you do not regard the loss of this town." He thanked her, and wished her a long and prosperous reign, "to the great comfort of all of us your Majesty's true and faithful servants". He signed it like a soldier: "Your Majesty's most humble and obedient subject to the death, Warwick." At the same time he wrote to Lord Robert, thanking God he had been spared from the plague, "rather to end my life upon the breach than in any sickness. . . . Farewell my dear and loving brother, a thousand times".*

The garrison returned to England in August, and they brought the plague with them. This caused the first serious outbreak of it in Elizabeth's reign. The dreadful disease was very contagious, and, though not inevitably fatal, had a very high rate of mortality. The symptoms were terrible: heat, thirst and loss of appetite were followed by hard and painful swelling of the glands, vomiting of blood, and the appearance of the dark, bruised-looking patches on the skin which had given it the name of the Black Death. In this epidemic de Quadra died. It was thought necessary to remove Lady Catherine and Lord Hertford from the Tower, and Lady Catherine was sent with her younger child to the house of her uncle Lord Gray at Pirgo in Essex, while Lord Hertford and the elder child went to his mother, the widowed Duchess of Somerset, at Hanworth.

On August 7th, Lord Robert wrote to the Queen, first thanking her for a letter written in her own hand, then regretting that he had so soon visited Lord Warwick, without waiting for the latter to observe quarantine. This meant, as he said, that he could not come to Court till he was out of quarantine himself. By September 1 Lord Warwick was cleared. A reporter deputizing for the Spanish Ambassador, whose successor had not yet arrived, wrote to Cardinal Granvella at Brussels: "The Earl of Warwick entered here yesterday. He carried his right leg tightly tied up with taffety and had a wide, large band of red taffety for a support."

*Forbes, *Public Transactions in the Reign of Elizabeth.*

The previous June another of the rumour-mongers had been brought to book. At Wilts Assizes Bart Huger declared that Robert Brooke had told him: "It is said my Lord Robert is fled out of the realm. He answered, why so? Then said Robert Brooke, Say nothing. It is told me he hath got the Queen with child, and therefore he is fled, and so ended: No words! Say nothing!"*

The public could not fail to know at least that Lord Robert commanded a great share of the Queen's generosity. In September of this year he received the most famous of all her gifts. She gave him the Castle and parklands of Kenilworth in Warwickshire.

This castle had been obtained from the Crown by Northumberland only three months before his execution, when it had reverted to the Crown again. It was one of the lake fortresses, sited as Camden says, "where the wild brooks, meeting together, make a broad pool among the parks". The natural streams that pour through the meadows had been dammed to form a mere, surrounding the castle on the south and west and covering one hundred acres. All built of cornelian coloured stone, the oldest parts of the castle were twelfth century in origin. The most noble addition was Lancaster's Building, built by John of Gaunt. This two-storied block, at right angles to the Norman keep, comprised on its first floor a hall, 45 by 90 feet, with a great fireplace at each end, a range of lofty, pointed windows in each side, and an oriel at the south-east corner looking on to the inner courtyard; and under this a vaulted cellar. At the end of the Norman keep, opposite Lancaster's Building, was a much less lofty wing of Tudor domestic architecture, known as Henry VIII's lodging. Lord Robert planned a great block, reaching from Lancaster's Building to Henry VIII's lodging, thus forming the fourth side of a square. He set about building it immediately.

* MSS. British Museum: Harleian, 6990, fol. 49.

VIII

LORD ROBERT PAID great attention to improving the breed of English horses by crossing them with foreign strains. It was not easy to import horses from Spain, for the Spaniards had regulations governing their export, as the English had. He thought some could more easily be obtained if he offered the Spanish authorities English dogs at the same time. In January, 1564, Sir Thomas Chaloner wrote to him from Aragon: "Touching the licence for twelve jennets, I will mention it, if by your next you still so desire . . . as yet, I have not bought a Spanish horse . . . your offer of dogs shall not be forgotten."*

In April the French Court were about to send Castelnau de Mauvissière on an embassy to England, to celebrate the signing of peace between the two countries. Word was sent to Lord Robert that the Ambassador would bring over in his train a man whom Lord Robert was anxious to employ; this was the Italian, Hercules Trinchetta, who "gave place to no other in the breaking of young and rough horses". The French Court were very careful now to cultivate Lord Robert Dudley. Montmorenci, the Constable of France, referred to him as Monsieur le Grand. Sir Nicholas Throckmorton had heard that Lord Robert was coming to France. This was perhaps the echo of the scene reported by Keyle a year ago when the Queen had checked and taunted him, and in offended dignity he had asked leave to go abroad, which the Queen had *readily* granted; or it may have referred to a later project of Lord Robert's. He several times spoke of wishing to go to France, but when they were in amity the Queen could not spare him, and when they were at odds Lord Robert would not put himself at the disadvantage of leaving the country. On April 14th, 1564, Throckmorton wrote to him saying that, if he did come, this was the sort of luggage he should bring with him: Silver vessels to set out three tables, slight cups and a light basin and ewer so that one horse could carry all of it, and he could have it all with him wherever he dined or supped. The whole service should not contain more than fifty pieces, and should be packed in leather baguettes to sling on each side of the

* H.M.C. Pepys.

horse. He should bring a light field-bed, and no more clothes than could be carried on one horse with his ordinary *malle*. Do not let him buy anything new, "three or four comely suits will suffice as your voyage is *en poste*". The French King had told de Maisse to bring him from England some good fighting mastiffs and two or three pretty curtals, or horses with docked tails, that would gallop; and the Queen Mother wanted two or three geldings. Throckmorton said: "These should be your presents to them if you come."*

On April 24th de Maisse, in London, sent word to Lord Robert: "I am sorry that her Majesty is not sending you to France, but glad to know of your affection for the King and the Queen Mother. I will tell them of your wish to give them a spaniel and mastiff and some cobs, and I thank you for those you have sent me."

The situation of Lady Catherine and her husband separated from one another, and in private custody, had not become easier. Over any offence that approached, even remotely, the sphere of her own regality, Elizabeth's steady, immovable anger had a quality like the burning coldness of liquid air. As matters stood it was improbable that her pardon would be granted for the stolen match; then something happened which quenched the slightest hope. In April, 1564, John Hales, Clerk of the Hanaper, or the Chancery Exchequer, brought out a book which he called *A Declaration of the Succession of the Crown Imperial of England*. Hales explained the purpose of his work; it was to get the claims of one of the pretenders universally accepted so that the horrors of the past should not be conjured up again. "The great and horrible murders and bloody battles that were between the factions of the Red Rose and the White, the House of York and Lancaster, for the Crown of this Realm, by the happy marriage of King Henry VII and Queen Elizabeth his wife were ended, whereby great quietness and peace (thanks be unto God) hath followed in this realm, God grant it may be continue."

There was only one way to ensure this, said Hales. People must be made to recognize the claims of the House of Suffolk, and then to support them, to the exclusion of any others. He expounded the rights of the Suffolks, as based upon the Will of Henry VIII, but that brought him down only to Lady Jane's surviving sisters, Catherine and Mary. If the Queen of Scots' claim were to be effectively blocked, Lady Catherine's marriage must be proved valid, and then the Suffolk line would be safe because there would be two little princes ready to hand. In the absence of witnesses or documents, the commission presided

* H.M.C. Pepys.

over by the Archbishop of Canterbury had returned the verdict: "That there had been no marriage between the Earl of Hertford and Lady Catherine Grey"; but Hales could not accept this; too much hung upon the answer. The Archbishop and his findings must be swept aside, and he consulted jurists on the continent, publishing their opinions where these were given in favour of the soundness of the marriage. He wound up his arguments by exhorting the reader to counter them if he could; if he could not, then, said Hales "I require him for God's sake and for the love of his country, to give place to the truth quietly".

Elizabeth had received such a lesson in her sister's reign of how the heir is courted at the expense of the reigning sovereign that she had determined with all her might never to put herself in a situation of such disadvantage. She said so, over and over again. To nominate an heir, she said, would be to have her winding-sheet hung up before her eyes. Apart from the danger to herself, such an act would have struck at the base of her whole policy; any heir must have been either Catholic or Protestant, and the setting up of faction would have destroyed the strengthening process of unification. As ever, her personal wish coincided with her political aim, and both of these demanded that the question of the succession be left in abeyance. On reading Hales' book she found herself adjured, first to understand Catherine Grey's claim, and then to accept it quietly. Not surprisingly, she was livid with anger. The book would have offended her deeply, whoever had been the candidate whose claims were set forth in it; but she was particularly enraged at the setting up of Catherine Grey. Elizabeth never forgot that Jane Grey had been proclaimed Queen, to exclude her own sister and herself.

Hales' book, as well as making her angry, had aroused her suspicions, never profoundly asleep, and two people who felt the force of this were Lord Robert's sister and brother-in-law, Lord and Lady Huntingdon. Later, the couple were to become very intimate with Elizabeth; at the end of the Queen's life Lady Huntingdon was much sought after because her access to the Queen was so good; they spent, it was said, "many hours together, very private".* In 1564, however, "Sister Kate", as Lord Robert spoke of her, was a young woman, apt to be startled. She was at Court in April, and the Queen, exasperated by Hales' book, saw in her, perhaps, not the discreet young Countess, affectionate and loyal, but the daughter of that Northumberland who, by putting forward Jane Grey, had tried to prevent Elizabeth from

* H.M.C. De Lisle and Dudley.

succeeding to her father's throne. And the Countess's husband—he claimed Plantagenet descent, did he not? Perhaps someone would write a book about *him* presently! In Lady Huntingdon's words, her Majesty gave her "a privy nip". The dismayed Countess went home to her husband, and her story drove Lord Huntingdon nearly to despair. His lineage was a Sword of Damocles, suspended above his head. He wrote a letter of passionate protest to his brother-in-law. "How far I have always been from conceiting any greatness of myself, nay, how ready I have always been to shun applause both by my continual low sail and my carriage, I do assure myself is best known to your Lordship and the rest of my nearest friends." He hoped that "a foolish book, foolishly written" would not cause the Queen so to mistake her faithful servant, "who desires not to live but to see her happy. What grief it hath congealed in my poor heart (but ever true) let your Lordship judge," he concluded. His brother-in-law's influence, he knew, "could effect a greater matter than this," and he begged it should be used on his behalf.* Lord Robert was fond of his sister, and he was on good terms with her husband. If he were able to use any influence in the matter, he no doubt honestly did so. In fact, the commotion died down of itself. Hales was given six months' imprisonment, but no further troubles arose from it.

Meanwhile, Lord Robert's foreign correspondence was interesting. In June Sir Thomas Chaloner sent him from Madrid "two skins, for a jerkin and harness, and half-a-dozen pairs of gloves all perfumed with flowers". He warned that these should not be put anywhere near apples or quinces, which would destroy the scent. "Such skins are rare this year," he explained, "because a late restraint suffered no more skins or gloves to pass from Valencia hither."† Lord Robert had his portrait painted in a leather jerkin, all covered with a pattern of perforations.** It may have been made from one of these skins.

The Queen's cousin, Lord Hunsdon, was on an embassy at Paris, to take the Garter to Charles IX. He wrote to Lord Robert telling him about the horse fair at St. Denis. It lasted till midsummer, and horses were brought there for sale from Flanders, Germany and Denmark. He had been there that afternoon and seen at least two thousand horses of all kinds, and at such prices—had Lord Robert been there, he would have spent one or two thousand crowns!

The next day, June 15th, Lord Hunsdon wrote to Cecil with considerable annoyance. He had been given the paraphernalia of the

* H. N. Bell, *The Huntingdon Peerage*, 2nd Edn.   † H.M.C. Pepys.
** See the portrait in the National Portrait Gallery.

Garter to present to the French King, and he now saw that it was such a miserable collection he wished "it had been better considered of". The Garter itself was much too big for the boy's puny leg, he could not wear it. The chains, now Hunsdon had unpacked and examined them, were such, he "would scant wear any of them" himself. He could see none that, for shame, could be given to the French King. When a member of the Order of the Garter died, his ornaments were returned; and when the Order had been bestowed on a foreigner, the latter returned his ornaments on the death of the sovereign who had bestowed them. Therefore, said Hunsdon, there were in the treasury many rich chains: he mentioned those that had been worn by Edward VI and Philip of Spain. Could not either of these be sent at once? He urged Cecil to get the Queen to attend to this. He seemed to think that his cousin, eager to practise her economies, had chosen this most inappropriate occasion for doing so. Cecil must speak to her. "It touches her honour more than any chain or garter or George is worth." Then he said with a note of bitterness: "Had I such as my Lord Robert hath, 'a should have one of mine."[1]

In June Don Guzman de Silva, the successor to de Quadra and most charming of the Spanish Ambassadors, presented his credentials. The Queen sent a gentleman to him the day after his arrival with messages of welcome and compliment. Before the Queen's messenger could arrive, Lord Robert Dudley had already sent one of his own, welcoming the Ambassador with every courtesy. De Silva returned a message of thanks and asked Lord Robert at the same time to convey to the Queen that the Ambassador would like an audience. He was impressed by the fact that Lord Robert obtained his for him at once. He went from London to Richmond on June 22nd, and was conducted to the Council Chamber. He was met at the door by young Lord Henry Darnley, who was in attendance on the Queen, and who brought him into the room where the Queen was standing listening to someone playing a musical instrument. She greeted de Silva with an enchanting courtesy, inspired with gaiety and enthusiasm.

In August the Queen was to visit Cambridge, and Lord Robert would attend her both as Master of the Horse and as High Steward of Cambridge University. This meant that he left London before August 5th. Sir William Cecil was the Chancellor of Cambridge University, and in spite of the weight of his work as First Secretary, he did not regard his Chancellorship as a sinecure. He kept a sharp eye on the behaviour of the undergraduates, and his observation led him to compose an edict which forbade them "to use very costly and disguised manner of apparel, and other attires unseemly for students in any kind of humane learning, but rather meet for riotous prodigals". If these youths were given their heads, they would set a bad example to the needy and be "more chargeable to their friends than was convenient", and the University, instead of being a storehouse of learning and virtue, would become "a collection of prodigal, wasteful, riotous, unlearned and insufficient persons".

Cecil, like Lord Robert, went over to Cambridge in advance of the Queen to make sure that all his suggestions and orders for her reception and entertainment had been properly carried out. He was suffering badly from gout, and he told the Vice-Chancellor: "As for myself I mean to lodge with my old nurse in St. John's College, and so, I pray you, inform the Master." On his arrival the Vice-Chancellor and Fellows were anxious to wait on him, but they were told not to come till he sent for them, as his sore leg was giving him so much trouble. The Fellows, eager to do everything which could make the Queen's visit a success, had written to say so, to the Lord High Steward. Lord Robert replied with the greatest courtesy and encouragement: "To my very loving friends, The Vice-Chancellor, with the rest of the Fellows in the University of Cambridge: Touching the matter in your letters, for doubt of your well-doings to the good liking of the Queen's Majesty, I may very well put you out of any such doubt . . . nothing can with better will be done by you than it will be graciously accepted by her . . ."

On Saturday, August 5th, at 8 a.m., Cecil sent for the Vice-Chancellor and Heads of Colleges and told them he had received word that the Master of the Horse was coming that morning "to know if they would require anything to be done of him". They assembled to welcome him at King's College, which was now the Court, and here he came riding, all the beadles going before him bare-headed. The Earl of Warwick was with him. First he examined the Queen's apartments in the Provost's Lodge; then he went into King's Chapel, where a great stage had been built across the nave, tapestries hung round it, and rushes strewn on the floor. He saw also a little retiring room in the middle of the rood loft, with glassed-in windows looking towards the choir, which had been specially built, "if the Queen Majesty would perhaps there repose herself". As it turned out, this was not used. Then he rode to his own lodging and that of Lord Warwick, in Trinity. Here the Master received him with an oration, and led him through the Great Hall, to his lodging "in the Master's Chamber, the doors and walls thereof were hanged with verses in his praise and well-coming", and here also he was given some presents on behalf of the University: two pairs of gloves, a confection of almond paste called marchpane, and two sugar loaves. These, made in conical shape and imported from the Middle East, were still an expensive luxury.

Lord Robert next went to Sir William Cecil's lodging in John's. Here several members of the University were present, and he shook hands with them all as Cecil introduced them.

In the early afternoon the Queen herself arrived; a little after two o'clock she and her retinue rode into the Court of Queen's College. Here everyone dismounted except the Queen, who, in black with her hair in a gold net, and wearing a black hat with gold-spangled black feathers, remained sitting on horseback while a long oration was pronounced to her in Latin on bended knee. An accomplished horsewoman on a well-trained mount, graceful and elegant, impervious to fatigue and heat, listening and observing with the united forces of intelligence and good will, she was a rewarding spectacle for the University that had laboured long and hard to give her a suitable welcome. At the end of the speeches she was conducted, still on horseback, to the west door of King's Chapel. Here another oration greeted her, at the end of which the orator "kissed her hand held out to him". Then she dismounted and a canopy was raised over her head, its four poles supported by four dignitaries of the University, and under it she walked into the Chapel. She was led into the choir, where the great east window is nearly all of blue and crimson, an intense, translucent sapphire, a glowing ruby, and here the choirboys sang a *Te Deum*, a sermon following. The Queen stood "marvellously revising at the beauty of the chapel, praising it above all others within her realm". She was then taken to her apartments in the Provost's Lodge.

The five days that followed were an almost ceaseless round of orations, dissertations, disputations, receptions, banquets and plays. The latter were acted at night, by torchlight on the stage in King's Chapel, and lasted usually till midnight. The Queen's interest, the attention she paid to what was enacted before her, her calling out to some speakers in a dissertation to speak up, and, when they did not do so, moving impatiently to the edge of her dais that she might be nearer to them, was remarked by everyone; but her intent listening all the time to this exacting programme meant that her energies gave out before the very end. On the last evening a performance of Sophocles' *Ajax* had to be cancelled, as the Queen was too tired to sit through it, and when on the morrow she sat on horseback at 9 a.m. ready to make an early start, and saw the Master of Magdalen prepared to deliver a farewell oration in the street, she begged to be excused listening to it, because of the press of people and the heat; but she softened the slight by asking for his copy of the speech to take with her.

The Court was in London again at the beginning of September, and de Silva, trying to form an opinion on what he saw as to the probability of Lord Robert's match, wrote: "I should not be at all surprised if it did take place or did not, so constantly are things changing."

It was clear the Queen thought that distant courts should be instructed what to think. The English agent in Germany was Sir Christopher Mundt, and on September 8th, 1564, Cecil wrote to him from a draft endorsed "Copy of a letter written to Mr. Mundt by order of the Queen". The letter said that he himself could see that the Queen would rather marry a foreign prince than an Englishman, and the greater the suitor were, the more likely would she be to accept him. He could not deny, the letter continued, that the Englishman of whom there was so much talk, namely Lord Robert, was eminently worthy of the Queen's hand. "His sole impediment is that he is by birth the Queen's subject," wrote Cecil, who for his own private guidance drew up table after table, listing Lord Robert's drawbacks as a husband for the Queen, balanced against the advantages of other suitors. "For that reason alone does he not seem to the Queen worthy to be her husband . . . Yet . . . on account of his eminent endowments of mind and body he is so dear to the Queen that she could not love a real brother more. And from this they who do not know the Queen as she really is, are often wont to conclude too hastily that he will be her husband. But I see and understand . . . that there is nothing more in their relations than that which is consistent with virtue and most foreign to the baser sorts of love . . . and this I wish you to believe and assert boldly amongst all when the occasion demands it."* On the draft was written: "P.S. Please send this letter back to me for I am very anxious not to have published what I write in this affair."

The letter was written, not only for a definite purpose, but at the Queen's command; but though it is impossible to assert what Cecil thought, he never, it would seem, wrote or said anything to anyone contradicting that this was the view held by "those who knew the Queen as she really was". A much more important confirmation of the view that Elizabeth was not Lord Robert's mistress, in the ordinary sense of the word, comes from the impression that she made on de Silva, who, so far from writing for effect, was trying to give his court

* Haynes. State Papers.

the unvarnished truth. On September 23rd he described a conversation he had had with the Marchioness of Northampton, whom he was cultivating because she was an intimate friend of the Queen; so intimate that there was some little coolness between her and Lord Robert. However, as a result of what she told him, de Silva said: "I understand that she bears herself towards him in a way that, together with other things that can be better imagined than described, makes me doubt sometimes whether Robert's position is so irregular as many think." It is nothing new, he said, for princes to have evil spoken of them, even without giving any cause for it.

The question of the Queen's marriage was indissolubly joined to that of the succession, and the latter, a peril like that of a sunken reef, was always disclosing itself in some new place by the waters that raced over it just breaking into foam: the foam twinkled and was gone, but it had warned the watchful eye. Lady Lennox, cousin to the Queen and mother of Lord Henry Darnley, was eighteen years older than Elizabeth, and had always been on bad terms with her. She was a Catholic, and had been a friend of Mary Tudor. When Elizabeth ascended the throne she showed Lady Lennox genuine kindness, but Lady Lennox viewed her cousin with hatred as the supplanter of her boy. As early as 1561 de Quadra had heard that Lady Lennox wished to marry her son to Mary Queen of Scots; a year later,* she was speaking of the time when her son and her niece should be King and Queen, uniting England and Scotland in one realm.

In the autumn of 1564 Lord Lennox asked leave to go to Scotland, for the Queen of Scots had promised to restore to him the Scottish estates he had forfeited by his part in Henry VIII's Scottish wars. This was granted, for Lennox's English property was so much greater than his Scottish that it was assumed he would not risk the loss of it through treasonable activity in Scotland. As he went north the Queen of Scots' envoy, Sir James Melville, came down to London to discuss with Elizabeth and her Council the question of Mary's marriage, with Lord Robert as a possible candidate, and the related question of her recognition as successor to the English crown if Elizabeth died without children. He had also secret instructions to tell Lady Lennox to get permission for her son to go up to Edinburgh.

In a series of interviews, in which Elizabeth both questioned Melville about Mary Stuart's charms and accomplishments and took care to display her own, playing on the virginals and dancing before him, and wearing the dresses of all the European countries in turn that he might

---

* Domestic MSS., Elizabeth, Vol. XXIII, quoted by Froude.

say which became her best, she nevertheless gave him an unexpected intimation of her sharpness. Melville had suggested that the Earl of Bedford and Lord Robert Dudley should be sent up to the border to confer with the Earls of Murray and Lethington. Elizabeth seized upon his words. He seemed, she said, to make small account of Lord Robert by naming the Earl of Bedford before him, but before he went back to Scotland, he should see Lord Robert made the greater Earl of the two! The Earldom she once meant to bestow and had then withheld, to Lord Robert's anger, was now to be conferred upon him: either as a proof of her personal favour; or to make him eligible to play the part of a suitor to the Queen of Scots; or perhaps for both reasons. It was an uncanny trait in Elizabeth that what she wished to do from personal motives was apt to turn to some political advantage. On September 29th, Michaelmas Day, 1564, the investiture was held at St. James's Palace.

In the Presence Chamber the Queen was sitting on a chair under a canopy. Nobles stood on each side of her, among them de Mauvissière and Sir James Melville. Lord Hunsdon approached, carrying over his arms a peer's velvet mantle lined with ermine. After him Lord Robert Dudley, wearing a surcoat and hood, was led forward between Lord Clinton and Lord Strange in their parliament robes. He knelt before the Queen, and Lord William Howard, the Lord Chamberlain, gave the parchment containing the letters patent to the Queen, who handed it to Sir William Cecil. The latter read aloud from it in a raised voice, and at the word "creavimus", we create, Lord Hunsdon gave the mantle to the Queen, who, rising, put it round the shoulders of the kneeling man. He was hereby created Baron Denbigh. Melville said in his Memoirs that when the Queen fastened the mantle about Lord Robert she could not refrain from tickling his neck, even before himself and the French Ambassador. With a deep reverence, the Baron withdrew to the sound of trumpets, and the Queen asked Melville how he liked her new creation? Melville replied with courteous praise; but with the suddenness of lightning the Queen pointed to the bearer of Sword of State. "Yet," she said, "you like better of yonder long lad!" Her finger pointed to the very tall, very slender, round-faced, round-eyed young nobleman, Lord Henry Darnley. Melville was taken completely aback. It was a first intimation, and a complete revelation all in one, that the Queen knew of his secret mission to Lady Lennox. An experienced diplomat, he collected himself and assured her that no woman could prefer a lady-faced boy to so fine a man as Lord Robert.

The second part of the ceremony now took place. Lord Warwick appeared, carrying a sword. Lord Robert was led forward once more, this time between Lord Huntingdon and Lord Sussex. Lord Clinton was now carrying the cap and coronet. Cecil again read aloud from the letters patent, and at the words "cincturum gladii", the girding of the sword, Lord Warwick handed the sword and its baldrick to the Queen, "who girt the same about the neck of the Earl, putting the point under his left arm; then she put on his cap and coronet". Cecil gave back the parchment to the Queen, who gave it to the new Earl of Leicester. Then the trumpets sounded once more and the Queen went to dinner in the Council Chamber, the trumpeters sounding all the way before her. [1]

At some time after this ceremony, Melville had a conversation with the Queen in her bedchamber. The great apartment was lit by candlelight; the Earl of Leicester and Sir William Cecil stood talking to each other at the far end of it; meanwhile the Queen opened a little cabinet, in which were some miniatures wrapped in paper, and other treasures. She took out a little paper-wrapped object on which was written in her hand: My Lord's picture. Melville caught up a candle and advanced to see more clearly. She seemed reluctant to unwrap it but he persuaded her, and saw that it was a portrait of Lord Leicester. Melville suggested she should send this to the Queen of Scots; but Elizabeth said she could not spare it, it was the only one she had. Melville glanced at the figure, talking quietly to the Secretary at the other end of the room. "Your Majesty hath here the original," he said. Then he saw in the cabinet an enormous ruby (the ruby, said Hilliard, "that flickereth and affecteth the eye like to burning fire, especially by candle-light"[*]). He said, if she would not send the miniature, would the Queen send the ruby to the Scots Queen as a token? But it was now late at night. The Queen said, if Mary Queen of Scots would be ruled by her, then in time she could expect to inherit everything Elizabeth possessed.[2]

Lord Lennox meanwhile had had his estates formally restored to him, and, saying he wanted to entail some of them on his elder son, he asked the Queen's permission for Lord Darnley to come to him in Edinburgh, explaining that the young man's presence was necessary for the purpose. Elizabeth gave the desired permission, but according to de Silva the day after she revoked it, telling Lady Lennox she had now discovered that Lord Darnley's presence was not necessary, for the entail could just as well be settled without him; and that she was

* Nicholas Hilliard, *The Art of Limning*.

much annoyed by Lord Lennox's deceit, for had he asked honestly for the permission she would have granted it.

On October 9th de Silva reported some words the Queen had uttered to him in confidence: "I am insulted both in England and abroad," she said, "for having shown too much favour to the Lord Robert. I am spoken of as if I were an immodest woman. I ought not to wonder at it: I have favoured him because of his excellent disposition and his many merits, but I am young and he is young and therefore we have both been slandered. God knows they do us grievous wrong, and the time will come when the world will know it also. A thousand eyes see all that I do, and calumny will not fasten on me for ever."

The boldness with which she spoke showed that at least she had no smallest fear of a pregnancy, that one event which would have blasted her, in reputation and in the exercise of independent rule. The calamity would have been overwhelming, and her confidence made it plain that she knew she ran no risk of it.

Elizabeth's instinct for toleration, and her policy which in the end produced the results she intended, meant that until it had taken root she had the support of neither side. The Catholics condemned her system which claimed that the head of the state was *ipso facto* the governor of its church; the extreme element among the Protestants made criticisms of her ecclesiastical policy every whit as severe and far-reaching. The Anglicans accepted the Catholic Church, but they went back to the fourth century A.D., before Rome had exercised its universal supremacy. The Puritans repudiated the Catholic Church under any form of its existence; they went back to the apostolic age itself. The Catholic Church, they said, was merely the work of anti-Christ; nothing was allowable in church services or church government unless warrant could be found for it in Holy Scripture. They therefore rejected the use of vestments, they condemned bell-ringing, sometimes even the use of the ring in marriage; but these were minor effects of their theory; they said archbishops must be abolished, and bishops themselves "de-lorded" and reduced to an equality with the rest of the clergy. They declared that a minister should be appointed by the decision of the congregation, thus doing away with the whole system of livings, and finally they denied that the monarch had any authority over the Church. These were the tenets in their extreme form, and it was hardly surprising that, while the Queen had considerable personal sympathy with Catholicism, Puritanism aroused her indignation and abhorrence. The sect, however, had the unquenchable vitality belonging to a movement that expresses the mood of a national development. The resistless growth of initiative and independence which was owed directly to the Queen herself, and to her life-long policy of conservation of the national resources, found a scope in this creed where personal judgment and perpetual weighing and testing of the worth of customs and ordinances replaced the acceptance of a completed system. The Puritans were not numerically formidable, but they had an influence out of all proportion to their strength, and their sympathisers were found among the bishops themselves and in the Privy Council. By 1564, it was known that Lord Leicester was one of them.

It is impossible to define where self-deception ends and hypo-crisy begins. Leicester's father had been conscious of general dislike and distrust, and had been anxious, by an almost over-emotional response, to conciliate where he might. Leicester himself must have known that his persistent ambition, selfishness, insincerity and greed made him widely disliked. He could not give up the pursuit of the things he wanted, but he longed to redress the balance: he wanted the strong moral and emotional support that comes from making one of a religious sect. His father, whatever his convictions, had been the head of the Protestant party, and it was natural that Leicester, once he had found that Catholic support could not avail him, should revert to the religious system of his childhood. There was a personal leaning in it, too. The Puritans had an edifying style of conversation peculiar to themselves, and it gave him a pleasurable stimulus to talk about God, to convince people who were genuinely religious that he was religious too: not for any worldly advantage, but for the soothing, exhilarating, reassuring mental sensations it procured him. That his conduct was widely divorced from his professions did not make him so very different from the majority of human kind; but there was something about Leicester that earned him the dislike due to a hypocrite, inevitably though not altogether justly. Leicester was very far from being a fool, but he never had the sense to realize that if you are going to be false, greedy, selfish and ruthless, prating is a luxury you cannot afford. But these utterances and exhortations to which he was so prone—as Naunton said, "I never saw letters fuller of the strains of devotion than his"—satisfied a deep need of his nature. The instinct that impelled him to cultivate so earnestly the friendship of Lord Shrewsbury, to justify himself so eagerly in his many quarrels with Cecil, to be more conciliatory, more flourishingly courteous to subordinates than anyone else thought of being, also made him fly to the practice of piety. Just as he was capable of friendship, he was no doubt capable of sincere religious feeling; who could say where one motive gave place to another, or at what exact point in the rainbow yellow becomes green, or blue violet? Strype said simply that Leicester set up as a patron of the Puritans "on some displeasure with the Archbishop, and for other ends". At all events, he was recognized as such by the end of 1564 when the Queen made Dr. Parker issue an ordinance imposing uniformity in church usage, including the use of vestments, which, because of their Popish origin, the Puritans called "meat offered to idols". Dr. Pilkington, the Puritan bishop of Durham, wrote to Leicester, calling upon him to expostulate with the Queen, while Whittingham, the Dean of Durham, who had owed his deanery to Leicester's influence, lamented the enforcement of vestments: "Alas my Lord, that such compulsion should be used towards us and so great lenity towards the Papists! O noble Earl, at length be our patron and stay in this behalf, that we may not lose that liberty which hitherto by the Queen's benignity we have enjoyed!"*

In January, 1565, de Silva mentioned the matter of vestments and Lord Leicester's intervention. In the same letter he said: "The Earl of Leicester . . . shows the same goodwill towards your Majesty. I believe he desires to please everybody as he seems well-disposed and has no inclination to do harm." But from this time, gradually but with increasing force, Leicester developed a hostility against the Catholics until he was recognized as one of their bitterest enemies.

* Strype, *Parker*.

IX

From whitehall to the Temple the Thames makes a curve, the Strand following its northern shore; on the Strand, at the middle of the curve, stood Durham House, "with a little turret that looked into and over the Thames".* It was Crown property, and while de Quadra was in England it had been leased to him for the Spanish Embassy. In 1565 it was occupied by Leicester.

In the New Year so hard a frost set in that the river was frozen over, and de Silva saw people walking on it as if it was a street. The Queen had been taken ill with a feverish cold on Christmas Eve, and on January 2nd she had only come out of her bedchamber as far as the Privy Chamber, and had as yet given no audiences. Leicester had, of course, been hovering over her; he told de Silva that though better she was very thin. De Silva told his King that her doctors regarded her constitution as a weak one; "Your Majesty should note that she is not considered likely to have a long life."

The first year of Leicester's earldom was signalized by the dedication to him of a book by Thomas Blundeville, a private gentleman whose passion was for horses. This was: *The Four Chief Offices belonging to Horsemanship, the offices of the Breeder, the Rider, the Keeper and the Farrier.* It was dedicated to: The Rt. Honourable and his singular good Lord, the Lord Robert Dudley, Earl of Leicester, Baron of Denbigh, Knight of the Honourable Order of the Garter, Master of the Queen's Majesty's Horses. The preface urged Lord Leicester to see to it that the Queen executed the statutes made "by her noble father and dear brother" touching the breeding of horses on commons, and also to see that she enjoined that "all parks within this realm which be in her Majesty's hands and meant for that purpose, might not wholly be occupied to the keeping of deer" (which, said Blundeville, is altogether a pleasure without profit) "but partly to the necessary breeding of horses for service". The country, he asserted, was very poorly off for horses at present, "the lack of which, if any invasion should chance, which God forbid, would quickly

* Aubrey, *Brief Lives. Sir Walter Raleigh.*

appear, I fear me". He besought Leicester to use his influence to ensure that "not only a sufficient number of able horses may be bred within the realm, but also that the same horses may be broken, kept, maintained and exercised accordingly". The book was illustrated by practical drawings; there was a series of designs for horse-shoes, including those for a perfect hoof, for a flat foot, for weak heels, for a false quarter, hinder shoes for perfect hooves, for a shoe with rings attached to make a horse lift up his feet, and a long, elegant drawing entitled "the true shape of a perfect horse-shoe nail".

The chief matter in connection with Leicester, in the opening of the year, was the discussion of that strange mirage, his marriage with the Queen of Scots. Cecil wrote to Sir Thomas Smith, the English Ambassador at Paris: "The Earl of Lennox's friends wish that the Lord Darnley might marry with the Scottish Queen . . . but I see no disposition thereto in her Majesty, but she rather continueth her desire to have my Lord of Leicester preferred that way." He said the plan had been talked over at Berwick with the Queen of Scots' half-brother, the Earl of Murray, and with Lethington, but so far nothing had been determined. The bait to the Queen of Scots was to be that, if she would accept this husband of the Queen of England's choosing, the marriage should bring with it her recognition by Parliament as heiress presumptive to the English Crown. The strange and interesting feature of Cecil's letter was that, as he saw it, Elizabeth was hesitating over the latter point, not over the relinquishing of her lover. He said: "I see the Queen's Majesty very desirous to have my Lord of Leicester placed in this high degree to be the Scottish Queen's husband; but when it cometh to the conditions to be demanded, I see her then remiss of her earnestness."[1]

On January 16th Leicester wrote to Baroncelli, his agent in the Low Countries: "The patterns of bodices you have sent me for the Queen are beautiful but not what she wants, having several of that make. She wants the kind used in Spain and Italy, worked with gold and silver. I desire you to make every effort that I may have the two white mares in good condition." In February Baroncelli replied that both geldings and bodices had been despatched. He hoped they would arrive quickly. As for the latter, he said, "If her Majesty had sent me a pattern I would have tried to supply her before now."*

On February 5th, Randolph, the English Ambassador at Holyrood, wrote from Edinburgh to Queen Elizabeth that the Queen of Scots now seemed genuinely willing to entertain Lord Leicester's suit.

* H.M.C. Pepys.

"I requested her humbly . . . to let her mind be known how she liked the suit for my Lord Leicester, that I might be able to say or write somewhat thereon to your Majesty." The Queen of Scots had replied: "My mind towards him is such as it ought to be of a very noble man . . . and such one as the Queen your mistress, my good sister, doth so well like to be her husband if he were not her subject, ought not to mislike me to be mine. Marry! What I shall do, it lieth in your mistress's will, who shall wholly guide me and rule me." This may not have seemed wholly convincing to everyone who had had experience of the Queen of Scots, especially to those who had tried to make her ratify the Treaty of Edinburgh. So far from being guided and ruled by Elizabeth, Mary was in point of fact still calling herself Queen of England. However, the bewitching manner of the Scots Queen enchanted Randolph and made him feel that everything was eminently satisfactory on that side; therefore he was the more surprised and disapproving that Lord Leicester showed himself so languid. "To woo a Queen without labour or travail, cost, charge, message, token, no, not so much as once signifying of your own good will." Randolph said that Leicester would be extremely fortunate if he could gain her so easily; speaking for himself, he wished he could, with a great deal more trouble than Leicester was taking, get hold of some elderly widow, with enough money to keep him in his old age! However, the scheme should not fail for want of exertion on Randolph's part. "I have said so much that if half were but true, your Lordship I am sure is half-consumed in love for her sake."[1]

To Randolph's consternation, in February Lord Darnley was allowed to come to Edinburgh to join his father. It was well known what the purpose of his parents and the Queen of Scots herself was in regard to him, and for that reason the permission had been withheld for the last six months. Possibly Leicester had convinced the Queen and Cecil that in no circumstances would he be made available as a husband for Mary Stuart, and therefore they released Darnley on his northward flight as the least undesirable of the other choices the Queen of Scots might make. This theory, however, is partially contradicted by the almost desperate efforts they made to recall him when it became known that the Queen of Scots had decided to marry him.

In spite of Darnley's arrival in Scotland, Randolph continued his negotiations for the Queen of Scots' hand on the unwilling suitor's behalf. It had now been intimated to Mary that Elizabeth would not pronounce her as heir to the English crown until Elizabeth herself should have decided never to marry, a decision which it was hoped everyone would assume to be out of the question. Mary had exclaimed angrily that she supposed she must be "content with her small portion", by which she meant her position as Queen of Scotland, until "better" came to her, by which she meant the Crown of England. When this should happen, she would give God thanks but not consider herself beholden to anybody else. Angry as she was, and in tears of disappointment and rage, Leicester's suit was not dismissed.

Holding the affair in this precarious balance, Randolph was horrified by a report of Leicester's behaviour which reached Edinburgh with the speed that only scandal can achieve. As he wrote to Sir Nicholas Throckmorton: "What is most secret among you is so soon at this Queen's ears, that some would think it should be out of the Privy Chamber door where you are!"

There had been a long-standing animosity between Lord Robert Dudley and Henry Howard, Duke of Norfolk. The latter, the premier Duke of England, had resented the fatmiliarity with the Queen enjoyed by a man whom he regarded as he upstart son of a traitor. Lord Robert had resented this attitude. When Norfolk had showed himself anxious that the Queen should accept the Archduke Charles, Lord Robert told him that no true Englishman wanted to see the Queen married to a foreigner. The situation was one in which neither could ignore the other. Norfolk had the prestige of the old aristocracy, and though he himself was nominally a Protestant, as the head of the great house of Howard he had so many Catholic sympathies and affiliations that in the north, a region remote and still predominantly Catholic, his name carried very great weight. In 1565 he was twenty-nine, three years younger than his adversary. He was plain and undistinguished in appearance; he had no ability, nor even a decided character, but the integrity of a man who, blundering from error to error and misfortune to misfortune, yet always meant to do what he thought was right. This, combined with the influence derived from a long line of noble ancestors, gave the Duke the sort of importance that Lord Robert with all his powers was not able to command. The quarrel had smouldered between the Duke and Lord Robert Dudley; between the Duke and the Earl of Leicester it now flared out.

On a day in March the two men were playing tennis, a fast indoor game, for which Henry VIII, who was very fond of it, had put up a building in Hampton Court, with a gallery for spectators. The

Queen was watching, and, as it was reported to Randolph, "My Lord Robert, being very hot and sweating, took the Queen's napkin out of her hand and wiped his face". The familiarity of the action drove Norfolk into a frenzy; he threatened Leicester's face with his racquet. The spectators were aghast at the commotion, and the Queen's indignation was directed against the Duke of Norfolk. The news of the episode ran the length of the British Isles and was thoroughly exasperating to Randolph, still working to bring about a marriage between Lord Leicester and the Queen of Scots.

Leicester was never a member of the government who contributed a policy of his own and influenced the rest to adhere to it; when in later years he took a strong line, he did it by throwing in his weight behind Sir Francis Walsingham. But what he had to give, he gave; he was clear-headed, with an aptitude for affairs; he liked to know what was going on. He liked it because it was interesting in itself, and because he was interested in the machinery of arbitrary government, with its innumerable opportunities for the well-placed man to gain some advantage, by selling his influence or his information, or dispensing patronage to gain supporters. For the first ten or twelve years of her reign, his determination was to marry Elizabeth. When he had seen that she would for ever elude him, his determination remained essentially the same though it was re-formed: it was to maintain himself perpetually in the inmost circle of the sphere of power; to keep his hands on as much as he could of the wealth and honours that the Crown had to bestow, to be "a preferrer of suits" so that when suitors gained some benefit they did it as often as possible through him, and to enjoy the intercourse, on the footing of an equal, with great persons of other countries. This could be gained only by hard work in the day-to-day tasks of governmental employment. This work, too, was the Queen's consuming interest, and any man who wanted to preserve a close personal association with her could only do so by playing his part in it. Leicester did it with an eager industry. The minutes of meetings of the Privy Council, year after year after year, show consistently that, of the six, eight or ten members present, the two almost invariably there were Cecil and Leicester. On April 14th of this year, 1565, Aylmer, then Archdeacon of Lincoln, wrote to Sir Nicholas Throckmorton about a scheme for reforming church government.* "Mr. Secretary took a note while I was with him, whereof I have also written to my Lord

* C.S.P. Domestic, Addenda, 1547–65.

Leicester. If Mr. Secretary forget, put my Lord in mind to call upon him for it."

The behaviour of the Queen and Cecil now appeared to contradict what they had done in giving Lord Darnley leave to join his father. In May, it was heard that the Queen of Scots proposed to marry the young man who had, after herself, the best claim to the English throne, if primogeniture only were consulted and Henry VIII's Act of Succession abolished. Indeed, as Darnley had been born in England, some would consider his claim sounder than that of the Scottish-born Mary Stuart. Whatever Elizabeth might have had in contemplation before, she now flew to a defensive action against this menace. Throckmorton was instructed to tell the Queen of Scots that "as for this matter of her marriage with Lord Darnley, the Queen simply mislikes it as a matter dangerous to the common amity of the two kingdoms". This dictatorial attitude to the Queen of Scots in her marriage plans was explained and justified by Mary's own conduct. Had she ratified the Treaty of Edinburgh, thereby admitting that Elizabeth was Queen of England and that she herself was not, her marriage would have been a matter which merely called for the exercise of English diplomacy; but since she had never withdrawn from the position she had originally claimed—that she was Queen of England—her intentions were so nakedly hostile that a marriage with one of Darnley's lineage and claims was almost tantamount to a declaration of war. Lady Lennox herself had so viewed it, and declared that all the Catholics in England were only waiting to acclaim the pair as King and Queen of both countries. Throckmorton was further instructed to say that, as regarded any public declaration of succession, the English Queen could only be brought to allow this if the Queen of Scots married Lord Leicester. Leicester himself remained passive; the last thing Elizabeth wanted to do, in any circumstances, was to make such an announcement. Perhaps he foresaw that, before she could be brought to such a step, the scheme for the marriage upon which the step was contingent would be allowed to disappear. It would have served its turn if a discussion of it had postponed a danger.

Meantime his own scheme received a fresh accession of help. The Emperor Ferdinand had been succeeded by his son Maximilian, who now renewed the suit to the English Queen of his brother, the Archduke Charles. Philip was not assured that the new Emperor's sympathies were entirely, rigidly Catholic—he might be intending some démarche towards the German Protestants—but Catherine de

Medici was making approaches on behalf of the boy Charles IX, and an Anglo-French marriage must be prevented at all costs. Not being yet instructed to support the suit of the Archduke Charles, de Silva seized upon that of Leicester, hoping to kindle its embers, so that it should distract the Queen's attention from the French proposal.

In May Leicester, while hunting with the Queen, met with an accident. It was not said that he had broken any bones, but he must have been severely bruised and sprained, for, athletic and powerful as he was, he was obliged to keep to his bed. De Silva went to see him on May 5th. "I sent to tell him that I was coming," he wrote. "My messenger had to wait awhile as the Queen was with the Earl before dinner." When de Silva entered the room himself he found Lethington there, and presently Cecil came in with Throckmorton. Lethington was returning to Scotland, and Throckmorton was going up with him. In the present position of affairs in Edinburgh, the English government needed some representatives more astute than Randolph. De Silva said that the others drew off, talking among themselves, and left him alone at Leicester's bedside. "I said to him very secretly . . . I am so much attached to you . . . you will be sorry you have lost so much time . . . I have done my best to urge your suit to the Queen. So has my King." Leicester protested his gratitude and loyalty to the King of Spain. Then he said: "The Queen will never decide to marry me . . . only some great Prince." She would never, he was sure, take a subject of her own; no one would do for her except Don Carlos or the Archduke. However, having said as much, his spirits seemed to revive a little. If de Silva were to press the Queen now, he might succeed. He went on: "She refused me before because she heard the Queen of Scots was to marry a great Prince; but since that Queen is marrying only Lord Darnley, she might now accept me." De Silva soothed him. "Well, leave it to me, I said", and he left the invalid in his weary, restless, unsatisfied bed. Later in the month, de Silva fulfilled his promise; he said to the Queen that if she wanted to marry within her own kingdom, she could not overlook the claims of "his friend". Elizabeth always like to hear those she loved kindly spoken of, and she thanked de Silva now for his remark. He commented: "It shows Lord Robert's affair is not off." He was not, however, at all pleased with Leicester, who was showing too much friendliness towards France; but, he said, "I always speak well of him to the Queen, to place him under obligations to us".

The letter de Silva received from the King of Spain, written on June 6th, showed how right the English government were to fear the marriage of Mary Stuart with Darnley. The King wrote: "Considering the Queen of Scots' good claims to the Crown of England, to which Darnley also pretends . . . the marriage is one that is favourable to our interests, and should be supported to the full extent of our powers . . . if they will govern themselves and not be precipitate, but will await a juncture when any attempt to upset their plans would be fruitless, I will then assist and aid them in the aim they have in view." All this, said Philip, must be most carefully concealed from the Queen of England and her friends, "seeing the great danger that would result to the business itself and all other of our affairs if it became known".

Meanwhile, in Edinburgh, Throckmorton, with far more acuity than Randolph, had found out that the marriage of the Scots Queen with Darnley was a settled thing, and that it formed the basis of a project, inspired by the Catholic powers, to depose the heretic Queen of England and gain possession of her throne. He told Cecil to take steps immediately to prevent further communication between Lady Lennox and the Spanish Ambassador. Lady Lennox was accordingly lodged in the Tower, and orders were sent post haste to Lord Lennox and Lord Darnley, commanding them, on their allegiance, to return to England. It was too late: their position at the Scottish court was already impregnable, and Lord Darnley's answer to the summons was: "I find myself very well where I am and so purpose to keep."

Throckmorton's personal attitude to Leicester had altered considerably since the death of the latter's wife, five years ago, when Throckmorton had feared that the Queen would marry him and so plunge herself in irretrievable ruin. He now congratulated Leicester on his unswerving devotion to Elizabeth and his constant refusal to court the Queen of Scots, which, he said, had saved him from a pitfall. "If persuasions and severe commandments of her Majesty from time to time, if evident presumptions and manifold assurances of your never enjoying her Majesty, and contrariwise, if proposals, arguments and vehement tokens were offered to move you to take hope *this* Queen was likely to be yours . . . if all these respects could have enchanted you to allow of this matter to yourself," then, said Throckmorton, "you had been very unhappy."

This was very well so far as it went, but that was not very far. Leicester, on his feet again, was making a renewed effort to overcome the Queen's resistance, and in the first week in July this brought him into violent opposition against Lord Sussex. The Archduke Charles had again been put forward as a suitor to the English Queen, and

Sussex was to go to Germany to conduct the negotiations. He was most earnestly in favour of the match, as a means of getting the Queen with child and as an alliance that seemed admirably poised between the two factions, for Charles, a Hapsburg, was necessarily a Catholic, but his family were obliged to concede a certain friendliness to German Protestant princes. Sussex did not know that no match arranged for Elizabeth would ever be concluded, for reasons that were not to be explained; he thought that his efforts were likely to be negatived because Lord Leicester would be courting the Queen behind his back. His feelings found vent in an open quarrel, and the Queen fanned it, for it gave her a temporary respite. "I am told," said de Silva, "that when the Earl of Sussex speaks to her, she tells him that Lord Robert presses her so that he does not leave her a moment's peace, and when Lord Robert addresses her, she says the same thing of the Earl of Sussex, that she is never free from him."

And now, news arrived from Sweden. An envoy, bringing with him a magnificent present of sables for the Queen, Lord Leicester and the Lord Admiral Lord Clinton, told the Court that the Princess Cecilia had married the Marquess of Baden, but that she had consented to the match only on condition that her husband should bring her on a bridal journey to visit the Queen of England, whom she had long regarded with romantic enthusiasm. The party were now, it appeared, at Emden waiting for a ship to carry them over; when they should arrive, Cecilia was to take the opportunity of urging again her brother's suit.

X

THE SUMMER OF 1565 was a troubled one for the Queen. The menace of Mary Stuart was growing nearer and more formidable. The Scots Protestants, headed by Murray, had told Mary that they objected to a Catholic's being made King of Scotland, and that Lord Darnley could not so be made without consent of Parliament. Her answer was to have Darnley proclaimed King at the market cross in Edinburgh. On July 29th she married him, though it was thought that a private ceremony had considerably preceded the public one. If Mary could hold the dissident elements of her realm in check, so providing herself with a secure base for operations, her next step would be to invoke the King of Spain's promised aid, and at the same time to call upon the English Catholics to support her as she advanced to take the English crown. In this project there were arguments upon her side which appealed to Catholics, but there was one against her which appealed to all English people, Protestant and Catholic alike: this was the seven years' span of peace and steadily increasing prosperity that was now associated with Elizabeth's name. The strength of this, however, could not be known till it was put to the proof; what was known was the imminent danger.

Private life itself was agitating and distressing. In this July Kat Ashley died. The Queen had been to see her only the day before her death. The Court was at Richmond, and the Queen told de Silva about the death of the lady who had brought her up, and he could see the grief it caused her. He also saw that she was by no means on her usual terms with Lord Robert. Was she, perhaps, angry, however unreasonably, that he had not done his utmost to prevent the peril of the Queen of Scots' marriage with Darnley? "Lord Robert," de Silva noted, "seems lately to be rather more alone than usual, and the Queen appears to display a certain coolness towards him." In August Cecil wrote to Sir Thomas Smith at Paris: "I will in a few words give you some light. The Queen's Majesty is fallen into some misliking of my Lord of Leicester, and he therewith much dismayed." He wrote in his diary: "The Queen's Majesty seemed to be much offended with the Earl of Leicester, and so she wrote an obscure sentence in a book at Windsor."

For the first time since the disappearance from the scene of Sir William Pickering five years before, Elizabeth was amusing herself with romantic conversation with someone other than Lord Leicester. "She has begun to smile on a gentleman of her court named Heneage, which has attracted a good deal of attention," said de Silva. Thomas Heneage, who had given the Queen the hourglass, combined characteristics not often found together; he was said to be a thorough courtier, yet he was kind and eminently good-hearted. He had been made a gentleman of the Privy Chamber in 1560, and the rest of his life was spent in posts of increasing responsibility in the Queen's household, until at his death he was Vice Chamberlain and a Privy Councillor. In his Will he left a jewel to the Queen, "whom, above all other earthly creatures, I have thought most worthy of my heart's love and reverence". But though Heneage was at present rapt up in a spell of romantic intercourse with Elizabeth, he was well known to be a friend of Leicester, and de Silva did not believe that the affair would become at all serious. But this did not say that Leicester's own ambition would succeed.

Sir Henry Sidney told de Silva that his brother-in-law "had lost hope of his business". Sidney said he himself was sure the Queen did not mean to marry, and that "they were in the most troublous state that was ever known in England; if the Queen were to die, there would not be found three persons in one opinion as to who was to succeed".

However writing from Windsor in the middle of August de Silva told his King: "I keep Leicester in hand the best way I can, as I am still firmly of the opinion that if any marriage at all is to result from all this, it will be his."

De Silva had seen, more clearly than most people, how Elizabeth's behaviour was motivated. "I do not think anything is more enjoyable to this Queen," he said, "than treating of marriage, though she herself assures me that nothing annoys her more. She is vain and would like all the world to be running after her, but it will probably end by her remaining as she is, unless she marries Lord Robert who is still doing his best to win her."

Leicester, indeed, still regarded himself as a lover, to whom favours shown to another man were a deliberate injury. Heneage, buoyed up by the Queen's favours, displayed an elation that made Leicester complain to the Queen of his rival's insolence and his own wrongs.

De Silva's account of this is exceptionally interesting, for it shows the method by which such information was collected, and how it sometimes was found wanting. Conversations with the Queen were held in the presence of other people, unless a private interview were granted, a fact which in itself was considered noteworthy. In the great rooms and galleries that opened one out of another, the Queen was never present without ladies in waiting, even if these stood at a discreet distance. Outside the door of the Presence Chamber were some of the fifty Gentlemen Pensioners who formed the sovereign's bodyguard. Out of doors, the Queen rode behind one body of riders and in front of another, larger retinue; if she were on foot in the gardens or the park, the utmost degree of privacy a companion could ensure was that the ladies and gentlemen in attendance should be out of earshot. It was from the numbers always about the Queen that the ambassadors derived most of the information about her not gained by themselves in personal intercourse. In recounting the quarrel, de Silva said that when Lord Robert complained to the Queen "she was *apparently much annoyed*", although "what she said *could not be heard*". However, Heneage at once left the Court, and Lord Robert did not see the Queen for three days; this was a method he nearly always found successful. He would not have dared to remove himself for too long, for after a certain point absence would have become dangerous to him; he depended upon the Queen's sending for him before that point was reached. Had she not wished to do so, she would have found no pleasure in the game. In the exquisitely delightful reconciliation Lord Robert, it was believed, suggested magnanimously that Heneage should be recalled, to avoid injurious tittle-tattle.

The Spanish Ambassador was not the only one who supported Lord Robert's suit. Catherine de Medici had failed to promote a match between the youthful Charles IX and the Queen of England, and she was eager that Elizabeth should at least be prevented from taking a husband in the Spanish interest. The French Ambassador, de Foix, told the Queen that she could do nothing better for the welfare of her country than to marry one of its great men. He had caught the Queen in a moment of unrestrained candour, and the reply to his remarks was somewhat startling. She told him that if she did marry, she was determined not to give up any of her power, property or revenue to her husband; the mere marriage would make him but too powerful. But, she exclaimed, "If I think of marrying, it is as if someone were tearing the heart out of my body . . . nothing but the welfare of my people would compel me to it!"*

Lord Leicester, however, was notoriously skilful at managing horses, and he had considerable confidence in being able to manage women. All the rebuffs, disappointments and deceitful encouragements he had so far encountered had only sharpened and intensified his determination. In the veering winds and currents of court life, Sir Nicholas Throckmorton had now placed his great ability at Leicester's disposal. The latter was sharp enough to value it; he was, besides, always pleased to gain a friend, and his suppleness never found it difficult to adopt the role of pupil, once his confidence had been gained. At the beginning of September Throckmorton, who, in de Silva's words, "ruled Lord Robert", advised him to test the Queen's affection by making up to Lady Hereford.

This lady was Laetitia Knollys, whose grandmother, Mary Boleyn, had been Ann Boleyn's sister. Mary Boleyn had for a short time preceded her sister as a mistress of Henry VIII; she had then married one of the Carey family. Her daughter had married Sir Francis Knollys, and their daughter Laetitia was thus Elizabeth's second cousin.

Laetitia, whose name was shortened to Lettice, was eight years younger than Elizabeth; in this year, 1565, she was twenty-four. Her portraits, both as the young wife of Lord Hereford and in her elderly years, show beauty and an extraordinary degree of sexual magnetism; a narrow face, black-avised, secretive, sullen, with the expression typical of the woman who is exceedingly attractive to men, and regards her equals in this sphere with grudging respect and her inferiors with scornful contempt. For the last seven years Lettice Knollys had been obliged to behave herself amiably to her cousin, and while no cause for sexual jealousy invaded the scene this was perhaps no difficult task. At all events it had been successfully accomplished, and in this autumn de Silva described Lady Hereford as "one of the best-looking ladies of the court, daughter of a cousin of the Queen, with whom she is a favourite". The Queen made many presents of dresses to the ladies of the Court, and the previous year the Wardrobe Accounts showed "From the store, 13 yards of black velvet barred, delivered by the Queen's order to Viscountess Hereford for a gown, £16.18.0".

Lady Hereford had been married for five years and had two small daughters, of whom the elder, Penelope, was destined to have a great importance in the life of Leicester's nephew, Philip Sidney.

* Von Raumer, *Elizabeth and Mary Stuart.*

Leicester's approaches were received with ardour, and the Queen, whose attention they were intended to attract, at once became jealous. He deepened the impression by a request that he might be temporarily released from his attendance at Court, "to go to stay at his own place as other men did". Since this would have taken him no further than the Strand, even if the Court remained at Windsor he would not be far removed from his vantage point; however, he did not press to be allowed to go, even so far. He merely remained shut up in his lodging within the Court till the Queen sent for him. De Silva heard that both Cecil and Lord Sussex tried to smooth matters, "though they are no friends to Lord Robert in their hearts". The result of their mediation was an interview between the mutually offended lovers. A blazing quarrel took place, in which both parties cried with anger and wounded feeling; the result of it was that Lord Robert returned to his former favour.

But a return to his former favour meant abandoning Lettice Hereford. No doubt he was sorry, but some desirable objects cost too much. Leicester was building his fortunes and he could not afford this liaison. His self-denial was rewarded. Towards the end of this year of varied haps, he achieved a spectacular advancement. The Queen created him Chancellor of the County Palatine of Chester.

A County Palatine had no local government; it was under the immediate jurisdiction of the Crown, and in its confines its Chancellor, representing the Crown, was accorded almost royal status. Thus the appointment was of a kind peculiarly agreeable to Leicester. A superb manuscript was prepared for him by Robert Cooke, Chester Herald. It contained "The most Ancient and Famous Pedigree of the noble Earls of Warwick and Leicester". Written on vellum, comprising eighteen pages, each page bordered with silver ragged staves and sprays of green leaves, two of its pages were devoted to Lord Leicester's arms; these contained forty-eight quarterings, surmounted by an earl's coronet and the devices of the bear and ragged staff, the crowned silver lion, a lion's head azure, and a cinquefoil; their margins were decorated with 189 coats of arms of foreign princes and English kings and noblemen from William the Conqueror onwards, whom the Herald had found to be a part of the Dudley pedigree. In this welter of heraldic splendour the most charming item was the little cinquefoil, a floweret with five petals in a circle like the blossom of a hawthorne. This had been the device of the twelfth century family of Bellômont or Beaumont, Earls of Leicester of the first creation. Leicester, whose earldom was of the fourth creation, adopted the earliest cognizance he could find. He made it particularly his own; it is scattered like stars on his buildings, his armour, his furniture, his books, his tomb.

In September the Princess Cecilia of Sweden, her husband the Margrave of Baden and their entourage arrived at Dover. The Princess's journey had lasted eleven months; she was pregnant and within four days of her delivery, but the hardships of travel had been borne by her as nothing; encamped at midnight on a frozen shore, she had exclaimed: "What do we care for cold? Let us talk about the Queen of England!"

Elizabeth was gratified by the visit of a member of a reigning house, and preparations of welcome had been made on a scale suitable to the occasion. The Earl of Bedford was in the north as Governor of Berwick, and his house by Ivy Bridge in the Strand had been taken over for the Princess's reception. Cecilia, her long pale hair loose under a crown, in a black velvet dress and a mantle of cloth of silver, created a sensation in the London streets.[1] The Queen was at Windsor and did not immediately come to visit a guest who was so far gone that her labour was expected to begin at any moment. In two days' time Cecilia was delivered of a Prince. The Queen then came to see her, spent the whole day with her and promised to stand godmother to the baby, for whom she chose the dear name of Edward. Fortunatus was added, to celebrate the happy outcome of his mother's perils.

On September 30th the child was christened in the Chapel Royal of Whitehall Palace, in a scene of magical brilliancy. It was late in the afternoon and the chapel was hung with cloth of gold and lighted with eighty-one wax-lights. Their deep-coloured radiance rested on an altar which bore a mother-of-pearl basin rimmed with pearls and jewels, a bejewelled agate bird, a coral basin ornamented with pearls, a crystal bowl and cover. The child was kept in a space curtained off with purple taffeta, where a fire was burning. In their gleaming copes the Archbishop of Canterbury and the Bishops of London, Salisbury and Rochester awaited at the altar rails the entrance of the Queen. When she was told that all was in readiness she came to her closet, which was entered from above, and remained there for the first part of the service. When the christening was to be performed she descended the staircase into the chapel, and "about her Majesty were borne six tapers of virgin wax". Though the Queen stood godmother "in her own person", she did not of course carry the baby to the font. Her cousin, Kate Carey, now Lady Howard of Effingham, was deputed to do this. Struggling and straining, the young Lady Howard found herself nearly overpowered by the weight of the child's jewelled mantle. Lord Ormonde came to her assistance, and between them they carried the infant to the waiting Archbishop.

"Name this child," said Dr. Parker, and the high, clear voice uttered: "Edwardus Fortunatus". After the ceremony the ceremonial washing of hands took place. The ushers gave a towel to Lord Northampton, a basin of water to Lord Leicester and an under-basin, to catch drops, to Lord Sussex. These three noblemen waited on the Queen as she washed her hands. The baby was brought for her to look at, and at the same time the cupboard of gold plate that was his royal godmother's present to him was carried forward. Then the Queen, surrounded by her lights, ascended the stairs once more. At the head of the stairs the baby's father was posted, who thanked "her and the others for their gifts and pains". The child was carried back to the Strand by torchlight "for it was then within night".*

In November another ceremony took place at Court, this time of great importance to Leicester's family. This was the marriage of his brother Ambrose, Earl of Warwick, to the Earl of Bedford's daughter, Lady Ann Russell. Leicester had assured the Earl of Bedford of his friendship for him, which he declared he had shown by supporting his brother's suit. "I know not how I might better show it than wishing him I love as myself to be so allied with him that next is, as dear a friend as can be to myself; which is, my brother the one, your Lordship the other." Now he knew that Bedford wished the match himself, he would do everything in his own power to forward it, and he could tell Bedford that the Queen favoured it also. "Her Majesty hath often times wished it to be brought to pass, and showed great liking thereof before ever I would say anything." He had told the Queen "that as you had, as it were, bequeathed your daughter to her, you would be ordered as pleased her Majesty". He assured Bedford the Queen was most willing "to deal" in the matter. "Only I," he said, "knowing her good mind will let your Lordship understand it." He wanted the father to give him *carte blanche* to make arrangements for the daughter: "Not to mislike if I think it convenient to bring her to Court if her Majesty will have her about herself, as she meaneth, out of hand."† It almost seemed as though the father, the intending bridegroom, the girl herself and even the Queen, could not with their combined good will bring about the marriage without

* Leland, Collectanea, II.   † *Notes and Queries*, 6th Series, iii.

the intervention of the Earl of Leicester. At all events the match was made, and proved not only happy to Lord Warwick but a source of great comfort to the nervous and exacting Queen. Mild-natured, honest and sweet, Lady Warwick became one of her closest female friends. "Lady Warwick presented" this or that person, "Lady Warwick was with the Queen", "the Queen, alone but for Lady Warwick" —such notes appeared more and more frequently as the years went on. On the wedding day, November 11th, 1565, the bridegroom was thirty-three and twice a widower, the bride a girl. The ceremony was performed at Whitehall Palace, where Lady Ann had slept the previous night; her father had not come down from Berwick, and the Queen and Lord Leicester managed everything between them. The maids of honour wore yellow satin dresses trimmed with green velvet and silver lace; otherwise it was a violet wedding. The bride's kirtle, the straight under-dress, was of silver shot with blue, the gown that opened over it was purple velvet embroidered with silver. The bridegroom wore a gown of purple velvet embroidered with gold and furred with sable; Lord Leicester, who gave the bride away, wore a gown of purple satin with a broad, gold-embroidered belt. The bridal party met in the Queen's Great Closet. The Queen came to them there and first there was some conversation; then the actual ceremony of marriage was performed, after which they all went into the Chapel Royal for the marriage service. When this was over, there was a great dinner in the Council Chamber.

The double event, the christening of Prince Edward of Baden and Lord Warwick's marriage, was celebrated by tournaments of extraordinary magnificence, lasting for two days. The Earl of Leicester and the Margrave took part not as defendants but "for pleasure". In the course of one of the actions, the purple tissue trappings of Lord Leicester's horse fell to the ground, so becoming a perquisite of the heralds; to get them again, the Earl sent the heralds twenty nobles. At the conclusion of these jousts and triumphs, Leicester made a great dinner at Durham Place.*

It seemed now, in December, that his ambition had come to life again. The French Ambassador, de Foix, told Catherine de Medici: "The friendship and favour of the Queen towards the Earl of Leicester increases daily." Cecil had told de Foix that Leicester had come to his room and there delivered himself of a speech, of which Cecil repeated to de Foix the gist, without comment; it was that Leicester not only aspired to the Queen's hand, but believed that his chances

* Leland, *op. cit.*

were better than those of anybody else; therefore he must ask Cecil
to relinquish any plan he might be considering of marrying the
Queen to a foreigner. The remembrance that Cecil had once been a
secretary to the Duke of Northumberland appeared to overcome
Northumberland's son at this point; he assured the Queen's most
trusted adviser, the man who carried greater weight in the government than anybody else, that he, Leicester, had long had a high
opinion of his conscientiousness and knowledge of affairs, and if
Cecil would now follow the line Leicester laid down for him, Leicester would see to it not only that he maintained his present position,
but that he was promoted as his abilities deserved. In de Foix's
words, Cecil thanked the Earl for his good opinion and for the friendship he appeared to entertain for him.[1]

The wish of Catherine de Medici and Charles IX, to encourage
Leicester so that he might checkmate the Queen's marriage with
anyone in the Spanish interest, had caused them to send the Earl a
most cordial invitation to visit France when they heard he had said he
wished to do so. This invitation was now in de Foix's hands, but the
hazards and delays of communication meant that by the time of
its arrival Leicester had regained his place at Court and no longer
wanted to leave it. To her surprise, Elizabeth hear the Ambassador
say that his King would be delighted if she would send the Earl to
France, and that the Earl himself had asked him to tell her so. Elizabeth sent for Lord Leicester, and in de Foix's presence asked him point-
blank if he wished to leave her? The situation required delicate handling. Leicester said that to see France again—he had not been abroad
since he fought for the King of Spain in 1557—was a thing he much
wished to do. The Queen was not pleased either by his proposing to
leave her, or by his making a plan behind her back. With disagreeable teasing, she said she could hardly send a groom, a horsekeeper, to
wait upon so great a King. Then she smiled and said to him: "I
cannot live without seeing you every day." Before he could con-
gratulate himself she had added: "You are like my little dog. As
soon as he is seen anywhere, people know that I am coming, and
when you are seen, they say I am not far off." This was what he had
brought himself to, and what he would put up with, if it would serve
his turn.

On December 19th de Foix was writing: "Leicester has very much
urged the Queen to decide upon her marriage by Christmas, but she
said, only wait till Candlemas, then she would satisfy him." Candlemas
was February 2nd, so the Queen appeared to be putting him off only

for a few weeks. De Foix had, in fact, heard it said that the Queen had promised marriage to Leicester before witnesses. If she had, this troth plight would legally have bound her to the marriage. However, the Ambassador said: "If she thinks fit to disengage herself, no one will call her to account or give testimony against her."*

* Von Raumer, *Elizabeth and Mary Stuart.*

XI

THE QUEEN'S SLEEPLESS vigilance matched even Sir William Cecil's: the latter might sometimes lament that she would not do what he wanted her do to; he had never to complain that she would not give her mind to the matter. The closest bond between Elizabeth and the man who worked hardest for her was that they shared the same consuming interest. Bohun said: "In her private way of living, she always preferred her necessary affairs and the despatch of what concerned the government, before and above any pleasures, recreations and conversation." What Cecil once said of himself could have been said equally well by her: "My service hath been but a piece of my duty and my vocation hath been too great a reward."

With this intellectual industry Elizabeth combined an imperious appetite for pleasure, but not of an altogether sensual kind. Her rooms, it is true, were splendid, and all her life she was multiplying the number of beautiful, brilliant and precious objects about her, of gold and silver, mother of pearl, crystal and glass. When her success and grandeur were at their height, the ceiling of her bedroom in Whitehall was entirely gilded, her counterpanes were cloth of gold or cloth of silver, lined with ermine. But she ate and drank very little; she seldom dined in public, and, when she did, she often left the table when the meal was only half-finished. She enjoyed Alicante, a dessert wine imported from Spain, but her ordinary drinking was the lightest sort of ale, or wine mixed with water. In spite of the visual splendour that surrounded her, as Froude said, she lived simply and worked hard.

She had an exacting standard of personal cleanliness, and her sensitive nose required that those about her should have the same. This was not so difficult to ensure as is sometimes supposed. The difference between the sixteenth century and the present was the very small number of people who then washed and wore clean clothes, compared with the majority who do so now; but, within that minority, a high standard was expected. Sir Henry Sidney's letter of advice to his eleven-year-old son Philip, a boy at Shrewsbury School, tells the child, among much general advice about behaviour, that he must always be very careful to see that his clothes and all parts of his body are clean. This, attended to, would make him pleasant and attractive to people; if he neglected it, they would think him "loathsome". The ideal of personal charm was much the same as it is at present:

> An alabaster neck, a turquoise eye,
> A cleaner, cooler, who did ere espy?

The versifier said he would like to be so near the girl's nakedness, he wished he were her smock, or

> A bath, or sweet compound-water,
> Her delicate limbs to bathe, both soon and later.*

Elizabeth herself had a travelling bath that she took about with her. In 1563 the ironsmith, William Hood, was called in to repair the hinges to the iron-work of "the removing bath for the Queen".

An immaculate person, charming at any time, and implying admirable instincts, was combined, in Elizabeth's case, with her demanding, desolate vanity. It was remarked by a traveller that at Windsor Castle two little "stove-rooms", for bathing or taking vapour baths, were "ceiled and wainscotted with looking-glass",† and the slenderness and whiteness of her own body was a theme of which she could never hear too much. The verses George Puttenham put into his *Art of Poetry*, a book for all to read, celebrated her beauties without reticence. He said "*her bosom, sleek as Paris plaster, held up two balls of alabaster*", and spoke of her having "*A slender shin, swifter than roe, a pretty foot to trip and go*". He gave, too, in a couple of lines, an impression of seeing this pale, bright apparition out of doors among greenery:

> As I would approach her near,
> Her head yshone like crystal clear.

This was the vision of herself, it seemed, that she wished to evoke, that she wished to be adored; and when, at the beginning of January, 1566, the French Ambassador assured the Spanish Ambassador that Lord Leicester had slept with the Queen on New Year's Night, the story was by no means improbable, though the scandal was not of the nature that he imagined.

On January 27th, de Silva had an audience with the Queen, who had a fall down five steps and had been much shaken. She was still

* Letter Book of Gabriel Harvey, 1573–1580.   † Paul Hautzner, *Travels in England*.

lame and looked, he thought, very thin; however, she was very much pleased to see him. Candlemas came and went, but there was no word of her marrying Lord Leicester. Indeed, de Silva heard that at a Council meeting on February 4th the Duke of Norfolk had reminded Leicester that he had said he did not aspire to the Queen's hand, and the Queen, for her part, had said she did not intend to marry him. For this reason, said Norfolk, the Council had re-opened negotiations with the Archduke Charles, and if any delay occurred in these, and the nation thought Lord Leicester was responsible, then Norfolk must point out to the Earl that his position would be highly unenviable. The safest thing for Leicester to do was to give all his support to the projected marriage immediately. Leicester's reply was in fact repeated by newsmongers and their spies, but he thought he was giving it in confidence to his colleagues, and it was very interesting. He said he would indeed support the match, if it could be so arranged that the Queen should not think he had relinquished his pursuit of her from lack of inclination. This "would cause her, woman-like, to undo him". It was not a thing any woman with a great attachment to him could endure without pain, but in Elizabeth's case it would imply more than mere disappointment and humiliation; where she had placed her affection she clung as a man clings to a spar to save himself from the horrors of drowning; when her mother no longer charmed her father, the King had cut her head off.

It appeared that Leicester took the Council's warning to heart and did his best to satisfy them and safeguard himself. Later in the same day, de Silva had an audience with the Queen, who gave it him because she was going to Greenwich next day. He walked with her up and down the Lower Gallery of Whitehall Palace, which was open to the garden and the February air. She told him how unselfish the Earl of Leicester was; he had just been urging her to marry, for the sake of the country, for her own sake, and even, he had said, for his, because, as things were, he was blamed for her single state. He must have put all this with a felicitous blend of emotion and regret, for the Queen exclaimed fondly that if the Earl were but a king's son she would marry him tomorrow.

But however well Leicester had acquitted himself in this difficult situation, de Silva's private comment was: "She deals with them in a way that deceives them all! When she speaks to the Duke of Norfolk she says one thing, and when she speaks to Lord Robert, quite the contrary."

The Queen of Scots' marriage to Darnley had failed of its great objective; it had not caused all the English Catholics to rise and demand that Henry and Mary should replace Elizabeth upon the English throne. Darnley, arrogant, stupid and weak, had gone to pieces under the test of his great advancement; as a husband, he was an infliction that aroused wide-spread sympathy for his wife. The doings of the Scots Court were punctually reported to England. The Queen of Scots had made a confidential secretary of the Italian musician David Rizzio. This man's position, since he managed all the Queen's correspondence with the Pope, would have made him in any case an object of suspicion and dislike to the Protestant Lords, but his underbred insolence exacerbated them to fury. Exploiting Darnley's jealousy, they secured his name to a conspiracy to rid themselves of what they considered an offensive and dangerous nuisance. On February 13th Randolph wrote alarming news to Leicester: "I know for certain that this Queen repenteth her marriage, that she hateth (him) and all his kin. I know that he knoweth himself that he hath a partaker in play and game with him." Here Randolph subscribed to the commonly held but quite unproved belief that Mary was Rizzio's mistress. He went on to say that Lennox as well as Darnley were in a conspiracy against her. "I know that there are practices in hand contrived by the father and the son to come by the Queen against her will. I know that if that takes effect which is intended, David with the consent of the King shall have his throat cut within these ten days." Randolph was only a fortnight out; on March 9th Rizzio was murdered with horrible barbarity in the presence of the Queen of Scots, who was seven months gone with child. Mary, summoning her great resources of courage and high spirits, gained her craven young husband to her side again and escaped by moonlight in a wild ride to Dunbar, the unspeakable Darnley goading his wife to speed by shouting brutally that if she lost that child they could get another.

Mary's dauntless bravery was rewarded. Darnley denounced the conspirators without saying he had been one of them, and they dispersed and fled. Having escaped from their hands Mary was able to reassert herself, and in spite of the fearful trials she had endured she was safely delivered of a son at Stirling Castle in June, 1566.

The Scottish scene, however, was becoming so dark that if Leicester had had any lingering pangs of renounced ambition they must have died away. But, to do him justice, neither his words nor his conduct ever suggested that he had the least wish for the position now so disastrously occupied by Lord Darnley. His unchanging attitude to Scotland was summed up in the comment he made in 1571, on the murder of Lord Lennox: "God defend all my friends from that soil!"[1]

In March Lady Huntingdon was ill, and Leicester, leaving the Court, went up to Ashby-de-la-Zouche to see her. Whether he combined with a genuine wish to visit his sick sister a wish also to pique the Queen was debated in certain circles, for there had now arisen a formidable successor to Heneage among those who distracted the Queen's attention from himself.

The Earl of Ormonde, the dark and handsome Thomas Butler, known as Black Tom, had been brought up at the Court of Henry VIII. He had gone over to Ireland in Mary Tudor's time to try to create order among his tenantry, and, strongly Anglophile himself, he did what he could to conciliate the Irish in the interests of English rule. The patriotic Earl of Desmond fell upon Ormonde's estates, and savage intermittent warfare ensued. In 1565 Ormonde returned to Elizabeth's Court to plead his case, and remained there for the next four years. His good looks, his Irish charm and his responsive gallantry, as well as his strong English sympathies, made him a very attractive companion to Elizabeth, and de Silva saw that by March Leicester had become conscious and resentful of Ormonde, whom the Ambassador described as "an Irishman of good disposition, thirty years of age".

The French Ambassador scanned the newcomer with characteristic sharpness. "The Earl of Ormonde is in high favour," he said. "Though he had neither ability nor means to maintain his ground, Leicester is nevertheless under some apprehension." Whatever his motives for the journey to Ashby-de-la-Zouche, and whatever the feelings entertained by the Queen for anybody else, once Leicester was away, with no date fixed for his return, Elizabeth wrote asking him to come back. He replied to this by a request for fifteen days' further leave of absence, whereupon the Queen told him to come back at once. When de Silva wrote, the Earl's return was expected that night or the day following. The Earl of Ormonde, meantime, was still rising in favour.

Unhappily, the Princess Cecilia and her husband were outstaying their welcome. There had been trouble quite early in their visit. Lord Bedford had written from Berwick to Leicester asking that, if the Princess herself were not still occupying his house in the Strand, her train might not remain in it either, "which, as I hear," wrote his

Lordship, "be but a homely company, and in as homely a manner do use my house, breaking and spoiling windows and everything".* The Queen entertained them generously, paying the expenses of their household, but neither the Princess nor the Margrave understood the manners and customs of the English; they were apt to see slights, and they both, the latter especially, thought it an impertinence on the part of shopkeepers to ask that their purchases should be paid for. The Margrave, making an unostentatious retreat towards the continent, was laid by the heels at Rochester and imprisoned for debt. Finding himself in the Round House, he threatened to shoot his way out, and the Mayor of Rochester sent to the Queen, asking either that the Margrave should be told he must keep the laws of the country, or that the town might be relieved of so awkward a prisoner. The Queen sent down the money to discharge the Margrave's debt, and he lost no time in getting away. First, however, he sent a servant up to London with a letter to Lord Leicester, demanding a horse. "I require an English horse for this journey," he wrote. "Looking round I cannot find a suitable one for sale here. But as I know you have plenty, I shall consider it an addition to your previous kindness if you will give one to the bearer, my servant, to bring with him." He added; "If you would like a German horse, you shall have one."*

It was well understood that Leicester's personal influence with the Queen was great, that in matters of private life she listened to him very readily, whether he spoke for himself or other people; but he could not encroach one inch upon the magic circle within which she bounded herself and her power. Generally speaking, he did not attempt to do so; he was notorious for his gentle-spokenness, his easiness combined with a deep reserve, for his ability to "put his passion in his pocket"; but had this tactful, grave manner concealed no hidden forces, it would not have been the potent attraction that it was. It concealed, in fact, the ravening self-assertion of his father Northumberland, and his father's rage at the least affront to his personal dignity. On the rare occasions when these instincts escaped the guard which was habitually imposed on them, Leicester was betrayed into misjudgment so extraordinary that a man far less clever, adroit and experienced could have been trusted to avoid it.

The famous instance took place apropos the entrée to the Privy Chamber. This apartment, opening out of the Presence Chamber, was the Queen's withdrawing-room, and it was the business of the

* H.M.S. Pepys.

official known as Gentleman of the Black Rod to allow no one to pass the threshhold whom he did not recognize. One day the Black Rod, whose name was Bowyer, checked in the doorway a swaggering captain and told him he must not go further. The man was a protégé of Lord Leicester's, and, having tried in vain to overcrow Bowyer with his patron's name, he went off, saying darkly that he might yet see Bowyer turned out of his place. Thinking, apparently, that the power of his name had been publicly slighted, Leicester himself appeared in fury, and, telling Bowyer that he was a knave, and should not long continue in his office, he made for the Queen's presence. But Bowyer was too quick for him; passing rapidly in front of him, the usher fell on his knees before the Queen, and on the spur of the moment put his case into words which the deepest calculation could not have bettered: explaining the matter in dispute, he begged only to be told, whether my Lord of Leicester were King, or her Majesty Queen? Unlike those whom anger deprives of speech, Elizabeth was stimulated by it to torrential eloquence. "God's death, my Lord, I have wished you well," she exclaimed, "but my favour is not so locked up in you that others shall not participate thereof, for I have many servants unto whom I have, and will at my pleasure, confer my favour, and likewise reassume the same; and if you think to rule here, I will take a course to see you forthcoming. I will have here but one mistress and no master." Her eyes went from the tall, standing figure of Leicester to the kneeling Bowyer; intuition sent its lightning message to her brain, and she added: "And look that no ill happen to him, lest it be severely required at your hands!" Sir Thomas Naunton, who told the story, said that "this so quailed my Lord of Leicester, that his feigned humility was long after one of his best virtues."*

So much for a scene of rage and command, for a humiliation that became public property; but on April 12th, 1566, a strange event was seen by passers-by in the streets between St. Paul's and the river-side. On the morning of that day Lord Leicester, followed by seven hundred footmen, his own and the Queen's, came to young Lord Oxford's town house, that stood opposite St. Swithin's Church, beside London Stone. When he found no one there to meet him, he departed with his following. Meanwhile the Queen, in a boat rowed by one pair of oars, attended by two ladies only, had come up against the tide from Greenwich. A landing could be made only where there were stairs, and the boatman brought her to those on the wharf known as The Three Cranes, from the three great machines that stood

* Naunton, *Fragmenta Regalia.*

there for loading and unloading. Here a blue-painted coach was waiting for her and she drove off to London Stone. Alas, no one was there. Lord Leicester, though refusing to wait for her at the tryst, had none the less posted himself at a point she must pass on her return to the wharf. "When she saw him, she came out of her coach into the high-way and she embraced the Earl and kissed him three times." Then he climbed into the coach with her and they drove across London Bridge and took the road to Greenwich. This vision of the lovers, inconsequent, unaccountable, rose and disappeared again like a happening in a dream.*

On April 29th, 1566, there took place, under difficulties, the departure of the Princess Cecilia. De Silva said she had always made a point of speaking well of Lord Leicester, but he had helped her little in her hour of need! Before the Princess's ship could put out to sea, creditors boarded her and at least threatened to impound twelve chests belonging to her ladies of honour. But one pleasant conse- quence of the visit remained. The youngest maid of honour, Helena von Snakenburg, fair-haired, exquisitely pretty, and at her arrival fourteen years old, had become a favourite with everyone from the Queen downwards. Lord Northampton's wife had died in 1565, and the fifty-three-year-old peer wanted to marry the delightful little girl, who was artlessly elated by his suit. "My dearest mother dear," she wrote to reassure an anxious parent in Sweden, "even if I brought him nothing but my shift, and gave him happiness, he would ask no other wealth." Northampton had said to the Princess: "If Elin wants to remain in England after your departure, I promise to keep her as though she were my own daughter . . . whether she prefers to stay with the Queen or at my house, she shall do as she likes." The Princess had at first given her consent to the match, but now in her exasperation with the English she withdrew it; but, as Helena told her mother, "she only wanted to revenge herself on his Lordship, who had done her nothing but good!" The little creature had no intention of allowing her prospects to be blighted by the whims of her mistress. As she said: "My dearest mother, I cannot imagine I shall ever want for anything, however beautiful or expensive, that his Lordship can buy, without his getting it at once for his Elin."

Elizabeth loved the child; she made her a Gentlewoman of the Privy Chamber, and Elin had a most enjoyable life at the English Court. She married Lord Northampton in 1571, and the Queen attended the wedding. Northampton lived only six months after-

* Stow, *Historical Memoranda.* Camden Society.

wards, but after this short time of bliss, it was said, "he sweetly ended his life". The Queen always spoke of Helena as "the good Lady Marquess", and the latter remained one of her intimate friends for the rest of the Queen's life.* At her death, the Marchioness of Northampton was the chief mourner in the funeral procession.

In May de Silva reported that Dr. Young, Archbishop of York, "a great friend of Lord Robert", had thought it only right to "admonish and counsel the Queen" about her way of life; people, said his Grace, were speaking ill of the favour she showed—to the Earl of Ormonde! So preposterous an admonition threw the Queen into a passion; Lord Leicester, however, magnanimously intervened, and begged her to think no more of it.

On June 15th de Silva encountered Leicester on the grand staircase of Whitehall. The Earl spoke with the utmost suavity and said that if the Queen would not marry one of her own subjects, then he hoped she would take the Archduke. Their conversation was broken off by a message from the Queen asking the Spanish Ambassador to come to her. He and Leicester went in together, and there they found the Queen with Lord Ormonde. "Certainly," said de Silva, "he and Leicester did not look very amiably at each other."

Cecil on several occasions drew up tables, analysing the pros and cons of Leicester as a husband for Elizabeth. He had made one last April, and among such disqualifications as: "It will be thought that the slanderous speeches of the Queen and the Earl have been true", "He is infamed by the death of his wife", "He is far in debt", he wrote down an observation formed at first hand, and reminding the reader of Leicester's portraits with the staring, sinister eyes: "He is like to prove unkind, or jealous of the Queen's Majesty."†

Leicester's frayed temper showed itself in the months of June and July. A violent quarrel broke out between him and Lord Sussex at Greenwich, at the Council table itself. The Queen with difficulty "made them accord", and a decent show of reconciliation was somehow brought about. In this month, Sir James Melville came posting south with the news that the Queen of Scots had been delivered of a son. Cecil conveyed the news to Elizabeth at Greenwich where she was dancing after supper. The story as given by Melville was that she exclaimed: The Queen of Scots is lighter of a fair son, and I am but a barren stock! Doubt has been cast on the authenticity of these words. If she did utter them, they could perhaps be explained, not as the lament of a childless woman, but as a poignant reminder of the

* C. A. Bradford, *Helena Marchioness o Northampton*.   † Haynes.

political disadvantage she was under of not being able to give the nation an undoubted heir; two sons had strengthened the power for harm of Lady Catherine Grey, and the birth of James Stuart would provide the Queen of Scots with an additional weapon in her attempts upon the English throne. Leicester might well have used the occasion as an opportunity to urge Elizabeth to give herself to him and let him put her in the state where she need no longer fear the child-bearing of other women. If he did, he met with no success, and another furious quarrel blazed out between Lord Sussex and himself less than a month after the first. This was over affairs in Ireland, where Sussex had been Lord Deputy till 1564. The disturbance was so great that the Chancellor, Sir Nicholas Bacon, and the other Councillors present were united in an attempt to restore order. The Queen was very angry at this indecorum, and insisted not only that the two Earls should be friends again but that they should be seen as such; at her command they rode back to London together, and dined together at a house of the Earl of Bedford's in Southwark.

In this year, two contradictory medical opinions had been given about the Queen's fitness for marriage and child-bearing. When the suggestion had been made of a marriage between Charles IX and the English Queen, Catherine de Medici had instituted searching enquiries on this point and a member of the French embassy had asked the opinion of one of the Queen's physicians, who had replied heartily: "Take no notice of what she says; if the King marries I will answer for her having ten children, and no one knows her temperament better than I do."* The author of this opinion remained anonymous, but Dr. Huick, who had been physician to Catherine Parr and had known Elizabeth since she was fifteen, when consulted on this matter, gave his advice in the opposite sense. Whether he formed the view that, since her nervous resistance was so great, sexual union would by physically impossible, or whether, when she told him what she felt and feared, he soothed her by saying she ought to be guided by her feelings, at all events it became public property that Dr. Huick had encouraged her in her determination not to marry, as Camden said, "for I know not what womanish infirmity".

The French Ambassador, La Forêt, who had replaced de Foix, had taken care to place himself on most friendly terms with Lord Leicester. As Zwetkovich the Imperial attaché, said, the French were doing their best to induce the Queen to marry the Earl so that she might not contract the Austrian match, "which would spell disaster for the

---

* De la Ferrière, *Projets du Mariage de la Reine Elizabeth.*

French King".* On August 6th La Forêt reported an interesting conversation he had had with Leicester. "The Earl has confessed to me, smiling and sighing at the same time, that he does not know what to hope or fear." This was the occasion of Leicester's making the famous statement: "I have known her since she was eight years old, better than any man in the world. From that time she has invariably declared she would remain unmarried." Leicester went on to say, he thought that if she were to marry an Englishman, he would be her choice. "At least," he said, "the Queen has done me the honour to tell me so, several times, when we were alone, and I am as high in her favour as ever,"† he concluded, with perhaps a wish that the new Ambassador should be under no delusion as to Lord Ormonde's position.

Whatever his hopes or fears, Leicester's position in the public eye was one of unclouded ascendancy. The year before, the Queen had paid him a brief visit at Kenilworth, where Leicester's Buildings were under construction, and she and her train had to be lodged in other parts of the Castle. Leicester had written to Antony Forster, who, as Steward of the Household, was in charge of all arrangements, about tapestry for the dining chamber: "I cannot have such hangings as I looked for" (from Flanders), but he heard some "very good" were to be had in London. "In any case, deal with Mr. Spinola . . . he is able to get such stuff better cheap than any man, and I am sure will do his best for me," and, with a touching eagerness, he exhorted Forster to make provision for everything, "against my chiefest day".

This year, 1566, the Queen was to come to Oxford on her summer progress. Leicester, as Chancellor of the University, was in the position of her host, and he was staying at Kenilworth a fortnight before the Queen should arrive, that he might supervise everything for which he was responsible. This was not confined to the doings of the University. His nephew Philip Sidney was now twelve years old, a wonderful child, clever, gentle, earnest and sweet, of "a lovely and familiar gravity", whom, even at this age, his father spoke of as "the light of my house". Sir Henry Sidney was now in Ireland as Lord Deputy, and Philip, when away from his mother, was in the charge of the invaluable family Steward, Mr. Marshall. The boy had been invited to join his uncle's party at Oxford, and Marshall brought him from Shrewsbury School to Kenilworth a fortnight before the festivities were to begin. There was much to be done. The Sidneys

* Von Klarwill, *Queen Elizabeth and some Foreigners.*
† Von Raumer, *Elizabeth and Mary Stuart.*

were not well-to-do for their station, and Philip's clothes were not suitable for this great occasion. Marshall had done his best; he had had the child's old black velvet cloak turned into a pair of trunk hose, "whereof the charges" included six shillings for "a yard of double sarcenet to line them with", "fourpence for quarter of a pennyweight of jean fustian for two pockets", and "four shillings for the making", but, do what he would, he could not turn the boy out looking fit to be seen. Leaving his charge at Kenilworth, he went over to Coventry, where the Earl was, "to speak with my Lord for the knowledge of Mr. Philip's apparel". The knowledge aroused Mr. Philip's uncle to prompt action. He gave Marshall an order on his London tailor, the same Whittle who had made his mourning, and Whittle ultimately delivered at Kenilworth a crimson satin doublet, a green taffeta doublet, a canvas doublet striped blue, a canvas doublet striped red and silver, a plain canvas doublet (not yet received, Marshall noted), a pair of crimson velvet trunk hose with crimson silk stockings, a pair of carnation woollen trunk hose with woollen stockings to match, green leather trunk hose with green stockings and blue leather trunk hose with blue stockings, a white leather jerkin trimmed with gold, a red and black leather jerkin, six pairs of double-soled shoes, two white, two black and two blue shirts, a double taffeta coat and a short damask gown trimmed with velvet.*
Whittle either did not supply, or had not in hand, the fringe and lace with which the short, full breeches were trimmed, so Antony Forster wrote to Mrs. Montagu, the Queen's silk-woman, who had knitted Elizabeth's first pair of silk stockings. "I pray you, deliver to this bearer, my Lord's hosier, as much crimson fringe and lace as will trim a pair of crimson hose for Mr. Philip Sidney, and so much purple as will trim a pair of carnation hose, also as much blue and green lace as will trim two pairs of leather hose."†

In the third week in August the Queen came towards Oxford and established herself at the palace of Woodstock. The party included the Spanish Ambassador. On August 27th he went out hunting with Leicester in Woodstock Chase, and he said: "I talked with him for a long while on the way, trying to direct the conversation to his affairs. It is easy to see he has not abandoned his pretensions from the way in which he treats the matter."

The Queen could not join the hunt on this occasion as she was

---

* Wallace, M. W., *Philip Sidney*.

† Dudley MSS. Longleat, quoted by Jackson, *Wilts Arch. and Nat. Hist. Magazine*, May, 1877.

unwell with an "issue" in her shoulder. This was a treatment to produce a "counter-irritant" which was supposed to relieve various conditions. A nick was made in the skin and a small gold or silver ball was inserted and sewn up; the resulting inflammation was thought to be useful. An issue was usually set up near the part it was meant to relieve, those in the shoulder being for lung troubles or headache. The Queen may have been suffering from the latter; she was the victim of migraine as a girl, and in view of the taxing engagements ahead of her she may have been advised to take strong measures. At all events, she could not hunt on the 27th, but she told de Silva she hoped he would go out with her ladies, and that Lord Leicester would take care of him.

At the impending visit to Oxford Leicester, as Chancellor of the University, was in his glory. He was worthy of his honours for his genuine interest in literature. Two years before, in 1564, Arthur Golding had published the first volume of his translation of Ovid's *Metamorphoses*, which was to prove one of the most popular Elizabethan books. Golding dedicated the book to Leicester as a patron of literary men who was "wont to encourage them to proceed in their painful exercise", which they undertook "to enrich their native language with things not heretofore published in the same". The second volume, published in 1587, he dedicated with an even stronger emphasis on Leicester's interest in translations, and his known kindness to all such students of foreign languages as beautify the mother tongue with foreign riches. May such writers, he said,

> *Proceed through thy good furtherance and favour in the same*
> *To all men's profit and delight and thy eternal fame.*

In this year 1566 Thomas Nuce dedicated to the Earl his Latin play *Octavia*, saying he had chosen Leicester as his patron "for his favourable and gracious humanity to scholars".

The Court was to arrive at Oxford on Saturday August 31st, and Leicester, attended by Lord Warwick and Lord Huntingdon, went two days before the Queen to supervise the arrangements for her reception. He met Cecil by appointment in the quadrangle of Christchurch, but a "vehement" rain drove them to take refuge in the Master's Lodge. The weather had cleared by the day of the Court's appearance, and in the evening of August 31st the Queen came from Woodstock. Though she usually travelled on horseback, she now rode in a coach, and de Silva said she looked very thin, but if she felt ill she did not show it. The fairy-like cavalcade approached: the coach which Court painters had been feed to decorate with vermilion and gold leaf, and inside it the pale-faced, glistering figure who alighted and to whom the waiting dignitaries were presented in their turn. When the Puritan Dr. Humphries approached to kiss her hand, the Queen said: "Master Doctor, that loose robe becomes you well; I wonder your notions should be so narrow!" Then she smiled and said: "But I do not come to chide."

The Queen was conducted immediately to a service in Christchurch Cathedral, during which a *Te Deum* sung to the music of cornets had been specially arranged to give her pleasure.[1]

Among the young men who made orations to her during her visit was Edmund Campion, whose only connection, so far, with the Earl of Leicester was that six years before he had taken part in the funeral ceremony of Lady Dudley. On this occasion he made a speech of welcome, complimenting the University on their magnificent Chancellor, and saying how fit it was that he himself should speak, in the name of Philosophy, Princess of learning, before so learned a Princess. He afterwards delivered for the Queen's entertainment a dissertation on the influence of the moon upon the sea. Many gifted young men were competing for Elizabeth's attention, but among them all Campion's brilliancy of expression and his unusual charm of manner marked him out. On the day the Queen's visit ended, the royal party withdrew to Woodstock for the night, and she asked de Silva how he had liked the young men's speeches? Excellently, he said, but after all they had had long preparation: he did not suppose they could have made much of a showing without it. He should see, the Queen told him, and at once a message was sent to Oxford that a few young men of the most distinguished sort should come out to Woodstock, to debate in Latin, impromptu, before her Majesty and the Spanish Ambassador. Campion was of course among those chosen, and he said afterwards that "the sudden great pomp in which the Queen came forth to hear him" took him aback until he reminded himself "that she was but a woman and he a man, which was the better sex", and that "all the splendour that glittered in his eyes was but transitory vanity and had no substance in it". In possession of himself once more, he spoke so brilliantly that when the display was over Elizabeth told Leicester to get into touch with him. Leicester sent for him, and with the gracious, cordial manner that was irresistible to a young and humble man he asked Campion what were his ambitions? The Queen, and Leicester himself, would be glad to further them: let Campion ask what he would.

With exquisite tact Campion answered that he would ask nothing; the Chancellor's friendship was worth more than any gift.*

Leicester determined to be the young man's consistent patron, and five years later Campion acknowledged how truly the Earl had fulfilled his intention. In 1571 he dedicated to him a *History of Ireland*. Campion was ingenuous, modest, grateful, but his enemies themselves could not have called him servile, and when he wrote: "There is none that knoweth me familiarly but he knoweth withal how many ways I have been beholding to your Lordship", it must have been the truth. "How often at Oxford, how often at the Court, how at Rycote, how at Windsor, how by letter, how by reports, you have not ceased to further with advice and to countenance with authority the hope and expectation of me, a simple student." He gave a picture of Leicester's courtesy and easy manner towards "an infinite resort of daily suitors", praising him for "so lowly a stomach, such a facility, so mild a nature in so high a vocation", and for the humility with which the great nobleman put himself under "the tuition of learned men". This friendship, in which both parties had been inspired by good feeling and good will, was to prove a sacrifice to events for which, ultimately, neither side was responsible.

On the return journey from Woodstock to London the Queen, accompanied by Leicester and a part of the retinue only, stayed at Rycote, the house of Sir Henry Norris whose wife Margery was the black-haired, black-eyed young woman whom Elizabeth called "Mine own Crow". Lady Norris adored the Queen, and her family had long been members of Leicester's intimate circle. The house-parties given for Elizabeth at Rycote had a private, idyllic air, surrounding her with the tender enthusiasm of her lover and her friends. Leicester, between the claims of the University, his brother's castle at Warwick and his own at Kenilworth, had reason to be fairly often in the neighbourhood, and Campion's dedication shows that he was frequently staying with the Norrises.

The birth of a son to the Queen of Scots had naturally sharpened the fears of those who did not want either a Catholic succession or a civil war; and the Parliament which was to assemble in October was prepared to force the Queen to undertake definitely to marry, if possible, but in any case to declare her heir presumptive. On September 6th de Silva said he had heard that Leicester was secretly using his influence to encourage Parliament in this design, because he felt sure, de Silva said, that the marriage with the Archduke would be

* Bede Camm, *Lives of the English Martyrs, Edmund Campion*.

scotched, and then, on the tide of public insistence for her marriage, he would catch the Queen for himself.

For the opening of this Parliament, the Queen's crimson velvet robes needed repair. The Wardrobe officials set to work "for making a new bodice and sleeves of crimson velvet for the kirtle for Parliament, lined with white satin; for mending the fur on the mantle, kirtle and surcoat of the Lady the Queen for Parliament, and hanging on the same four ermine furs and two hundred powderings."[1] The Queen did not make much of this occasion of the opening of Parliament. Instead of being carried through the streets, robed and crowned, she went by water from Whitehall to Westminster and put on her crimson robes when she got there. De Silva heard that, having made the speech from the throne, she recommended the Houses to be resolute in their voting and not too long in their speeches, and then she went home to dinner.

There had been no need to tell Parliament to be resolute; the members had come up from their constituencies, charged that they should not vote any money without a promise from the Queen to marry at the first possible moment. They expressed their determination amid scenes of unprecedented uproar. The Lords sent a deputation to the Queen, who answered haughtily: "My Lords, do whatever you wish. As for me, I shall do no other than pleases me. Your bills can have no force without my assent and authority."[2] In the same week she was subjected to a private harrying on the matter, and her terrified spirits rose to a desperate pitch. Norfolk, Pembroke, Northampton and Leicester himself sought an audience, and they entered the Presence Chamber all together, a quartet of relentless men, advancing implacably upon her, to force her to the nameless horror. The fear, the anger, the hatred that she could neither control nor explain animated the burning reproaches that poured from her lips, of disloyalty, of ingratitude, of dishonesty, of treason. In the midst of her passion she turned upon Leicester, crying, she had thought that though all the world abandoned her, he would not. In self-defence, Leicester exclaimed that he would die at her feet! But how would that appease Parliament or release her from her nightmare? In furious impatience she told him his words were beside the point. For some days after this Leicester and his friend Pembroke were not allowed to enter the Presence Chamber.

The discussions about the Succession which Elizabeth had tried to prevent had encouraged the Queen of Scots to send, not to Elizabeth herself, but to the Privy Council, an imperiously worded demand for a recognition of what she termed "our hereditary right, as has lately been mentioned in the Parliament". She appeared to think that if only the English would have the common honesty to produce the Will of Henry VIII, it would be found to contain something of great benefit to her. She demanded to be shown it on many occasions, and it was a great pity that it was never produced for her. There she would have read, once and for all, that, however many people might be willing to see her ascend the English throne, Henry VIII had not been among them.

The session had begun in such stormy manner, it was almost impossible to see how the Queen could extricate herself from her troubles, since the one thing demanded of her was the one thing she could not grant. She achieved it by a stroke of genius, which, however, was only within her power as the result of eleven years of unremitting conserving of her resources and building up the nation's confidence in her. She said that, of the subsidy she had asked for, which was necessary to pay the expenses of her intervention in France and to maintain her programme of shipbuilding, she would accept two-thirds; the rest, she said, was as good as in her exchequer if it were in her subjects' pockets. The effect of this gesture was so powerful that the House, expressing their gratitude and approval of her "great clemency", voted the two-thirds of the money without standing out further for the one impossible condition. Sir Richard Baker said of Elizabeth and her subjects: "She thought the money did as well in their coffers as in her own, and indeed she never wanted it when they had it, and they always had it when she needed it."

Christmas came on with its revels, and *The Tragedy of Tancred and Gismunda* was acted on Twelfth Night by the gentlemen of the Inner Temple. The gloomy piece was a composite production, of which Act IV had been written by Christopher Hatton, a tall, good-looking lawyer, twenty-six years old. The Queen had noticed his graceful dancing in a masque put on by the Temple two years before. He was now one of the Gentlemen Pensioners, a position for which his height, his handsomeness and his personal devotion to the Queen made him eminently suitable.

XII

IN JANUARY, 1567, the Court was at the palace of Nonsuch in Surrey, de Silva wrote: "The Earl of Leicester not being in very high favour with the Queen just now, I was walking out of her chamber when she called me back, and said she would be glad if I would show some love and friendship to Lord Robert as I was wont to do." De Silva was astonished at this wistful plea. He told the Queen there was no lack of good will towards Lord Robert on his part; he had only acted with reserve towards him out of consideration for her.

The Court had returned to London when all topics of every kind were banished by the fearful news from Edinburgh that in the early hours of February 11th Kirk o'Field, the small, outlying house in which Lord Darnley was recovering from the smallpox, had been blown up by gunpowder, and the bodies of himself and his servant had been found strangled in the garden beside it. The Queen of Scots had left her husband's bedside two hours before the explosion took place; she said she must return to Holyrood to grace the wedding feast of one of her servants. As she made her way from Kirk o'Field to the palace, she sent back a page to bring away a rich counterpane that covered her bed in the room below her husband's.

The news was received in many forms, but one aspect of it was accepted immediately and universally. The Queen of Scots had now no future as a reigning sovereign in any country. So completely was this realized that those in England who were anxious and determined to stand well with the next heir were obliged to bethink themselves. Lord Leicester had been markedly indifferent to the fate of Lady Catherine Grey; but on the night that Darnley's death was known in London he sent Lord Warwick to wait upon the Earl of Hertford "to offer his services in the matter of succession", while he himself, as the more experienced tactician, went off and applied his powers to dealing with Hertford's mother, the formidable Duchess of Somerset.* Contact could not, or not immediately, be made with Catherine Grey herself, for she was under the guardianship of Sir Owen Hopton

* C.S.P. Spanish.

at Cockfield Hall in Suffolk. The extreme rapidity of Lord Leicester's action on the very night the news was brought to London recalls Lloyd's saying that "he was always before-hand with his designs, being a declared enemy to after-games".*

The Queen of Scots' affairs proceeded in a series of sensational episodes of such overpowering effect that it seemed scarcely credible that, between the murder of Darnley in February and her own imprisonment on the island in Loch Leven in June, only four months had elapsed. In that short time she had, against Elizabeth's most earnest, disinterested advice, married Bothwell, who was generally believed to be the prime mover in her husband's murder, and had aroused the implacable hatred of her nobles not only by marrying him but by placing the fortresses of the kingdom in his control. The risings against her began in June. On June 15th she was forced to capitulate at Carberry Hill, where Bothwell left her on the field, and she was brought back to Edinburgh, exclaiming that she would hang and crucify the rebels, while her subjects crowded the streets of her capital, shouting *Burn the whore!*

Elizabeth was in a state of the most wearing apprehension about the Queen of Scots, in connection with whom she had only exchanged one set of fears and problems for another. She had wanted to see her in eclipse, so that she could not work harm in England; but the sight of a monarch imprisoned by subjects was one which filled Elizabeth with indignation. She divined that, once such a thing was tolerated, no other Sovereign was safe. Mary, she decided, must be released and restored to her throne, but under such conditions as would safeguard the Protestant religion in Scotland, her own nobles and Elizabeth's kingdom. Sir Nicholas Throckmorton in Edinburgh saw that Elizabeth's peremptory manner towards the Scots was not only prejudicial to the Scots Queen's cause but likely to drive the Scots themselves into a French alliance. He wrote warning Leicester on July 24th that "if the Queen will still persist in her former opinion towards the Queen of Scots (unto whom she shall be able to do no good)" then he saw plainly that "these Lords and all their complices will become as good French as the French king could desire".[1] All the French wanted was an opportunity to return to Scotland; they would not mind on whose side they were asked to intervene.

Throckmorton wrote to Leicester again on July 26th: "It is to be feared that the tragedy will end in the person of the Queen violently,

* Lloyd, *State Worthies.*

as it began in Davy's and her husband's." He wanted to be recalled, "seeing I do nothing here but spend the Queen's money".[1]

On August 6th Leicester wrote, telling him from the Queen that he was "to use all means to let the Queen of Scots know the Queen's great grief for her . . . the Queen takes the doings of the Lords to heart as a precedent most perilous to any Prince". To which Throckmorton replied bluntly: "The way to amend this Queen's fortune and treatment is for the Queen of England to deal more calmly in her speech of them than she does."[2]

De la Mothe Fénélon was now the French Ambassador at St. James's, and he poured into the avid ears of Catherine de Medici that the Duke of Norfolk and his father-in-law, the Earl of Arundel, had spoken to Leicester very gravely about his behaviour with the Queen. If Leicester could tell them that she wished to marry him, then they would support his suit. If he could not make this claim, then they must tell him that his conduct towards her was very improper. They charged him with being in her bedchamber before she was out of bed, and with handing her the shift she meant to put on. They further instanced his kissing her without being invited thereto. If he were not troth-plight to her, then such conduct was injurious to her honour. The peers did not allow themselves to concede, even by implication, that Lord Leicester could not have been at the Queen's bedside unless leave had been given him; they merely told him that, unless he would claim the privileges of a betrothed lover, these doings must cease.

Leicester was affronted by this conversation, but he dared not say so. He could not say the Queen had promised to marry him, and therefore he was obliged to listen to the rebukes of Norfolk and Arundel, for though the Queen had often taken his part in a quarrel she had never given him the confidence that he could defy all comers because he held her affection. This fact in itself was enough to tell so acute an observer as Cecil that he had never possessed her. "The most reserved man of the age", he veiled his feelings now. He said the Queen had shown him such affection that he had been led to hope she would marry him, but he would try to bring the matter to a head; if he could not gain her promise, he would cease his habits of intimacy with her. As a faithful councillor, her honour and that of the crown must be dearer to him than his own life. The strange contrast between the outer and inner positions occupied by Leicester was thrown into relief by this interview with the heads of the nobility, who took him to task for the impropriety of his conduct, and by the publication of his portrait as one of the frontispieces of the Bishops' Bible, issued in 1568. This was an edition of the Old and New Testament produced by the Bench of Bishops as a popular work meant to rival the Genevan Bible of 1560, for the latter bore marginal comments of a strongly Puritan tenor. In the usual ambivalence of his conduct, Lord Leicester's portrait was used with one of the Queen's to give attraction to a work conceived in a spirit of hostility to the Puritans, though he himself was regarded as a leader of the Puritan party.

The unfortunate Lady Catherine Grey, who had for many months been in a decline, perpetually grieving and unable to eat, died on the morning of January 27th, 1568, while the tolling of the passing bell which she had asked them to ring was heard in her bedchamber. De Silva, writing in February, said he had heard that a rapprochement was expected to take place between Leicester and Cecil, and that they would lay their heads together over the succession. Since the official view was that Lady Catherine's marriage was not proved, her two sons were reckoned illegitimate, and the only surviving claimant in her immediate family was her sister Mary, a dwarf, who had made herself further unacceptable by a stolen match with a giant, a Mr. Keyes, sergeant-porter to the river-gate at Westminster. This match had been discovered three years before, and like her sister she had been separated from her husband. Lady Mary was at present living under the unwilling guardianship, in his town house, of the exasperated Sir Thomas Gresham. This was not a strong prop on which to support the Protestant interest.

The project of the Queen's match with the Archduke had now no more life in it. The ostensible cause of its failure was the problem of religious observance. In fact the marriage had never been a possibility, but there had been many advantages in pretending that it was. The disagreeable feature of the case was the deception of so honourable and decent a man as Lord Sussex. Sussex came home convinced that the failure of the negotiations was due simply and solely to Lord Leicester's own pursuit of the Queen. He knew, he said, who had been at work in the vineyard while he was away. "If God should ever put it into my dear mistress's heart to divide the weeds from the grain, she should reap the better harvest here," he said. His loyalty to the Queen was largely the outcome of his own loyal nature; but considering the annoyance and frustration which her exactions inflicted on him, the chivalrous affection he felt for her showed something remarkable in Elizabeth. Meanwhile the situation was a little easier. England's vulnerability, and the desire of Spain and France to possess her, meant that England was safest when Spain and France had their hands fully occupied. France was now distracted by the religious war; Spain was about to launch an onslaught upon the religious and economic freedom of the Netherlands. The Queen of Scots, the third menace, was immured on an island in the waters of Loch Leven.

Elizabeth had done her best, in the teeth of her own Council, to take Mary's part against the lords who had imprisoned her. The Queen of Scots had been forced to sign a deed of abdication, and the Earl of Murray was now Regent for the two-year-old James. Elizabeth's own wish was to see the Queen of Scots restored to her throne, but under such limitations that she could not bring French or Spanish help into Scotland to cow her own subjects, and then attack Elizabeth's. The English Queen, in short, wanted to see her a Queen in name, dependent upon English support. This arrangement, with its guarantee of security for the Reformed religion, would have satisfied the majority of the Scots; by exorcising the nightmare of France or Spain using Scotland as a base for the invasion of England, it would have satisfied the English government, and by according Mary a titular respect it would have soothed Elizabeth's agitation and fear at the sight of a crowned queen held a prisoner by her subjects. The person whom none of this would satisfy was the Queen of Scots herself. She had learnt nothing and she had relinquished nothing. In May, 1568, it was heard with consternation that she had escaped from the island; on May 13th her followers fought an action with the Regent's forces and were defeated at Langside; within four days Mary, with eighteen companions, crossed the Solway and arrived at Workington in Cumberland. She was escorted to Carlisle, and while she wrote to Elizabeth from here, demanding help and clothes, the neighbouring Catholic gentry poured in to pay their respects to the woman who in the eyes of many was their Queen already. Eight years ago, in France, Mary had declared herself Queen of England, and had had the English Royal Arms engraved on her possessions. She had never ceased in her efforts to make good this claim. She had demanded in peremptory terms to be pronounced heiress presumptive of England; among her intimates she declared that she was the English Queen. She had been an imminent danger to Elizabeth ever since the latter's accession; she was now actually in the kingdom, holding Court among Elizabeth's subjects. The horror of hearing of her arrival was increased when Mary sent a message, asking first for clothes, and then for an escort to bring her to Elizabeth's presence.

Sir Francis Knollys was at once sent north to take charge of the situation. The parcel of underlinen one of the Queen's maids had prepared for him to take to the Queen of Scots was so far from answering the latter's expectations that rumour transformed its contents into ragged shifts and worn-out shoes. Mary had wanted Elizabeth to send her clothes and jewels in which she could appear as a Queen, and it was beyond Elizabeth's powers of self-control to help her to make such an appearance in Elizabeth's own kingdom, which Mary had frequently stated to be hers. Though Mary had come as a suppliant, her intentions were those of a very different order. Bright, appealing, gracious, bewitching as she was, her presence on English soil was acutely dangerous to Elizabeth and to the government of the country; to what extent only time would show.

Though possible successors to the English throne were sought out and their claims scrutinized with anxious care, while the Queen of Scots asserted that, if right alone decided the issue, she herself occupied it already, the sovereign who in point of fact was Queen of England was fulfilling the office with remarkable success. The confidence the Queen's government inspired was based on an avoidance, after the brief intervention in France, of ruinous war with its inevitable consequence of heavy taxation, a religious policy so tolerant for its time that both Catholics and Puritans condemned it, the absence of any odious and cruel foreign husband, an encouragement of ship-building that recalled the days of Henry VIII, and a firm administration which, while Elizabeth should live, banished the spectre of civil war. The Queen's life became increasingly precious as the only assurance that these benefits would continue, and Elizabeth in her own person was a dazzling symbol of her government's success: high spirited and elegant, vital and dignified, intensely interested in everything she saw, graced with the charisma of exciting enthusiasm in the people around her. In July, 1568, de Silva accompanied her on an expedition to Reading, to visit a house the Duke of Norfolk owned in that neighbourhood. "The Queen," he said, "came by river as far as Reading and then through the country in a carriage open on all sides that she might be seen by the people who flocked all along the roads as far as the Duke of Norfolk's house where she alighted. She was received everywhere with great acclamations as she always is."

The Queen of Scots was now removed, under the care of Lord and

Lady Scrope, to Bolton Castle. She had expected, and demanded, to be received by Elizabeth and entertained by her as a royal guest, while an English army was sent into Scotland to chastise her rebels and replace her upon the Scottish throne. That her secret expectation was of an English Catholic rising in her favour, she revealed by her furious exclamations when she was removed against her will to Bolton: "I have made great wars in Scotland—I pray God I make no trouble in other realms also!" In August Sir Francis Knollys wrote to Leicester about a stud for her: "You had need send two or three horses hither for her own saddle . . . I have essayed one of mine with a woman's saddle to serve her, but as yet no woman hath ridden on him and . . . his service is doubtful, though he be well liked of her servants that have ridden him with a woman's saddle." Leicester's duties as Master of the Queen's Horse from henceforward included the administration of the stables kept for the Queen of Scots, the charge of whose maintenance from now onwards was met entirely by the English crown. In 1576 Prospero D'Osma wrote in Italian a MSS. book on the Royal Stud at Tutbury, Lord Shrewsbury's castle in Staffordshire where the Queen of Scots then was. The book was in Leicester's library.*

In this year, a very secret passage in Leicester's life began. He accompanied the Queen to a house-party, said to have taken place at Belvoir Castle, belonging to the Earl of Rutland.† Here among the guests were John, second Earl of Sheffield, and his wife Douglas, née Howard, the daughter of Lord William Howard, Queen Elizabeth's great-uncle. Lord Sheffield had been one of those granted honorary degrees at Oxford two years before at the hands of "the magnificent Chancellor". His wife was now five and twenty. She bore a strong resemblance to her dead kinswoman Queen Katherine Howard; like her, Douglas was feather-headed and dazzling, "a star in the Court for beauty and richness of apparel". The history, written ninety years later from the standpoint of the Sheffield family, declared that Lord Leicester "found her an easy purchase". When she returned home, with a recklessness worthy of Katherine Howard herself, she was carrying about with her one of Leicester's love-letters. The story asserts that the letter promised or at least spoke of the murder of Lord Sheffield. This must be discounted as a later elaboration, since, even if Leicester had such a thing in mind, he was the last man to commit it to paper, and then entrust the evidence to an impulsive woman. The

* W. E. Moss, *Bindings in the Library of Robert Dudley, Earl of Leicester.*
† There is no record of this visit in Nichols' *Progresses.*

letter, however, was sufficiently compromising for Lady Sheffield to become panic-stricken when she realized that she had lost it. She asked all her women if they had seen it, and they said no. She asked her sister-in-law, who also said no; but this lady had indeed picked up the letter on the great staircase, and, having read it, determined to show it to her brother, who was then from home. On his return she did so, and when Lord Sheffield discovered from it that he had been cuckolded by the man who with such dignity and grandeur had bestowed on him the degree of Master of Arts, his rage was violent and bitter. "He parted beds that night," and next day went up to London to see about getting a divorce. Before he could set matters in train, he was seized with illness and died suddenly. The narrator, who was the great nephew of Lord Sheffield's sister, had no hesitation in saying that Leicester had had him poisoned.*

There was no evidence to show that Leicester had done any such thing, and the idea was refuted by the presumptive evidence afforded by his conduct afterwards. The object of the crime, if it had been committed, must have been his marriage to Lady Sheffield, and it was precisely his unwillingness to marry her, and his denial that he had ever done so, that caused a thirty years' story of tragic unhappiness. In the meantime, her mourning over, Lady Sheffield returned to Court, where for the next few years she received numerous offers of marriage, all of which she steadily refused, though no one, not even her sister, appeared to understand the reason for this behaviour.

In the autumn of 1568 an enquiry was opened at York, under the commission of the Duke of Norfolk, the Earl of Sussex and Sir Ralph Saddler, to examine the charges made against each other by the Queen of Scots and her adherents on the one hand, and the Regent Murray and the party of the Scots Protestants on the other. Mary had instructed her representative, the Bishop of Ross, that he was to treat the proceedings as an occasion merely for her to accuse her subjects of treason; if countercharges were brought against her, he was to make a formal withdrawal from the proceedings immediately. She had already told Elizabeth that she would consent to no process in which she and her subjects appeared to be arguing with each other as parties of equal status. Elizabeth strongly urged her to lay aside this attitude, saying if she had a defence of her own conduct as regards her husband's murder, let her make it in God's name. A refusal to do so would do her infinitely more harm, Elizabeth assured her, than she would incur by derogating from her royal dignity in pleading her

* Gervase, Holles, *The Holles Family.*

cause. Mary, however, since she could not prove her innocence, made an effective gesture by saying she would not stoop to do so. The Duke of Norfolk was anxious that the charges should not be pressed against her. He had another prospect in view for her besides that of Queen of England. A number of people were beginning to feel that a marriage between Mary Stuart and him might be the solution to many difficulties. With a Protestant, English husband, she would no longer be a menace in Scotland, nor in England, and the succession might thereby be assured on terms that both Catholics and Protestants would accept.

Some rumour of secret undertakings had probably reached Elizabeth, for she ordered the Commission to remove from York and re-open at Westminster; in the new session, Cecil and Leicester were added to the commissioners. As Murray now moved from defence of his own conduct to accusations against Mary, the Bishop of Ross announced that the proceedings were null and void and that the representatives of the Queen of Scots would give no further attendance at them. Mary renewed her demand for a personal interview with Elizabeth, and Elizabeth replied that she could not grant it, "considering the multitude of matters and presumptions now lately produced against her, to all of which she had refused to make any answer". Elizabeth now terminated the enquiry, saying that nothing had been produced to impair Murray's honour as a subject, but that on the other hand the charges against the Queen of Scots were "not sufficiently proven". This verdict absolved the Queen of England from having either to antagonize the Scots or to support, in the eyes of the world, the charges they had made against their sovereign, although the proceedings had left Mary utterly discredited.

Murray at once returned to Scotland to resume his regency on behalf of the child James. The Queen of Scots was kept in England. She was maintained like a Queen, with thirty of her own servants beside her ladies, secretaries and physicians. The expenses of her whole establishment were paid by Elizabeth, while her pension as a widowed Queen of France was paid into her own hands. It was, legally, unfair that, while neither side had been pronounced guilty, one should be allowed to return to Scotland and the other prevented from doing so; but Mary's fate was the direct result of her determined policy of claiming to be Queen of England. Right or wrong, it could not be expected that she should now be set free to collect French or Spanish forces to bring into Scotland. Nor was the English decision the only one affecting her. Next year, at the Congress of Perth, the Scots positively refused to allow her back in Scotland as Queen, as Regent, as co-Regent, or as a private person. From the English point of view, it was safer to have her shut up in England than elsewhere, but, even so, her presence was like the dreaded underground fires that in a time of drought break out and send up the land in flames. Now that she was here Elizabeth was never to know peace again till, nineteen years later, in her last attempt to destroy the English Queen, the Queen of Scots destroyed herself.

In November the Portuguese Ambassador told Dr. Wilson, the Master of the Court of Awards, that he had a piece of unicorn's horn he wanted to show Lord Leicester. This precious substance, supposed in fact to be the horn of the narwhal, was highly prized as a protection against poison, and small pieces of it fetched a very high price. Leicester may have bought a piece of this one, for next year he sent some to the Queen of Scots as a tender of his regards.

XIII

At the end of 1568 de Silva, to the great regret of the English Court, was recalled to Madrid, and his place was taken by Don Gerald de Spes, a fanatic whose desire for prompt action against the heretics was equalled only by his short-sightedness. He arrived in England possessed by the conviction that, if everyone concerned would exert themselves, Queen Elizabeth could be disposed of, Mary Queen of Scots placed upon the English throne, and Catholicism restored as the state religion of England without loss of time. He was hardly in the country before he established communication with the Queen of Scots at Bolton. At his arrival the commission was still sitting at Westminster, and de Spes heard that Lord Leicester sat nearly every day, "discussing with great fervour the affairs of the Queen of Scots". Leicester's great réclame as the Queen's favourite determined de Spes to establish a close relationship with him, but this did not turn out to be a mere matter of ask and have. On December 12th, 1568, he reported of the Earl: "He said he would come and speak to me but subsequently sent to excuse himself"; but Mary, alight with hope on hearing of the activities of the Duke of Alva in the Netherlands, wrote to de Spes saying: "Tell your Master if he will help me, I shall be Queen of England in three months, and Mass shall be said all over the kingdom!"

It had been decided to place her in the guardianship of Lord Shrewsbury, whose integrity and influence, as well as his enormous wealth and possession of so many castles and manors, made him, from Elizabeth's point of view, eminently suitable for the trust. He himself had written to Leicester saying: "The Queen of Scots coming to my charge will make me soon grey-headed." Lady Shrewsbury wrote saying that such short notice had been received that they were to expect the Queen of Scots and her train at Tutbury, it would be hard to have everything prepared in time, but if necessary she would supply what was needed from her own apartments, and "lack furniture of lodging" herself rather than fail in duty to Queen Elizabeth.*

* H.M.C. Pepys.

Sir Nicholas Throckmorton, who continued to be Lord Leicester's political guide and mentor, formed one of a party with Leicester, Pembroke and Norfolk to prepare a second version of the plan for Norfolk's marrying the Queen of Scots. They went so far as to discuss it with the Bishop of Ross, from whom de Spes heard of it. The terms proposed to Murray were: that the abdication forced upon Mary at Loch Leven should be cancelled, that no more should be said about Darnley's murder, that Mary should be divorced from Bothwell, who was now in Denmark, that Catholics and Protestants should be allowed equal freedom of worship, and that no foreign alliances were to be contracted; finally, the Queen of Scots was, at long last, to ratify the Treaty of Edinburgh, and at the same time to be pronounced by Parliament heiress presumptive to the English throne. On paper there was much in all this of benefit to everybody. The obvious objection to it as a matter of practical politics was that such a man as the Duke of Norfolk, however honestly he undertook to do it, would never be able to control such a woman as the Queen of Scots. When the plan came to Elizabeth's ears, she put the matter in a nutshell. If she consented to any such thing, she said, she would be in the Tower before four months were out. It is strange that so sharp a man as Throckmorton should have believed that a mere undertaking on Mary's part not to call in foreign soldiers would prevent her from doing so, if the French or Spanish seized the first-rate opportunity of her having the English crown almost within her grasp to press their services upon her. Neither Norfolk nor Pembroke was a statesman, however, and whatever claims Leicester had to political insight were at this time countered by his ambitions. It had been suggested at one stage of these negotiations that he might take the Queen of Scots himself. He replied that for many reasons he was not the man for the position. He did not suppose, he said, that even the Duke of Norfolk would consider the match "were it not for the benefit of Queen Elizabeth and her realm". It was to be quite a sacrifice on the Duke's part; but the scheme held out another much weightier inducement to Leicester. If the succession were to be settled on the Queen of Scots, then, since her son was in being, the next generation was already provided for, and it would cease to be a matter of great moment whom Elizabeth married; if she married at all, she might as well marry Leicester. If she had children by him, that would re-open the question between her children and Mary's, but the prospect was uncertain and in any case distant. The immediate result, from Leicester's point of view, would be his assuming the position of King

Consort. Better to be the husband of the reigning Queen than of the heiress presumptive; a bird in the hand was worth two in the bush.

However, Leicester sent a courteous letter to the Scottish Queen. He had heard that she feared attempts on her life by poison, so he sent her three preservatives: a gold box containing a stone (many precious stones, such as agate and ruby, were said to be preventives against poison), a silver box containing mithridate, a substance of many ingredients made into a paste with honey, an antidote to poison and infectious diseases, and thirdly "a piece of the horn of some beast",* possibly the piece he had bought from the Portuguese Ambassador.

It was decided that as soon as the Queen of Scots' assent to the proposal and its conditions was received, Elizabeth should be taken into the general confidence. Mary replied accepting Norfolk's offer, and a message was despatched to Murray, who, if he could get the consent of the Scots, would then send Norfolk a formal acceptance. Mary, who wrote to Norfolk as "Mine own Lord" and vowed herself unalterably his, assured de Spes that she would much prefer a Spanish husband, and that though she had promised religious toleration for the Protestants she would nevertheless hold herself entirely at the disposition of the King of Spain for the benefit of the Catholic Church.

De Spes had his hands full of conspiracy, and he now suffered the inconvenience of having to remove his embassy. This was at present established in Paget Place, one of the great houses on the Strand, immediately opposite St. Clements Dane, beside Temple Bar. In June, 1569, Lord Leicester took a lease of this house from the Paget family, and de Spes and his staff had to cross the river and occupy Winchester House on the shores of Southwark. This was a nuisance to the Ambassador, and the Bishop of Winchester did not care for the arrangement either; he "raised some difficulties", de Spes said, though the Earl in person wrote to him about it. The matter was settled by an order from the Council. Leicester not only directed that the Bishop should give up possession of his house, he decided what rent should be paid for it. "We have agreed," wrote de Spes, "that the Earl of Leicester's valuation shall be accepted, and I shall move into it." Meanwhile Lord Leicester's establishment was transferred from Durham House eastward along the Strand to Paget Place, which became henceforward Leicester House.

The gatehouse, one of the row of houses lining the Strand, opened

* *Confession of the Duke of Norfolk*, quoted by Froude.

into a forecourt; beyond this stood the house, built round the four sides of an inner court. The south front, lying parallel with the river, was a block whose roof rose in four gables, terminating at the eastern end in a battlemented tower like that of a church. In this block, the ground floor was occupied by the great hall. Over the hall lay the great chamber, the withdrawing chambers, and the entrance to the upper rooms of the tower. South of this block, the oblong-shaped garden ran down to the river shore. The great hall gave on to a terrace, from which a flight of steps led down to a pleasure-ground laid out in four knot-gardens, or plots of flowerbeds. Beyond the beds a second flight of steps descended to a ground laid out in two large rectangles of turf, cut into curious shapes with paths running between them. This area led down to the river stairs where the water of Thames ran by, clear and fast, sometimes bearing fleets of swans.*

The great coagulation of houses that comprised the City of London, with their crowding, their stench, their unmade, miry roads, their teeming, noisy life in the daytime, their darkness of night fitfully dispelled by ruddy light from windows but deep and dangerous elsewhere in the streets, began almost immediately east of Temple Bar; but west of this, all along the curve of the river as far as Westminster, there was but a single row of houses on the opposite side of the Strand, facing the river-side houses; behind them were their gardens, but behind these again was an illimitable stretch of field, copse and open heath: Lincoln's Inn Fields, St. Giles-in-the-Fields, St. Martin's-in-the-Fields showed their wild, open surroundings in their names. Leicester House was almost the last of the great houses standing outside the City's congestion.

Leicester occupied this town house to the day of his death. He already possessed Kenilworth as a country seat, his peerage had given him Denbigh Castle, and two years after this he acquired Wanstead, six miles out of London, a rural retreat within easy distance of the capital. But the great town house was the centre of his social and political existence. His own apartments were contained in the southern block. The three wings behind the river frontage contained the household offices of a large community: the kitchens, bakehouse, buttery, laundry, the armoury, the napery, and a wardrobe in which was stored furnishings that were needed when the rooms were all occupied, including close-stools and chamber pots and wicker screens to put round them while they were being used. The rooms in Leicester House were gradually appropriated to the members of

* *Archeologia*, 73.

Leicester's family who used them most, and called after them. Lord Warwick had no town house, only a right, as Master of the Ordinance, to a lodging at Court. It was natural that a suite in Leicester House should become known as the Lord of Warwick's bedchamber, the Lord of Warwick's closet, the Lord of Warwick's dining parlour. The bedchamber was hung with tapestry and the bed with green and silver lamé, embroidered with the bear and ragged staff and trimmed with carnation velvet; a chair, a low stool, a footstool, were all upholstered with green cloth of silver, "suitable" to the bed. In the dining parlour the tapestry showed a woodland scene, the chairs were covered in green velvet.

Leicester spent nineteen years in the collection of beautiful and luxurious things to fill his houses. He was much interested in Oriental carpets. At the beginning of Elizabeth's reign, Turkey carpets were used to hang at windows and to cover tables; the floors of palaces were still strewn with rushes, though Henry VIII had rush-matting made for those of Nonsuch. Leicester was among the early users of Oriental carpets as floor coverings; he had them on the floor at Wanstead and Kenilworth. A velvet carpet, however, was almost certainly used as a curtain or tablecover; at Leicester House was a beautiful one of dark tawny velvet with a border of copper-gold and silver. Some of the windows were hung with Turkey carpet. There was in the house a canopy of purple velvet, the curtains of purple taffeta trimmed with silver lace. This would dignify a chair for the Queen to sit in, on any but quite private occasions. His household possessions included services of silver gilt and silver plate, gilt bowls with covers, gilt spoons, blue glass flagons, a mother of pearl salt cellar in the shape of a swan. He was at all times fond of putting his armorial bearings on his possessions. In Leicester House was a "sweetwood" table standing on four bears; the covers of his books were stamped with the bear and ragged staff in gilt; and at Kenilworth, among the great state beds carved and decorated with the bear and ragged staff, was a charming one ornamented with the cinquefoil; its carved posts were painted crimson and silver, and the canopy, bed head and valance, all of crimson velvet, were powdered with silver cinquefoils.[1]

An exquisite small painting of Queen Elizabeth forms the frontispiece to *Christian Prayers* which was published in 1569. It shows her kneeling, with elbows extended and hands palm to palm, at the seat of a chair over which is thrown a white drapery scattered with golden fleurs-de-lys; a small crown lies upon it, and an open prayerbook.

Behind the Queen is a little alcove containing a window, its walls apple green painted with flowering rose branches; above her head two massive crimson curtains are looped up. Elizabeth is wearing a dark crimson dress ornamented with gold. Her pale, sharply outlined profile, the hair strained back from the forehead and temples and pushed into a net with a garland twisted round it, emerges from the background with eerie delicacy. The space between the small pie-dish ruff that supports her chin and the low-cut bodice is filled with gold net. The narrow bodice ending a little below the natural waist and the bell-shaped skirt show the graceful fashion of the first two decades of the reign. This little view of the Queen, in the coiffure and the dress, and the interior decoration of 1569, shows what she looked like in the year Lord Leicester took possession of Leicester House.

In June of this year Dr. Chaderton, who had been Leicester's chaplain and was now Master of Queen's College, Cambridge, consulted Leicester about his own wish to get married. Leicester replied first by thanking the Doctor for his good opinion and the desire he showed for Leicester's approval. Discretion and a suitable choice, said the Earl, were essential; beyond this, he could only observe that "marriage, as it is lawful, so it is convenient for such as cannot otherwise contain". He scarcely knew what else he could say; he would give Chaderton his advice, if he knew the party. As it was, he could but wish the matter "to turn to his comfort and consolation". He remained Chaderton's friend and patron, and the latter ultimately became Bishop of Chester, the Palatinate of which Leicester was Chancellor.[1]

The Earl had news in August of another friend to whom he was always kind. This was the Duke Hans Casimir, second son of the Elector Palatine. This young man had visited England, and in 1564 he had wished to propose for Elizabeth's hand through Sir James Melville, who was then at the Elector's Court in Leipzig. Melville had refused the embassage, saying it was useless because, from something he had heard said in her Court, he knew that Elizabeth was incapable of bearing children. Four years later Melville dilated to Elizabeth on the agonies the Queen of Scots had suffered in childbirth, saying that he did so to give the English Queen "a little scare from marrying". Either his original statement to Casimir was untrue, or he had seen reason to discount it since. He had, in any case, another reason for refusing to be the matchmaker; he said he had discovered from Elizabeth that "first and last she despised the said Duke Casimir". Leicester's friend Sir Henry Killigrew now wrote from Leipzig sending him a message from "Cass", as Leicester spoke of him, that "he wished (for) you this hunting time when he was in at the death of eighty stags in one day".[1]

Leicester's enthusiasm for hunting, like his passion for fine clothes, beautiful furniture and all the splendour of Court life, made his Puritan sympathies sit strangely on him; but beside the instinct he had inherited from his father to adopt the leadership of their party, and any emotional support he may have derived from being looked up to by men of their intense earnestness, he had another motive for association with them. Huntingdon, his brother-in-law, looked up to Leicester as the most highly placed and influential member of the family into which he had married; but it was Huntingdon himself whose veins carried the precious infusion of royal blood that might, as Leicester's father had foreseen when he arranged the marriage, make him a connection of supreme value to the Dudleys. Such a contingency was the last thing Huntingdon wanted to dwell upon, but, despite himself, he was a card in the Earl of Leicester's hand, bequeathed to the latter by his scheming father.

Leicester's Puritan convictions were scarcely such as would in the previous reign have carried him to the stake, but Huntingdon's were devout. In 1569 he asked the Queen's leave to sell his estates and equip an army for the aid of the Huguenots. He was probably influenced in this scheme by the fact that, though he had been married seventeen years, he had no children to provide for and now scarcely hoped for any. Needless to say the Queen, ruling a population of little more than four millions, and regarding every good and loyal subject as of great value to herself and the nation, refused out of hand to allow the Earl of Huntingdon to withdraw himself and his wealth "in this strange sort". But his wishing to do so showed the strength of his convictions, and it was plain that, should he ever come to that state of supreme importance which he so much deprecated, no one would have any influence with him unless they subscribed to his religious views.

A divergence in religious opinion was making itself felt among the supporters of the plan to marry the Queen of Scots to the Duke of Norfolk. The two most northern of these were the Earl of Northumberland and his friend and neighbour the Earl of Westmorland. Uncompromising Catholics as they were, they began to think that the marriage of the Scots Queen to a man whose eligibility was supposed to consist in the fact that he was not a Catholic was unlikely to be of much use to the Catholic religion. The development of the plan was meanwhile going forward: Leicester, Pembroke and Sussex had got so far as saying in open council that they were in favour of the match, but Sussex added that before he would go any further in the matter the Queen must be told of it. It was generally agreed that she must be told; the point was, who was to do it?

Norfolk, who had written a letter to the Queen of Scots assuring her that Elizabeth would not dare to refuse her consent to their marriage, suggested that a posse of peers should wait on the Queen at Greenwich and announce their determination; but none of the gentlemen who would be expected to give their attendance could agree to this plan, and Lord Leicester said "he thought it not well to have it broken to her Majesty by a number because he knew her Majesty's nature did like better to be dealt with by one or two". He undertook to do it himself, if Cecil would support him, but Cecil was not there to ask, nor had he been at the Council meeting. Norfolk could not make up his mind to speak to the Queen when he had the opportunity. The Court moved from Greenwich up to Richmond, and Norfolk followed it. On the way he went by Leicester's house at Kew, and there, under the August skies, stood Leicester, fishing in the river. Leicester said to him, he must tell the Queen at once. The news had got out among her ladies, and some of these babblers had made her Majesty believe they had meant to get the marriage actually performed without telling her of it. He had persuaded her that this was not true, but what the outcome would be, he was not prepared to say.*

At Richmond Palace Norfolk met Cecil, who urged him to tell the Queen everything. Elizabeth herself gave him a direct opening, in Richmond garden. She asked him if he had no news to tell her of a wedding? Lady Clinton came up to her with a basket of flowers, and as the Queen turned to look at it Norfolk snatched at the chance of escape and slunk away. The Court moved on to Guildford, and here Norfolk came upon the Queen and Leicester together privately. Cushions had been placed for coolness in an open doorway; the Queen sat upon them and Leicester knelt beside her, while she listened to a child playing the lute. As Norfolk entered at the other end of the apartment, Leicester got up and came towards him. He assured Norfolk that the Queen had been speaking of the match, and not unfavourably.* The Court went on into Hampshire, the Queen going to Lord Winchester at Basing House, Leicester to Lord Pembroke at Titchfield. And here Leicester, probably in consultation with his friend, decided to tell Elizabeth before further concealment

* *Confession of the Duke of Norfolk*, quoted by Froude.

should make the final revelation disastrous. He took to his bed, either really unwell or, as Camden suggests, "counterfeiting the sick", and sent a message to Basing, begging the Queen to come to him. Elizabeth, who feared to lose her friends by death, was always agitated by their illness and visited them in their sick beds readily. She came at once to Leicester's bedside, and in these favourable circumstances, with her affection increased by anxiety for his safety, he poured out to her the details of the plan, telling her that his loyalty and devotion forbade him to keep them secret any longer. However necessary it might be to restrain indignation before a patient in so critical a state, the Queen on her return spoke to Norfolk with great sharpness. She asked him how he dared go about such a thing behind her back? Norfolk replied haughtily that he had no wish to marry the Queen of Scots. He needed no aggrandizement. When he was on his estates in Norfolk, he felt himself the equal of a king.

In September de Spes related the progress of the affair to the Duke of Alva: "One day the Queen of England will allow the marriage, next day she will not hear of it. Leicester is said to take the Duke's part; the Duke gives him hopes that after the expected changes he will be allowed to keep his present position and even to marry the Queen . . .*However," de Spes continued jubilantly, "all is arranged in the Scottish Queen's favour, and if she is once at liberty, your Excellency can make your game as you please, with one Queen or the other."

Mary and her Court at present occupied Lord Shrewsbury's manor of Wingfield, a pleasant house, and without the fortifications of a castle. It was from here that the Duke of Norfolk planned to rescue her. He left Court abruptly to make his arrangements in London.

Elizabeth now acted with energy. She sent for Lord Huntingdon: if he wanted occupation in the Protestant interest, he should have it here at home. She ordered him to proceed at once to Derbyshire, remove the Queen of Scots from the unfortified manor of Wingfield, and escort her, with Lord Shrewsbury, to the fortress of Tutbury. Huntingdon fulfilled his commission with brilliant speed. In less than a week he had reached Derbyshire, shown his warrant to Shrewsbury, and despite the violent outcry of the Scottish Queen had separated her from half her retinue and brought her to Tutbury, which he garrisoned with five hundred men. Mary was beside herself with anger. She protested passionately that she should never have been put into Lord Huntingdon's power, since she was the heiress to

* MSS., Simancas, quoted by Froude.

the English crown and he a pretender to it. She told him she would make him feel what her credit was in England!

A letter from Alva to Philip written on September 25th, remarked that "the Earl of Leicester and Cecil . . . entirely govern the Queen and do and undo as they please". This showed, at least as far as rumour went, that however deeply Leicester had been involved in the scheme for Norfolk's marriage, the revelations had caused him to moult no feather. Indeed, Elizabeth may have encouraged him to take part in it, so as to keep her *au courant* with whatever was going on. Her nickname for him was Eyes, and in letters to each other they used two circles with a dot in the centre, as a symbol of the word.

The rapid removal of the Queen of Scots to an impregnable stronghold, and a peremptory summons from Elizabeth to present himself at Windsor, had broken Norfolk's nerve. He sent a message to the Earls of Northumberland and Westmorland that the southward advance they were planning, which was to have been met by one made by himself and his followers towards the north, and reinforced by arms and men sent over by Alva from the Netherlands if matters had gone forward as Norfolk hoped, must now be indefinitely postponed. But the northern Earls had gone too far to stop. On November 14th, with an army of retainers at their back, they entered Durham Cathedral, tore up the English translation of the Bible and trampled it underfoot; then they began their march southward.

Their object was Tutbury. Alva and Philip, in the various conspiracies against Elizabeth, always made it a point that before Spanish troops were sent into England the Queen of Scots must be released. Alva was watching the Earls at a distance. If they succeeded in getting Mary Stuart out of custody, Spanish soldiers would be sent across the Channel; it was said that Alva would lead them in person. This was a perilous moment. Despite the fortifications and the garrison, Huntingdon and Shrewsbury did not believe that Tutbury would stand a siege of more than a few days. Not without some quarrelling—for Shrewsbury was jealous of Huntingdon's commission, and Huntingdon threw some doubts on Shrewsbury's loyalty—between them they took the Queen of Scots southward by forced marches to Coventry. The Earls, meanwhile, having failed of their objective, began a march towards London, on which they expected innumerable Catholics, anxious for the overthrow of Elizabeth and her government, to fall in behind them. When they had got as far as Staffordshire without anyone joining them, their peril was too great to be ignored; they wheeled and retreated northward.

Lord Sussex, who, as President of the North, had done his best to prevent them from starting, assuring them that the Queen would show them clemency if they confessed and relinquished their treason, now led his forces from York to the attack, while two armies were sent up from the south under Lord Warwick and Lord Hunsdon. The main part of the rebellion was crushed by the end of November, when the Earls were driven over the Border.

The seriousness of the rebellion was unnerving after eleven years of successful government, and, by obliging the Queen to put on foot three armies, it had desperately injured her economy. She had been made savage by fear and anger, and overriding Sussex, who thought that the ringleaders only should be hanged and their humble followers released, she insisted that seven hundred peasants should be hanged by martial law. The leaders were tried for treason so that their lands should be forfeit to the Crown. Of these, some were executed and some spared if they had only a life-interest in their estates.

This was the sole rebellion of Elizabeth's reign, and she knew whom to thank for it. She composed some verses on the occasion, in two lines of which she both coined an immortal synonym for Mary Queen of Scots and gave the reason why the attempt, dangerous as it was, had proved a failure:

> The Daughter of Debate that eke discord doth sow,
> Shall reap no gain where former rule hath taught still peace to grow.

It was true, but it could never to relied on entirely; the menace was perpetual. Nevertheless, the first of the striking demonstrations in favour of Elizabeth had been given: not in the form of shouting crowds about her, but, where the rebels had expected numberless supporters, in appalling silence and vacancy. The last demonstration was given in 1601, when the Earl of Essex walked through the City of London calling aloud on the citizens to rise, and found the streets empty.

At the end of 1569 Lord Leicester and Sir Walter Mildmay, Chancellor of the Exchequer, each wrote down his views on the safest manner of dealing with the Queen of Scots.[1] Leicester's were written in the form of a letter to Sussex, the latter being still in the north. It showed a very strong desire on Leicester's part to conciliate Sussex, treating him with both cordiality and respect. He said the matter was in such debate he could not tell Sussex of any settled opinion, but he owed it to his friendship with Lord Sussex, and the high position the latter occupied at present, to let him know as much as Leicester knew himself, "and how we rest among us". The crux of the matter was, ought Queen Elizabeth to support the party of the Queen of Scots, or of the infant James and his Regent? Leicester admitted that, considering her conduct towards England, there were many reasons against supporting the Queen of Scots, but said none the less: "I must confess myself to your Lordship to be on the opposite side." If Elizabeth supported James' party, she must inevitably go to war over it, and a war begun with Scotland would probably end as a war with France or Spain, and "that she hath treasure to continue any time in war, surely my Lord I cannot see it". As regards the value of the Queen of Scots' promises, this involved moral as well as realistic considerations. "In worldly causes men must be governed by worldly policies," he wrote, "and yet so frame them as God, the author of all, be chiefly regarded. And though in some points I shall deal like a worldly man for my Prince yet I hope I shall not forget that I am a Christian, nor my duty to God." The brittleness of Princes' promises was but too well known, and yet, he said, they must keep *some* of them, and were, in fact, sometimes obliged by a promise to do what their wishes would lead them to shun. The Queen of Scots might be securely bound—to say she relinquished her claim to be the present Queen of England, to respect the Reformation, to make no foreign alliances. She might be forced to cede as gages some Scots cities, any except Edinburgh, and told that if she defaulted on any point of the agreement she should be removed altogether from the succession. "There, I would think, would be sufficient bonds to bind any Prince, specially no mightier than she is." Leicester had not, of course, seen the letters Mary had written to de Spes, but neither had Elizabeth; yet the latter had no difficulty in divining that Mary would drive a coach and four through any such agreement as this.

Sir Walter Mildmay's paper, dated October 26th, 1569,[1] was perhaps a minute prepared for the consideration of the Privy Council. His point of discussion was, whether to keep the Queen of Scots in England or send her back to Scotland? "Keep her," he said. He admitted one argument on the other side, and he thought it a powerful one. "The Queen's Majesty of her own disposition hath no mind to retain her, but is much unquieted therewith." Therefore, he agreed, "when it is said that the Queen's Majesty cannot be quiet so long as she is here, but it may breed danger to her Majesty's health, that is a matter greatly to be weighed, for it were better to adventure all, than her Majesty should inwardly conceive anything to the damage of her health". But Mildmay thought that, if the matter were sympathetically argued with her, the Queen might think better of it. If the Queen of Scots were kept here, he went on, the most stringent precautions must of course be employed. He suggested keeping her very near the Court, that it might be "more easier to understand her doings", diminishing her train of forty persons by half, and cutting her off from all access, letters and messages. And he concluded, let other Princes be told why she is so straitly kept; say that it is on the grounds of her conspiracy with the Duke of Norfolk; assure them that she shall be used honourably, but kept safely from troubling the Queen's Majesty or this state.

In 1569 it was Leicester who, of the two advisers, recommended the tolerant and large-minded course. Eighteen years later he was urging Mary's death so determinedly that, when Elizabeth stood out against her execution, he recommended that she should be secretly poisoned.

XIV

In the cold weather of January, 1570, the frosty ground was as difficult for a messenger's horse as mire in milder weather. Lord Leicester wrote to the Queen from Kenilworth on January 10th, heading his letter: "From your house. Fearing," he said, "in this hard weather for a messenger to be the slower, I have prayed this good man to take the more pains; whose desire is as much to see you, as my longing is to hear from you, thinking it now very long since I heard." Lord Warwick should have been at Court, but he had been so much occupied in the Rebellion that he had not had time to present himself there, since he returned "from the discharge of your service". He was at Kenilworth now. "After a little rest with your o o he will attend according to his duty." On the 16th, the Earl was having a house party for his brother and sisters, Lord Warwick, Lady Mary Sidney and the Countess of Huntingdon. He wrote to Elizabeth again "From your house at Kenilworth", saying: "If it lay in the power of so unable creatures to yield you what our will would, you should feel the fruits of our wishes. We two here, your poor thralls, your Ursa Major and Minor, tied to your stake, shall for ever remain in the bond chain of dutiful servitude. . . . So long as you muzzle not your beasts, nor suffer the match over hard, spare them not." Sister Mary, he said, was with him, and Sister Kate, "well amended" since he had gone up to see her in her illness at Ashby-de-la-Zouche.[1]

On January 30th de Spes noted the fact of Leicester's being at Kenilworth. He had supposed that Leicester's retiring there might have been a cover for a visit to the Queen of Scots in Derbyshire, but he now knew this was not so. "The going of Leicester to the country was with the object of fortifying a place of his called Kenilworth." For this purpose he had taken with him Julio Spinelli, an Italian who had had engineering experience in the Netherlands. Leicester had said he greatly feared civil wars in this country.

By 1570 Leicester either owned or occupied a house at Teddington, in the country air near Richmond. In February he had come up from

Kenilworth, seen the Queen, and gone off to Teddington in the throes of a bad cold about which she had been anxious. On February 13th he wrote from Teddington his grateful thanks to her "for sending so graciously to know how your poor ○ ○ doth; I have hitherto so well found myself after my travel as I trust I am clearly delivered of the shrewd cold that so hardly held me at my departing from you. I have always found exercise with open air my best remedy against those delicate diseases, gotten about your dainty city of London, which place, but for necessity, I am sorry to see you remain about, being persuaded it is a piece of the sacrifice you do for your peoples' sake."[1]

After the extinguishing of the Rebellion, the Queen had issued to the parishes of the realm a statement saying that the rebels had falsely declared "some general severity intended by us or our ministers against them only in respect of religion, when no such thing did appear or was anywise meant or thought of". No persecution of anyone was intended, whatever his belief, so long as he should not show himself "manifestly repugnant and obstinate to the laws of the realm". The government, however, were now driven from the position in which they could say that a man's religion, privately held, had no bearing on his duty as a subject. In May the Pope, Pius V, published his Bull excommunicating Elizabeth, "the pretended Queen of England"; on the morning of May 12th, a copy was found pinned to the door of the Bishop of London's house in St. Paul's Churchyard. In it the Pope freed the Queen's subjects from the duty of all allegiance to her, and laid under his curse anyone who should dare obey any of her laws, directions or commands. Catholics who were both devout and loyal were now placed in an agonizing position. On June 5th John Fitzwilliam wrote from abroad to Leicester and Cecil: "The Pope has given England to anyone who will undertake to go and get it."*

In August the Queen made her usual progress, but having got as far as Chenies, the Earl of Bedford's house in Buckinghamshire, she developed an ulcer on her shin and was obliged to stay many days longer than she had intended. She received the French Ambassador, de la Motte Fénélon, in négligé, with her feet up, and said she was sorry her condition had prevented her from seeing him earlier. She was now appearing to entertain an idea of marrying Catherine de Medici's second son, the Duke of Anjou. His relations, the Guises, had suggested to him that he should marry the Queen of Scots and

* C.S.P. Foreign.

take the English crown by force; the mere possibility that the English Queen herself might marry him made the Queen Mother and Charles IX agog with eagerness. So long as these delusive negotiations were entertained they, at least, would give no support whatever to any fresh alliance with Mary Stuart.

De Spes, in this month wrote: "The Queen's opinion is of little importance and that of Leicester still less; Cecil unrestrainedly and arrogantly governs all." This seems so strangely unapt a description of Cecil's actual manner, it is a most interesting sidelight on the unassailable strength of his influence.

The progress made its way into Oxfordshire, and Sir Henry Norris, who was Ambassador in Paris, wrote to Leicester, hoping the latter would go and hunt at Rycote and "be master" of Norris' "poor game" there.

The perennial rumour that the Queen had had a child or children by Leicester sprang up again this year, and one Marsham, for declaring in public that Leicester had given her two children, was sentenced to lose both his ears or pay a fine of £100.

An altogether contradictory rumour came from Madrid, where the adventurer Thomas Stucley, who was said to be a bastard of Henry VIII's, when asked why the Queen did not marry, exclaimed she never would: "For she cannot abide a woman with child, for she saith these women be worse than a sow."* Stucley's remarks show that, as well as scandal such as Marsham retailed, there existed an impression that Elizabeth had a nervous horror of the normal sexual relationship.

Thomas Blundeville, who five years before had dedicated *The Chief Offices of Horsemanship* to the Earl, in 1570 dedicated to him another work, "A very brief and profitable treatise declaring how many counsels and what manner of Counsellors a Prince that will govern well ought to have". The dedication said candidly that the little treatise represented to the Earl, "as it were in a glass, many of those virtues and qualities that do reign in you, and ought to reign in every other good counsellor". The book was an implied tribute to the Earl's handsomeness. As a horse-fancier, Blundeville attached paramount importance to physical traits. "The over-fat man," he said, "bellied like a barrel, and the over-lean man, shaped like a dried conger, besides giving with their presence cause for laughter, are therewith seldom seen to be serviceable. The body of a Counsellor ought to be well-proportioned." In Blundeville's opinion, appearance

---

* R. Simpson, *The School of Shakespeare.*

was the index to disposition. In that picture of the mind, the face, the Counsellor should be somewhat long, rather than altogether round, "and therewith neither too blowghty nor yet too shrimp". Eyes should be neither sullenly downcast nor wantonly rolling, noses neither too long nor to short, neither big nor small, and not turned up. Without being willing to go as far as Blundeville, the Queen herself thought that physical appearance was a qualification of some importance for official positions. She once said to Francis Bacon: "Bacon, how shall the office be respected if the man is despised?"

On New Year's Day, 1571, Leicester gave the Queen a ruby and diamond bracelet with a "clock" set in the clasp. Lord Warwick gave her an ornament combining the roses of Lancaster and York, a white-enamelled rose with a ruby at its centre surrounded by six red-enamelled roses centred with diamonds; Lady Warwick a mother-of-pearl pendant encircled with garnets, on a gold chain; and Lady Mary Sidney a diamond-encrusted ring. De Spes told Zayas, the Duke of Alva's secretary, that Leicester had given the Queen a jewel in which she herself was represented as seated on a throne with the Queen of Scots in chains at her feet, and France and Spain being submerged by waves, "with Neptune and the rest of them bowing to this Queen". The description had exasperated him. "It is really necessary," he declared, "though we possess so much power, not to let it slip through our fingers."

Early in January Sir Francis Walsingham was sent to Paris on a special embassy, as it appeared that the Queen was seriously considering a match with the Duke of Anjou. Walsingham, a man of exceptional ability and also of fanatical Protestant sympathies, was a colleague of Sir Nicholas Throckmorton. Leicester was naturally led to become his friend, and Walsingham was of course very glad to have him as such. Leicester's access to the Queen made him invaluable, his adherence to the Puritan party made him sympathetic to one of Walsingham's own leanings, and Leicester's cordial charm could not but please anyone for whom it was exerted. Throughout this embassy, Leicester maintained a close correspondence with him. The Earl made a hobby of collecting portraits of crowned heads. In the first month of Walsingham's stay in Paris Leicester asked for portraits of Charles XI and Anjou. Walsingham had to tell him none were available as people were not allowed to paint them without a licence; if they did, the punishment was great.

In February Leicester, who had been unwell, was away from Court. He wrote on February 17th to the Queen: "Your great favour, thus oft and so far to send, to know how your poor ⊙ ⊙ doth, is greatly beyond the reach of his thanks, that already for a thousand benefits stand your bondman." He spoke of her plans for the summer progress: "Nothing is better for your health than exercise, and no one thing has been a greater hindrance thereto than your over-long stay in that corrupt air about the city; but you have so earnestly promised a remedy, as I hope to see you in time this year put it into practice, respecting yourself before others." Her house at Grafton, in Oxford-shire, he said, would be ready for her by the end of May (this suggests that he was writing from Kenilworth). "Meanwhile, other good places shall see you, which if they could speak, would show how sorry they are that you have been so long from them. Wishing you above all earthly treasures, good health and long life, I take my leave; rejoicing in your post-script, that you have felt no more of your wonted pangs." Elizabeth appeared to suffer from neuralgia—she was often said to have a pain in her cheek—and also from fevers and pains in the limbs which were perhaps due to malaria, from which Leicester suffered himself. The pangs he speaks of must have been something to which she was regularly a victim.[1]

On February 25th, the Queen created Sir William Cecil Lord Burleigh, Baron Burleigh. At this ceremony, Lord Leicester and Lord Cobham led him between them, and Lord Hunsdon carried his mantle. The Queen's Latin Secretary read aloud to the assembly her reason for bestowing this honour: it was "the faithful and acceptable duty and observance which he hath always performed from the very beginning of our reign, and ceaseth not daily to perform many ways, not only in the great and mighty affairs of Council but generally also in all other enterprises of the realm, and also for his circumspection, energy, wisdom, dexterity, integrity of life, providence, care and faithfulness".

It was most true, and no honour could be more deserved. Leicester, however, did not think the better of his colleague for the eulogium so publicly pronounced. In talking with de la Mothe Fénélon about the prospects of the French match, Leicester told the Ambassador that Cecil was strongly opposed to any husband for the Queen, "except (metaphorically speaking) Cecil himself, who was more King than she was Queen". This account of Burleigh's views was patently untrue; the latter was intensely anxious to see Elizabeth married and a mother. It was Leicester himself who secretly wished ill to the match; these negotiations gave him the first real uneasiness he had had since the early days of the Archduke Charles. Though he more than once admitted the fact of Burleigh's paramount influence with the Queen, he never reconciled himself to it. In July Sir Henry Neville wrote to Burleigh: "My Lord of Leicester sings his old song unto his friends, that is, that he had the Queen in very good tune, till you took her aside and dealt with her secretly, and then she was very strange suddenly."*

However, he was obliged to work in a close, harmonious partnership with Burleigh, writing the letters which were essential in keeping Walsingham in touch with his Court. The latter, like Burleigh, was personally very anxious for this match to take place. He viewed it as a means of getting the Queen with child, and of cementing an Anglo-French alliance which, being *ipso facto* inimical to Spain, must turn to the advantage of the Protestants in the oppressed Netherlands. Burleigh and Leicester wrote to him in July: "As for the inward intention of her Majesty in this case, we cannot certainly give you to understand more than it pleaseth her to utter. To the matter itself she yieldeth, as to a matter necessary to her estate and realm, otherwise we see no particular forwardness such as is common between persons that are to be married."

Down at Warwick on September 29th, Leicester wrote to the Queen: "Thinking it long since I heard of your good estate, according to the duty of your bounden ○ ○, I have sent this bearer to understand the same, meaning not to be long after in coming to give my attendance." He was attending to some family business with Lord Warwick, and he thanked her for his leave of absence: "It had been no small hindrance both for my brother and myself if I had not been here. All that we both have hath proceeded from your only goodness." He had come away in some discomfort; he had been out of training and knocked himself up by over-exercise. The Queen had been afraid that his pains meant something serious, but he reassured her: "To satisfy your over-great care of my present state: though I departed away in some pain yet in no suspicion at all of what you feared; only, it seems, for lack of use, my late exercise wrought some strange accident, through my own negligence, to take more cold than was convenient after such heat. I was well warned by you, but neither fearing nor mistrusting any such cause as followed, I have felt some smart for my carelessness, whereby I am driven to use the commodity of a bath to ease the pain." Not, he said, that the pain was worth telling her about, "but to satisfy your

* H.M.C. Hatfield.

good pleasure, being more careful of me, poor wretch, than the loss of a thousand such lives are worth."[1]

The tone of this, as of Leicester's other letters to the Queen, would have enlightened anyone who, unlike Lord Burleigh, imagined that Elizabeth's relations with Leicester were those of a mistress in the ordinary meaning of the word. The misapprehension was of course unavoidable. When the occasion arose to draft bills about the succession, and reference was made to the Queen's "lawful issue", Elizabeth had the phrase altered to "the Queen's issue". Having regard to the number of stories current about her having borne children, of which new versions were occurring almost to the end of her life, Elizabeth felt that "lawful issue" was a term to avoid since it implied the existence of unlawful issue. Such was the public dislike and mistrust of Leicester that the alteration was attributed to him for a purpose of his own. Camden said: "I remember, being then a young man, hearing it said openly by people that this was done by the contrivance of Leicester, with a design to impose, hereafter, some base-born son of his own upon the nation as the Queen's offspring." But writing in the next century, in all the misery entailed by the ruinous incompetence of the Stuarts, Francis Osborne looked back to the days when a political genius occupied the throne, and only wished the rumours had been true, that even a bastard child of that unmatched strain might have done away with the necessity for the Scottish line. "This I may safely attest," he wrote, "the smallest chip of that incomparable instrument of honour, peace and safety to this now unhappy nation, would then have been valued by the people of England above the loftiest branch in the Caledonian grove."*

The rumours of such a child's existence, however, gained no credence wherever the Queen was known. Catherine de Medici, when the marriage proposals were afoot, had asked Fénélon whether these stories about the Queen of England had any truth in them? The Ambassador answered that they were the usual slander that base-minded people liked to utter about their betters. He said: "She is a very great Princess", and that the authority she exercised and the respect she commanded could never exist if she were a woman of notoriously evil life.

Like Burleigh, Leicester took his duties as Chancellor of the University seriously; so seriously, indeed, that Anthony à Wood said: "In those years in which he held his Chancellorship he altered almost the whole government of the University, in some things for

* Francis Osborne, *Historical Memoires of the Reigns of Queen Elizabeth and King James.*

the better, but in most things for the worse." Before Leicester took office, the domestic government of the University had been carried on by the whole body of resident teachers, who drew up the agendas for the meetings of Convocation. Leicester deprived these of their powers, which he vested solely in the Vice-Chancellor, Doctors, Heads of Colleges and Proctors. As the posts of the senior officials were bestowed by patronage, the new arrangement concentrated power in the Chancellor's hands, and he used it invariably to strengthen the Puritan interest. Cambridge had had a vigorous Reformed element since the time of Erasmus, but Oxford had been the stronghold of Catholicism, and Leicester's interference in this direction brought him a fresh accession of unpopularity.

However, two at least of his enactments were of great benefit: he got the Queen to grant the University incorporation by Act of Parliament, confirming all privileges previously bestowed; this meant that Oxford had no longer to seek a new charter from each succeeding sovereign. He also secured great financial advantages to the University by overhauling their system of leases, in the light of the fact that the value of money was going down while that of land was soaring. He made the Fellows say that leases should not be granted for more than twenty-one years, and that one-third of a rent was to be paid in corn and malt. All this was very well, but when the Chancellor began to concern himself with the undergraduates' behaviour, their "looseness of apparel", their absence from lectures their disorderly football, and to follow these admonitions with severe rebukes to the Masters and Fellows because they had not been attended to, the University began to feel about him rather as the Frogs felt about King Stork.[1]

Leicester's personal relations with men of letters were, however, of the happiest kind, and the fact was celebrated over and over again. Campion had declared how friendly, how helpful, how encouraging, Leicester had been to a humble student, and in 1572 William Malim gave the same testimony. He translated from the Italian "A true Report of all the Success at Famagusta", which described the action of the Venetians in repulsing the Turks from Cyprus. In his dedication to Lord Leicester he said: "I can justly witness that for the five years last past, since my return from my travels beyond the seas, that your Lordship's lodging in the Court (where I, through your undeserved goodness, to my great comfort do daily resort) hath been a continued receptacle or harbour for all learned men, coming from both the eyes of the realm, Cambridge and Oxford." He said that as the Moon spread abroad the light derived from the Sun, so Leicester bestowed "all that favour and credit which he hath gotten at the Princes' hands to the help and relief of the worthy and needy".

This goodness of nature was so often praised, it is not possible to doubt that Leicester had it; it shone to admiration when he exerted it of his own free will. When he was called upon to exercise forbearance in any matter touching his self-importance, it was apt to disappear alarmingly, as the burgesses of Warwick found to their cost.

In October, 1571, Charles IX having, as a compliment to Elizabeth, conferred on Lord Leicester the Order of St. Michael, the ceremony of investiture was to take place by proxy in St. Mary's Church, Warwick. Lord and Lady Warwick owned Warwick Castle, and Leicester's seat at Kenilworth was only five miles away. Warwick, therefore, was a town which Leicester regarded almost as family property. He meant to make a handsome endowment in the neighbourhood, and in this year he had gained a charter authorizing him by Act of Parliament to establish a hospital in either Warwick or Kenilworth "for sustentation and relief of needy, poor and impotent people", which hospital should be able to hold property to the value of £200 a year. It had now been decided that the site of the hospital should be in Warwick, and news of the intended benefaction had been made public among the townspeople.

Lord and Lady Warwick were at the time in residence in Warwick at Mr. Fisher's house, and the ceremony was to be attended by other members of the nobility, who came down with the Earl. These included Sir Henry Sidney, Lord Hertford, the widower of Lady Catherine Grey, and Lord and Lady Northampton, whose marriage had taken place the previous April.

When it was known that Lord Leicester would arrive at Warwick on a certain day, the bailiff of the town and the burgesses decided that a present must be made him. They knew the Earl had fine sheep at Kenilworth, so they thought a yoke of oxen would please him best. Repairing to the Church, where their strong-box was kept, they took out £10 odd, which was all their store, and with it they bought two splendid oxen. The question then arose as to how these were to be presented. Here it was that a calamitous misunderstanding took place. Some had heard that the Earl would come on Thursday, others thought it would be Friday. It was assumed that if he did come on Thursday it would be incognito, and that the official reception would be expected on Friday. So it was that, when the Earl and his troop of fine friends rode into Warwick on Thursday afternoon, no group of burgesses was there to meet them. Under the eyes of his brother-in-law, to whom he was so great a man, of Lord Hertford, who was his grateful protégé, of Lord Northampton and his Elin, Lord Leicester was obliged to ride through the streets of Warwick as if he had been nobody at all.

The burgesses were not slow to realize their mistake. By eight next morning they and the oxen were at the gates of Mr. Fisher's house, but the Earl had already departed, riding through the autumnal early morning to Kenilworth. The burgesses stood their ground for seven hours. While they waited, Lord Leicester's servants came out and talked at them, uttering their astonishment that the burgesses "would not so much as bid the Earl of Leicester welcome, but hid them-selves", saying that if his Lordship had showed himself in Bristol or in Norwich, towns with which he had no particular connection, where he was not founding a charity worth £200 a year, what a welcome he would have received! "But this town was so stout, it regarded not of his Lordship." The burgesses endured as well as they might, till at three in the afternoon the Earl and his company were seen riding back. The burgesses tried to make their present, but Leicester swept them aside, hurrying on and saying bitterly, "he would not charge the town so much".

The dismayed burgesses implored the retinue to intercede for them with his Lordship. After some negotiation, they were taken into the garden behind Mr. Fisher's House, where the Earl could see them out of his window, "but they could not see him". Here, when they had poured out explanations, apologies and entreaties, "it was signified to them, My Lord had great marvel that they would no better present themselves to him, coming to his brother's town, but he had, at their instance, remitted the offence, upon condition that thenceforth they would serve themselves more dutifully to his Lordship".

On October 30th, Michaelmas Eve, the state and ancientry was enough to soothe even his Lordship's wounded dignity. "In the morning, word was brought that my Lord of Leicester was ready to come to church, and stayed but for the Bailiff and his company, where-upon, *making the more haste*, the said Bailiff and Burgesses and their assistants came to the Priory, where they were placed and appointed to wait upon the said Lord." Dragon Pursuivant at Arms and Claren-cieux King at Arms led the procession with their attendants, and then came "my said Lord Earl of Leicester apparelled all in white". The Earl's clothes were the finest the onlookers had ever seen. He wore a jerkin and short breeches of white velvet slashed with cloth of silver; his stockings were white knitted silk, his shoes white velvet. Over these garments he wore a white satin robe with an embroidered gold border a foot deep; his hat was black velvet with a white plume. Round his neck was the Order of St. George, and the Garter was on his leg. Magnificent as his garments were, it was not they alone that took the gazers' eyes. "All the proportions and lineaments of his body" were so fine, his carriage so attractive and graceful, the beholders declared him "the goodliest male personage in England".

After the ceremony in the Church, the Earl returned to the Priory in the same state as he had come, and "kept the Feast with great liberality and good cheer"; he himself, "sitting in a parlour by himself without any company, was served with many dishes, and upon the knee with assay". Such was the state Leicester arrogated to himself on this occasion, that he was not only served kneeling, but with a servitor to taste the dish, to show it was not poisoned—a ceremony reserved for royalty. After dinner the Earl remained sitting alone, in his robes, till evening, silently experiencing his grandeur. "He was minded to go again to evensong, but the weather being foul, and of very great rain, he could not go forth according to his intent."*

* Dugdale, *Warwick and Warwick Castle*.

XV

THE DUKE OF NORFOLK, who had been imprisoned in the Tower during the Rising in the North, was released, on his signing a paper promising that he would have no more dealings with the Queen of Scots. He told the Bishop of Ross that though he had signed the document he would not abide by it, and he became at once involved in a scheme spun between the Queen of Scots, de Spes and a Florentine banker, Ridolfi. Its objects were that the Queen of Scots should be released; that the Duke of Alva should send ten thousand soldiers into England to place her on the English throne, and that Elizabeth, as a necessary part of the enterprise, should be assassinated. When Alva was consulted, he said he could not spare any men for such a purpose unless Elizabeth were dead already. While breath remained in her, the English would defend her so furiously that he would find himself engaged in a full-scale war for which he had not the means at his disposal. Let Ridolfi and his friends murder Elizabeth and release Mary, then Alva would send troops to safeguard the latter's accession. Ridolfi had been living in England, and he declared light-heartedly that it would be easy enough to have the Queen shot or stabbed. Alva had not set foot in England, but he doubted very much whether the thing would be easy, and he wanted to see it done before he made any move. His opinion, confided to the King of Spain, was that Ridolfi was a babbling fool. Ridolfi went to Madrid, and, laying the plans before Philip and his Council, assured them that a dozen men could be found to murder the English Queen. The Count de Feria heard him; he abominated Elizabeth, but he had lived eight years in England, and he told Ridolfi he did not agree with him that her murder could be easily procured. While Ridolfi was still abroad, the whole conspiracy was exposed by the discovery of a mass of incriminating letters concealed in the Duke of Norfolk's town house. Norfolk was put on trial and inevitably found guilty of high treason. Elizabeth ordered that it should be announced to the Mayor, Aldermen and citizens in the Guildhall that the Queen of Scots and Norfolk had tried to get ten thousand Spanish soldiers sent into the country;

but she resisted the strongest efforts of Parliament to have Mary Queen of Scots executed or even removed from the succession, nor could she be brought to sign the Duke of Norfolk's death warrant.

The distress of mind brought on illness. In March, 1572, a severe attack of internal pains seized her, which, as she told Fénélon, for five days "so shortened her breath and clutched her breast, she thought she was dying". Such pains, until they were relieved or accounted for, always carried with them the terrifying suspicion of poison. Fénélon was told that for three nights running Lord Burleigh and Lord Leicester sat up with the Queen, so great was the alarm.

The conditions about her in illness were a mixture of splendour and lack. There was an infinite number of attendants to keep a patient clean, warm and soothed by such comforts as home-nursing could supply, but medical aid was not of much effect. The doctors could make the patient unconscious by an opiate, but they could do little to relieve continual pain or discomfort. Their infusions of herbs could purge and reduce fever, but in the main the doctors' work was to estimate the severity of the illness and its probable length, and to say that the patient must be kept quiet and his constitution spared un-necessary handicaps in fighting its battle. One of the Queen's beds had hangings of cloth of silver lined with shot taffeta, its posts topped with bunches of ostrich feathers spangled with gold.* In some such bed, shadowy and gleaming in the candlelight, with such help as physicians and anxious ladies could give, while her most trusted adviser and her best loved friend were both within call in the great room, the sick Queen wore through the evil hours, and at last came out again, still looking ill but saying she was better. But the three nights of acute anxiety had acted upon Leicester's sense of self-preservation. He had heard some report of the Queen of Scots' conversations in which she had spoken of him as one of those who bore her ill will, and he wrote to Lord Shrewsbury: "Touching the talk that Queen hath had of me as of her enemy, I beseech your Lordship to friend me so much as to gather, as near as you can, the cause thereof?"

When Thomas Wilson published his *Discourse on Usury*, he said in his dedication to Leicester: "I know and therefore will not fear to say that you have been, next to the Queen's most mild and gracious disposition, a great help and means of this most calm and merciful government, a thing so joyful to all good people as nothing could be more." A dedication to a patron may be regarded with suspicion, but

* British Museum, Addit. MSS., 5751, fol. 38.

at least the numerous protégés of Lord Leicester all used the same words; they said he was kind to them, and that his disposition was kindly. Yet there ran beside this vein another which made him alarming and sinister when crossed. In April, 1572, a year after he had fallen foul of the Warwick burgesses, he encountered a serious rebuff in Wales, where his title made him Lord of the Manor of Denbigh. He had written to the bailiff aldermen and burgesses of the town, requiring them to nominate as their representative in parliament his own nominee, Henry Dynne. The burgesses had ignored his letter and put forward a candidate of their own election. Leicester expressed considerable anger at their conduct, and insisted that they should cancel their election and accept his: "Not," he wrote, "for any account I make of the thing, but for that I would not it should be thought that I have so small regard borne me at your hands who are bounden to owe me, as your Lord, thus much duty as to know mine advice and pleasure." They might say they had made their choice before his letter reached them; in that case, they should not have done so without consulting him; "So have I thought good to signify unto you that I mean not to take it in any wise at your hands."[1] But the burgesses of Denbigh were made of sterner stuff than those of Warwick. They persisted in returning their own candidate, Richard Candish, and a process of anger and vindictiveness towards his Welsh interests formed itself in Leicester's mind.

He did, however, enjoy the exercise of kindness, and particularly towards his own family. Philip Sidney was now eighteen; while he was at Oxford, Leicester had written to Archbishop Parker asking for a dispensation to eat meat in Lent, for his health's sake, "for my boy, Philip Sidney". In May, 1572, Sidney's father had him sent abroad, and Leicester wrote to Walsingham about him: "My nephew Philip is licensed to travel . . . I have thought good to commit him by these my letters, friendly to you, as unto one I am sure will have a special care of him during his abode there. He is young and raw and no doubt shall find those countries and the demeanour of the people somewhat strange unto him."

About another young man the Earl showed himself in a somewhat different light. A page had, it seemed, run away from his service and entered that of the Cardinal de Guise, who had refused to send him away. Leicester wrote to Walsingham: "As for the boy Clarke, since I cannot obtain him as I desire, I must content me. I wish I had one of my Lord Cardinal's monks, to see how devoutly he should be kept here . . . The boy hath sought many ways to return unto me as well by letters to his friends as by supplication to myself, but I mind not to have him so. The cause that I did so earnestly seek him was to punish him in example to others, which, if it will not be, I will leave it for a time, and hope to give you knowledge where he is shortly, trusting you will give order that he may be suddenly apprehended."[1]

The Council, backed by strong demands in Parliament, had twice brought Elizabeth to the point of signing the warrant for the Duke of Norfolk's execution, and twice she had recalled and cancelled it. As the clamour for the execution of the Queen of Scots was now violent, she could not stand out against both demands. On June 2nd Norfolk was beheaded, and the letter he wrote to the Queen, asking her forgiveness and commending his children to her, shows that, black as his record was for treason, he was not a villain, but a weak, stupid, misguided man in a wilderness of conflicting loyalties. This was the first execution of Elizabeth's reign. The scaffold on Tower Hill was falling to pieces from disuse and they had to build another.

The marriage with the Duke of Anjou was now understood to be abandoned: religious differences, it was said, had proved an insuperable obstacle. But in April, 1572, the French and the English had signed the Treaty of Blois, a settlement of the greatest importance. By it they were to send help to each other if invaded, "for any reason none excepted", and they were both to keep out of Scotland. In the whole of the treaty, Mary Stuart was not mentioned once. The English had done exactly what they hoped to do.

The fruits of a marriage negotiation with the House of Valois being so valuable, when Catherine de Medici asked whether Elizabeth could "fantasy" her youngest son, the Duc d'Alençon, though he was twenty years younger than the English Queen, the latter returned a temporizing reply, and a new era was begun of these glittering mockeries, whose real significance was that they were part of a life and death struggle of a small nation against almost overpowering odds.

The Queen, whatever her secret intentions might be, always entered upon marriage negotiations as if their details were of an importance vital to her happiness. She had heard disquieting rumours of Alençon's appearance; the nineteen-year-old Prince was said to be short, puny, and pitted with smallpox. Leicester, who knew no more than anyone else whether she would ultimately marry, was aware that, if she seriously considered doing so, the personal traits of the Prince would be a matter of considerable moment. Anxious for every reason to form some idea of where he stood, he approached Lord

Clinton, who had just been created Earl of Lincoln and despatched on an embassy to Paris. Lord Lincoln was sixty years old and his third wife was living, nevertheless, he seemed to be thinking of another connection. When he went to Paris he was obliged to leave a lady behind him. He wrote to Lord Burleigh on June 18th, signing himself "The lover in Paris". Leicester wrote to him about Alençon: "I would be glad to receive a word or two from your Lordship, what you think of him, I mean his person." Then he said the Queen, thank God, was well, and so were all Lord Lincoln's friends, adding a teasing remark about "my best beloved, whom, I know, ye least long to hear of!"[1]

Lord Lincoln's affairs were not more mysterious than Leicester's own. The first public account of his amour with Douglas Sheffield was given in that entertaining but unreliable work *Leicester's Commonwealth*, published in 1584; and though an effort to bring the matter into court was made after Elizabeth's death, when Leicester's son by Lady Sheffield attempted to prove his legitimacy, that he might claim his father's earldom and that of his uncle Warwick, the issue of whether the young man's parents had been legally married was not tried in court: the action consisted in proving that he had gone the wrong way about bringing his case, and he was forbidden to bring it again. A good many depositions had been taken, however, before he was estopped, and though many of them are said to contradict each other certain facts are not in dispute.

Lady Sheffield said she was contracted to the Earl at a house in Cannon Row in 1571, and that he made before witnesses the formal declaration: I vow to take you for my wedded wife. At the same time he told her, she said, that the matter must be kept deadly secret.

There came to light some years ago the draft in Leicester's hand, of a letter written to an unnamed woman whom internal evidence showed to be a widow, and to have a liaison with him of long standing, and whom he was reminding of their compact that she accepted the position of his mistress, knowing that she could never be his wife. The circumstances of the woman, and the extremely important place which she occupied in the writer's life, would appear to put her identity beyond question. The letter is perhaps the most revealing document ever found in Leicester's hand; it shows, what for so much of the time can only be assumed, the attraction that his personality exercised over women. No one reading it can doubt either his fondness for the woman, or his merciless determination that she should not interfere with his comfort, his well-being, and above all his

ambition. She was begining to be a nuisance, and after some hesitation, he said, in case she should misunderstand his motives, he was
writing to her, because he thought honesty and good-will obliged
him to it. "I have, as you well know, long both loved and liked you
and found always that faithful and earnest affection at your hands
again that bound me greatly to you. This good will of mine, whatsoever you have thought, hath not changed from that it was at the
beginning towards you." He reminds her, "after your widowhood
began, upon the first occasion of my coming to you", he had clearly
explained to her that he could not marry her, and he had thought she
fully accepted the position, "without any further expectation or hope
of other dealing". This state of things had continued to his "contentation", until "this last year" she had begun to press him "in a further
degree than was our condition". He reminded her that he had then
had the matter out with her, and after "a great strangeness" they had
made it up, and he thought she had determined to say no more of her
grievance. But such resolution had been, clearly, beyond her powers;
for five or six months past the "strangeness" had continued, and she
assumed, but quite wrongly, that the good-will he bore her had clean
been changed and withdrawn, and besought him to tell her what his
feelings really were and "what I intended towards you". His affairs
had been so engrossing, he had not been able for some time to have
this interview with her, but he had at last made time for it, not many
days before the writing of this letter: "For many days are not passed
since our first meeting for this last reconciliation." Now although the
tone of this meeting was one of reconciliation, and had renewed their
loving intercourse, yet, "at the last being with her of all", she had
said something which made him fear she was again harping on what
she had said last year. This had made him determine once and for all
to go into the matter thoroughly and examine it from the point of
view of both of them.

   He assured her, first, that he loved her as much as ever; and for
that reason he must so arrange things as not to do her irremediable
injury. "God forbid I should any way be found so unthankful. For
albeit I have been and am, a man frail, yet am I not void of conscience
towards God nor honourable meaning toward my friend; and having
made special choice of you to be one of the dearest to me, so much the
more care must I have to discharge the office due to you. And in this
consideration of the case betwixt you and me, I am to weigh of your
mind and my mind, to see as near as may be that neither of us be
deceived."

For his own part, he was completely determined against marriage, for a single reason. She might understand how strong this reason was, considering that, apart from it, the inducement for him to marry was so powerful; for his not marrying was causing him to be "almost the ruin of my own house . . . my brother you see long married and not like to have children", and the only prospect of heirs resting in himself. But he put this over-mastering reason into a few lines, using, as people have always used, the discreet "they" for the distinctive pronoun: "If I should marry, I am sure never to have favour of them, that I had rather yet never have wife than lose them; yet is there nothing in the world, next that favour, that I would not give to be in hope of leaving some children behind me, being now the last of our house. But yet," he said, "the cause being as it is, I must content myself and cannot but show my full determination to you that you may shrewdly know my mind and resolution as it is." So much for his own part; "now for the second, which concerneth yourself". He would remind her of what she had complained of herself: her person, her time of youth being consumed, and the hardship a woman endures in such a liaison, "the daily accidents that hap by grieving and vexing you, both to the hindrance of your body and mind . . . the subjection you are in to all reports to the touch of your good name and fame". Now, what was the remedy? If only he knew her mind he could advise her better; but he knew that many offers of noble marriage had been made to her and she had refused them for his sake. "It is not my part to bid you take them, so it were not mine honesty to bid you refuse them", but this position of affairs made him very uneasy. "To carry you away for my own pleasure to your more great and further grief hereafter were too great a shame for me." When the time for receiving these advantageous proposals should be past, his repentance would be unavailing, "when no recompense could be made on my part sufficient to make satisfaction". In short, his love and care for her were so great, he must earnestly hope that she would marry somebody else. It must be said in Lord Leicester's defence that, within the limits of this classical situation, he had shown more tenderness and more real affection than he might have done, and that few men could read such a letter without being almost entirely on the writer's side. He ended by committing Lady Sheffield to the Almighty, and signed himself: "Yours, as much as he was, R. L." But, even then, he felt a post-script would make things safer: "I pray you think, and so I do faithfully assure you, this doth rise upon no other cause in the world but upon your last speech with me, by which methought it seemed you conceived somewhat, and (it) were not honest to leave you in doubt, being resolved, as I am and ever have been, for certain, otherwise and in all things, the same I was I will be."*

From this letter it is clear that, whoever the woman was, no contract of marriage had been made with her; if it were Lady Sheffield, then either the letter was written before 1571, or there was no contract in that year. One of the few facts not in dispute was the birth of her son by Leicester on August 7th, 1574. Her pregnancy would have begun in December, 1573, and she said that after she had told him she was pregnant, and had claimed a promise of marriage in such a case, a marriage ceremony between the Earl and herself was performed, in her chamber at Esher, "in the wintertime at night".

In May, 1573, Lord Shrewsbury's son Gilbert Talbot, who kept his father regularly posted with Court news, wrote about Lord Leicester: "There are two sisters now in the Court that are very far in love with him, as they have been long, my Lady Sheffield and Frances Howard. They, of like striving who shall love him better, are at great wars together, and the Queen thinketh not well of them and not the better of him; by this means there are spies set over him."

This shows the restless, wretched state of Lady Sheffield, unable to claim his undivided attention. It has been said that, if Lady Sheffield were troth plight to Leicester, it was strange that she did not tell her sister so and put a stop to this painful rivalry; but there is no proof that she did not tell her sister. If she did, the latter knew that Lady Sheffield dare not make her claim publicly; and if Leicester indulged in a flirtation with Frances Howard, Lady Sheffield could not control either of them. Leicester would have the sound excuse that his behaviour was diverting suspicion from his secret association.

Obviously the letter was written before the pregnancy was known, and the prospect of a child was the one consideration of sufficient importance to Leicester to make him, when he was faced with it, alter his determination, strongly as it had been expressed. He had no longer to decide whether to beget a child or not. The child was in the making, and it was an even chance that it would prove a boy. If the mother did not think herself married, as the law then stood her power over the child would be absolute; the bastard could not claim maintenance from his father, but the father had no control over the bastard: such a child was entirely the mother's property. In practice, it was naturally almost always the mother's strongest wish to get the father to take control of the child, but he had no legal claim to it.

* Conyers Read, *Huntington Library Bulletin*, April, 1936.

This child might be the son who, if legitimate, would be the longed-for heir to the earldoms of Leicester and Warwick, and the one who would carry on the strain of Dudley.

When Lady Sheffield swore that she had been married by a clergy-man and that he produced a licence, the fact that neither she nor the witnesses knew his name, and that no trace of any such licence could be found in the Archbishop's records, does not *ipso facto* prove that no form of marriage took place; it is possible that a ceremony was performed by a man who was not a clergyman, whose licence was a forgery. The evidence, which was not produced until 1603, fifteen years after Leicester's death and twenty-nine years after the birth of the child, was inconclusive. Lady Sheffield stated that Sir Edward Horsey gave her away (but Horsey died in 1583), and that seven witnesses were present besides Giulio Borgherini, Leicester's Italian physician, who was commonly known as Dr. Julio. None of these was available in 1603, but two whom she could produce as with her at the period of her child's birth, which according to her occurred two days after the ceremony, were Mrs. Erisa, who stayed with her for a fortnight during her lying-in, and a servant, Magdalen Frod-sham. This woman said she had been present at the marriage cere-mony; but she had been hunted up by a man called Drury, who had offered to get evidence together for the claimant, and who wrote of her that he had "made her" subscribe to the note, adding: "She is very forward to depose, for a further consideration." When first approached, she had exclaimed: "What would they have me do? I was very young and I cannot remember anything." This was after-wards altered by her into two statements: one, that she was nineteen years old at the time, and was asked by Lady Sheffield to be present at the ceremony; the other, that she was a small child who wandered into the room by mistake and was about to go out when her cousin made her stay there with the rest.

The most apparently reliable witness produced by Lady Sheffield was Mrs. Erisa, and this lady's recollection was that Magdalen Frodsham had not entered Lady Sheffield's service till after the child was born. Her testimony also casts doubt on another piece of evidence. When the boy was born, Leicester's man Will Clewer went post to his master, who was attending the Queen on a progress down at Gloucester. He brought back a letter from the Earl full of joy and congratulations, signed, as Lady Sheffield declared, Your very loving husband. Mrs. Erisa had seen this letter—but she could not remember that it had been signed with these words. She had not been present at any ceremony either. She did remember Lady Sheffield's "tears and bitter complaints that Lord Leicester was false to her", but her testimony was consistent only with a *promise* to marry, except for one instance: the month after the child's birth, in September, 1574, she went down to Cornwall, and on the way she met Lord Leicester by arrangement at Salisbury, as he was returning with the Queen's progress. She remembered that he greeted her then by saying: "How do my Lady and my boy?"

Lady Sheffield and her son were together for a year or two, and all this while the child was called Robert Dudley, as if he had the right to his father's name. Presently Leicester separated them, and the boy was brought up at Stoke Newington, in the house of his father's relative, John Dudley. Leicester was, like his own father, a kind, affectionate parent. Robert Dudley's upbringing was of course private, but he was reared with all the care and given the education appropriate to Leicester's son. In 1584, when he was ten, Leicester placed him with a tutor at Offington in Sussex, where Lord and Lady Warwick had a house in the neighbourhood. Another piece of evidence was produced for Lady Sheffield by Owen Jones, who had been the boy's attendant at Offington. The latter declared that once, when Leicester visited him there, the Earl said to Jones: "Owen, thou knowest that Robin my boy is my lawful son, and as I do and have charged thee to keep it secret, so I charge thee not to forget it, and therefore see thou be careful of him."

Whether Leicester ever said this or anything like it, at least he never denied parentage. The boy was sent to Oxford, and when he matriculated at Christ Church in 1588 he was entered as Filius Comiti, Earl's son.[1]

The dark and obscure reaches of Leicester's private life were in the greatest contrast to the openness and brilliancy of his public existence. In 1572 the Queen's visit to Warwick, as the guest of Lord and Lady Warwick, attended by Lord Leicester, was a sort of house-party in which the whole town of Warwick took part. She entered the town sitting in a coach beside Lady Warwick, and it was long before the welcome prepared for her allowed the coach to be drawn up Castle Hill and inside the Castle gates. At the last moment, when the Queen had already said: "I thank you, my good people," and was desirous to be going, Mr. Griffin appeared with something written on a paper. "If it is a request," said the Queen, "I will read it in the Castle", and she gave it to Lady Warwick. But it was not a request such as might have been anticipated; it turned out to be a Latin acrostic, urging the Queen to marry and have a baby.

The exquisite beauty of the grounds about Warwick, where the river, appearing quite still so that it looks like dark glass, winds, in May, through fields powdered thick with daisies, appears in Drayton's *Polyolbion*, in an early morning of summer, the burnished east drying up the dew on bushes and knolls, while

> *. . . the mirthful choir with their clear, open throats*
> *Unto the joyful morn so strain their warbling notes*
> *That hills and valleys ring, and even the echoing air*
> *Seems all composed of sounds about them everywhere.*

When Drayton speaks of a vision of Diana in Warwick Chase *. . . following thy fleet game, chaste, mighty forest Queen*, it recalls the sight, in Warwick Castle, of a saddle used by Queen Elizabeth, of emerald velvet, embroidered all over in silver thread and fringed with silver.

The Queen stayed with Lord and Lady Warwick, who were still occupying Mr. Fisher's house, from Monday till Wednesday. Then, leaving her household at Warwick, she rode out by the North Gate through Mr. Fisher's grounds and made her way to Kenilworth. Here she stayed in blissful retreat till Saturday, returning to Warwick late on Saturday night. She surprised Lady Warwick at supper and sat down with them all, but "ate little", and, not thinking it necessary to wait till the others had finished, she left the table and went out into the gallery. There she encountered Mr. Fisher himself, who wanted to fall down on his knees, but as he was suffering from gout the Queen would not allow him to do so. This interview, occurring on the evening of the Queen's return from her private visit, inspired Mr. Fisher afterwards to indiscreet conversation, "reporting such things as, some for their untruth, and some for other causes, had been better untold . . . what these things mean", added the writer, "is not for everyone to know."* The climax of the party was a tremendous display of fireworks, so let off as to be reflected in the river, enhanced by cannon brought from the Tower at Lord Warwick's expense, who, as Master of the Ordinance, was able to command their removal.

The progress went on to Kenilworth, which Elizabeth now entered publicly; and it was while she was riding in Kenilworth Chase that a despatch was brought to her, which she read on horseback, telling

* Dugdale, *Warwick and Warwick Castle.*

her of the Massacre of Saint Bartholomew. She returned at once to the Castle, and the French Ambassador, who was of the party, was told that he could not be allowed to speak to her. He was not given an audience till four days later, when the Court had arrived at Woodstock. Here he was at last received by the Queen, who was standing in the middle of a semi-circle of Councillors and ladies, all of whom, like herself, were dressed in black.

This progress extended to Gloucestershire, and here Lord Leicester played a *mauvais tour* on Henry Lord Berkeley, against whom he and Lord Warwick were engaged in a long and acrimonious lawsuit. On the death of Edward VI certain property had reverted to Lord Berkeley, but the lands had originally been claimed by the Dudleys' ancestress Joanna Beauchamp. Her claims descended to Warwick and Leicester, and litigation was not finished till 1609, twenty-seven years later. Anyone at law with his brother and himself was regarded by Leicester as a sort of noxious animal. He considered that Berkeley Castle was his own and his brother's property, and though such a thing was not in the schedule of the progress, and Lord Berkeley himself was absent, he persuaded the Queen to let him take her hunting in the Castle park. Part of these grounds, known as the Worthy, Lord Berkeley had turned into a game preserve and stocked with deer. The sport was so good that in one day the Queen's party killed twenty-seven stags. When Lord Berkeley came back and heard what ravages had been made, his anger against Leicester was intense. He "disparked that ground" so that there should be no more hunting there for anybody, and his comments on the episode were carried to the Queen, losing nothing by repetition. The Queen was angry in her turn; she thought that, as Lord Berkeley had not been there to welcome her, he should have been glad that she had amused herself in his park, and, had it been only she, Lord Berkeley very likely might have been. As it was, he saw the whole thing as a piece of deliberate impudence and spite on the part of Lord Leicester. The Queen, after hearing a choice selection of his remarks, exclaimed that he had best take care. Lord Leicester might presently take the castle as well as the deer; she was told he had good title to it.

Leicester was greatly interested in the art of manège, of teaching horses the movements of stopping suddenly and wheeling in a small space. The practice was well known in Italy and France but still new in England, and he wanted a "rider" who could train his horses in it. He thought that, of the many French Lords murdered in the Massacre of St. Bartholomew, some might have had riders in their service who would now be unemployed, and in September, 1572, he wrote asking Sir Francis Walsingham if there were such a one at liberty, "appertaining to any of the late Lords that were murdered"? He would give him £30 a year, meat and drink, "and his horse found in my stable". Walsingham replied at once. He had asked Captain Lassety to be on the look-out, "who is most willing to do your Lordship any service", but all the riders Lassety could discover demanded 300 crowns a year, "and the least they can be reduced to is 200 crowns". The captain was trying to make them believe that "150 crowns in England will go further than 300 here, but as yet, no persuasion will serve to make them so to think". In the end Captain Lassety, in despair of finding any French trainer who was skilful and not exorbitant, "hearkened out" one in Italy who was willing to come at a reasonable figure. Walsingham said: "If your Lordship will have him, you must send into Italy a bill of credit for so much money as may defray his charges into England."*

In October, the Queen had had a sharp attack of some illness which had been accompanied by a rash; they had feared it was another bout of smallpox, but, as Smith wrote to Walsingham: "Now it makes no matter what it was; thanks be to God she is perfectly whole." The next night, however, she had a relapse, and he had to inform Burleigh "Her Majesty hath been very sick this last night so that my Lord of Leicester did watch with her all night". But he was able to add: "This morning, thanks be to God, she is very well. It was but a sudden pang."

Leicester possessed the high degree of physical magnetism which makes a very good nurse, and he was, plainly, a capable manager of the Queen in her ailments. In the first week of November his soothing influence and his skill were urgently needed.

The pressure exerted by Parliament upon Elizabeth to have Mary Queen of Scots put to death after the disclosure of Ridolfi's conspiracy had been intensified by the horror felt by Protestants at the Massacre of St. Bartholomew. Elizabeth continued her resistance to their demand, but the Scots had originally threatened to execute Mary Stuart themselves: since her flight into England, she had been the cause of the first and only rebellion of Elizabeth's subjects, she had tried to get Alva's ferocious troops sent into England, she had sent Ridolfi to discuss with the King of Spain's council the possibility of having Elizabeth murdered; and the English Queen began to think whether the Scots could not be encouraged to carry out their original

* Digges, *Compleat Ambassador.*

intention. Sir Henry Killigrew, under the seal of absolute secrecy, had been sent to Scotland on a mission known only to the Queen, Burleigh and Leicester; it was to sound the Regent Mar as to whether, if the Scots Queen were returned, he would guarantee to have her executed in a matter of hours after she had crossed the Border. Mar received the proposal favourably, but he began to make conditions, as that, after the execution, Queen Elizabeth must pay annually to the Scots what she now paid for Mary's upkeep. The negotiations were brought to an end by the sudden death of the Regent himself. But while they were still being entertained Elizabeth was a prey to such agitation that she became hysterical. Leicester wrote to tell Walsingham, so that he should not be misled by rumour into thinking her worse than she was. "The fits that she hath had hath not been above a quarter of an hour, but yet this little thing in her hath bred strange bruits here at home."

Burleigh wrote to Leicester explaining that the scheme for having the Queen of Scots put to death by judicial process in Scotland had failed, and they could now only hope that God would inspire Queen Elizabeth to take the strong-minded course. Leicester replied that he had not been able to take Burleigh's letter to the Queen immediately, as it had arrived at six in the evening when "she was at her wonted repose". He agreed that it was a matter of urgent necessity to get her now to assent to bringing the Queen of Scots to trial in England, and said with great candour that Burleigh was able to exert more persuasion over her in one than anyone else could in seven years; therefore he wished Burleigh were with her even then.[1]

In this year, an edict of the City Corporation forbade players to go on tour unless they were attached as servants to a nobleman. The company of which Lord Leicester had become patron some years earlier therefore wrote to him, "humbly desiring your honour that you will now vouchsafe to retain us at this present as your household servants: not that we mean to crave any further stipend or benefits". They asked only their liveries and "your honour's licence to certify that we are your household servants when we shall have occasion to travel amongst our friends, as we do usually once a year and as other noblemen's players do". The letter was signed by six of the company, headed by James Burbage, the father of the greatest actor of the Elizabethan stage.[2]

It was the duty of the Revels Office, among others, to read the plays to be put on at Court to make sure they contained nothing offensive. In December the office put down: "Perusing and reforming of plays:

The expenses and charges when My Lord of Leicester's men showed their matter of *Panecia*. Gloves for my Lord of Leicester's boys that played at Court: For the carriage of their stuff and for the carter's attendance that night. For the hire of a horse two days to the Court to furnish my Lord of Leicester's Players, the frost being so great, no boat could go and come back again; for holly and ivy for my Lord of Leicester's servants." "When I came to Mr. Peters to receive the money," the clerk wrote, "I could not, without further order of my Lord Treasurer . . . for my boat hire to and from Westminster to receive the money, one shilling."

In transporting trunks of clothes and properties, one shilling was paid to the watermen for expedition; eight pence bestowed upon them in drink; and one and six pence to carry the trunks to the Court from Mortlake on men's shoulders, because time would not serve to go by water.

Edmund Tilney, Master of the Revels, and his men were paid for boat hire, when they came to the Lord Chamberlain and the Lord Leicester, "for showing of patterns".*

* Feuillerat, *Accounts of the Office of Revels.*

XVI

LEICESTER'S POWER WAS great, but it was based on his personal influence with the Queen, and the possibility of losing that influence through a withdrawal of her affection, though not a strong one, was always present at the back of his mind. His attention was kept on the stretch because Elizabeth was never wholly under his influence. Not only had he to give place to Burleigh in political matters, but in the spheres of romantic amusement, friendship and intellectual interest she was, all her life, responsive to other men; it was part of her success. In so small a nation the Court was a magnet of almost every ambition, and the Queen was the centre of it, not only by virtue of her place, but also because of the inspiration of her personality. Lord Leicester was the great favourite, but he was never the only one, and it was always possible that a rival might encroach disagreeably on his preserves. After the alarms aroused by Lord Ormonde and Sir Thomas Heneage had subsided, the greatest threat he had as yet encountered was in the person of Christopher Hatton, who never displaced him, indeed, but came uncomfortably close. Leicester's great influence had begun in a passionate mutual attraction of young people, but its growth was based on the capacity of a man who thoroughly understood women to give Elizabeth the support she wanted: an appearance, at least, of unaltering admiration and faithful love. No one, not even Lord Burleigh, was allowed to take from Elizabeth the management of what she considered her peculiar sphere—as Sir Francis Walsingham once said: "I would her Majesty would be content to refer these matters, as other Princes do, to them that can best judge of them"* but the things she wanted arranged and managed for her Leicester performed with ability, promptness, and a knowledge of how to please her combined with an anxious desire to do so. The cares and fears, the burdens of her state, oppressed and ailing as she often was, and always preoccupied with some political or social problem of overwhelming importance, made the soothing, reassuring quality of Leicester's support invaluable to her comfort.

* Conyers Read, *Mr. Secretary Walsingham and the Policy of Queen Elizabeth*.

The support was enhanced by the delight of his personal presence: his height, his strength, his grace. He was not, perhaps, the less attractive to a temperament such as hers because she might suspect that beneath his devotion, his tenderness, his grave carriage, his profoundly attentive demeanour there was a predatory animal whose teeth would be in her throat if she relaxed her vigilance.

The affection and reassurance which Hatton's devotion supplied was without any sinister attribute. He had the personal traits Elizabeth always found attractive: height, gracefulness, ready speech and sound intelligence. He also entertained for her a passion that, since it is difficult to estimate the strength and sincerity of Leicester's, must be described as the most ardent and genuine she ever inspired. He once gave a very good idea of the charm of Elizabeth's responsive, sympathetic conversation, her capacity for calling out the interest of the man to whom she was talking and listening. He said: "She fished for men's souls with so sweet a bait, no man could escape her net-work."

Loyalty and even personal devotion to Elizabeth were not devalued by the mere instinct of self-preservation which obliged men to keep open a communication with the Queen of Scots in case the turn of Fortune's wheel should bring her up again. Lord Burleigh could not do this, or even hope to do it; if Mary Stuart attained the English throne, his head would be off. Sir Francis Walsingham's would probably follow. But, for the rest, care and adroitness were at least worth trying. Lord Shrewsbury told the Queen of Scots that though he was obliged to act as her keeper while Queen Elizabeth, to whom he owed his present loyalty, was in being, if Elizabeth died he himself would place the crown on her head; and Christopher Hatton took occasion to let Mary know that if Elizabeth died he would himself bring her the news.

These instincts of caution were sharpened by the fact that in the years 1573 and 1574 Elizabeth, who was now forty, appeared very frail, and there was a widespread rumour that she had not long to live. The prospects of the Queen of Scots brightened, and for nearly ten years she remained quiescent, without lending her name to plots for Elizabeth's assassination or even for her own release; chance might crown her without her stir. Lady Lennox was influenced by the prevailing mood; passionately, frantically as she had denounced her daughter-in-law as the murderess of her son, she now made secret approaches to Lord Darnley's widow as the possible Queen of England. Mary, as the price of a reconciliation, demanded and obtained from her a signed statement that she had been forced by

Queen Elizabeth and her Council to accuse the Queen of Scots of Darnley's death, and that she herself had never believed Mary to be guilty. Some inkling of this transaction reached Elizabeth, who asked Lady Lennox if she were reconciled to the Queen of Scots? Lady Lennox said: "I asked her Majesty if she could think so, for I was made of flesh and blood, and could never forget the murder of my child."*

To the English nation as a whole, however, whether Catholic or Protestant, the idea of Mary Stuart's accession wore one aspect and one only; though consistently ignored by succeeding generations, the vividness with which it was present to those living at the time is seen plainly in their exclamations and utterances. The fearful and sustained onslaught made by Philip of Spain upon the religious, political and financial independence of the Netherland States had started in good earnest in 1567, the year before Marys' arrival in England. The Dutch mounted one of the most heroic resistance movements in the history of the world, but for years it seemed that they must be doomed to fail. The task of subduing a terrain inter-sected with dykes, and defended by cities whose inhabitants were inspired with an almost superhuman courage, was a long and immensely hard one even for Spanish forces commanded by the Duke of Alva, but slowly, and by the exertion of treachery, bestial cruelty and overpowering force of arms, the Spanish campaign was making headway. By the committee known as the Council of Blood, Alva announced that it was high treason to question the King of Spain's right to deprive the provinces of their liberties, or to maintain that he was bound to respect any of their laws or charters. In the first three months of its sitting, the Council put eighteen hundred persons to death; but this was as nothing beside the fate of the besieged cities when they had been reduced. Haarlem was sacked in 1573, and the unspeakable tale of the tortures wreaked on its inhabitants, combining savage ferocity with ingenious cruelty, was repeated in the fates which befel, one after the other, the great cities of Mons, Mechlin, Nimwegen, Zutphen, Naarden and Maestricht, and after the accounts of burning, slaughtering and hideous torment, which reached English ears, a terror of a different kind succeeded: the English merchants and craftsmen heard that in some of the once-thriving centres of Netherland industry, densely peopled and humming with prosperous activity—grass was now growing in the silent streets. After the fall of Zutphen, no one dared approach its walls for days; and Count Nieuwenar wrote to Prince Louis of Nassau: "A wail of agony was

* *MSS. Domestic, December 10, 1574,* quoted by Froude.

heard above Zutphen last Sunday, a sound as of a mighty massacre, but we know not what has taken place." After the fall of Naarden, Alva wrote to Philip: "We have cut the throats of the burghers and all the garrison and not left a mother's son alive." It can only be said that those who died in Spanish hands by having their throats cut were exceptionally fortunate. At the end of his career in the Netherlands, Alva advised the King of Spain to burn down every single city still standing, except a few which would serve as garrisons for Spanish troops.*

In an aggressive war when men must be cruel, and in an age when much cruelty was taken for granted, this army of picked Spanish veterans terrified Europe by the horror of the methods it pursued; and this identical army was the one which Mary Queen of Scots made three distinct attempts to bring into England to her assistance. In Ridolfi's Plot, in Throckmorton's Plot, in Babington's Plot, the basis of each was that the Spanish army in the Netherlands should be brought over to exterminate English resistance. Spanish help did not mean an expedition sent from Spain; it meant, in Ridolfi's Plot, that Alva was asked to send troops to Hartlepool, in Throckmorton's Plot that the Duke of Guise was to land Spanish soldiers at the English south coast ports, in the Babington Plot that Parma, who had succeeded Alva, was to send a force to Newcastle or Scarborough. It was only the fact that Philip's generals had too much of his ghastly work to do in the Netherlands that prevented the Spanish troops from being sent; they were but a few hours' sail away, before a favouring wind.

"Tell your master if he will help me I shall be Queen of England in three months!" Mary had written to de Spes in 1568. At the time of Norfolk's trial, Elizabeth had insisted that the citizens of London should hear that he and the Queen of Scots had asked Alva to send ten thousand of his terrible troops into England; Parliament knew, the nation knew, what Mary would do if she could. Considerations of the legitimacy or illegitimacy of Elizabeth, the validity or invalidity of the Will of Henry VIII, even, to many, the issue as to whether Catholicism or Protestantism should be the national religion, became diminished in importance as they were met by the annihilating argument of the blazing, starving cities of the Netherlands and the sickening tale of their agony. The lovely and gracious Queen of Scots, a helpless, innocent captive, devoted to piety and fine needle-work, is a posthumous creation. To the people living at the time she

* Motley, *Rise of the Dutch Republic.*

was lovely indeed: of a blemished reputation which, in the eyes of some, was cancelled by the fact that she was a Catholic and would, if Queen of England, restore the Catholic faith. On those who had come into contact with her she exerted an extraordinary personal charm. How she appeared to the rest can be seen in the letter which an unknown writer sent to Lord Leicester, begging and imploring him to use his influence with Queen Elizabeth, whom he reproached bitterly for exposing England to the nightmare horrors of invasion and civil war, for the sake of sparing "one horrible woman, who carries God's curse with her wherever she goes".[1]

The royal blood in the Lennox-Stuart family flowed in another branch besides the son of Darnley and the Queen of Scots. In October, 1573, Lady Lennox formed an alliance with the termagant Lady Shrewsbury. Lady Lennox' younger son, Lord Charles Stuart, was introduced to Lady Shrewsbury's daughter by her previous marriage, Lady Elizabeth Cavendish, while Lady Lennox and her son were staying with Lady Shrewsbury at Rufford. Had Lady Shrewsbury not wished the young people to come together, her chaperonage of her daughter could have been Argus-eyed; as it was, the mothers shut themselves up together and the pair found themselves oddly at liberty, with the result that Lord Charles Stuart "so entangled himself" with Lady Elizabeth "that he could have none other". The young people were married without one word of announcement to the Queen; as the whole manoeuvre had been arranged on the grounds that Lord Charles Stuart was a prince of the blood this secret marriage was, of course, a punishable offence. The elder ladies were both given a term of imprisonment; but from Lady Shrewsbury's point of view it was well worth it. In 1575 the Lady Arabella Stuart was born, first cousin to the King of Scots and claimant next after him in the Stuart line to the English throne. Lady Shrewsbury's elation knew no bounds. When both the young parents died she brought her grandchild up herself, in preparation for the day when she should see her on the throne of England. The unfortunate little girl became an object of speculation to everyone who had an eye on the succession. Leicester already had Lord Huntingdon as a brother-in-law; he waited his opportunity to bring the little Arabella into his toils.

Between 1574 and 1575 Zuccaro visited England and painted an allegorical portrait of the Queen, wrapped in a russet satin robe embroidered all over with ears and eyes; a serpent was coiled on one of her sleeves, and her dress under the robe was embroidered

with the wild flowers grown on English soil. He also executed a
couple of drawings in red chalk of the Queen and Lord Leicester in
ordinary clothes. The Queen is wearing the graceful, full-skirted
dress of the seventies, with a small ruff outlining the chin, and a little
head-dress from which floats about her a long, full, diaphanous veil.
Her hands are crossed in front of her, one of them holding a plumed
fan. One like this was given to her by Leicester in 1574; "a fan of white
feathers set in a handle of gold, the one side thereof garnished with
two very fair emeralds, the other fully garnished with diamonds and
rubies; on each side a white bear and two pearls hanging, a lion
ramping with a white muzzled bear at the foot".* The drawing of
Leicester shows him in armour except that he wears a hat instead of a
helmet; a mailed glove, a mailed shoe, a breastplate, two helmets
and a sword are grouped about him as if he were trying on accoutrements. The interest of the drawings is that they are a pair. Zuccaro
had clearly caught something characteristic in the pose of each
subject, the Queen's upright carriage, Leicester's easy, graceful,
confident attitude, but judging from other portraits the facial like-
nesses are not strong. In the Queen's face, however, one thing seems
to have struck the artist, so that he reproduced it with particular
accuracy; the eyes are very clearly drawn, with the iris shown in its
full circle and the pupil a hard contrast, giving a look of piercing
observation.

On New Year's Day, 1575, Leicester gave the Queen a white satin
doublet fastened with eighteen pairs of gold clasps enamelled and
studded with diamonds and rubies. Lord Warwick gave her a black
velvet girdle set with emeralds and pearls. The Queen gave them, as
she gave all the nobility who brought her presents, gifts that were
catalogued as being so many ounces of gold plate.*

In this year, while his son by Lady Sheffield was less than twelve
months old, Leicester entered on another liaison, with the singular
force that inspires an old passion revived.

Viscount Hereford, the husband of Lettice Knollys, had been
created Earl of Essex in 1572. In 1573 he had gone to Ireland in an
attempt to colonize Ulster. The plan had added one more to the list of
lamentable failures by the English to govern that wild, beautiful and
unhappy land. Essex was recalled early in 1575 to explain his doings
to the Privy Council, and when he was before them it was noticed
that Lord Leicester seemed most anxious for all previous short-
comings to be overlooked and for Lord Essex to be sent back to

* Nichols, *Progresses of Queen Elizabeth.*

Ulster immediately. Sir Henry Sidney, who served three terms as Lord Deputy in Ireland, and managed to create there some approach to order and security, wrote to the Council in defence of Lord Essex, who was his personal friend; but this letter, earnest as it was, was not strong enough to please Lord Leicester. An English correspondent told Sir Henry on March 21st, 1575: "It seemeth your letters to the Lords were not agreeable to the Earl of Leicester's mind, whereby he took occasion of some offence against your Lordship that you had not made it apparent enough to her Majesty and the Lords that you earnestly wished the Earl's return ... But your Lordship did much better, and far more agreeably to my Lord of Essex' mind, who, notwithstanding my Lord of Essex' conceit, did forthwith satisfy his Lordship of your most friendly and effectual dealing."* This report of what actually happened in a Privy Council meeting is a confirmation of Camden's words, who said that in 1575 the Earl of Essex "threatened the Earl of Leicester" for the latter's behaviour towards Lady Essex, and that thereupon Leicester adopted that system of "striking and overthrowing men with honour", and used all his influence to get Essex sent back again to Ireland "with the empty title of Earl Marshall", which was achieved in a few months' time.

The country house of the Earl and Countess of Essex was Chartley in Staffordshire, but they now occupied Durham House as their town house, and here Lady Essex remained in her husband's absence, with her two sons Robert and Walter and her daughters Penelope and Dorothy. The twenty-year-old Philip Sidney, who had made the Grand Tour and been attached to Sir Francis Walsingham's embassy in Paris, where he had witnessed scenes of the Massacre of St. Bartholomew, had now returned to England, and spent much of his time with his uncle at Leicester House. Lord Essex was very anxious that this paragon of a young man should marry his daughter Penelope, but Sir Henry Sidney did not take the matter up and Philip Sidney passively allowed it to pass him by. Penelope Devereux was but twelve years old. When, six years later, she was married to Lord Rich and a passion for her seized him, all too late, he looked back in despair to the time when he had known her as a child

> ... yet could not, by rising morn foresee
> How fair a day was near. Oh, punished eyes!

At the riverside village of Mortlake, near Richmond, lived Dr.

* Collins, *Sidney Papers*.

Dee, who had cast Elizabeth's horoscope while she was still a princess. Here he was often called on by members of the Court; Sir Francis and Lady Walsingham, Sir Christopher Hatton, Sir Philip Sidney were among his visitors, as well as less distinguished members, such as the Queen's Lady in Waiting, Mistress Blanche Parry, who was Dee's cousin, and the Queen's dwarf, Mrs. Thomasin. Dee had several glasses which he used for scrying, a large one which he spoke of as "my great chrystalline globe" and a much smaller one of a dark and livid hue. This may have been the one he called his magic glass. He said it had been brought to him by an angel, which sounds like an *apporte*. The Queen heard of his magic glass, and on a day in March, 1575, Dee said: "The Queen with her most honourable Privy Council and other her Lord, ladies and nobility came riding across the fields from Richmond." When the cavalcade arrived opposite Dee's house, they heard that his wife had been buried only four hours since. The Queen therefore refused to come in, but Dee carried out the glass to show her. "Her Majesty being taken down from her horse by the Earl of Leicester, Master of the Horse, at the church wall of Mortlake, did see some of the properties of that glass, to her Majesty's great contentment and delight."* What Elizabeth wanted most in the world was to hold the love of the English people by being a great Queen of England. Her life was a brilliant achievement of this wish, and any of those supernatural processes which indicate future success or failure, must have shown her something to her great contentment. Had the process been expounded to her in detail, it would also have shown her something greatly to her dismay and anger in the conduct of the man in whose arms she had just alighted from her horse.

Lord Leicester continued to embellish Leicester House, and he now set in hand a little banqueting house on the river's brim, on the left-hand side of the garden facing the water. It was two storeys high. The first floor was the state room, the ground floor was divided between "the lower room" and "the gardener's chamber".† Burleigh helped him to get some stone for this building, though Leicester's letter of thanks does not show from where Burleigh got it himself. Leicester wrote: "I have to thank your Lordship very heartily . . . that your Lordship is pleased to help me that I may have some stone toward the making of a little banquet house in my garden." If Lord Burleigh would give Leicester's man Hawthorne instructions about this, "the pleasure will be great you do me and I will be ready to the best of my power to requite. And so, committing your Lordship to

* John Dee, *The Compendious Relation*.   † *Archeologia*, 73.

the Almighty the 17th of May, Your Lordship's very friend: R. Leicester."[1]

The chief object of Leicester's preparations, however, was the party he was to give for the Queen at Kenilworth. Sir Henry Killigrew had discovered an Italian maker of fireworks, and he sent Leicester this man's suggested programme for a pyrotechnical display, saying that it would take two months to prepare it. The plan so submitted to Leicester provided for live dogs, cats and birds to be thrown out of the body of a flaming, flying dragon; but as detailed accounts of the fireworks seen at Kenilworth make no mention of this feature, it may be assumed that it was cancelled. For the first evening, serpents of fire in the meads were suggested; for another, a display in the Castle courtyard of a fountain throwing water, wine and fire for seven or eight hours continuously, and "three wonderful wheels of scented fire of different colours", a combination of colour, light and scent, the three ideals of Elizabethan pleasure.[2]

Leicester had made himself the patron of Robert Laneham, a clever, pushing man who knew several languages, and had got him made Keeper of the Council Chamber Door. Laneham's enthusiastic gratitude was expressed in his account of himself, his office and the great doings at Kenilworth. His description of his office gives a vivid impression of the closed doors behind which Elizabeth's Council was actually sitting. If Laneham found people babbling in the ante-chamber, " 'Peace,' I say. 'Wot you where you are?' " Then he gives a glimpse of those methods employed by spies on which so much of an ambassador's despatches were built up: if Laneham saw people "spying through the lock-hole or, unmannerly, through the chink of the door", he pounced on them immediately. "Here," he said, "doth my languages stand me in good stead, my French, my Spanish, my Dutch, my Latin; sometimes among the Ambassador's men, sometimes with the Ambassador himself, if he bid call his lackey, or ask me what's o'clock." Leicester had been a kind and generous master, giving Laneham some of his own clothes and providing for his old father, and fortunately Laneham was eager to set down as much as he could of the Earl's magnificent entertainment at Kenilworth.

The artificial mere lay east of the castle and embraced the south wall as far as the bridge leading to the entrance in Mortimer's Tower. This stretch of water, to the left of the bridge as the Tower was approached, was the pool on which the water-pageants were performed. Leicester's Buildings were now complete, and Laneham expatiated on "the rare beauty of building . . . all of the hard quarry stone, every room so spacious, so well belighted and so high-roofed within . . . by day time on every side so glittering of glass, a' night by continual brightness of candle, fire and torchlight, transparent through the lightsome windows". Against the darkness of wood panelling the furniture displayed a fairy-like beauty, for some of it was upholstered in coloured lamé; there were chairs covered in "purple-silver", in "peach-silver" and in "crimson-silver". The great beds, their curtains of satin or velvet, crimson, green or blue, were embroidered all over with twinkling gold or silver, their posts were carved with the Earl's armorial bearings, their counterpanes, of satin to match the curtains, bore in the centre the bear and ragged staff worked in gold or silver thread. On the north side of the castle, between the twelfth century keep and the outer wall, Leicester had created a pleasure garden. At its eastern end stood the Swan Tower, overlooking the mere. All along, just inside the castle wall, he had reared a terrace, ten or twelve feet broad; on this, against the wall, was a marvellous aviary protected by a gilded mesh; inside, nesting holes for the birds were hollowed out of the wall itself. Along the terrace stood obelisks surmounted by spheres, and white bears mounted on curious bases. Below the terrace lay the pleasure ground, with paths sanded, "not light nor too soft . . . but smooth and firm, pleasant to walk on as a sea shore when the water has avoided". Here on the grass was a magnificent fountain "of rich and hard white marble", whose jets, falling into an octagonal basin, maintained there "two feet of the fresh falling water". The apple, pear and cherry trees in fruit, the beds of flowers, the breeze on the terrace where one could pick "delicious strawberries" and eat them from the stem, the sight and sound of the water, the fluttering and warbling in the aviary, all seemed to Lancham to form a terrestrial paradise which glorified the great Earl who had called it into being.*

The Queen, on her summer progress, was approaching Kenilworth through Oxfordshire, by way of Grafton where she had a house of her own. Burleigh was going to join the party at Kenilworth, and Leicester wrote to him from Grafton, saying the Queen was very well, and was very much pleased with the house there, as he had told her she would be when he saw it in 1571. There had been an awkward situation at her arrival at Grafton: "being a marvellous hot day at her coming, there was not a drop of good drink for her". In other people's idiom the drink was only too good; the ale was so heady the Queen could not take it. Elizabeth never took strong drink;

* Robert Laneham, *Entertainment at Kenilworth.*

her wine was always mixed with water, and when after a hot journey she found that the light ale she was accustomed to was not available, discomfort and indignation made her very angry. Water was not drunk freely in great houses, the sources were so apt to be tainted, so she was not able to quench her thirst as she might have done at the side of a brook. Nor was she on this occasion unreasonable; the ale was too strong for Lord Leicester himself: "No man was able to drink it; you had been as good to have drunk Malmsey. It did put me far out of temper." Fortunately, "by chance" some ale light enough for the Queen to drink was found in the neighbourhood, and the horrid crisis was past. "God be thanked, she is now perfect well and merry," he said, and he expected to bring her to Kenilworth on Thursday week. At the castle, where arrangements were being made in his absence, his stewards made this memorandum: "If the ale of the county will not please the Queen, then it must come from London, or else a brewer to brew the same in the towns near."*

In the evening of July 9th, Leicester brought Elizabeth and her train to the bridge leading to Mortimer's Tower. The weather was heavenly, hot and still, with a few refreshing showers. The beauty of the fields, and the groups of trees gradually thickening into the woods at the west of the castle, were the setting of the steep walls, rising cliff-like, of cornelian coloured stone. On the bridge seven pairs of columns were adorned with votive offerings; wheat, grapes, branches laden with fruit, cages of birds, platters of fish protected by fresh grass; the sixth pair were in the form of two ragged staves, from whose branches hung glittering armour; the last pair were two bay trees, hung on all sides with lutes, viols, flutes, recorders and harps.

A salute of cannon greeted the Queen's entry, and at that moment the clock on Caesar's Tower, with its blue dial and gold figures, was stopped; time was to stand still for these enchanted days. The castle was filled with ladies and gentlemen and their servants; thirty guests had been invited beside the Queen, and these included Sir Henry and Lady Mary Sidney, Philip Sidney and the Countess of Essex.

To all the diversions in the open air, the bear-baiting, the fireworks, the tumblers, the rustic plays and the romantic, elegant entertainments with their exquisite accompaniments of music and dancing, the people of the district were allowed to come. Five miles away, in Stratford, William Shakespeare, a boy of eleven, was living with his parents. Some twenty years later he wrote *A Midsummer Night's Dream*, a play to be enacted at Greenwich Palace during the wedding

* H.M.C. Pepys.

festivities of Lord Burleigh's granddaughter, Elizabeth Vere, and the
young Lord Derby, and he put a speech of extraordinary and fascinating implication into the mouth of the Fairy King. Oberon says to
Puck

> . . . thou rememberest
> Since once I sat upon a promontory
> And heard a mermaid on a dolphin's back
> Uttering such dulcet and harmonious breath
> That the rude sea grew civil at her song
> And certain stars shot madly from their courses
> To hear the Sea Maid's music.

This allusion to Mary Queen of Scots, called the Queen Dolphin as
her first husband had been the Dauphin of France, and to her fatal
encouragement of the northern Earls to join the rising of 1569, has
long been recognized; but Halpin* pointed out the similarity between
the imagery in the speech and the sights recorded of the Kenilworth
festivities. One evening the Queen stood on the bridge by Mortimer's
Tower, and watched a pageant on the mere, where a mermaid swam,
drawing her tail through the water, and Harry Goldingham, dressed
as Arion and wearing a mask, sat astride a floating dolphin. The
mermaid and the dolphin form one image in the speech; in the pool
they were side by side. The waters were thrashed about, until the
figure of Triton ordered them in Neptune's name to cease their
turmoil. His words were:

> You winds, return unto your caves, and silent there remain,
> You waters wild, suppress your waves and keep you calm and plain.

So much for the sea's growing civil. As for the stars that shot madly
from their courses, Laneham described the fireworks in these words:
"Blaze of burning darts flying to and fro, gleams of stars coruscant,
streams and hails of fiery sparks, lightening of wild fire, a' water and
a' land." A reminder of the water pageant occurs in yet another part
of *A Midsummer Night's Dream*.† As Queen Elizabeth stood upon the
bridge, looking at the pageant, Arion was overcome by his sense of
the occasion. He brought out a few of his lines, then pulled off his
mask, exclaiming that he was none of Arion, not he, but honest
Harry Goldingham. The Queen broke into peals of laughter and
said afterwards this was the best part of the show. In the rustics' play
of Pyramus and Thisbe acted before the great, Snug pulls off his

* Oberon's Vision.
† I am indebted for this suggestion to Mr. Arthur Hildon Nations, of Midland, Texas.

lion's mask and explains that he is not a lion but only Snug the Joiner.

The visual images in Oberon's speech do indeed bear a striking resemblance to the descriptions by eye witnesses of scenes at Kenilworth. If their resemblance be accepted as grounds for assuming that Shakespeare was drawing an actual recollection of what he had seen, then it may be believed that in this speech he was drawing also on recollection of what he had heard.

Oberon gives the story of the flower he sends Puck to gather, and he begins the narration like this:

> That very time, I saw but thou couldst not
> Flying between the cold moon and the earth,
> Cupid alarmed, a certain aim he took
> At a fair vestal throned by the west
> And loosed his love shaft smartly from the bow
> As if to pierce an hundred thousand hearts.

The splendid hospitality at Kenilworth, a tribute of Lord Leicester's devotion, might be symbolized by Cupid's attempt to pierce the Vestal's heart; it was common knowledge that Leicester had long sought to marry the Queen, and had at least clothed the ambition in the guise of romantic love, and that the cold brilliance of the moon had quenched the shafts aimed by his desire; but the line "flying between the cold moon and the earth" is capable of a less obvious interpretation. Ten years later, John Lyly's courtly comedy *Endymion* made a flattering allegory of Leicester's passion; he and the Queen were represented as the shepherd Endymion and the Moon whom Endymion adored. But in Lyly's play Endymion is shown as entangled against his better nature in a base, earthly love; this figure, whom Lyly calls Tellus, the Earth, has been convincingly expounded as an image of Lady Sheffield. The Moon and the Earth represented Leicester's two loves in a play performed at Court nearly ten years before *A Midsummer Night's Dream* was written.

Oberon now describes the flower to Puck—the shaft, he said, missed the mark of the Queen's heart:

> Yet marked I where the bolt of Cupid fell,
> It fell upon a little western flower,
> Before milk-white, now purple with love's wound
> And maidens call it Love-in-Idleness.

Oberon's words: *I saw, but thou couldst not,* suggest that something secret had been going on to which ordinary people had not the clue.

And in the midst of the gaieties at Kenilworth, in the full tide of the ceremonious devotion, the sparkling entertainments, the boisterous merrymaking, the idyllic twilight interludes when music was played upon the waters of the mere, something did happen, suddenly; something which was overcome and lost sight of as the radiant tides of pleasure flowed over it, but which for a few hours had threatened the ruin of the whole extravaganza.

On the twelfth day of the Queen's visit, a Wednesday, arrangements had been made for her Majesty to go three miles off to Widgen Hall and sup there in a pavilion; but the Queen stayed within doors all day and would not come out to see "a ready device" that had been prepared "of goddesses and nymphs". And, said Laneham, "all this day was such constant talk and appearance of removing that I gave over my noting and hearkened after my horse". Meantime the poet Gascoigne, who was one of the men responsible for the revels, was given orders to prepare a *pièce d'occasion* at once. In this hastily put together interlude Sylvanus, the Man in the Woods, met the Queen on her return from hunting, declaring that there was nothing heard among the dwellers in the forest but weeping and lamenting, mourning and moan . . . "the which sudden change he plainly perceived to be for that they understood . . . that her Majesty would shortly and too suddenly depart out of this country". The climax of the piece was the appearance, to the strains of music, of Deep Desire from out an arbour, who begged that her Majesty would give her gracious consent—not to new favours, but only that he might be restored to his former happiness.

This hurried contrivance shows not only that there had been some cause of anger on the one hand, and considerable anxiety on the other; it also illustrates the practice of the playwright or entertainer of putting into dramatic form comments on the private concerns of their patrons; it rested with the former not to make themselves offensive through tactlessness or impertinence. On this occasion, it seems, the Queen accepted the apology, the denial, the tribute; the episode which had given rise to it, though, as Oberon said, it was concealed, may well have concerned Lady Essex. In Lyly's *Endymion* there is a character who appears to fill, in relation to the rest, the part enacted by Lady Essex in real life, although Lyly's version of her is of a most respectable and pure-minded lady, who, when asked somewhat sharply by Cynthia, the Moon, whether she is in love with Endymion, replies: "With his virtues, Madame." This character is called by Lyly "Floscula", the Little Flower. The Moon, the Earth and the Little

Flower are all identifiable in Endymion, and they all occur in one speech in *A Midsummer Night's Dream* in a passage of the play that seems to be firmly based on recollections of Kenilworth in 1575.

Lady Essex was connected with these events by a grimmer episode. Edward Arden of Park Hall, Warwickshire, was a man of independent character and good local standing; he had been High Sherriff of Warwickshire in 1574. Lord Leicester, to make the most glorious appearance he could, had required the neighbouring gentry to present themselves at the Kenilworth fêtes wearing his livery, the blue coat and the silver badge of the bear and ragged staff, which the players had asked to wear as a privilege. Most of the local gentry viewed it in the same light; the protection it conferred was thought very valuable; but Edward Arden indignantly refused, and Dugdale says he went out of his way to add offensive comments about the Earl's conduct "touching his private access to the Countess of Essex". Sir Richard Baker said bluntly: "Arden called him whore-master." Eight years later Arden was put to death for treason. The circumstances were horrible. Arden was a Catholic, so was his son-in-law, John Somerville, who lived with him, and the household included a resident priest named Hall who disguised himself by dressing as the gardener. Somerville was of low mental standard; he conceived the idea that it was his duty to murder Queen Elizabeth, and, since the Pope had said that anyone who did this should have absolution, it was not unnatural that Hall should encourage him. Arden had sat at table and heard them both talking about this project without checking them; he may well have thought Somerville too foolish to merit serious opposition. Somerville published his determination to go to London and shoot the Queen with his pistol, saying he hoped to see her head set upon a pole for she was a serpent and a viper. He had not gone far on the road when his babble caused his arrest. When he was put in the Tower he charged Arden and Hall with being his accomplices. All three were tried, convicted, and sentenced to the horrors of a traitor's death. Somerville hanged himself in his cell, Arden was hanged and quartered, but Hall, upon whose evidence Arden had been convicted, was pardoned. Bohun says: "Hall, the procurer of all this mischief, was preserved by the intercession of Leicester." Arden's lands escheated to the Crown, and in their disposal some of them were given to the Earl. It was to appear that no one was on safe ground who spoke slightingly of Leicester's liaison with Lady Essex during the great Earl's lifetime.

The Queen and her party, accompanied by Leicester, went on

from Kenilworth to Chartley in Staffordshire, where, in the absence
of the Earl of Essex in Ireland, Lady Essex acted as hostess. After the
to-do at Kenilworth this house party, with all three persons concerned
under one roof, must have been electric in its atmosphere, but it was
a measure of Leicester's powers that he had both persuaded the
Queen that she had no cause to be jealous of her cousin, and succeeded in controlling Lady Essex into noncommittal behaviour.

Five months after everyone's return to London, in December,
1575, the Spanish commissioner, de Guaras, wrote to Alva's secretary,
Zayas: "As the thing is publicly talked of in the streets, there can be
no harm in my writing openly about the great enmity between the
Earl of Leicester and the Earl of Essex, in consequence, it is said, of
the fact that while Essex was in Ireland his wife had two children by
Leicester. She is the daughter of Sir Francis Knollys, a near relative
of the Queen and a member of the Council, and great discord is
expected in consequence."*

Thus, as early as this, the rumour was abroad that Leicester had
fathered a child on Lady Essex. De Guaras had heard there were two,
and *Leicester's Commonwealth*, published eight years later, confirmed
this, saying that one child was made away with by abortion, and the
other brought up by Lady Chandos, the sister-in-Law of Lettice
Essex. As no mention of this daughter was made in Leicester's Will,
though he there made ample provision for his son by Lady Sheffield,
the child must presumably have died before him. There is no
evidence of the birth, or of the abortion, for *Leicester's Commonwealth*
cannot be regarded as such; but De Guaras' having heard the rumour
in December, 1575, gives some weight to its repetition in 1584.

* C.S.P. Spanish.

XVII

THE QUEEN'S FONDNESS for emeralds is suggested by the number of jewels she was given that contained them. Sir Christopher Hatton gave her a great emerald set in a gold flower; Lady Paget Carey gave her "two emeralds, pendant, for earrings, hanged in gold," on New Year's Day, 1576, Lord Leicester gave her a gold cross containing five great emeralds, with three pearls hanging from it.

Leicester's handsomeness was said to be impaired in his later years by floridness, a bald foreheard, white hair and increasing weight. A man of his height would carry off the last disadvantage better than many, and neither his physical nor his mental activity suffered, but in 1576, when he was forty-three, he was ordered by his physicians to take the baths and drink the waters of a spa. The treatment may have been meant for the effects of over-eating and hard living; as he spoke of a fever, it may have been recommended for his malaria also. In July, 1576, he went to Buxton, and this he did for three years running, while the crisis in his matrimonial affairs during those very years showed how fascinating he still was to women, with his physical ascendancy, his mature handsomeness, his manner "at once great and engaging".*

Buxton Spa was on the Derbyshire property of Lord Shrewsbury, who had built a bath house there to enclose the waters of St. Ann's Spring, and had put up a row of houses where bathers could take lodgings.

William Turner, in the third part of his herbal, *Of the Nature and Properties of Baths*, gave a fair idea of how the patient was treated. To begin with, said Turner: "Ye must at no time go into the bath except ye have been at the stool, either by nature or craft." Furthermore, you should go in on an empty stomach; but if this is found too taxing, you may take a little bread steeped in barberry or currant juice, or a little syrup made of these fruit juices, or two spoonfuls of raisins soaked in wine and water, or a few stewed prunes. While

* James Dark, *Memoirs of Robert Dudley*, 1706 (a version of *Leicester's Commonwealth*).

in the bath you must take nothing unless you feel faint and require a stimulant, but you should use your sense about this. "Let no man tarry in the bath so long till he be faint or weak, but let him come out before that time." He should take "reasonable" sleeps during the day, and moderate walking exercise, "and all the time a man is in the bath he must keep himself chaste from all women". At home again, let him maintain the improvement; "beware of surfeiting in any wise, and of anger, and of too much study or carefulness".

When Leicester had returned from the bath at Buxton he found himself, in August, 1576, the object of a stern remonstrance. Thomas Wood, a Puritan, was not in orders, but he engaged in the weekly meetings known as "prophesyings", "a most fruitful and comfortable exercise" which took the form of "exercises of interpretation of the scriptures" and spiritual admonition of members. Wood was on intimate terms with Lord Warwick and Lord Leicester; he had been with the former at Havre in 1562, and on the return of the army to England he was the first man to bring Leicester news of his brother's wounded leg. Wood was now a farmer in Leicestershire, a county where Puritans enjoyed the protection of Lord Huntingdon.

"Prophesyings" were regarded by Elizabeth with suspicion and indignation, since the underlying conception of extreme Puritanism was utterly disruptive of the Anglican Church; the Puritans wanting to weed out of church ceremonial and church government everything for which they could not discover warrant in Holy Scripture. Meetings, therefore, which were held for "exercises in interpretation of the scriptures" were something which the Queen was not prepared to tolerate. Archbishop Parker had forbidden the prophesyings himself two years before, but they had flourished just the same. In 1576 a particularly flagrant case of the comfortable exercise was found going on at Southam in Warwickshire. The Queen drew Leicester's attention to it and told him she would not have it; these excesses must be restrained or the meetings put down altogether.

It seems that Leicester, and other members of the Privy Council, made a move to control the Southam Puritans in their own interests so that their prophesyings should not be summarily extinguished; but Leicester himself took no active part; he said he knew nothing about the Southam meetings, either bad or good. Wood, however, up in Leicestershire, heard of the proceedings and assumed that Leicester, as the agent of the ungodly, had destroyed the Southam prophesyings in person. He at once wrote a letter of stern rebuke on this subject, and while he was about it, he said, he would refer to "other bruits, very dishonourable and ungodly" about Lord Leicester's conduct. He would not write them down; he had wanted to speak to Leicester about them at Kenilworth last year "if opportunity had served". Since these bruits in all probability concerned Leicester's liaisons with Lady Sheffield and Lady Essex, it was small wonder that, in the middle of a house-party given for the Queen, opportunity had not served to make them the subject of a godly admonition.

Wood enclosed his letter to Leicester, unsealed, in one to Warwick, so that Lord Warwick might read it before sending it on. "It is plain, and peradventure may be thought too plain," Wood said, but if the part touching Lord Leicester's ungodly life were as true as the part about Southam, then Leicester had not much time to repent, God's judgments on him would be so speedy.

Lord Warwick replied on August 16th. He said Wood was altogether mistaken as to what his brother had done at Southam and was grossly unfair to him. "I cannot a little marvel," he said, "that you or any other will so lightly condemn him upon every slight report, who hath done so great good among you as he has done . . . Assuredly, Thomas, you did well in writing that they came to you as reports, and that you hoped they were not true, yet I must advise you as a friend somewhat to qualify your affection from henceforth and not to write after so vehement a manner as that a man may rather judge you believe it than otherwise." As for the other matter, Lord Warwick would not comment on it since Wood had not said what it was; but he wrote: "I hope you shall find the one as true as the other, although I must needs confess we be all flesh and blood and frail of nature and therefor to be reformed."

Leicester's own reply, in a letter of over three thousand words, defended himself, rehearsed what he had done for the Puritan party, and told Wood exactly what he thought of the unChristian spirit animating Puritan society at that time, of which he considered Wood's letter a fine example. "There is no man I know in this realm, of one calling or other, that hath showed a better mind to the furthering of true religion than I have done, even from the first day of her Majesty's reign to this." When Puritan clergy were in trouble for refusing to wear vestments, "who did more for them, both at the Bishop's hands and at the Prince's? . . . I defy their worst, for my conscience doth witness the contrary." He reminded Wood of how he had employed the patronage that Elizabeth's accession had put into his hands. "Look at all the bishops . . . that I have commended to that dignity since my credit any way served . . . Look at all the deans ... Look into the University of Oxford likewise, whereof I am Chancellor. .... I have manifest wrong," he exclaimed, "to be thus charged, to be a slider or a faller from the Gospel or I cannot tell what." He said: "I take Almighty God to my record I never altered my mind or thought from my youth touching my religion, and you know I was ever from my cradle brought up in it." (He had twice offered to hand over the government of the country to Spain and to see Catholicism forcibly reimposed, if Philip would help him to Elizabeth's hand; but so his father Northumberland, after his persecution of the Catholic Church and his attempt to exclude Mary Tudor, had declared that he had always been a Catholic at heart.) Leicester asseverated, reverting to the matter several times over, that he had not attempted to suppress the Southam exercises, he had merely, for their own sakes, associated himself with a warning to them. Of exercises as such he had always approved. As regards the matter of his ungodly life: "I will not justify myself for being a sinner of flesh and blood as others be. And besides, I stand on the top of a hill where I know the smallest slip seemeth a fall. But I will not excuse myself. I may fall many ways and have more witnesses thereof than many others who perhaps be no saints neither, yet their faults less noted, though some ways greater than mine." And he made a fine riposte to Wood's censures: "I never saw or knew in my life more envy stirring, and less charity used, every man glad to hear the worst, to think the worst, or to believe the worst of his neighbour, which be very uncomfortable fruits of our profession."*

The remarkable aspect of the letters is that neither Warwick nor Leicester objected to Wood's admonitory tone; they merely said that in this instance his charges were unjust. Leicester denied that he had given the weight of his influence towards putting down the Southam prophesyings, and as to his private life, he said it was no worse than that of many other people who escaped censure altogether; but neither he nor Warwick adopted the view that it was gross presumption on Wood's part to take Leicester to task at all. It was indeed clear from the tone of Leicester's reply that he valued Wood's good opinion; he eagerly justified himself against the latter's accusations, and though he blamed him as a fellow Christian for a lack of Christian charity, he did not show any anger or resentment against Wood's treatment of himself as a nobleman. Leicester was born in 1533, so, if he had indeed been taught the Reformed religion from his

---

* Letters of Thomas Wood, Puritan, 1566-1577, *Bulletin of the Institute of Historical Research*, Special Supplement, No. 5, November 1960.

cradle the Duke of Northumberland's household was a Protestant one nearly fifteen years before the death of Henry VIII. At all events, Leicester had thoroughly accepted the Puritan discipline, which allowed one of the godly, though he were not in orders, to admonish any backslider, even among the highest in the land.

In September, 1576, the Earl of Essex died at Dublin. His death was apparently due to dysentery, a disease whose symptoms were consistent with those of acute poisoning, and the inevitable inference was drawn: in the mournful procession of Lady Dudley and Lord Sheffield, Lord Essex, it was declared, had now made a third. A post-mortem was performed, and no trace of poison was discovered, but the truth was hopelessly outdistanced by the rumour. This would have flourished in any case, but, as Camden said, the suspicion of poisoning was the more readily believed, "because Leicester so quickly afterwards abandoned Douglas Sheffield by whom he had a son (whether she was his wife or paramour I will not say)".

Leicester had declared in writing that he never would marry Lady Sheffield; whether he had made a pretence of doing so remained for ever open to doubt. What was not in doubt was that he wanted to marry Lettice Knollys.

According to Lady Sheffield's deposition, when the Court was at Greenwich he came to her in the Arbour, and there asked her "to disavow the marriage". The truth or otherwise of this statement was, of course, of pivotal importance; if Lord Leicester used these words, her claim was proved to the hilt. At all events, he told her that he wanted the connection dissolved whatever it were, and for her connivance he offered her, she said, one thousand pounds down and an income of seven hundred pounds a year. Lady Sheffield refused the suggestion passionately; Leicester, according to her, became furiously angry in his turn; he swore that "he would never come at her again", and that she should not receive one penny of support from him thereafter.

The question of whether a man in Leicester's position would dare to contract a bigamous marriage was not then to be decided quite so readily as such a matter would be now. Bigamy was not a felony; it was one of the misdemeanours dealt with in the ecclesiastical courts, and, though it was thought reprehensible, it did not carry the modern stigma of a crime punishable with a sentence in gaol. Leicester's physician, Dr. Julio, had three years before married a woman who already had a husband. He was summoned before the Bishop of London in 1573, but means were found of getting the hearing of the case postponed. The Master of the Rolls took a hand, and Dr. Julio indignantly petitioned Lord Burleigh "that he might not any more be disturbed by that powerful, crafty man". The case was spun out for three years, but in 1576 the Puritan Dr. Grindal was appointed Archbishop of Canterbury. He tried this outstanding case immediately, and gave a decision against Dr. Julio.

Grindal was instructed by the Queen that he must put down the comfortable exercise of prophesying; no more were these meetings to threaten the Church of England as by law established, once a week. Grindal told the Queen he approved of the prophesyings and his conscience would not allow him to suppress them, whereupon in 1577 he was suspended from his office. The grounds for the Queen's disapproval were clear, and it was plain, too, that Grindal's policy was one with which Leicester had long been associated; but such was the latter's vulnerability to rumour and scandal, it was widely repeated and believed that Leicester had procured the Archbishop's disgrace because of the sentence given against Dr. Julio.

XVIII

IN 1577 a charming book was dedicated to Leicester, called *Flowers of Epigrams*, a collection of verses made by Timothy Kendall, who repeated the universal praise of Leicester as a patron. "Your courteous nature doth minister encouragement to presume," he said. "Who knoweth not that your honour is a special patron of learning and learned men?" The hardness of life during the winter months made poets as a rule treat cold, snow and ice as a matter of horror or at best of gruesome comedy.* *Flowers of Epigrams* contained what was, for its time, an extremely rare instance of a bright and lovely snow scene, in a verse written "of certain fair Maidens playing in the Snow" by "the late Bishop of Norwich". It ran:

> *You virgins, fairer than the snow*
> *With which you sport and play,*
> *The snow is white and you are bright;*
> *Now mark what I shall say.*
> *The snow betwixt your fingers fades*
> *And melteth quite away.*
> *So glittering gleams of beauty's beams*
> *In time shall soon decay.*

In February, 1577, the Sidneys lost their elder daughter Ambrosia, called after her uncle Warwick. The Queen wrote a very sympathetic letter to Sir Henry Sidney, and offered, if the parents would like it, to have their younger daughter, the fourteen-year-old Mary, at Court, "whom . . . if you will send her to us before Easter, or when you shall think good, assure yourself that we will have a special care of her". The offer was gratefully accepted; Mary Sidney came to Court, and within the year a splendid marriage was arranged for her. William Herbert, the formidable first Earl of Pembroke, who had always been Leicester's friend, had died in 1570, and his son Henry Herbert was now Earl. He was forty-two, but it was not thought inappropriate that he should take for his third wife a girl just fifteen.

* Cp. "When icicles hang by the wall".

Sir Henry was highly elated, and ascribed this grand connection to the influence of his brother-in-law; "which great honour to me, my mean lineage and kin, I attribute to my match in your noble house". The marriage was indeed a great one. Lord Pembroke was very rich. His town house was Baynard's Castle, while his great country seat was Wilton in Wiltshire. The very youthful Countess does not seem to have been made unhappy by the difference between her own and her husband's ages, while her situation gave her many compensating advantages. Seven years younger than her brother Philip, she was said to be astonishingly like him; in their youthful portraits, her serious girl's face and his gentle boy's one could be exchanged without remark, Aubrey said: "She had a pretty sharp-oval face. Her hair was of a reddish yellow." Philip, he said, was "extremely beautiful. He much resembled his sister but his hair was not red, but a little inclining, viz., a dark amber colour." The wedding was held in April, and in May Leicester went down to visit his niece at Wilton.

So young a bride needed the society of her family, and she made the great house a paradise for her relations. In 1580 Sir Henry Sidney, then Lord President of Ireland, stayed at Wilton so long, the Queen sent a message saying she would be glad to hear that he had returned to the scene of his duties. The relation to whom the house meant most, however, was the Countess's brother Philip. From a tormenting passion for Penelope Rich, from the false, brilliant, cruel world of the Court, at which he began to feel the poet's sickness, he took refuge in the beautiful house, the serenity of its woods, and the society of a young sister by whom he was profoundly admired and most dearly loved. To amuse her he began to write the elaborate and well-nigh endless romance which became known as *The Countess of Pembroke's Arcadia*. "You desired me to do it," he wrote, "and your desire to my heart is an absolute commandment. Now it is done, only for you, only to you . . . Your dear self can best witness the manner, being done in loose sheets of paper, most of it in your presence."

The work carries in its meandering stream uncounted charms, one of these being its treasury of contemporary detail. It confirms, parenthetically, the craze for black and white that marked the late seventies and early eighties. Black embroidery on white linen or cambric was immensely fashionable, and the Queen herself was given handkerchiefs, smocks, coifs, even pillow-cases and sheets embroidered in black silk, often with the addition of gold and silver thread. The pure vegetable dyes, and the gold and silver wire twisted round silk thread, made the objects washable as rags. In 1577 the Queen was greeted on her progress in Suffolk by two hundred Suffolk squires, the young bachelors in white velvet, their elders in black velvet. In Book I of *Arcadia*, the protagonists encounter "a coach drawn by four milk white horses, furnished all in black, with a blackamour boy on every horse, they all apparelled in white, the coach itself very richly furnished in black and white".

In June Leicester went again to Buxton; Warwick accompanied him, and Pembroke joined them a little later. Leicester wrote to Burleigh, saying the treatment was doing them a great deal of good. "We observe our physician's orders diligently and obediently, and to say truth there is no pain or penance in it but great pleasure both in drinking and bathing in the water." If Burleigh came himself, Leicester advised him to bring the smallest retinue possible. The ever present menace of smells from a sanitary system without drainage required the utmost prevision and care to keep it under. "The house is so little," Leicester said, "a few fills it, and hard then to keep sweet." However, the Shrewsburies had done what they could to make the lodging comfortable: "My Lord and Lady Shrewsbury have dealt nobly with us every way."[1] The sarcastic letter which the Queen wrote to Lord Shrewsbury about this visit suggested that, though nothing had as yet emerged about Lord Leicester's marrying, she was inclined to treat him with a cat-like teasing that looked like irritation rather than gaiety. With a glance at Leicester's fondness for good fare and his increasing weight, she said his daily ration should not be more than two ounces of meat and the twentieth part of a pint of wine at dinner, "and as much of St. Ann's sacred water as he listeth to drink". On festival days he might have "the shoulder of a wren, and for his supper a leg of the same, beside his ordinary ounces". Lord Warwick should be allowed the same diet, except that as he was stouter than Leicester he had better omit the wren's leg, "for that light supper agreeth best with the rules of physic".[2]

The previous year Leicester had bought and largely rebuilt a house in Essex; it had been a bleak property known as Naked Haw Hall. He made it a long building with lofty windows, five gables in the roof, and a gabled porch projecting upon pillars. He called it Wanstead, the White House. It was habitable by 1577, and in that August he wrote to Walsingham from it: "I am loth to trouble you with the whole discovery that passed last night between her Majesty and me, upon the discussion of your letter." Walsingham wanted vigorous aid given to the Huguenots, by means of employing Duke Casimir to bring a mercenary army to their assistance. According to

Leicester, the Queen was now sorry she had not accorded this. "She is now in a mind to repair the oversight." Now the question would arise, how to find the money quickly enough to serve Casimir's turn? Leicester said, "he could only think of two plans, either by borrowing from her own merchants at Hamburg or Frankfort", or by calling in the sum she had already lent the Netherlands states. "I think she will agree to either, but the latter soonest. . . . In haste and in bed this Friday morning."[1]

William Davison, the English agent resident at Antwerp, was a confidante of Leicester's and executed many commissions for him. On September 28th, 1577, Leicester wrote to him: "Many thanks for all you have done and daily do for me . . . I am glad to find your service so agreeable not only to those there, but her Majesty here conceiving so good an opinion of you that you have cause to rejoice." Leicester seldom seemed able to give the time to writing his letters comfortably. "I know not if this letter hang together, being written at hasty fit. I leave it to your discretion to understand, and commit you to the Lord."[2]

As early as 1577, Leicester was recognized as one whose influence was used in the direction of persuading the Queen to send help to the Netherlands in their struggle with Spain. The matter was one of the utmost difficulty for Elizabeth to consider. The expense of such a measure would almost cripple her, and yet that was not the worst; intervention might so incense the King of Spain that he would declare war upon her and decide to suspend operations against the Netherlands until he had crushed England. On the other hand, if the Dutch resistance collapsed, England would be his next objective; therefore it was essential to England to support the Dutch, as far as this could be done without attracting full-scale reprisals. The Queen had already lent the States money; in 1579, she advanced them the very large sum of £50,000 in money of the time; but the great William of Orange, who was organizing the revolt with almost superhuman patience, courage and ability, was anxious that England should declare herself unequivocally as his ally, and he regarded Leicester as the means to work upon the English Queen to this end. Davison wrote to Leicester in October that the Prince of Orange greatly wished that he should come over to help them with his influence and advice; but at the same time Orange would not wish him to be absent from the English Court, as he was sure that Leicester's influence there was all upon their side. Orange would like him to come over for a short time to put things in order, "and to bring with you some such qualified person, as in case you should be revoked, might be fit to take charge". Davison had suggested as a substitute Lord Warwick or Mr. Philip Sidney. Either would be acceptable to the Prince of Orange, "but he would have all referred to your own discretion".[1] Such words from the great Stadtholder, the hero of the Netherlands revolt, were incense to Leicester.

His passion for self-advancement, and the care he took to fling his net so wide that nothing might escape him, were unexpectedly illustrated at the end of this year. Though he had two connections already, at the end of 1577 he offered his hand to the now widowed Princess Cecilia, and his letter was supported by one from Queen Elizabeth advocating his suit. That Leicester, with his anxiety to connect himself with royal blood, should have proposed to the Princess, whom he remembered as beautiful and ebullient from twelve years ago, was not surprising, except in view of his other commitments; but that Elizabeth should have encouraged his suit is at first sight astonishing, and suggests that she had once been seriously prepared to see him married to Mary Queen of Scots. A match of diplomatic character, arranged by herself, with a woman he had never seen, or with one whom he had not seen for twelve years, was of course in a different category from a secret marriage with a woman for whom he entertained an engrossing passion.

On receipt of the letters from England, Cecilia wrote for advice to her brother Karl, who had succeeded Eric upon the throne of Sweden. The King wrote in January, 1578: "We have received our beloved sister's letter and perceived from that, what the Queen of England has desired of our beloved sister on the Earl of Leicester's part, in which matter our beloved sister has asked our counsel and advice." All the King could say was, he should have thought that after everything she had suffered in England, his sister would not want to go there again.* This letter must have confirmed the Princess's own views; was she to come back and try conclusions with her former lady-in-waiting, the Marchioness of Northampton? She declined the Earl of Leicester's proposal.

It had been made at the end of 1577. By September, 1578, Lady Essex was in an advanced state of pregnancy. Lady Sheffield had been disposed of by sheer weight of personality; to disembarrass himself of the sensual, scheming Lettice, who had an egotism as tough and rampant as his own, would have been a very different proposition;

* Fridolf Ödberg, *Om Princessan Cecilia Wasa.*

and as her father, Sir Francis Knollys, was living, a connection of the Queen's, a Privy Councillor, Treasurer of the Royal Household, and a Puritan, had it turned out that Leicester had given her a child, but could not marry her because he was betrothed to a Princess of Sweden, the situation would have produced a very general unpleasantness. There was plenty of this in store as it was.

XIX

On new year's day, 1578, Lord Leicester gave the Queen an enamelled gold necklace, set with diamonds, rubies and opals. Lady Essex gave her ruffs of lawn edged with seed pearl, and two of the fashionable wigs, one yellow and one black. There was no description, and no portrait, of the Queen wearing any coloured wig except a red one, but periwigs were made in all colours,* and it was reasonable to offer her a flaxen and a black, to see if she would like either of them.

Early in the year Duke Casimir came to England to find out if the Queen would subsidize him to help the Netherland States with his troops, and in February Leicester took him up to Oxford, where, as the Chancellor's guest, Casimir could witness his friend's grandeur. Leicester was perpetually urging the Queen to intervene openly in the Netherlands; so was Sir Francis Walsingham. Elizabeth was reluctant and afraid, and Lord Burleigh shared her view. The two of them were in a different alignment from Walsingham and his supporters. Walsingham was a man of extraordinary, of unequalled, abilities in the organization of an intelligence service; he could conduct an embassy with clear-headedness, force and tact; but as a statesman he was limited by his religious prejudices. He thought creed came before nationality. He wanted to see England joined with Scots Presbyterians, French Huguenots, German Lutherans and the resisting Netherlanders, to assail the Spanish-Catholic domination in Europe Such a policy had much to commend it, but it carried very heavy risks. Walsingham was prepared to take them because he thought righteousness demanded it; the Queen refused to take them because she though expediency forbade it. Walsingham said: "What juster cause can a Prince that maketh profession of the Gospel have, to enter into war, than when he seeth confederacies made for rooting out of the religion he professeth?" Elizabeth's reply might have been given in the words of the collect appointed for the Communion Service, in which it was

* See *Two Gentlemen of Verona*, IV 4.

8—E & L

prayed on her behalf that she might "study to preserve Thy people committed to her charge, in wealth, peace and godliness".

Leicester found, by March, that she was not going, for the time at least, to send a force to the aid of William of Orange. He wrote to Davison: "I have been so troubled by the alterations of resolutions that I had no mind to write . . . For my own part it cannot but grieve me, putting myself forward as I did. I have done my best and bettermost to get it forward, as I thought safest for her Majesty, and God knows how little I sought any jot of my own particular."[1]

In May, Gilbert Talbot wrote to his father in the perennial idiom used by friends behind each other's backs: "My Lord of Leicester threateneth to come to Buxton this summer." Before going to Buxton, however, Leicester gave a house-party for the Queen at Wanstead. This house, like Leicester House, had rooms appropriated to particular guests. The Queen would hardly stay the night at Leicester House, which was within sight of Whitehall Palace, but at Wanstead, six miles out of London, a room was known as the Queen's Chamber. The bed in this room was hung with cloth of tinsel; the bed in my Lord's Chamber had gilded posts, curtains of yellow damask and a quilt of straw-coloured taffeta. There were besides the Red Chamber, the Green Chamber, the second Red Chamber, the Corner Chamber; there was the usual very long room known as the Gallery, a Withdrawing Chamber, and the Chamber next the Gallery. There was also a hot house, for taking baths.[2]

The party for the Queen was given in May, and Philip Sidney had written a masque to be played out of doors called *The Lady of the May*. As in many entertainments devised for her, the Queen was drawn into the action; at its close she was entreated to give her voice for one or other of the suitors of the Lady of the May. This lovely creature, a boy in girl's clothes, exclaimed that though she herself was the Lady of the May, she submitted herself to the Queen; not because of the latter's richness of apparel, for May's flowers were as fair as that; "Nor", she said, "because a certain gentleman hereby seeks to do you all the honour he can in his house"; but because of something in the Queen herself, "the beautifullest lady these woods have ever received". The words are empty compliment, but some of the lines give a curiously evocative impression of Elizabeth.

> Your state is great, your greatness is our shield,
> Your face hurts oft, yet still it doth delight.

The farewell of the Lady was made in the words of a poet: she took herself away with a reverence, saying: "I will wish you good night, praying to God . . . that as hitherto it has excellently done, so henceforward the flourishing of May may long remain in you and with you."

Such a holiday was a brief respite from heavy cares. Elizabeth had now allowed the marriage negotiations with the Duke of Alençon, which had been brought forward when those with the Duke of Anjou had lapsed, to be renewed, for a very subtle diplomatic purpose. The Spanish onslaught on the Netherlands States was being so courageously and doggedly resisted that the defence was no longer assumed to be hopeless; the French thought that, as the native resistance was so strong, a moderate assistance on their part might gain them the whole terrain as a sphere of influence, a prospect which alarmed the English almost as much as that of a complete Spanish domination. The Duke of Alençon, always at odds with his brother Anjou, who had succeeded Charles IX as Henry III, thought that he saw an opening for himself as Protector of the Netherlands. The question deeply engaging the Queen and Lord Burleigh was whether Alençon would enter the scene as an emissary of the King of France or in an independent capacity. If he could be encouraged and helped to do so independently of France, this might prove the best means open to England to avoid the menace of a French or Spanish control of the Netherlands. This was the object of Elizabeth's throwing out before Alençon's eyes the glittering possibility of his becoming King of England by a marriage with herself. It was essential to the success of the negotiations that Alençon should believe them to be sincere; this he would not do if the Queen were surrounded by able councillors all of whom knew that the whole process was a sham. She took none of them into her confidence; they all believed that, though the inherent difficulties might prove insuperable, the Queen personally was willing, even eager for the match.

That she was able to make this impression was owing to her obsessive fondness for being flattered and wooed, a fondness that was a part of her very being. Nature intensifies the faculties she is about to take away, and Elizabeth, at the age of forty-five, played her favourite game with a madder intensity than she had ever shown before. When the negotiations were halting, her councillors told her that if she wanted to withdraw they would take the blame upon themselves, and the Queen wept, asking why she, alone, was to be denied marriage and children, so great was the conviction with which she played the rôle. Yet every near approach to success was checked by herself; she spun her delusive webs until even the French King's eagerness for the alliance was exhausted, and he threatened to sever diplomatic relations. On Alençon's departure she took leave of him in an access of sensibility and grief, and at the same time she made a point of showing him and his train the dockyards at Chatham, where the sight of the ships under construction made the Frenchmen gasp. All this, seen in the perspective of the Queen's previous conduct, in which the entertaining of proposals of marriage, carried on publicly with all the apparatus of letters, presents, embassies, interviews and discussions in Council, went on at the same time that the Queen was making involuntary exclamations—that she wanted her tombstone to say only that she had lived and died a virgin, that the very idea of marriage made her feel as if someone were tearing the heart out of her breast, to say nothing of such remarks as that a pregnant woman was worse than a sow—it all carried out the impression she had given throughout her life, of a sickening loathing and a fierce resistance. It calls to mind what Mauvissière said she told him, apropos a marriage with one of her subjects: "*Si elle pensait que l'un de ses sujets fut si présomptueux que de la désirer pour femme elle ne le voudrait jamais voir, mais contre son naturel, qui ne tenait rien de la cruauté, elle lui ferait un mauvais tour.*"

Don Bernardino de Mendoza was now the Spanish Ambassador, and, like all his predecessors except the charming de Silva, was hostile to Elizabeth. When he was accredited in March 1578, there had been no Spanish Ambassador in England for six years, since de Spes had been summarily dismissed when his doings in the Ridolfi Plot had been discovered. It was not easy for Mendoza to pick up the threads immediately, and he was inclined to think that a conspiracy was hatching where there was no such thing. On June 3rd he wrote to his Court: "They say the Earl of Leicester will leave this week for Buxton near Derby, ostensibly to take the baths there; the place being only twelve miles distant from where the Queen of Scotland is, great suspicion here is engendered about his going, as Walsingham who is his familiar spirit will be away also, and the abandonment of business by both of them at the same time seems to prove that the matter they have in hand must be one of great importance. All the Council are extremely jealous and distrustful as the design, whatever it be, is kept closely between the Queen and Leicester. Some even say she is the one being deceived." The only matters of indisputable fact here were that Leicester was going to take the baths at Buxton, the Queen of Scots was at Sheffield, and Walsingham, accompanied by Lord Cobham, was about to go to the Netherlands to try to discover on what terms the Duke of Alençon was to adopt their cause. Mendoza added a few words about the notorious Dr. Julio. He was usually said to be an Italian, but Mendoza thought he was a Morisco. Julio, he said, spoke eight or nine languages beautifully and was in a position of the greatest confidence. He spent hours every day shut up with Leicester and Walsingham, and sometimes with the Queen.

On June 13th Lady Shrewsbury was in London to see the Queen, probably, Mendoza thought, on some matter connected with Mary Queen of Scots. Leicester had long been on most friendly terms with Lord Shrewsbury; the Shrewsburys had been very kind and hospitable to Lord Warwick and himself at Buxton, and Lady Shrewsbury had the additional claim on his services that she was now grandmother to one of the heiresses to the English throne. Lord Leicester, going north, met the Countess as she was coming to London, and when he went on to Buxton she came south and was put up, in his absence, at Leicester House.

While he was at Buxton he received a most interesting confidential letter from Sir Christopher Hatton. The latter began by saying that the Queen did not like the reports she heard of Leicester's health, and Hatton said: "She much misliked that your Lordship had not Julio with you." Hatton thought she would probably send Julio up to Derbyshire, "for in truth this matter troubleth her". But something else troubled the Queen. She knew nothing of Leicester's plans with regard to Lady Essex, but her acute intelligence, directed to a matter in which she was painfully interested, could not but give her some premonitions and foreshadowings. "Since your Lordship's departure," Hatton went on, "the Queen is found in continual and great melancholy, the cause whereof I can but guess at . . . She dreameth of marriage that might seem injurious to her", and, said Hatton, talked to him as if *he* were the man involved. He had tried to reason with her and to soothe her. "I defend that no man can tie himself to such inconvenience as not to marry . . . except by mutual consent on both parts." Then came the warning: "My Lord, *I* am not the man that should thus suddenly marry, for God knoweth I never meant it . . . I think you shall hear more of the matter." Someone, Hatton thought, had aroused the Queen's suspicions. "I fear it will be found some evil practice."* Meanwhile Leicester wrote to Walsingham from Buxton on June 24th. "I find great good in this bath already for the swelling you felt in my leg, not by drinking but

* Dudley MSS., Longleat, quoted by E. M. Tenison, *Elizabethan England*, Vol. III.

by going into the bath . . . I would fain write to Lord Cobham, but I am pulled away from this, being forbidden to write much, as this day I have to her Majesty and others."[1]

To Hatton, whose passion for the Queen had once seemed to threaten his own influence, Leicester wrote about her quite differently from the way in which he wrote about her to anybody else. On July 9th he sent Hatton a letter saying: "I hope ere long to be with you, to enjoy that blessed sight I have long been kept from. A few of these days seem many years, and I think I shall feel a worse grief ere I go so far for a remedy again. I thank God I have found great ease by this bath." He had heard from Hatton that the Queen had paused at Wanstead when travelling in the neighbourhood. He lamented that her "Eyes" had not been there to welcome to her; had he known in time of her coming, he would have bolted away from the sacred spring! "St. Ann should have had a short farewell." Dr. Bailey, who had accompanied him, was keeping him in hand, however, "especially because the late hot weather has returned again"; but Leicester meant to get home as soon as he could. "I long to hear of Mr. Walsingham's news; by this time you have it all, I am sure."[2]

Leicester came south very soon after his letter. He joined the Queen's summer progress, and on July 27th the royal party had reached Audley End, on the borders of Essex and Cambridgeshire, where she was received at Lord de Walden's house, Audley House, a converted abbey, standing in a great park.

The Vice-Chancellor of Cambridge University and the Masters of the Colleges had come out from Cambridge to greet the Queen, and the Vice-Chancellor gave her a Greek New Testament bound in crimson velvet and a pair of gloves, deliciously scented, wrapped in paper. Someone was deputed to hold the book, the Queen took the smaller packet herself, and the Vice-Chancellor began a Latin oration. As the Queen stood listening, "it fortuned that the paper in which the gloves were folded, opened". Her eyes catching "the beauty of the said gloves", she drew them half-way on her hands, "smelling to them". Inhaling the scent helped her to stand, almost exhausted as she was, listening to the oration. When it was finished she thanked them all heartily, but then, "alleging that she was weary, hot and faint after the journey, departed out of the chamber". Lord Burleigh attended her out of the room, and she sent him back with a courteous message to the members of the University.*

* Nichols, *Progresses of Queen Elizabeth*.

This visit was of special interest, for in the course of it a young scholar of Pembroke College was presented to the Queen. He had been brought to Lord Leicester's notice, and the latter was anxious that the Queen should see his protégé. "Is this your man?" the Queen asked him, as Edmund Spenser knelt before her.

Spenser was accompanied by the man who had introduced him to Leicester, his elder friend and mentor, Gabriel Harvey. The latter is famous for reading a part of *The Faerie Queene* and advising the poet not to go on with it; this, however, was because he thought Spenser's poetic capacity so distinguished that only Latin, or English quantitative verse, was worthy of it. Harvey himself wrote a collection of Latin verses to celebrate the Queen's visit to Audley End, which he called *Gratulationum Valdinensium*, the Joyful Welcome of Walden. The first section was dedicated to Elizabeth, the second to Lord Leicester, the third to Lord Burleigh; Lord Oxford, Sir Christopher Hatton and Mr. Philip Sidney divided the fourth between them. The verses to Leicester were, at this moment, had anyone but known it, peculiarly mis-timed. They said: "There is no one who does not assign royal honours to you, and expect to see a crown upon your head. The future is unknown, but everyone prays that you may become a royal bridegroom." In his verses about the Queen Harvey said that she gave him her hand to kiss and told him he looked like an Italian; he gave a glimpse of her departure:

> *Thus dost thou speak, and mount'st thy noble charger*
> *Through crowds, through seas of faces thou art borne,*
> *A mighty shout arose and pierced the sky:*
> *Long live the Queen! with welcomes and farewells.*

For Spenser the visit was the opening of intensely exciting prospects. By 1579 he was living at Leicester House, as secretary, messenger, protégé of the Earl, and accepted, though on a humble footing, as a member of the circle of Philip Sidney and his friends, whose interests were the reading, writing and discussing of poetry.

The Queen's progress continued through Cambridge, Suffolk and Norfolk. The yearly summer excursions fulfilled many purposes; they allowed the people to see her, always a means of strengthening loyalty and affection, and they gave great pleasure to the Queen herself. Bohun said she was especially fortunate in her weather, and that she loved the varied sights of wood, meadow, cornfield, flowers and fruit as she went about her kingdom. In this year, 1578, *A New Herbal or History of Plants* was dedicated to her by Henry Lyte of

Lytescary, wishing "our most dread and redoubted sovereign Lady Elizabeth . . . long life, perfect health, flourishing reign and prosperous success, to God's good pleasure, in all your most Royal affairs". The book speaks, among other English flowers, of "the March violet, the black or purple violet and the white. The sweet violet groweth under hedges and about the borders of fields and pastures; it is also set and planted in gardens." This flower, whose scent can be reproduced more truly than almost any other, was greatly used both for perfume and for confectionery. Platt gave recipes for violet fondant, "so shall your paste be both of the colour of the violet and of the smell of the violet"; and for "a most excellent syrup of violets, both for taste and tincture, clear, transparent and of the violet colour". He also said that one of the best scents for scenting gloves was made from violet, orange and lemon, "duly proportioned". Lyte described the hawthorne, so characteristic of English fields in early summer: "Sometimes a low bush, sometimes a tree. The boughs are set full of long, sharp, thorny prickles, the flowers be white and sweet-smelling . . . it flowereth in May." The white water-lily brought the influence of the cool depths in which it grew. A decoction of it was of use "against Venus or fleshly desires". A conserve made from the flower was "very good for hot, burning fevers and headaches; it causeth sweet and quiet sleep and putteth away all venerous dreams". Lyte noted many roses, calling their stamens "the yellow hair that grows in the midst of the rose". He described the enchanting wild-rose, with its variant, the sweet-briar or eglantine. The wild rose, with flowers, as Lyte said, either white or red, whose sprays and wreaths adorn the hedgerows in high summer, was one of Elizabeth's emblems. This fact was loyally commemorated by Lady Shrewsbury when she built Hardwick Hall. The plaster frieze of the Great Chamber shows the stags of the Cavendish arms and the Tudor rose, with the motto:

> The fragrance of the Eglantine
> We stags exalt to the divine!

And Philip Sidney's friend Fulke Greville, writing a verse about the Queen's combining in herself the Red and White Roses of Lancaster and York, gave in a few lines the essence of the power Elizabeth wielded over the people's hearts, by virtue of what she was and what she did:

> Under a throne I saw a Virgin sit,
> The Red and White Rose quartered in her face . . .

State in her eyes taught Order how to sit
And fix Confusion's unobserving race

The Queen came, in August, to Long Melford Hall in Suffolk, a red-brick mansion with turrets surmounted by domes occupying three sides of a court; showing the sort of fantastic gracefulness which Hall censured in his Chronicle, when he described the houses of the mid-sixteenth century "like midsummer pageants, with towers, turrets and chimney tops . . . for show and pleasure, betraying the vanity of men's minds." At this house-party the Queen was met by the Frenchman de Bocqueville and his train, who had come to begin courting in earnest for the Duke d'Alençon. During the progress, Leicester wrote to Walsingham: "It may be I do not give you light enough on our doings, so much as you would wish, but I assure you, you have as much as I can learn . . . For the matter now in hand of her marriage, no man can tell what to say, as yet she has imparted with no man, at least not with me, nor for aught I can learn with any other. In much haste, her Majesty ready to horse-back."[1]

The progress reached Norwich and began to retrace its steps and to return towards London, coming through a part of Cambridgeshire once again. From Monday, September 1st, till Wednesday before dinner, the Queen stayed with Lord North in his house at Kirtling, where, in the village, a public house called The Kirtling Queen, with a picture of Elizabeth on its sign, still commemorates this visit. Lord North was one of Lord Leicester's intimate friends, and Camden described him as "a person of great briskness and vivacity, with a hand and heart fit for a Prince". His house, in a remote, deeply wooded part of Cambridgeshire, had been nobly stocked for the Queen's reception. Preparations had been made of beer, ale, claret, sack, manchet bread, white bread, mutton and veal, and a variety of birds—geese, capons, turkeys, swans, mallards, cranes, snipes, plovers, pheasants, quails, curlews; of fish, including sturgeon, crayfish, crabs, oysters, turbots and anchovies; cheeses, and sweet things under the heading of "banqueting stuff". Lord North's incidental expenses included payments "to sundry persons labouring and taking pains about this business; charges of the banqueting house, the new kitchens and trimming up of chambers and other rooms, wax-lights and torches". To help, Leicester sent his own cooks to Kirtling, who were paid £4, and his own company of players, who received forty shillings. In return he was to call upon Lord North for an act of special friendship.[2]

The royal party left Kirtling on Wednesday, September 3rd, and a few days later Leicester withdrew from the progress and took his way back to Wanstead. He arrived on Monday, September 8th, and wrote from there to Walsingham on Wednesday. He had some very important business to prepare for at his own house.

In a deposition afterwards taken, Lord North* said that Lord Leicester, having been "very conversant with him for the past ten or twelve years", told him "there was nothing in this life he more desired than to be joined with some godly gentlewoman, with whom he might lead his life to the glory of God, the comfort of his soul, and to the faithful service of her Majesty, for whose sake he had hitherto forborne marriage, which long held him doubtful". The lady he had in mind was the Countess of Essex. Hearing him speak like this, Lord North "comforted his Lordship therein and heartened him thereunto". Therefore, on September 20th, 1578, Lord Leicester took Lord North with him when he went to his house at Wanstead for the night. North found there already the Earls of Warwick and Pembroke, Sir Francis Knollys and the Countess of Essex. After supper, Leicester told North "he meant to be married next morning, by leave of God, and therefor prayed Lord North to rise somewhat betimes for the purpose". This North did, and, being up, found the Earl "walking in the little gallery looking towards the garden". Leicester, saying he would fetch the Lords and Sir Francis Knollys, gave North his double-key, "praying him to go down and bring up thither by the privy way, Mr. Tindall, a chaplain of his Lordship's". North fetched Mr. Tindall, and he and the chaplain waited in the little gallery for the arrival of the others. Presently the bridal party came in. Mr. Tindall performed the ceremony, Sir Francis Knollys gave his daughter away, and the witnesses were Lord Warwick, Lord Pembroke, Lord North himself and Sir Francis Knollys. There was, half-present, another witness still. As Lord North "looked aside", he saw "Mr. Richard Knollys, brother to the Countess, stand in the door which came out of the Earl's chamber with his body half in the gallery and half out, who together with the persons before mentioned, both saw and heard the solemnity of the said marriage".

Three years afterwards, Mr. Tindall also made a deposition. He repeated the gist of the reasons Leicester had given him for wanting to be married, and they were the same as those related by Lord North. He then said the Earl had appointed him to attend at 7 o'clock the next day. "Between seven and eight of the clock next morning, being

* Collins, *Peerage*, Vol. IV.

Sunday, he was conveyed up by the Lord North into a little gallery at Wanstead House, opening upon the garden." Here came the gentlemen mentioned by Lord North, "and within a little while after this, the Countess of Essex herself, as he now remembers, in a loose gown", the dress worn, in an age of rigid corseting, either as a negligé or as the garment of a pregnant woman. Tindall then performed the marriage "with the free consent of them both". He repeats a second time the names of the witnesses, adding that of the gentleman half in, half out of the door, "one Mr. Richard Knollys, as he remembereth". This deposition, unusual in giving the names of the witnesses twice over, bore further testimony to the anxiety of the bride's father. Mr. Tindall wrote down at the end of his deposition a statement that at that time he was a full minister, that he had been ordained by the Reverend Father in God the Bishop of Peterborough in 1572, "for proof whereof he exhibited, at the time of his examination, his letters of orders, under the authentical seals of the said Bishop".[1]

Two days later, on September 23rd, the Queen reached the last stage of her progress, and this station was none other than Wanstead House. All trace of the early morning wedding had disappeared, as dew dries off the grass. Leicester feasted the company with a lavishness that was the theme of admiration, and the Queen returned to London, knowing no more than she had known already, with no more causes for uneasiness than those that had long agitated her. Leicester appeared secure—but his secret was known already to six people; of these, Warwick was his brother, Pembroke his nephew by marriage, and both Pembroke and North his great friends; but the number of confidants was dangerously high for a secret of so damaging a nature.

There was, of course, no reason why Leicester should not marry Lady Essex, supposing he were not married already to Lady Sheffield. He had the right to say to the Queen, and should have said to her: "I have given you every proof of my love except the one you would never allow me to give you. I want now to marry and have some children, and I am contracted to Lady Essex. If you dismiss me I shall have to leave you, but that will be because you wish it; my wish is to remain with you for ever, your devoted friend, admirer, companion and servant as I have always been." Had he said this, Elizabeth's anger would have been devastating but, as was proved by the event, it would in the end have worn itself out. Leicester, however, could not be absolutely sure that it would. Elizabeth might not be reconciled.

If she were not, and his career at Court were over, he could still live luxuriously with the woman of his choice, on the revenues the Queen had given him already; but this would go only a very little way towards satisfying him. Prestige, influence, power were the things he cared for above anything in the world. He would run the risk of losing them for ever, and, speaking candidly, Lady Essex was not worth it. By the time a woman is nearing the end of a second, perhaps even a third, pregnancy, the most exciting passage of an amour is over. Great willingness for marriage may remain, with affection and solid esteem, but not that goading instinct which will make a man of forty-five, who has a very great deal to lose, feel that all will be well lost. The reasons against his marrying, which Leicester had described to Lady Sheffield, were cogent still. He was no doubt more attached to Lady Essex than he had ever been to Lady Sheffield, for the former was much more highly-powered than her hapless rival; but he did not attempt to marry her till she was within a month or two of being brought to bed of his child, and then her father appeared to be taking a considerable part in the proceedings. Even Sir Francis Knollys could not get him to acknowledge the marriage publicly; Sir Francis had to be satisfied with taking every precaution to see that the ceremony was legally binding. Leicester must have known that concealment could not be indefinitely prolonged, but have thought, none the less, that any respite was worth having. The strength of his position was also its weakness: though he was perfectly adequate to the demands of the offices he filled, unlike Burleigh or Walsingham he was far from irreplaceable. He had a unique personal relationship with the Queen, because of all men he was the one she liked best to have near her; but if he were to become odious to her his posts could be ably filled by Ormonde, by Hatton, by Heneage, or half-a-dozen other men, eager to exert their considerable intelligence, their experience and their devotion in her service.

The realization of how swiftly and how completely he *might* lose his ascendancy was perhaps one of the motives behind the letter which, within a week of his marriage, he wrote to Lord Burleigh. The letter says he has never taken the step before of writing to complain of his treatment; now he seemed to feel that he could not afford even an appearance of any loss of standing with the man on whom the Queen placed her utmost reliance. The letter reproached Lord Burleigh because the latter, as chairman of a committee that sat to decide affairs of the Mint, had issued orders to the Mint without having them countersigned by all the commissioners. Leicester made this the occasion of a long and detailed statement of what he took to be Burleigh's attitude towards him. "I had more cause to think unkindness," he wrote, "to be in your Lordship's company all this summer as I was, and so often talked of these Mint matters, and would not acquaint me with your resolution, being joined as I was, in Commission . . . Either must I think it was for want of desire to confer with me, or some weak opinion conceived of my insufficiency to judge further in this cause . . . and yet, to none is my care and good will for the service of her Majesty better known than to your Lordship." Nevertheless, he said, "if I have not both long since and of late perceived your opinion better settled in others than in me, I could little perceive anything." Burleigh might think it strange of him to write like this, but, though he had never done so before, it was not for want of provocation. He recalled that he and Burleigh had been together in the Queen's service these twenty years. "What opinion you have indeed of me, I have, for these considerations alleged, somewhat in doubt, though I promise you I know no cause in the world in myself that I have given you, other than good . . . And surely, my Lord, where I profess, I will be found both a faithful and a just, honest friend."*

Having said his say and made his bid for sympathy and support, Lord Leicester appeared that autumn, as ever, in the centre of the Queen's circle. She twice postponed an audience for the French Ambassador, saying she had a pain in her cheek, but Mendoza heard that none the less she had been out to dine with Lord Leicester.

With much that was necessarily ambiguous in his conduct, Leicester sometimes gave utterance to some straightforward expression of decency. As Chancellor of the County Palatine of Chester, he wrote in this year to the Mayor and Justices of the city, reproaching them for the fact that, through a combination of neglect of legal obligation and sheer inhumanity, some prisoners in their gaol had died of starvation. He said: "It is very pitiful to hear of, that prisoners are dead of famine since the last Assize." He reminded the justices sternly that prisoners must be relieved, "at the leastwise as far as by the law you are bounden to relieve them".[1]

This humanity was strangely accompanied by a selfishness and ruthlessness which, in the public estimate of him, it could not offset. Among Leicester's numerous profitable appointments was that of Ranger of Snowden Forest, which meant that he exercised rights

* Conyers Read, *Lord Burleigh and Queen Elizabeth*.

over estates within the forest's boundaries. He hit upon the expedient of enlarging the limits of Snowden Forest to such an unheard-of extent that they took in lands in Caernarvon, Merioneth and even the Isle of Anglesea; for he read of a stag hunted in Merioneth by a king of past times, which stag had swum the Menai Straits, and, being killed upon the Isle, was said to be brought down "in our county of Merioneth". The freeholders, from whom Leicester now demanded exorbitant rents, banded together to resist him. Their case was tried before a jury, who, sitting to hear the case in the Earl's blue livery with the silver bear and ragged staff upon their sleeves, gave their verdict in his favour. But the victims had a powerful supporter. Sir Richard Bulkeley had estates in Cheshire and Beaumaris; he preferred his Welsh one and made it his home. Here he lived, a dignified local figure, prosperous, hospitable, honest and independent. He had, however, been a member of Elizabeth's household; this must have been when she was a Princess, for he was the same age as herself, and she said: "We brought him up from a boy." He had always been on affectionate terms with her, and of his loyalty she refused to entertain any suspicion. Sir Richard came to London; he had an interview with the Queen, and put the whole case before her, the mystical enlargement of Snowden Forest, the gross injury and insult of the demands for rent, the packed jury with the bear and ragged staff upon their sleeves. Elizabeth listened to it all, and in 1579 she granted a charter, confirming the abused freeholders "in quiet possession of their lands". Sir Richard returned to Beaumaris; he had delivered his neighbours, but he had not heard the last of Lord Leicester.*

*Pennant, *A Tour in Wales.*

XX

THE OPEN SECRET was still hidden from the Queen. On New Year's Day, 1579, Lord Warwick gave her "a very great topaz, set in gold enamelled, with eight pearls pendant", Lady Warwick a gold tooth pick, set with one large emerald and small diamonds and rubies. Lady Mary Sidney gave her a salt cellar of neo-classical form "resting on pillars" and made of lapis lazuli. Lord Leicester himself on this occasion gave the Queen several presents: a diamond and ruby clock, a pair of gold bodkins for the hair, set with diamond and ruby, and a set of fourteen larger and thirty-six smaller buttons, engraved with the bear and ragged staff and lover's knots, all set with diamonds and rubies. He had often placed his crest on something he gave the Queen, but this combination of it with lovers' knots on ornaments for her to wear had perhaps a particular significance in the year beginning in 1579. From the lady who was still known as Lady Essex the Queen received "a great chain of amber garnished with gold and pearl". The necklace cannot have been given in person, for this must have been almost the time of Lady Leicester's lying-in. That the Queen should not have heard of it, or of the terms on which Leicester stood with her cousin, was owing partly to the sparsely populated state of the country, the great houses widely separated from each other by unihabited landscape, and the slow, laborious means of communication—on horse-back, by horse-drawn coach or litter, by oars upon the water, impeded by weather, the state of the roads or the trackless down, and shortened by the hours of darkness, which divided journeys into stages between hospitable houses or country inns. It was said also that Leicester had taken great pains, "carrying her up and down the country" to keep her out of the Queen's way.

On January 5th Alençon's friend and confidential agent, Simier, arrived in London to make protestations of his master's ardour. The Queen found him so accomplished at the game, and he found her so elegant, distinguished and amusing, they were mutually charmed; and as the Queen thoroughly enjoyed the process of courtship, and she wanted the negotiations to wear an air of passionate sincerity, she and Simier became on such intimate terms that the Council as a whole believed that she would accept the French Prince if matters could be arranged. Leicester, and Hatton also, from being merely jealous and annoyed, became, as the year advanced, thoroughly uneasy and alarmed. Since, if the marriage took place, the English Parliament would view it as a hope of producing an heir, the Queen's doctors had had a consultation to decide whether she could expect to bear children if she married. The opinion of the majority was, that they saw no reason why she should not, and Burleigh, examining the matter with acute deliberation, made a memorandum based on this report. He began by saying that if the Queen had married when younger "it would have been better for her and the realm also", but considering the proportions of her body, that she was not diminutive of frame nor was she too large, and that she had "no sickness nor lack of natural functions in those things that properly belong to the pro-creation of children, but, by judgment of physicians that know her estate in those things, and by the opinion of women being most acquainted with her Majesty's body in such things as appertain", she was probably capable of bearing children "even at this day."* This opinion shows that people in a position to know best thought that there was no physical impediment to a sexual union. They said nothing about the horrified resistance, the nervous agonies that constituted an impediment every whit as great. Dr. Huick, it seemed, had understood something of this when in 1566 he had infuriated the Council because, having heard what Elizabeth had to say, he had agreed that she had better not undertake marriage and child-bearing. Either the doctors now regarded the condition as mere foolishness, or, since the Queen was said to be seriously considering the marriage, they assumed that the trouble would be overcome in the embraces of a husband to whom she willingly gave herself. Meantime the French Ambassador Mauvissière reported to his court: "She is gayer and more beautiful than she had been these fifteen years. Not a woman or a physician who knows her but says there is no lady in the realm more fit for bearing children than she is." But Walsingham, who was now in England, wrote to Davison in the Low Countries: "The affair of Monsieur takes greater foot than was looked for. She thinks it the best means to provide for her safety that can be offered . . . though otherwise not greatly to her liking."

On January 22nd Duke John Casimir came to England again, for a

---

* Conyers Read, *Lord Burleigh and Queen Elizabeth*.

visit of three weeks. Leicester was in charge of his entertainment, and on February 12th he wrote to Davison: "Cousin Davison, the cause that of late I have not written to you is for that since Duke Casimir is come hither, I have been almost always in his company, or otherwise so busied in her Majesty's affairs that I assure you I have had no leisure to write." He was indeed occupied by Casimir. Mendoza said: "When the Queen was in Council the other day, she twice asked for Lord Leicester and was told he was with Casimir. When he came, she said: 'You have quite forgotten us all, and business too, apparently, since we cannot get you here for the discussion of it!' Words, added Mendoza, "which were not displeasing to Sussex and Burleigh, who smiled at them."

The great Earl was still, however precariously, balanced on the crest of his fortune. The French King, according to Mendoza, had written to him, assuring Leicester on his word of honour that his position should not be injured when the Queen of England married the Duke d'Alençon; Leicester would then be the trusted guide and friend to the French King's brother.

The Queen was not only gay and elegant herself. She wanted her whole Court to appear *en beauté* for the Prince's arrival, and the Council themselves were ordering new suits. On March 27th Davison reminded Leicester that the latter had asked him for prices of the exquisite velvets and satins, woven in the northern provinces of the Low Countries, into which all the industry and prosperity of the country had retreated. He said: "I sent you a rate of the prices . . . and have since been expecting your answer." On April 25th Leicester replied: "I wish you to take up for me 4,000 crowns' worth of crimson and black velvet, and satins, and silks of other colours, and if there be any cloth of gold of tissue, or of gold, or such other pretty stuff", then Davison was to reserve it for him, "to the value of £300, of £400, or whatever the charge shall be".*

Lord Warwick owned Northall, an estate in Hertfordshire, where he had enclosed some of the common. In April of this year riots broke out, in the course of which some men broke down his palings. The disturbance grew too great for the local authorities to handle, and Sir Christopher Hatton was sent into Hertfordshire to deal with it. Leicester wrote to him, affectionately as always, and gave him a message from the Queen: "She would have you take some rest before you put yourself to travel again." Lord Warwick himself was with him, but Leicester could not, as he would otherwise have

* C.S.P. Domestic.

done, send Hatton any word from him: "For he is abed and asleep, it is now past eleven o'clock, and besides troubled with his gout."

Leicester, always on courteous and cordial terms with the Shrews-buries, had a conversation on May 10th with Gilbert Talbot just before he was leaving for Wanstead. Talbot told him that "the unreasonable people" of Ashford in Kent resisted the claim of Lady Shrewsbury, who had acquired property on a progressive scale in the course of four marriages, to some land in their neighbourhood. Lord Leicester was all on her Ladyship's side. He told Talbot that he himself "had angled and fished at that end of the town", and had always thought "that it belonged wholly to my Lady".[1]

And now sudden exposure came upon him. It was August, and the Court was at Greenwich. Simier had not been in England for six months without using his ears; his sharpness and address, and his instant recognition of Leicester as the person most hostile to his master's interests, made Leicester's secret Simier's oyster. Whenever he might have discovered the truth, he chose his own time for using it.

He had on several occasions urged Elizabeth to sign the passport for Alençon without which the Prince could not enter England, and always the Queen, though showing the utmost eagerness for Monsieur's arrival, had found some reason that made granting the passport impossible at the exact moment. At last, in July, Simier had obtained her signature to it. Her animation in talking of the Prince and listening to Simier's reports of his devotion, of which she could never hear enough, had worked such a change in her, of youth and radiant spirits, that Leicester was genuinely alarmed. When he heard that the passport had been actually given, against his known wishes in a matter so concerned with emotions of the heart, he went off to Wanstead in a sullen rage. Here he gave out that he was ill. Elizabeth came down to see him, to reassure herself as to his condition, to console him if she could. She stayed with him quietly for two days and then returned to London.

Shortly after this, one of the Queen's guard fired upon Simier in the grounds of Greenwich Palace. It was once assumed, and put about, that it had been done at Leicester's instigation. No evidence was produced to confirm this, but Simier had sustained the shock of attempted assassination. It was enough for him that Leicester was known to be the enemy of his negotiations. He decided to strike. He told Elizabeth that the infinite kindness she had always shown Lord Leicester had been undeserved. He was acting the part neither of a loyal subject nor of a true friend in trying to prevent her marriage. His conduct was the more detestable since he was married himself. Aghast, Elizabeth listened to the evidence he produced.

The woman whose behaviour indicates that she will make a scene if she is told the truth asks to be deceived. So much must be said for Leicester; but it was true also that Elizabeth suffered under the stroke even more than the ordinary woman in this situation. She had twice shown that she was prepared to see Leicester married to some-one else, but both these suggested marriages were those of ambition; what agonized her to the point of fury in the present case was that he had made secretly a marriage of passion with her sly, voluptuous, beautiful cousin: the godly gentlewoman whom he had wished to marry that he might live to God's glory and Elizabeth's own advantage, who had been led in to her wedding ceremony so far gone with child that she had had to abandon stays. So far Elizabeth's sufferings were of the kind that can't be cured, must be endured; but the desertion was not merely a cause of the searing pain of sexual jealousy; it inflicted a deeper injury. The cataclysmal events of her childhood had led her to place an abnormal reliance and value on the few people whom she felt she could trust. When her governess was taken from her she had cried the whole night long. Ascham had wanted to leave her for a few days, to pay a visit to his friends at Cambridge, but he had had to give up the plan; Elizabeth could not bear him to go away. Such had been her behaviour as a child. As a woman and a Queen, she gave her servants a loyalty and protection which was in striking contrast to the behaviour of other crowned heads, including her own father; but the exactions of her service were unremitting. In the sphere of politics, devotion to her was devotion to England, and, as in every aspect of her nature, the Queen's personal wishes were inseparable from the great aim of her existence. That this should come first with everyone who worked for her, and with her, was axiomatic, and the axiom added a more vivid tinge to her egotism when this demanded that in the sphere of the affections she must come first also.

When Simier spoke, the jealous pain natural to a woman in such a situation was reinforced by the demands for affection of a person with the classical symptoms of hysteria. She received the disclosure in an outburst of unmitigated fury. She raved. She swore that she would exercise her power of arbitrary arrest and send Leicester to the Tower. Most fortunately, the one man capable of controlling her in this crisis was present in the Palace in his official capacity. As Lord

Chamberlain, Lord Sussex was at hand. In the end Burleigh could always impose his will upon Elizabeth, but Burleigh was not a man of physical impressiveness; it often required time and reflection for his influence to make itself felt, and here there was no time to spare; something must be done at once, or the Queen would expose herself in a manner that would never be forgotten. Compared with Burleigh, Sussex was not a clever man, but he had the solid courage of a soldier; he was truth-telling to the point of tactlessness; he had often aroused the Queen's ire, and it distressed him, but it had never taught him not to say exactly what he thought. He saw her faults clearly, but he forgave them for the sake of her great virtues, and, however she might prefer the company of more amusing men, no woman so quick at assessing character could fail to give him credit for his loyal disinterestedness, his absolute integrity. In this terrible exhibition of rage and pain, Sussex acted with the nerve of a man who goes into a loose box to rescue a panic-stricken hunter that is kicking itself to pieces. He agreed with Elizabeth that she could send Lord Leicester to the Tower, but he told her that she must not do it. She must think of her own dignity. No one, he said, should be penalized for contracting a lawful marriage, "a thing always accounted honourable". He detested Leicester; the Queen herself had often had her work cut out to make them behave decently to each other in her very presence; but Sussex took no advantage of the present situation. He had once been prepared to support the scheme for her marrying Leicester, if she had wished it herself. He now bent the whole of his energies towards mitigating her anger against him and bringing her back to some degree of self control.

The great point was at last gained; the Queen conceded that the public act of committing Leicester to the Tower should not take place; but it was plain that he must keep himself out of the way. In Greenwich Park, on a mound overlooking the Palace, was a little tower, built by Humphrey of Gloucester, and called by Henry VIII the Tower Mireflore, because it had been used as a lodging for Ann Boleyn. Here, Leicester was told he must incarcerate himself. He did so, and, to make his retirement as little suspect as possible, he gave out that he could see nobody because he was taking medicine. After a few days, though still debarred from the Queen's presence, he was allowed to go to Wanstead.

Elizabeth's tempests of rage were violent, but they were brief. When this one had exhausted itself, certain aspects of the landscape had been irreparably altered, but the ground was still firm beneath

Leicester's feet. The relationship was there still, and it was open to
him to regain a good deal of the influence he had possessed so short a
time ago. Lady Leicester, it was understood, was not to show her
face at Court. Lady Mary Sidney found the situation too painful
and, relinquishing the apartments at Court the Queen had given her,
retired to Penshurst, but Lord Leicester was not forbidden to show
himself in his usual place, if he cared to appear before rivals and
dependents as a man humbled.

Sir Christopher Hatton as Vice-Chamberlain issued summonses
to a meeting of the Privy Council, and Leicester replied saying he
was "most unfit at this time to repair to that place where so many
eyes are witnesses of my open disgrace delivered from her Majesty's
mouth. Wherefor, if by silence it may be passed over (my calling for
being but in general sort), I pray you let it be so." If, however, his
presence were actually desired, he would of course come, if Hatton
could let him know in time. He signed, "in haste, this afternoon at
one of the clock."*

The French Prince arrived in August, and now the Queen appeared
to be all gaiety. She threw herself into the wooer's company.
Alençon caused surprise to those who had heard of him merely as
puny, undersized, with pock-marked face and a swollen nose. He
was all this, but he was brilliant in conversation, with a lively mind,
fascinating manners, and a direct method of making love which
Elizabeth would have enjoyed at any time, and which in her present
soreness of mind both elated and soothed her. She declared herself
enchanted with him.

Leicester's chagrin and his alarm were now acute, and he had lost
the means of making the Queen attend to his feelings. He had an
interview with Elizabeth, perhaps the first of a formal nature since
the explosion, and, Mendoza said, everyone who saw him come
away from it could perceive what a state he was in. That night,
August 25th, he supped with Lord Pembroke at Baynard's Castle.
Sir Henry Sidney was there, and other friends of the Dudleys'.
It was assumed, by those who heard of the meeting, that the party
discussed what steps they should take if the French marriage became
a fact; it was said that Leicester was meditating treason. However,
his affairs in France obliged Alençon to leave England in September,
though he declared that he should return immediately. He, at least, did
not consider the Earl of Leicester a spent force. While he left on one
of the Queen's fingers a diamond worth ten thousand crowns, which

* Nicholas, *Sir Christopher Hatton.*

his mother had given him for his bride, he gave Lord Leicester as a parting present a cap-band full of jewels, worth three thousand crowns.

Leicester was never popular with the nation, as his father had never been, but in his objection to the French match he had, for once, the people on his side. John Stubbs, a loyal, warm-hearted Puritan, issued a pamphlet which he called *The Discovery of a Gaping Gulph, into which England is like to fall, by reason of the French Marriage.* It set forth the dangers of the match, to the Protestant religion, and to the Queen herself, who would almost certainly die in childbirth, if it were forced upon her at her years. Stubbs' portrait of Monsieur was libellous; the Prince's person was declared repulsive, his morals unspeakable. That of Elizabeth was drawn with strong affection, but Stubbs stated plainly that, since she was so much older than the Prince, the latter's professed love for her must be a deception assumed for the evil purposes of the French, and it was the duty of loving subjects to save her from a bad husband, "the greatest cross that can be laid on a poor woman's shoulders". Elizabeth would have been angry at any attempt to interfere with a political manoeuvre of her own; much more depended on convincing Alençon that his romantic devotion was believed in and returned than Stubbs was able to understand. The pamphlet was exasperating to a degree in its political aspect, but the sexual insult it conveyed, the worse for being uttered in all kindness and sincerity, and coming as it did a few weeks after the discovery that Leicester had married Lettice Knollys, drove her to vindictive fury. A statute against libellous publications, enacted by Mary Tudor and allowed to lapse, was resuscitated for Stubbs' case, and his right hand was struck off by the executioner. With his left he pulled off his hat and cried God save the Queen! before he fell down in a faint; but his voice was the only one that uttered the words. An angry crowd received them in dead silence.

The feelings of the people found vent in a popular song:

> *The King of France shall not advance*
> *His ships on English sand,*
> *Nor shall his brother Francis have*
> *The ruling of the land.*
> *Therefor, good Francis, rule at home,*
> *Resist not our desire,*
> *For here is nothing else for thee*
> *But only sword and fire!*★

★ J. D. Furnivall, *Ballads from Manuscript Sources.*

On November 12th, 1579, Leicester wrote to Burleigh a letter of lamentation upon the Queen's displeasure with him for his hostility to the French match, and her unreasonable conduct in refusing him herself and then condemning his marriage to someone else: "My Lord, I have desired my Lord of Pembroke to excuse me to you and to pray your Lordship to help to excuse my not coming this day. I perceive by my brother Warwick your Lordship hath found the like bitterness in her Majesty towards me in that others (too many) have lately acquainted me withal." That men should know he was out of favour was an added bitterness to the loss itself. He said he did not deserve this treatment at the Queen's hands: "Her Majesty is grown into a very strange humour, all things considered, towards me, howsoever it were true or false as she is informed, the state whereof I will not dispute." Here he neither admitted nor denied his marriage, a curious ambiguity to preserve so late as this, but it gives point to the remark in *Leicester's Commonwealth* about his conduct towards Lady Essex, "now confessing, now forswearing, now dissembling, the marriage". Apropos his known disapproval of the French marriage, he reminded Burleigh that he had offered, "for avoiding such blame as I have, generally, in the realm, mine own exile, that I might not be suspected a hinderer of that matter which all the world desired and were suitors for". This statement echoes a letter written from Antwerp in 1582, which said Leicester knew there would be no place for him in England if Queen Elizabeth married the French Prince, and he had "procured a place in Germany, to dwell there, should the marriage take place".* He went on to say, with much reason: "I carried myself almost more than a bondman many a year together, so long as one drop of comfort was left of any hope, as you yourself, my Lord, do know." Then he said: "So being acquitted and delivered of that hope, and by both open and private protestation and declaration discharged, methinks it is more than hard to take such an occasion, to bear so great displeasure for . . ." The Queen might now regret the benefits she had bestowed on him, but if it came to that, had he nothing to regret? "So may I say, I have lost both youth, liberty, and all my time resposed in her, and, my Lord, by the time I have made an even reckoning with the world, your Lordship will not give me much for my 20 year's, service; but I trust she that hath been so gracious to all, will not only [sic] be gracious to me . . . In haste this Thursday afternoon, Your Lordship's thankful friend, R. Leycester."†

* C.S.P. Foreign.   † T. Wright, *Queen Elizabeth and her Times.*

Leicester was not only justified in what he said about his marriage; he should have taken such a stand from the beginning. But when he said he had lost youth, liberty and time reposed in the Queen, one can only ask, what could his youth, liberty and time spent in any other direction have gained him, that so ambitious and worldly a man would have liked better? As for what he had gained being little for twenty years' service, it is only right to say what some of these gains had amounted to by the year 1579. In every year from 1559 to 1579, Leiester had received from the Queen either grants of land, or the lordship of manors—which meant that he drew the rents of properties on the manor lands—or a licence to export some commodity free of duty, or some salaried office, or the wardship of a minor from whose estate he was entitled to large dues when the ward came of age or married. The Crown was, of course, continually maintaining its servants by grants and gifts, as statesmen were not salaried, but Leicester was recognized as drawing an unusually large share of the royal bounty. A few years chosen from the twenty-year-long procession of benefactions to him illustrate the scale on which Elizabeth provided for her dearest friend.

In 1562 he received an annuity of £1,000 to be paid out of tonnage and poundage, until the Queen should give him lands of equal value, three licences to export woollen cloth, and the estate of Sir Andrew Dudley, which had reverted to the crown on his attainder in 1553.

In 1563 he was given Kenilworth Castle, lands in Lancashire, Yorkshire, Rutland, Surrey, Carmarthen, Cardigan and Brecknock, and made Constable of Windsor Castle.

In 1566 he was given a licence for twenty years to export all manner of wood and timber growing in Shropshire, and lordship of manors in Worcester, Hereford, Gloucestershire, Somerset, Dorset, Denbigh, Brecon, Warwickshire, Hertfordshire, Bedfordshire, Norfolk and Lincolnshire.

In 1568 he was given the manor and the presentation to the living of Middlefoy in Somerset, and £1,303 2s. 1d. for surplus value of trees on manors he exchanged with the Queen.

In 1574 he received a wardship, the Old Palace at Maidstone and lands in twenty counties.

In 1578 he was given lands in Merioneth and Caernarvon, made Chancellor of Merioneth, Caernarvon and Anglesea, and given a wardship.

In 1579, the year of his letter to Burleigh, he got two wardships and a lease of Woodgrave Manor in Essex. The only two years in which the flow of gifts was stayed, 1569 and 1570, were those in which Hatton's ascendancy was first felt; in them, the chief grants were made to the new favourite, but, even so, Leicester was given three grants and the reversion of the office of Queen's Remembrancer.*

Without knowing the value of the lands, the rents produced by the manors and the income from the licences, it would not be possible to say which year's gifts were the most valuable, and some of the lists containing fewest items might equal or exceed in value the longer ones. These lists deal only with matters of lands, rents, offices and annuities. The general opinion, well or ill founded, was that Leicester exorted a great quantity of money from the Queen simply by importuning her for it and by turning any dispute with her to good account. It was said: "He makes gainful to himself every falling-out with her Majesty",† and that "he was never reconciled to the Queen under £5,000".**

Leicester's marriage to Lady Essex being now public property, there was nothing to prevent Lady Sheffield from following the advice given in his letter, and accepting one of the many eligible proposals made to her. On November 29th, 1579, she was married to Sir Edward Stafford, the resident English Ambassador at Paris. Her son Robert was five years old and living in his father's care, and Lady Stafford might now look for a new era in her life: a distinguished social position and a loving husband who would restore to her the years that the locust had eaten. She had, of course, by marrying Sir Edward Stafford tacitly admitted that her marriage with Lord Leicester had not been valid; but if she herself were prepared to do this there seemed, at present, no reason why she should not. The struggle came twenty-five years later, when her son married Alice Leigh, the daughter of Sir Thomas Leigh of Stoneleigh in Warwickshire. Robert Dudley's father-in-law then worked upon him to prove the legitimacy of his birth, which, if proved, would make Sir Thomas' daughter Countess of Leicester and Countess of Warwick. But in 1579 after five years of misery under desertion, culminating in a quarrel in which Leicester repudiated her with the utmost brutality, all Lady Stafford now asked was to live as the wife of the man who was willing to love and protect her.

Her troubles, however, were not yet over. Elizabeth had known something of Leicester's previous liaison, but mere common sense

---

* Walter Rye, *The Murder of Amy Robsart.*
† Leicester's *Commonwealth.*   ** David Lloyd, *State Worthies.*

demanded from her that she should not expect him to deny himself to other women altogether; and though in 1573 she had been described as watchful and displeased at the appearance of Douglas Sheffield and her sister "at great wars together" for his regard, the vast difference in her attitude to Douglas Sheffield and to Lettice Essex was the difference not only between her view of a keeping and a marriage, but between the powers of the two women themselves. Now this half-forgotten episode recurred to her. Might there be some evidence of at least a betrothal contract with Lady Sheffield, which, if not cancelled by mutual consent of the parties, prevented a legal marriage with anybody else? Leicester's own statement would be worthless; competent investigation must be made, and if it turned out that he had had a binding contract with Lady Sheffield, then, the Queen swore, "he should make up her honour with a marriage, or rot in the Tower!"

Sir Edward Stafford, who had married Douglas Sheffield for love, could not look upon this prospect with any enthusiasm, even when the Queen hastily promised that if he had to give up his bride "she would better the estate of the Staffords". However, at her order he questioned his wife very closely; as a result, he reported that she had said she had no evidence of a previous contract. Newly married as she was, her views no doubt had changed; she might now wish to conceal such evidence if she had it; her husband's report was not sufficient. The Queen took counsel with Lord Sussex, who agreed with her here; if it were possible to clear the matter up, once for all, the effort should be made. It was arranged that in the Queen's presence he should interrogate Lady Stafford. Sussex had every reason to abominate Leicester; his sympathies were all with Lady Stafford, who was a relation of his wife, but, however painful to her, it was necessary that anything she knew should be made available. He was a Privy Councillor, and when the Council set themselves to extract information they usually succeeded. Alone of any authority under the Queen's, they could order the use of torture for this purpose. There was, needless to say, no suggestion of any such method being applied to Lady Stafford, but this was the background of authority against which she was being questioned.

With relentless thoroughness, Sussex obliged her to go once again over the events of six years ago, of the troth-plight which at this time was all she claimed. Was there nothing, he asked, that she could produce? No contract of betrothal, no deed of settlement, no attestation of witnesses? No documentary evidence of any kind whatever?

Under his probing the newly healed wound broke out afresh. The past rushed upon her, and she broke into hysterical weeping as between her sobs she exclaimed that "she had trusted the said Earl too much to have anything to show, to constrain him to marry her". Sussex was obliged at last to tell the Queen that they could get nothing further. The result of the interview was the demoralization to Lady Stafford, the bitter anger of the Queen, an intensifying, if such a thing were possible, of the indignation and contempt in which Sussex held Leicester, and a complete vindication of the position of Lady Leicester.

On December 28th, Holy Innocents' Day, the Earl of Leicester's Players had prepared "A History" to be played at Whitehall; the company was in readiness "to have enacted the same", as the Revels Accounts put down, "wholly furnished with sundry things of this office, but the Queen's Majesty could not come forth to hear the same, therefore it was put off".*

* Feuillerat, *Office of the Revels.*

XXI

At the end of 1579, or the beginning of 1580, was born the little Lord Denbigh, Leicester's son by his wife Lady Leicester. Several pictures were painted of him during his short life: "Of the Lord Denbigh, naked; of the young Lord Denbigh; of the Countess of Leicester and my young Lord standing by her". In Leicester House he had a cradle draped with crimson velvet, with trains of crimson taffeta, and a little chair upholstered in green and carnation cloth of tinsel.[1]

The Queen's affection for Leicester was so deep-rooted that it renewed itself after being laid waste. When the fateful year 1579 was out his influence began to revive, if it never regained its former strength. The meeting of the Feast of St. George at Windsor in April, 1580, was celebrated by Teshe in his *Verses on the Order of the Garter*, which relate that the Earl of Leicester was present among his peers. Teshe described the Knights waiting expectantly for the Queen's speech, as if looking forward to some happy tale.

> *Behold the Queen stand up amongst them all,*
> *Heralds cried Silence! Hushed was all the hall.*

The Queen delivered a speech on the words *Honi soit qui mal y pense*, and *Dieu et mon Droit*. Then she sat down and each knight approached to do homage. Teshe puts lines into the mouth of each, incorporating the motto of his arms. Lord Leicester was said to advance "with stately look and with a pleasant cheer", and the words ascribed to him were:

> *Right, firm, just, true, whatever shall befal*
> *My word imports my will: Droit et loyal.*

Well, he was allowed to return, to prove it if he could. The Queen, however, was adamant in refusing to receive Lady Leicester. The Countess must at times have been obliged to remove herself from the scene, in Wanstead, or Leicester House, for the Queen sometimes met the Council at Wanstead, and on one occasion at least she

was present at a very important meeting in Leicester House; but
Lady Leicester undoubtedly occupied these houses. Both of them
were furnished in the height of comfort and splendour. In Leicester
House, the Countess's bed chamber contained a bed of walnut hung
with curtains of scarlet, trimmed with gold and silver lace, a square
stool upholstered to correspond, and a chair covered in crimson velvet,
while a cupboard and four coffers held her clothes. Rooms were
appropriated to her own family. Her son Robert Devereux, 2nd
Earl of Essex, was thirteen at the time of his mother's marriage to
Leicester. He was a ward in Lord Burleigh's house, but a room in
Leicester House was called my Lord of Essex' Chamber. His sister
Penelope was seventeen and married to the wealthy Lord Rich.
The marriage turned out unhappily, but she had a welcome at her
stepfather's splendid house, where the room she used was called my
Lady Rich's Chamber.

In beauty of furniture, of curtains and bed-hangings, and in the
comfort of feather beds, down bolsters, fine bed-linen and woollen
blankets, with fires on their hearths and windows overlooking
Thames with its sailing swans, the bedchambers of Leicester House
were among the finest and fairest to be found.

One thing marred all this: the standing drawback of privies without drainage. The nuisance was age-old, and people had come to
terms with it. In the large rooms of the gentry it was slight, but it
might always become serious, and the perpetual changes of the
Queen and her great household from one palace to another were
made largely with a view to cleaning out the cesspits and thoroughly
airing the vacated building. In the following decade the Queen's
godson, John Harington, published in *Ajax* his scheme for a water-
closet which had originated in Italy. *Ajax* was a wordplay on "A
jakes", and the work was couched in a facetious idiom. A covert
reference to Leicester, who was then dead, gravely offended the
Queen and she sent Harington away from Court, but she then tried
the scheme of a water-closet at Richmond Palace, and finding, as
Harington had promised, that "it would give you a clean and sweet
privy all the year round", she allowed him to return. The reference
to Leicester, which annoyed the Queen because it had all the painful-
ness of truth, was to the Earl's somewhat sanctimonious reputation.
Harington said he would not end his flighty work with a sermon or
a prayer, "lest some ways liken me to my Lord ——'s players, who,
when they have ended a bawdy comedy, as though that were a

preparative to devotion, kneel down and pray all the company to pray with them for their good Lord and Master". The book, however, contained unexceptionable references to Leicester and his interest in sanitation. Sir John Young had an invention of his own, of keeping the cesspit air-tight. Meeting Lord Leicester at Bristol "he commended to my Lord that fashion and showed him his own, of a worse fashion, and told him that at a house of his at Peter's Hill in London, there was a very sweet privy of that making".

The members of the family used close-stools in their bedchambers, where wicker screens were provided, and the pans were carried away by servants. The household used the privies or "house of easement", sometimes placed in the garden, whose contents were carried away by men who called regularly for the purpose. In the country, a privy was sometimes built over a brook, or a brook was made to run through the cellarage of a house so that it was "daily cleansed with water". Harington thought the great cold this entailed outweighed the advantages. Whatever was done and whatever care was used, it was impossible, in large households, to banish the annoyance all the time. This accounted for the lavish use of burning-perfumes, some of which not only diffused a sweet scent but destroyed all other smells in their neighbourhood. Bohun said that Leicester "so accustomed himself to the scents of musk and civet . . . that he could not live without them".

The members of the Earl of Leicester's household ranged from Mr. Atye, his Lordship's private secretary, to the men and maids indoors and the grooms and gardeners without. On his appointed level was Edmund Spenser.

Spenser was high-minded, moral and sincere, but he longed, he yearned for some appointment that would establish him permanently at Court, in the centre of excitement and brilliance. Philip Sidney had had experience of this society from boyhood; he was sick of the spectacle which intimacy with it revealed, of the poison of self-seeking and the withering heat of ambition; and like the hart seeking the waterbrook he fled to Wilton surrounded by its woods, where the elegant retirement of a great house was illumined for him by the companionship of an adoring sister. But Spenser had risen from humble antecedents, and his greatest achievement so far had been a scholarship to Pembroke College. To him Leicester House upon the Thames, within the view of Whitehall Palace, the home of the great Earl of Leicester, the haunt of the angelical Philip Sidney, the resort of the greatest in the kingdom, even of the pale and dazzling Queen herself, had given a draught of intoxicating happiness. The sight of the great personages acted as a stimulant to the intelligence of the retiring, ingenuous but very clever young man, as the visual splenddour of Leicester House called up a response in the imagination of the great poet. The wine was at his lips and he was avid for more of it; the last thing he wished was to retire to an unpeopled solitude, however lovely.

At first, Leicester House was a sphere beyond anything he had hoped. He boasted to Harvey of the use Lord Leicester made of him, of the familiar kindness with which he was treated by Philip Sidney and his friends, but he ardently desired some advancement that would keep him where he was, in a greater and more assured success. The brightness faded, and in its place grew the gnawing discontent and misery of the man perpetually waiting for half-promised favours. The patronage of Leicester, which, it had seemed, would translate him to the seventh heaven, he mysteriously lost.

In the poem *Virgil's Gnat*, dedicated to Leicester but published after the Lord's death, the introduction runs:

> *Wronged, yet not daring to express my pain*
> *To you, great Lord, the causer of my care,*
> *In cloudy tears my case I thus complain*
> *Unto yourself that only privy are . . .*

If any one should divine this riddle, the poet says,

> *Let him rest pleased with his own insight,*

and say nothing about it.

> *But what so by yourself may not be known,*
> *May by this gnat's complaint be easily shown.*

The fable describes a beautiful shepherd, leading his flock into the shade at midday and falling asleep beside a stream. A dangerous serpent glides up to him, but he is awakened in time by a gnat who stings his eyelid; a brush of the hand kills the gnat, but the shepherd saves himself from the serpent.

This poem, "Long since dedicated to the most noble and excellent Lord the Earl of Leicester, late deceased", suggests that Spenser had attempted to warn Leicester of some impending danger and that his warning had been taken amiss. If its occult meaning could be read it would perhaps explain why, instead of being retained in Leicester House and given a place at Court, which was the longing of his heart, Spenser was provided for by being sent away to Ireland as a secretary to the Lord Deputy, Lord Grey de Wilton.

Like Lyly, like Shakespeare, Spenser thought that the lives of the great, whether public or private, were legitimate material for his verse; part of the interest of his great body of work is its reflection of contemporary happenings. When a search was made for some poem that might have conveyed a warning which Leicester resented as presumption, it was suggested that *Mother Hubbard's Tale* might have been the one. This work deals with the dangers to the country inherent in the proposed French match. Alençon is represented by an Ape, in a knave's confederacy with a Fox who is a most offensive personification of Lord Burleigh. But Lord Leicester was thoroughly against the marriage; he did not need Spenser to point out its disadvantages to him. A much more convincing suggestion is advanced by Professor Mounts. On December 5th, 1579, was published Spenser's first work, *The Shepherd's Calendar*. It consists of twelve conversations in verse, among shepherds, one for each month. In the Eclogue for March, the shepherd Willy says to his friend Thomalin that spring is almost with them, the hawthorns are budding:

> Then shall we sporten in delight
> And learn with Lettice to wax light.

If Lady Leicester's name had been Bridget or Mary or Ann or Joan, she might have shared it with any shepherd's lass, but neither Laetitia nor its familiar, Lettice, has ever been a usual name in English, even in the educated class. In a work emanating from Leicester House and dedicated to Philip Sidney the association was inescapable, and its indiscretion breathtaking.* It was believed that Leicester pursued Edward Arden with deadly malice because Arden, speaking of Leicester's association with Lady Essex, had called him a whoremaster. What was he likely to think, more important, what was Lady Leicester likely to think, of this impertinence from a protégé? Much of the matter remains obscure: the March Eclogue does not convey a warning, it merely makes a slighting reference; it could not, in itself, be the matter for which the faithful gnat was swept into annihilation; but it seems to show that Spenser was alive to the situation between Leicester and Lettice Knollys, though he probably had not heard of the secret marriage of 1578, which had taken place

---

* Charles E. Mounts, *Spenser and the Countess of Leicester*, Journal of English Literary History, Baltimore, September, 1952.

very shortly before his own introduction to Leicester House. If he had known of this, there would have been no grounds left for a warning. But if he knew of the connection which he supposed a liaison merely, he would have known, too, of the Queen's impending anger. Young and humble though he was, he was on an anomalous footing with his patron: a poet was regarded as an inspired creature, though he was liable to be put into the street. He may have thought that he could save the Earl by pointing out to him what he had to lose, thus performing for him a service that no one else in the great household had the courage or the unselfishness or the sense of gratitude to undertake. Such a notion, though not possible in anybody else, was not impossible in a young, devoted and totally inexperienced man.

When he took this step, if he took it at all, is not easy to determine. In April, 1579, he was carrying letters from Leicester to France. In October of the same year he wrote from Leicester House telling one of his friends that he was going to Spain and to Rome on the Earl's affairs: "I go thither as sent by him and maintained mostwhat of him. I am there to employ my time, my body, my mind, to his Honour's service." In December, while he was absent, *The Shepherd's Calendar* was published; it had a great, an instantaneous success. Was the line in the March Eclogue like the pomegranate seed that, lingering in Persephone's mouth as she came to the upper air, meant that she must go back again to the shades?

Spenser returned to Leicester House in April, 1580, and by that time the Countess of Leicester was installed there as its mistress, mother of its heir. There was no evidence of a quarrel between Spenser and his magnificent patron; indeed, all the references to him in Spenser's poetry, except the lines in *The Gnat*, breathe gratitude and devotion. It was clear from those lines themselves that the matter, whatever it might be, was kept profoundly secret; but three months after his return, in July, 1580, Spenser sailed with Lord Grey de Wilton, and with brief visits to England he remained in Ireland for nineteen years, quitting it at last barely a month before his death.

His career there was a sufficiently prosperous one, but it was not the one he wanted, and whenever his poetry speaks of his own fortunes he laments a torturing disappointment.

The bulk of his poetry, particularly of *The Faerie Queene*, consists of narrative cast in an allegorical or pastoral or fairy-tale form; and it is a matter of extraordinary interest to detect how much of the description assumed to be merely visions of fairyland, by a comparison with eye-witnesses' reports of Elizabeth's Court, and of relics of the age, can be seen as actual recalling of *chose vue*; these are not necessarily what he described, but they indicate the sort of visual experience available to him.

The Faerie Queene was projected in twelve books, and, of the eight written, each deals with the adventures of a knight who rides out in armour and encounters adventures that are allegories of good and evil. To Spencer's audience the mounted figures encased in plate armour were not archaic, for, though gunpowder had destroyed the medieval method of making war by an attacking force of men completely covered in plate armour, this armour was still used in the tilt yard; the elaborate and skilful game of tourneying was one of the diversions of Elizabeth's Court. The pictures of the tilting armour worn by Leicester and Hatton are miracles of beauty and strangeness. A suit belonging to Hatton, signed 1588, is made of steel, stained russet, striped lengthwise with broad bands of engraved gilt, the intervening russet stripes filled with gilt spirals. On the gilt stripes a crowned E is repeated. The scabbard is tawny, and each piece of armour is lined with tawny leather which shows as a piping. One of Leicester's suits is of russetted steel with gilt stripes; another was of white enamelled steel, with gilt bands running down it in the shape of the ragged staff, while a muzzled bear was engraved on the elbow caps; this suit was lined and piped with scarlet. A man covered up in this armour, with great head and shoulders, narrow hips and hands and feet scaled like some prehistoric dragon, presented an appearance both savage and exotic. The method of tilting, in which a barrier was erected longwise down the lists, the mounted opponents approaching each other from either side, each seeking his moment for the blow that would unhorse his rival, had a sinister excitement for the packed spectators. Great physical strength, great agility, poise and quickness of reaction were essential.* The recurring descriptions of conflict between mounted men in armour in *The Faerie Queene*, were addressed to an audience who found the spectacle of the tilt yard absorbing.

Spenser's eye was particularly caught by a use of gold and silver. When Elizabeth had a banqueting pavilion built beside the river in the gardens of Whitehall, for the second visit of Alençon in 1581, the ceiling, painted with clouds, sun and stars, had baskets depending

* E. St. John Brooks, *Sir Christopher Hatton*; Lord Dillon, *An Almain Armourer's Album*.

from it full of fruit spangled with gold.* Spenser must have seen some such arrangement, for, in Book II of *The Faerie Queene*, the Bower of Bliss was wreathed with bunches of green and purple grapes.

> *And them amongst, some were of burnished gold,*
> *So made by art, to beautify the rest.*

He described over and over again the cloth of silk and gold or silk and silver, which he had probably seen first in Leicester House, and a wonderful visual impression of "green gold" occurs in Book III, where, in the House of Busyrane, the walls were hung with it,

> *Woven with silk and gold so close and near*
> *That the rich metal lurked privily . . .*
> *Yet here and there, and everywhere unwares*
> *It showed itself and shone unwillingly,*
> *Like a discoloured snake, whose hidden snares*
> *Through the green grass his long bright burnished back declares.*

One of his allegorical set-pieces of Elizabeth, who figures under several names in different books of the poem, though presented as a fairy vision, has a recognizable source. The writer of the News Letter to the Fugger Banking House saw Whitehall Palace in 1585, and said that behind the Queen's chair of state was "a tapestry of cloth of silver on which heraldic beasts were embroidered in gold". Spenser, describing Elizabeth as Mercilla, sitting in state, says (Book V) that over her head was spread a cloth like a cloud,

> *Whose skirts were bordered with bright sunny beams,*
> *Glistering like gold among the pleats enrolled*
> *And here and there shooting forth silver beams.*

In the April Eclogue, one of the most charming in *The Shepherds' Calendar*, Elizabeth is sitting on the grassy green, clothed in scarlet trimmed with ermine, with a crown of spring flowers on her head. Not wearing ermine on a summer progress, but in spreading dresses covered with jewelled clasps, and a small high crowned hat on top of a gold net—this was how people of villages and country towns did see her, and amidst all the elegance and fineness, the glitter and the scent, a pale, high-nosed, piercing-eyed face, concentrating like the sun's rays through a glass, upon them, their neighbourhood, their fortunes, their complaints. Spenser evoked a procession of the nine muses with their violins, running to play and dance before the Queen;

* Holinshed, *Chronicles o England.*

when Lord Hertford entertained Elizabeth at Elvetham, the Fairy Queen came into the garden, dancing, with her maids about her. They sang a song of six parts "with the music of an exquisite consort, wherein was the lute, bandora, base viol, cithern, treble viol and flute. This spectacle so delighted her Majesty that she caused to hear it sung and to be danced three times over."

The extraordinary beauty and strangeness of the great houses built in the second half of Elizabeth's reign show that Spenser's fairy vision was much closer to visual experience than would be supposed by the present age; the epitome may be seen in Hardwick Hall in Derbyshire, where the enormous windows are filled with small diamond shaped panes of greenish glass, that outside show a scattered twinkling like dew on the grass and inside bestow a greenish acqueous light. The light from these windows, falling upon the set of superb tapestries put up by Lady Shrewsbury, depicting Hero and Leander sundered by transparent waves, the waters filled with sea nymphs, corals, pearls and fish, recalls the passage in Book III of *The Faerie Queene*, where the wounded knight Marinell is left for dead on the shore and the sea god in sympathy casts treasures about him—gold, amber, ivory and pearls—and his mother the sea nymph takes him down to the bottom of the ocean, where her bower

> *Is built of hollow billows heaped high,*
> *Like to thick clouds that threat a stormy shower,*
> *And vaulted all within like to the sky.*

"Glassy" is a favourite word of Spenser's, and the transparent, silver-shining effect he so often produces is one of the ideas of beauty characteristic of the age. Hawsted Hall in Suffolk, which the Queen visited in the progress of 1578, was built of timber and plaster, and the plaster on the front was thickly stuck with fragments of glass "which made a brilliant appearance when the sun shone and even by moonlight".*

The allegorical themes of *The Faerie Queene*'s eight books cover the main currents of topical affairs, the chief protagonists appearing under allegorical forms: Philip of Spain as Orgoglio, Alençon as Braggodochio, Simier as Trompart, the Queen of Scots as Duessa, Leicester himself as Prince Arthur. The whole is dedicated to Queen Elizabeth, to whom the poet consecrates his labours, "to live with the eternity of her fame"; and Elizabeth, under various names—Mercilla, Britomart, Belphoebe, and Gloriana the Faerie Queene—glimmers

---

* Nichols, *Progresses of Queen Elizabeth*.

through the poem's enchanted landscapes. The conception of Belphoebe, the virgin huntress who salved the knight's wound but could not understand his continued sickness, which was caused by his nearly dying of love for her (Book III), has a strangely touching air; though the picture bears no likeness to the day-by-day relations of Elizabeth and Leicester, yet it is that of a woman who cannot give herself to a man. In the description of Britomart, a girl of impregnable chastity who dons armour and rides out to find adventures, there is a reference to the colour of Elizabeth's hair. When Britomart has overthrown a lascivious knight, to refresh herself she unlaces her helmet and her hair falls down her back, "crested all with lines of fiery light".

Spenser's other poems contain several references to the Dudley family. *Prothalamion*, celebrating the double marriage of Lady Elizabeth and Lady Katherine Somerset and written after Leicester's death, mentions Leicester House as the scene of the wedding, and it is thrilling to read the lines describing the progress down the river of the bridal party, to the point on the shore where the arched brick water-gate of the Temple stood:

> *Next whereunto there stands a stately place*
> *Where oft I gained gifts and goodly grace,*
> *Of that great Lord which therein wont to dwell,*
> *Whose want too well now feels my friendless case . . .*

and to look at Agas' map showing, on the north shore of the Thames, the Temple water-gate and the garden of Leicester House running down beside it. In *Prothalamion* the two brides are figured as swans floating down the river, pure white, of silken feathers, a natural association of ideas when thinking of Leicester House and the Thames flowing before it; Agas himself drew swans on the reach.

In *The Ruins of Time*, another poem published after Leicester's death, and dedicated to the Countess of Pembroke, commemorating Leicester and many members of the Dudley family, there is a pointed omission of any reference to Lady Leicester, but a wild and strange evocation of Lady Sheffield's disastrous love. The poet sees a magnificent bed draped with cloth of gold and wreathed with flowers

> *. . . as if it should*
> *Be for some bride, her joyous night to hold,*

and in it the fairest lady lying.

I heard a voice that callèd far away
And her awaking, bade her quickly dight
For lo, her bridegroom was in ready 'ray
To come to her and seek her love's delight.

The lady started up:

When suddenly, both bed and all were gone,
And I in languor left there all alone.

XXII

Nearly two years had elapsed since the disclosure of Leicester's marriage, and time had proved that, however damaged, his relationship with Elizabeth was still intact. They were now forty-eight, and their long friendship, since it had weathered the storm that threatened it with shipwreck, could now be expected to survive any shocks or reverses. A violent and bitter quarrel had not disrupted it, and boredom and indifference would never blight it. Elizabeth had still her fondness for his society, and for whatever reasons, what she was or what she had, she stimulated and enchained him still. He had, in fact, returned to his position at Court, eager as ever to play his part as a man of affairs, to wield his influence and discharge his duties.

One of these, connected with the office of Master of the Horse, was purveyance, the demanding of a certain number of horses from a district for the Queen's service. Leicester's zeal in this respect bore hard on the Palatinate of Chester. Since he was their Chancellor he naturally wished for a fine response to his demands. On April 5th, 1581, the Commissioners of Musters were obliged to tell him that it was impossible for the gentlemen of the city to raise the number of horses for which he had asked. Next month, however, he gained an unexpected addition to the royal stables. John Brown wrote to him from the Netherlands that he was shortly bringing over, from his colonel, a present for her Majesty "of six Hungarian horses . . . which horses I hope your Lordship will like well, for they are very well suited, as I ever saw, for her Majesty's coach. Their colours are all light grey and their manes and tails dyed into orange-tawney, according to the manner of their country. They are horses of light shape and good of travel and very young."* These six beautiful creatures, with their orange manes and tails, were seen by a foreign visitor, drawing the Queen's coach as she went to open parliament in October, 1584. They then wore bridles studded with pearls, and had diamond pendants on their foreheads.†

* Wright, *Elizabeth and her Times.*
† Von Karwill, *Queen Elizabeth and some Foreigners.*

In the month of April the Queen went to a dinner party of extraordinary interest and brilliance. The *Golden Hind*, in which Drake had sailed round the world, had been laid up at Deptford, and on April 15th Drake entertained the Queen on board with a dinner of such lavishness as had not been known since the days of Henry VIII. Elizabeth had not inherited King Henry's gastronomic powers; as at the banquet at Kenilworth, where she ate "smally or nothing", she may have done scant justice to the food and drink, but another aspect of Drake's hospitality she thoroughly appreciated; he gave her a silver casket and a frog made all of diamonds, a graceful reference to Monsieur, whose confidential agent Marchaumont accompanied her on board.

Leicester was *au fait* with the negotiations for the French match even if he could not alter their course. He was privately in Marchaumont's confidence; his position was too great for any advance of his to be ignored by a secret agent. In June Alençon came to England unexpectedly, to treat over the heads of the French commissioners already in London, and Mendoza reported that the moment the French Prince had arrived, "Marchaumont sent to Leicester a jet ring which was to be the signal of his arrival. Leicester and Walsingham could not believe it," Mendoza said, "for there was no reason which demanded his coming".

Leicester had found no difficulty in establishing a rapport with Marchaumont, but his approaches to the commissioners themselves were rebuffed. When the Secretary Pinart was about to leave, the Earl suggested to him that they should keep up a private correspondence. Pinart told him that Secretaries to the French King did not do such things. When there was any business about which Lord Leicester wished to correspond with his Majesty, his Lordship should communicate it to the French Ambassador, who would forward it in due course, without Pinart's mediation.*

Alençon remained in London two days. He was incognito, but during this brief time he did untold harm to the commissioners' efforts, for Elizabeth extracted from him the information that the King his brother no longer supported his venture in the Netherlands. Alençon would henceforward be dependent on English aid to keep him in the field, a matter of high significance in Elizabeth's policy.

In July the enmity between Leicester and Sussex blazed up again with such violence that it broke out in a shocking scene in the Queen's presence. Dr. Dee heard of it in his house at Mortlake, and noted it

* Martin Hume, *Courtships of Queen Elizabeth*

in his diary: "The Earl of Leicester fell foully out with the Earl of Sussex, the Lord Chamberlain, calling each other traitor, whereupon both were commanded to keep their chambers at Greenwich where the Court was." Walsingham also sent word of it to Burleigh since the latter had not been present.

"The Queen ordered each to keep his chamber and will commit them in case they shall not yield to stand to her order." Such stubborn savageness as that was unlikely in either party; but what Sussex had seen of Leicester's doings in the past two years, added to long-standing dislike had made his feelings, when tried, almost unmanageable.

In the following year, 1582, Dr. William Tresham, a Catholic, wrote to Lord Sussex from Paris; he wanted to explain to Sussex, whose good opinion he valued, why he had departed suddenly from Court without the latter's knowledge, "and contrary to my duty". "I beseech you," he wrote, "whilst perusing these lines, to suffer your judgment to cease as a Councillor of State and to weigh my cause as a private man. If I had seen any means to preserve myself from the persecution of the Earl of Leicester, whose favour has been lost without defect of mine, and for recovery whereof I have used such humility as has never been used at Court even to Princes . . . as appears by my letter to her Majesty which I beseech you may be read in her hearing, wherein is manifested the just occasion that has forced me to this desperate act. . . . No dishonest act or lewd practice either against Prince or Country or your Honour have moved me thereto, but only the extreme fear of the cruelty of the Earl of Leicester."[1]

In 1581 there returned to England, in company with a colleague, a Catholic priest who, one of the picked men in the Counter Reformation movement of the Continent, now came back to his country prepared to face the unspeakable agonies of a traitor's death, that he might rescue lapsed Catholics and open to as many heretics as possible the gates of everlasting life. This was Lord Leicester's former protégé, Edmund Campion.

Elizabeth's Religious Settlement by 1559 had been, by the standards of the age, exceptionally tolerant, as a glance at Mary Tudor's policy shows. The Act of Uniformity was binding on everyone: clergy who refused to use the Prayer Book were liable to life imprisonment; parishioners who refused to go to church once a month were liable to a fine of one shilling for each absence. The provisions were the less onerous because they were irregularly and slackly enforced. In many districts, where Catholic sympathies were

strong, they remained a dead letter. This state of things had been
rudely shattered by the publication of Pope Pius V's Bull of Excom-
munication. From May, 1570, all Catholics were laid under the
Pope's curse if they dared once to obey Queen Elizabeth or any of her
laws. From this hour the identification of a profession of the Catholic
religion with allegiance to a hostile foreign power was inevitable,
and the severe anti-Catholic legislation began.

The priests who had been trained in the seminaries of Douai,
Rheims and Rome were not appalled by the prospect of the semi-
strangulation and disembowelling which was the statutory penalty
for treason, and was only converted into a sentence of beheading for
those who were of noble birth. It was estimated that by 1580 one
hundred of them were at work in England. They themselves, it can
scarcely be doubted, were there on a purely spiritual mission; but the
wording of the Bull had made it impossible for non-Catholics living
at the time to acquit them of seditious intentions. It was assumed that
they must be there for the purpose of overturning the government of
Elizabeth, whom the Pope had called "the pretended Queen of
England". Gregory XIII, who succeeded Pius V, made a concession.
In his Explanation, published in 1580, he had said the Bull was still
binding on Elizabeth and the heretics, but Catholics might obey her
so long as her government remained in being, and while no directive
had been received that they were to overthrow her. This caused the
English Council to devise a question for which the Catholics naturally
execrated them but which, in fact, went to the root of the matter.
It was this: If an invasion, sponsored by the Pope, were directed
against Queen Elizabeth, would you fight on her side? It has been
said that it is not legal to question people like this on something which
has not happened; but, whether legal or not, it cannot be ignored
that this was the one question to which the government needed the
answer, and that no answer could satisfy them except a straightforward "yes".

In 1581, the rising tide of fear and anger against Catholicism
was intensified by the Pope's having provided funds for an army of
Italians, Spaniards, French and Irish which, accompanied by the papal
emissary Dr. Nicholas Sanders, landed in Munster to attack the
English government in Ireland. The expedition was put down, but
it showed how vulnerable Elizabeth might be in the west as well as
in the north. Fresh enactments in 1581 raised the penalty for non-
attendance at church to £20 a month. Saying Mass was punishable
by a fine of 200 marks and a year's imprisonment, hearing Mass was

punishable by a fine of 100 marks and a similar sentence; and it was decreed that whoever should seek to withdraw the Queen's subjects from their natural allegiance, or, for that intent, from the religion as by law established, was guilty of high treason. This was the legal position when Campion and his fellow, Parsons, re-entered England in May, 1581.

He was captured at a country house in Berkshire at the end of July and brought to London, where through a yelling mob he was carried to the Tower, and lodged in the vile cell known as Little Ease, where there was no room either to stand or lie down. At the end of forty-eight hours he was released from this durance. It was night-time, the night of July 25th, and he was taken under guard to an unnamed destination. It proved to be Leicester House, and there in a small room, accompanied by the Earl of Bedford and two secretaries, were two other people; his old patron the Earl of Leicester, and the Queen herself. Fifteen years before he had seen her at Woodstock, where she had almost bereft him of presence of mind by appearing suddenly before him in her glittering state. Fifteen years had added to her impressiveness, by a steady increase in peaceful and prosperous government and in the admiration and love she commanded as the symbol of it, and she met him now in a vehement attempt to make him understand and participate with her in her effort to keep this achievement safe, protected from the depredations of hostile powers. But fifteen years had worked a change in Campion too. His inspired nature was now completely absorbed in the duty of ministering to the Catholics who were lapsing for want of a priest, and of leading into the Church as many heretics as he could. He was infinitely more self-possessed, more balanced, more determined, more tranquil than he had been all those years ago. The traits that had not altered were his gentleness, his simplicity and his sweetness.

In this extraordinary interview, held in the hours of summer darkness by candle-light, Elizabeth asked him whether he acknowledged her as his Queen? He said yes, as his lawful Queen. Then the question was put to him that had been devised to test loyalty. Campion refused to give, not only the required answer, but any answer. His own motives were entirely spiritual—he said, we are dead men to the world, we only travel for souls—but his refusal showed that his first allegiance was given to the power that had already sanctioned the murder of Elizabeth.

The Queen did him no injustice; she possessed too much penetration and sense to believe that he had any wish to injure her, and she tried to impress on him why, from her point of view, it was necessary to impose a degree of observance to the religion of the state. She urged her reasons, she promised that in his case this observance should be reduced to a minimum; let him attend a Protestant church once only, that should be enough. It was useless; every argument fell short in Campion's ears, because it ignored what was to him the one all-conquering argument. The Queen could do nothing further. The interview was over, and Campion was taken back to the Tower, but the Earl of Leicester sent a message to the Governor, Sir Owen Hopton, that the prisoner was to be well-treated. This meant that he was no longer to be kept in a dungeon; it did not save him from being racked, in an effort to make him disclose the names of the families who had sheltered him. With fourteen other missionary priests he was tried and found guilty of high treason; the same hopeless deadlock prevailed through his trial, and at the scene of his death. He said at the gallows: "If you consider my religion treason then am I guilty. Other treason I never committed any, as God is my judge", and a voice from the crowd cried out: "In your Catholicism all treason is contained." Lord Hunsdon and Sir Francis Knollys, among the crowd of gentlemen who witnessed the execution, were in charge of the proceedings, and when Campion was hanging one of them ordered the executioner to leave him till he was dead, so that the quartering was performed on his lifeless body. Someone, able to command, had wished him well.

In July Mendoza, in writing about the Queen, told the King of Spain: "Walsingham and Leicester persuade her she can only insure her own safety by troubling your Majesty in all ways. Only the other day . . . they said . . . while the Queen of Scots lived . . . this Queen could not be sure of her personal safety, much less of that of her crown."

In this year 1581 Leicester, as Chancellor of Oxford University, used his influence to inforce that the oath acknowledging the Royal Supremacy and The 39 Articles of Religion should be administered to every undergraduate over sixteen years old. The University by this became exclusively Anglican. At the same time, all tutors were to be licensed to examine their students with a view to finding out whether they were secretly Catholics. These injunctions were not carried out by the authorities with any enthusiasm, and a year later the Chancellor wrote to the Vice-Chancellor and the Fellows, to complain of their being neglected.

In November, Alençon returned for the last phase of his courtship.

Walsingham was *en poste* in Paris. Leicester and Hatton were not in the Queen's confidence, and for some hideous moments it seemed to them both that this repulsive match was about to become a reality; but the Queen was not acting irrespective of policy. She had already written to Stafford at Paris, apropos the people's dislike of the match: "Hitherto they have thought me no fool; let me not live, the longer the worse . . . my mortal foes can no ways wish me a greater harm than England's hate."* Burleigh was confined to his bed with gout, and when Alençon's arrival was announced she sent him a note, saying: "Let me know what you wish me to do." A few days later she was walking with Alençon in the gallery at Greenwich. She kissed him, and said to the French Ambassador: "You may tell his Majesty that the Prince will be my husband", and drawing a ring from her own finger she put it on Alençon's.

Leicester thought the decision was now irrevocable. In his anxiety to know the truth, he put a question to her which showed that he himself had never deflowered her: with the French Prince's self-satisfied moppings and mowings before him, he demanded of her bluntly, whether she were a maid or a woman? Elizabeth laughed gaily and said: a maid. She told him not to be distressed. The business of extricating herself had now to begin, and the painful, ludicrous process occupied the next three months. An exchange of letters between Spanish spies at Antwerp said: "The Earl of Leicester knows well enough that if the Duke should be married in England, it would be the end of his own prospects." The rumour of Elizabeth's incapacity for child-bearing had always been counter-balanced by reports of her illegitimate children. This letter went so far as to say that the Queen had two daughters, one of whom was to be married to Alençon. The Queen, the writer said, thought of nothing but being shut up with the Duke, "from morning till noon, and after, till two or three hours after sunset. I cannot tell what a' devil they do."†

The writer, who thought the Queen attended to nothing but love-making with Alençon, could not tell what the devil she did. Lord Burleigh could have enlightened him. In the position he occupied, and in the pressure of the times, the handling of this insignificant young man was a matter of the greatest significance. At the beginning of the year the King of Spain was annexing Portugal, and the forces of the Counter-Reformation had launched a military attack on Ireland and a civil invasion by missionary priests. The Guise family

---

* Wright, *Elizabeth and her Times*.   † C.S.P. Foreign.

had sent their agent, Lord Esmé Stuart, to the Court of the young Scots King, where the ascendancy he quickly gained over the latter was intended to pave the way for an invasion led by the Guises, which should move from Scotland southwards, calling up all Catholics to unite in the overthrow of Elizabeth and the setting of Mary Stuart in her place. In this posture of affairs, it had been open to the Duke of Alençon to enter the Netherlands as an auxiliary of his brother and bring them within the French sphere of influence, so that, opposite to the southern shores of England, the whole coastline from Brest to the Hague would be in French control. His departure in February, 1582, after scenes of indescribable absurdity, of tears, broken vows, recriminations and protestations (with, it was true, £50,000 of good English money in his pocket), preparing to counterpoise Spanish power in the Netherlands and yet separated from the power of France, in firm alliance with England but not the husband of the English Queen—this was a diplomatic triumph worth every concession, moral and financial, that it had cost.

Mendoza heard that Alençon had thrown upon Simier the blame for the failure of his wooing, because Simier had destroyed the Earl of Leicester's influence with the Queen by exposing his marriage to her, and had thus deprived Alençon of his services. Simier himself had assumed the opposite; he told the Queen that everyone was astonished that Lord Leicester still enjoyed her favour. She had replied, according to Mendoza, that she could hardly put the Earl down, as he had taken advantage of the authority she had given him to place kinsmen and friends of his in almost every port and stronghold in England. "This is quite true", Mendoza said, and added that until she had time to get some of these places out of their hands it was not possible for her to deprive him of the position he held.

Actually this was not true; although Lord Bedford, Lady Warwick's father, was governor of Berwick, Sir Henry Sidney Lord President of Wales, Lord Grey de Wilton Lord Deputy of Ireland, Sir Edward Horsey (who Lady Sheffield said had given her away at her marriage to Lord Leicester) Governor of the Isle of Wight, and Lord Warwick Master of the Ordinance, it would have been in Elizabeth's power to recall any of them by a stroke of the pen. If she had indeed made the remark to Simier, it was another falsehood. She never showed herself in the smallest degree afraid of Leicester. With so much support available to her in other people's dislike of him, there would have been no obstacle to his removal had she wished it. The plain truth, which would not have been very easy to explain to

Simier, was that she did not wish it. Many waters cannot drown love.

At Alençon's departure for the Netherlands, Mendoza said: "Leicester managed to get appointed to go with him, to gain credit with the heretics, whom he gives to understand that he has been the cause of Alençon's departure." The Prince, with £30,000 in hard cash and bills for £20,000 more, was taken over to Flushing in a fleet of fifteen large vessels, attended by Lord Leicester, Lord Hunsdon, Lord Willoughby and Mr. Philip Sidney. He had not, formally, relinquished his position as the Queen of England's lover. The month before, on New Year's Day, he had given her lover's gifts of an enchanting gracefulness. One was a gold bracelet, inscribed *Serviet eternum dulcis quem torquet Eliza: May it serve for ever the sweet Eliza it entwines.* Another was an ornament of enamelled gold in the shape of a white rose and a ruby, diamond and sapphire butterfly; a third was one of a diamond and ruby ship with spread sails. On the sails was a word which the makers of the inventory could not translate. That New Year's Day, Lady Huntingdon's gift was most appropriate; it was "a green frog, the back of emeralds, small and great, with a pendant emerald, with a small gold chain to hang by".

While Lord Leicester was making his first visit to Antwerp, where he had escorted Alençon from Flushing, the Prince of Orange showed him how the States could reward those who helped them. In a private room, he and the Earl were received by two burghers of the city; presently they were joined by two men, booted and spurred, who had just ridden in from Ghent. Each of the four now produced a key, and these keys unlocked four locks of a casket. When this was opened, it revealed a gold cup, set with such a blazing galaxy of precious stones that Leicester was astounded. He knew at once who would be enraptured at the sight. Why, he exclaimed, had they not sent this miracle to London? The Queen of England would do anything in return for it.[1]

He returned to London. He had brought Alençon in safety and in great state to Antwerp, but at Flushing a sandbar in the harbour had interfered with the immediate landing of the ships, and Leicester, in recovered intimacy and freedom to play the jealous lover, told Elizabeth scornfully that he had left the Duke stranded on a sandbank. She said she would give a million pounds to have her Frog swimming safely in the Thames again. To celebrate his home-coming, Leicester gave a supper-party for his two sisters, his brother and sister-in-law and other kinsfolk. A spy told Mendoza that during the conversation Leicester declared that a man who had attempted to murder the

Prince of Orange had been seen leaving the Spanish Embassy in London a month ago, and he would try to get the Queen to expel Mendoza. Lady Warwick, with her usual candour and sweetness said that she had never seen anything to complain of in his behaviour.

In July, Mendoza reported to Philip that he had secured Lord Henry Howard to the Spanish interest on an official basis: "I have given him 500 crowns and promised him 1,000 a year and have induced him to continue in your Majesty's service." He then spoke of Sir James Croft, the Queen's Comptroller of the Household, who was also on the Spanish payroll; but he, said Mendoza, "has been almost dumb with me for some months past . . . in consequence of Leicester's having set the Queen against him, and he therefore avoids such business". By November Mendoza was quite sick of the uselessness of Sir James. "He must make himself useful for some years before your Majesty can be expected to make him another grant, since he is so very silent now. I understand that his reticence is caused by Leicester who has quite terrified him." As early as 1582, therefore, animosity between Sir James Croft and the Earl had been noted.

In the autumn Lord Shrewsbury lost one of his sons by death. The age demanded that a letter of condolence should be written in a strain of high piety and religious resignation, but Leicester's letter to the bereaved father is markedly different, for instance, from the letters Elizabeth sent to her friends on their children's deaths; letters urging resignation, indeed, but in terms both loving and brief. Leicester's letter to Lord Shrewsbury ran: "Be thankful to Him for all His doings, my good Lord, and take all in that part which you ought; be you wholly His and seek His kingdom first, for it passeth all worldly kingdoms." He did not know, as he wrote, how terrible a blow impended over himself and how soon he would be called upon to take his own counsel.

Elizabeth had to write a letter of condolence herself to Lord Burleigh the following month; his daughter Elizabeth had made a very happy marriage, but within the year the young husband, Lord Wentworth, died of the plague. The Queen's letter to Lord Burleigh made him weep. He exclaimed: "My sovereign sweet lady, whom I pray God to preserve from all grief of mind and body."*

In November Lord Sussex developed the final stage of an illness that was to prove fatal. It was said that he had never recovered from the rigours of the campaign in the Rising of the North, when he

* Conyers Read, *Lord Burleigh and Queen Elizabeth.*

caught cold lying on the hard ground. Mendoza said: "He is consumptive and cannot attend to business." Burleigh, Mendoza heard, had told the Queen that two more Privy Councillors must be appointed, and he was taking care they should be of his own party. This meant that they would favour a pacific foreign policy and not attempt to commit the Queen to the suicidal hazards of a war against Spain. Burleigh needed such ballast, for now that Sussex was laid up "it was not possible to oppose Leicester and his gang".

In September the Norrises had been greatly looking forward to the Queen's coming to Rycote. Elizabeth must have been in the neighbourhood, for the September wet weather only prevented her coming at the last moment. Leicester and Hatton both dissuaded her from a journey over roads in such a state, and Leicester went on to Rycote by himself. He wrote to tell Hatton of the intense disappointment his sole appearance had caused Lady Norris, when he arrived at ten o'clock at night, over as foul and ragged a way as he had ever travelled in his life. Lady Norris scolded him for having dissuaded the Queen, "but I was fain to stand to it . . . and would not for anything, for the little proof I had of this day's journey that her Majesty had been in it". Lady Norris was so sorely disappointed, Leicester said, "if it had not been so late, I think I should have sought another lodging, my welcome awhile was so ill . . . but I dealt plainly with her that I knew she would have been sorry afterwards to have had her Majesty come at this time of year to this place". Hatton must do his part to pacify Lady Norris, "but her Majesty must especially help somewhat, or we have more than half lost this lady". To make amends, Leicester promised that if the Queen stayed at Oatlands, the palace in Surrey where, as Master of the Horse, he had official accommodation, Lady Norris should come there and occupy his lodging. "They had put the house here in every good order to receive her Majesty," he told Hatton, "and a hearty, noble couple they are, as ever I saw, towards her Majesty. I rest here this Sabbath day to make peace for us both; what remains, you shall do."*

Nothing could show more plainly that Leicester had regained his privileged footing. He had not given up, either, any of his favourite schemes except the one his marriage had finally put out of his reach. Like his father, he could not resist the attempt to get his hands upon any possible heirs to the English throne. With the young King James of Scotland he had long been on ingratiating terms, sending him dogs and a fine piebald horse; but another claimant in the Stuart line

* Nicolas, *Sir Christopher Hatton*.

was growing up. The seven-year-old Lady Arabella Stewart was living in the care of her grandmother, Lady Shrewsbury. Little Lord Denbigh was some four years old, and his father thought yearningly of a match between the children. If the sixteen-year-old King James were to die, or to be assassinated, even—and in the wilds of Scotland there was no saying what might occur—then Lord Denbigh might be what Lord Leicester had once meant to be, the husband of the Queen of England.

XXIII

AFTER THE CRACK that flawed their intimacy in 1579, Leicester's presents to Elizabeth either denoted from habit an affectionate relationship of long-standing, or were chosen with a view to asserting it. He was, like the other Councillors, accustomed to using a cipher for his correspondence abroad; in 1571, he had told Sir Francis Walsingham he would like an easier one, but he was able to handle the complicated process. In the collection of his books now at Lambeth Palace, Lt.-Colonel W. E. Moss* discovered on the fly leaves of several volumes an assemblage of letters which he deciphered as a codeword, giving "R. Leycestir" and "Elizuabeth", the forced spelling of the latter being a concession to the demands of the cipher. On New Year's Day, 1583, Leicester's present to the Queen was a necklace of twenty pieces, consisting of letters "and a cypher in the midst", every piece set with diamonds, two pearls between each letter, and from each letter a diamond hanging.

At the beginning of March, 1583 the English Catholics on the Continent were saying that there was a "practice" between Lord Leicester and Lady Shrewsbury for the marriage of Lord Denbigh to the Lady Arabella. Now the Earl was credited with another scheme. Lady Leicester, by her first husband Lord Essex, had two daughters; one, the *éblouissante* Penelope, was now Lady Rich; the other, Dorothy, was still available. Mendoza heard that Leicester, in concert with Walsingham, had told the young Scots King that if he would marry Dorothy Devereux, and would assure them that he would not change his religion, they would have him declared by the judges to be the heir to the Crown of England. "Notwithstanding this offer," said Mendoza, "Leicester still perseveres in the match I mentioned, of his son with the granddaughter of the Countess of Shrewsbury, who after the Queen of England they say is the nearest heiress. With Walsingham's aid he is thus trying to get his son made king in right of the latter's wife. His relatives and friends," continued Mendoza, repeating what he had said some months before, "have

* Bindings from the Library of Robert Dudley, Earl of Leicester.

possession of the ports of entry of the country, the only thing wanting . . . being control of the sea-forces, which the Queen has
promised, after the death of the Earl of Lincoln (who is now more
than seventy), to Lord Howard, with whom Leicester has made an
arrangement before hand to exchange the office of Admiral for that
of Master of the Horse which Leicester holds."

The last sentence shows, unfortunately, how totally unreliable
Mendoza's reports could be. The Queen made appointments with a
keen eye to suitability and merit; once they had been bestowed, it
was not open to the recipients to exchange them with each other as
if they were children bartering their playthings. The idea that Lord
Howard of Effingham, who five years later commanded the naval
forces against the Armada, should have conceived the notion of
exchanging the office of Lord High Admiral for that of Master of
the Horse was so ludicrous, it was astonishing that an ambassador
resident in England could credit it. "The Queen of Scots," Mendoza
went on, "has earnestly pressed the French Ambassador to let the
Queen know of this design of Leicester's for the marriage of his son,
as she is certain it would arouse her female jealousy and make her
very indignant. The Ambassador, however, has refused." The Queen
of Scots and Lady Shrewsbury had for a time been on very intimate
terms. The intimacy had turned sour, and Lady Shrewsbury now
had little interest to spare for the past importance of the Queen of
Scots, or even for her possible future importance as Queen of
England; she thought only of the heiress she was bringing up in her
own family. The Queen of Scots' enmity to her and to Leicester was
understandable; since her household was under the same roof as
that of Lord Shrewsbury, her servants would have had no difficulty
in picking up the information as to Lady Shrewsbury's plans and
ambitions for the little Arabella.

Once again, the morbid and unhappy William Tresham appeared
in letters from abroad. In April he wrote to Sir Christopher Hatton—
whose friendship for Leicester was known to everybody—"How
may it be thought that even you would have rejected me, your devoted
poor friend, for the sole pleasure of the Earl of Leicester . . . knowing
as you do . . . that he affecteth you only to serve his own turn?
Take heed of him in time ! . . . all the harm I wish you is that you will
with the eyes of wisdom look into him thoroughly, and there you shall
find that he knoweth only to gain friends and hath not the good
regard and grace to keep them." This was indeed not true of Leicester :

Lord Shrewsbury, Lord North, Sir Francis Walsingham and Hatton himself were conspicuous instances to the contrary.

Philip Sidney was knighted in 1583, and in March of this year a marriage was arranged between him and Walsingham's daughter Frances. This matter was much less spectacular than his passion for Lady Rich, but Frances Walsingham was very beautiful, dark while Penelope was yellow-haired, and the match was one of mutual affection. Neither family could put down much money, and Sir Henry Sidney said frankly that he was looking to Sir Francis Walsingham to "move the Queen to certain suits", so compensating for lack of that settlement which he would have got if his son had married elsewhere; but he thoroughly approved the match in itself, and his letter, in which he spoke of the suits, spoke also of "the joyful love and great liking between our most dear and sweet children, whom God bless". The match had not been mentioned to the Queen before it was concluded, and, as Sir Philip Sidney occupied a prominent place at Court, Elizabeth made this reticence a ground of displeasure. Secret marriages were something she abhorred; as she said when her lady-in-waiting Frances Vavasour was clandestinely married to Sir Henry Shirley: "She [the Queen] hath always furthered any honest and honourable purposes of marriage or preferment to any of hers, when without scandal and infamy they have been orderly broke to her." She took the line now that she should have been told of the match between Philip Sidney and Frances Walsingham. Sir Francis Walsingham was incensed. He wrote freely to Sir Christopher Hatton. The reason he had said nothing to the Queen was that: "I am no person of that state, but that it may be thought a presumption for me to trouble her Majesty with a private matter between a free gentleman of equal calling with my daughter." He told Hatton peremptorily: "Let her understand, first, that the match is for concluded, secondly how just cause I shall have to find myself aggrieved if that her Majesty shall show her mislike thereof." This was all very well; it was easy enough telling someone else to bell the cat. However, Hatton did his best. The wedding took place in September, and the Queen was godmother to the first child of it. The marriage of Leicester's nephew to Walsingham's daughter increased the friendship and warmth of feeling between Walsingham and himself.

In May Lord Burleigh gave a house party for the Queen at Theobalds, his newly built house in Hertfordshire. It had been transformed from a small house called Tongs into a red-brick palace enclosing three successive courts. The road that led to it out of

London is still called Theobalds Road. The notes remain that Lord Burleigh made for this visit, allotting their accommodation to the various guests. The principal ones were lodged in the inner court. "In the corner, a chamber with a bay-window, with an inner room opening towards the great garden," was set apart for the Queen's robes. The Hall was converted to the Queen's Great Chamber; on the third storey, at the south side, was "a gallery for the Queen's Majesty". At the south side, in a tower, one chamber with two pallet chambers was reserved for the Earl of Leicester. This was a bed-chamber for the Earl and two rooms for his servants. Lord Hunsdon was next to him. At the north-west end of the gallery was a bed-chamber in a tower; this was for the Queen's Majesty. There were also provided an inner dining chamber, the Queen's withdrawing chamber and the Queen's Privy Chamber. In the fourth storey, above the Queen's room, was that of her very old lady in waiting, Blanche Parry; on the same floor was Sir Christopher Hatton and "a closet vaulted with stone for avoidances". One delightfully-sounding room, "a chamber with a pallet chamber, having a stair downward towards the east into a garden", was given to the Lady Marquess of North-ampton,* still so-called though she had for seven years been the wife of Sir Thomas Gorges.

The hostess, the blue-stocking Lady Burleigh, was some years older than the Queen; she had been educated in the same academic tradition, but there the likeness ended. Lady Burleigh, frosty and austere, though deeply beloved of her husband, disapproved of the Queen. Her daughter Ann, however, the unfortunate young Lady Oxford, was artlessly fond of her great godmother; Burleigh spoke of her to the Queen as "Your Majesty's most humble young servant". When she asked Lord Sussex, as Lord Chamberlain, to allot her some rooms at Hampton Court, she said she was asking for them because she thought it would please her husband to come there and because, she said, "methinks it long since I saw the Queen".

In June, 1583, Lord Sussex died. His chivalry and integrity, his brusque honesty and protective tenderness had been Elizabeth's assets ever since she came to the throne twenty-five years before. He had served her at her coronation banquet while she sat exhausted and speechless and developing a severe cold, and he had seen her, through a policy of caution, economy, vigilance, self-dedication and single-minded passion, come to a state of hived-up riches and power, and a place in the people's hearts which even her father had not surpassed.

* Murdin, ed., *State Papers.*

He knew, too, what the dangers were surrounding her, abroad and at home, and of these he thought he knew the chief. As he lay dying, Hatton sat by his bed. Hatton did not know, or did not credit, the far-reaching nature of Leicester's plans; nor had he been obliged to see the Queen in the humiliation of her ravings, or to question Lady Sheffield in her hysterical crying; he was deceived by this smiler with the knife. Sussex made a last effort to warn him. "Beware of the gipsy," he said, "he will be too hard for you all. You do not know the beast as well as I do."

He died on June 9th, and was buried in Westminster Abbey, where his splendid tomb in St. Edward's Chapel commemorates a great nobleman and an honest man.

Meanwhile Lady Leicester, to whom common sense should have dictated a behaviour that was altogether inoffensive, had rekindled the Queen's anger. The anecdote rests upon Mendoza's authority, and it is perhaps proper to make a distinction between his statements as to what certain people intended to do—which gave large grounds for making mistakes even in those who knew them well and could estimate their probable course of action—and what his spies had over-heard them actually say. Mendoza was told that the Queen had made enquiries among certain of the Scots as to whether Leicester had in fact begun negotiations for the marriage of James with Lady Dorothy Devereux. They told her, no; but she was not satisfied. She was reported to have exclaimed, that she would sooner the Scots King lost his crown, than that she should see him married to the daughter of such a she-wolf; and that if she could find no other way to check Lady Leicester's ambition she would proclaim her all over Christendom for the whore she was, and prove her husband a cuckold. In order to mollify the Queen, Mendoza was told, Lord Leicester was now making efforts to get the girl married to a private gentleman; but this proved unnecessary. Lady Dorothy who was bursting with exuberance saved her stepfather the trouble of arranging a *parti* for her by eloping with Sir Thomas Perrot, to whom she was married in Broxbourne church in the nick of time, while pursuers galloped up to the porch.

What the evidence might be on which Elizabeth called her cousin a whore is conjectural. Whether Lady Leicester had already begun a liaison with Sir Christopher Blount—whom she married with remarkable haste after Leicester's death, when she was forty-eight and Blount twenty-four—or whether the Queen knew or assumed her to be engaged on one with somebody else, whether the whole accusation were groundless, or if indeed it were made at all, can scarcely be determined; but the report of it shows the impression in the public mind of the Queen's attitude towards the Countess.

Leicester's position was outwardly undamaged, but he felt himself at a disadvantage; this was clear from his conversation with the French Ambassador. Mauvissière wrote to the French King saying he had been to dine with Lord and Lady Leicester at Leicester House; his letter gives an interesting view of the sort of position Lady Leicester occupied. Mauvissière said: "He especially invited me to dine with him and his wife, who has much influence over him and whom he introduces only to those to whom he wishes to show a particular mark of attention." In other words, Lady Leicester was seen only on occasions. Mauvissière wrote of this same dinner party to the Queen of Scots, with whom he was in active correspondence.[1]

The Duke of Guise and his brother the Duke of Mayenne were planning what was called The Enterprise of England. Guise's plan to invade England through Scotland had had to be abandoned because of the exposure and expulsion of their agent Esmé Stewart. It was now determined that Guise should land in Northumberland with four thousand men and Mayenne in Sussex with another four thousand, while their ally Duke Albert of Bavaria was to bring five thousand more from Dunkirk into Norfolk. But Dr. Allen and the English Jesuits did not want The Enterprise carried out by French forces; they were unalterably committed to Spain. Let the Duke of Guise command, they said, but the whole matter must be in the hands and under the authority of the Spanish King. Dr. Allen assured the conspirators that England was waiting to welcome the invading army.

Mary Queen of Scots, who was kept in close touch with every development by Mendoza, by her Paris agent Thomas Morgan and by Francis Throckmorton, a nephew of Sir Nicholas Throckmorton, who was the manager of the plot in England, was attempting to come to a settlement with her son. Her demands were that he should become a Catholic and admit her as co-ruler with himself of Scotland. In return, she promised him massive support from English Catholics, who would secure for him the succession to the English crown; without her assistance, she assured him, he would never gain this coveted end. James, objectionable but pitiable, with a shocking heredity and every neurotic tendency increased by the rigours of his upbringing at the hands of Scottish presbyterians, had, nevertheless, considerable intellect and shrewdness; for the last three years, though not independent, he had been a force in his own government. He had now to decide for himself where his advantage lay. If he embraced Catholicism, he would lose the support of Elizabeth and the English parliament to his claims to inherit the English crown. If he rejected his mother's overtures and The Enterprise should succeed, then she would be Queen of England and Scotland, and he would be reduced to total insignificance.

This was the situation in which Mauvissière was involved when he dined at Leicester House. "I dined today," he wrote to the Queen of Scots, "with the Earl of Leicester and his lady to whom he is much attached. They both received me very kindly and . . . expressed a wish that the Countess and my wife should be on intimate terms. After dinner the Earl walked out with me and vowed that he had never been your Majesty's enemy, but had now lost his influence with Elizabeth, the King of France and your Majesty." The near possibility of her own elevation, at last, to the English throne had caused Mary to ask for some information on Leicester's attitude to the claims of his brother-in-law. "As for the Earl of Huntingdon," Mauvissière assured her, "Leicester would be the first to combat him, and in the event of the death of his Queen, he, with all his relations and friends, would willingly render some important service; he told me I might acquaint your Majesty with this, but was on no account to let anyone else hear it, as it would ruin the whole affair. . . . In a word, the Earl has never promised me more for your Majesty's service, and the means to keep him in this humour is to gain his wife and assure her that you will be her friend. Let me know if I shall continue the negotiations in this manner, for if Leicester does not dissemble, he wishes to serve your Majesty, only not a soul, not even Walsingham shall know it."[1]

"In the event of the death of his Queen", was all that Leicester had said. The possibility of her death, even of her assassination, was one which was continually present at the back of many minds, in some with hope, in others as anxiety amounting to nightmare. Leicester showed no eagerness for it; he could scarcely be accused of indifference towards it because he was trying to provide for his safety and welfare if it should occur. The long-standing affection between Elizabeth and himself had life in it still, and the old habits of tenderness asserted themselves on any occasion of illness. In October he was seized by what was probably his malaria, for it was some illness with which the Queen was familiar and for which she had been accustomed to suggest remedies. She did so now, sending frequently for news of him, and he caught at the opportunity to express his ardent gratitude and his devotion. "Thanks for your great grace to your poor . . . by your oft and most comfortable messengers, who hath brought best help and remedy to your old patient, that always has from that holy hand been relieved. I have no more to offer again but that which is already my bond and duty: the body and life, to be as ready to yield sacrifice for your service, as it has from you received all good things."*

* C.S.P. Domestic. Addenda, 1580—1625.

XXIV

On new year's day, 1584, Lord Leicester gave the Queen a porringer, standing on four feet; it was made of bloodstone, a dark green stone spotted with red, and had two gold handles in the form of snakes. He also gave her a more intimate gift, asserting his right to hang round her neck a diamond necklace made of his cinquefoils interspersed with lovers' knots.

His marriage had been acknowledged for four years, and, though his wife was not received at Court, Leicester House was the established home of the greatest noble in the land. The life of a family man was reflected in the inventory of its pictures and properties. Besides the portraits of Lady Leicester and his child, there was one of the Earl, "full length . . . with Boy his dog by him". There were portraits of Penelope Rich and Dorothy Perrot, "of Mr. Sidney when he was a boy". There was even one "of Lady Sheffield in a frame". There is no mention of any work by Nicholas Hilliard: his small, full-length picture of the Earl is dated 1588, but Leicester had, it appears, been a patron of this exquisite miniaturist for three or four years at least.

Hilliard had worked as goldsmith, carver and painter to the Queen, and in consideration of two years' service she had granted him a lease of certain property which produced a rent of £23 3s. 4d. a year. The letters patent enabling Hilliard to enter on the property remained uncompleted in the office of Sir Walter Mildmay, Chancellor of the Exchequer. On June 24th, 1582, Lord Leicester had written to the Chancellor, explaining Hilliard's case, saying, "wherefor I heartily pray your good favour towards him for his speedy going through therewith; it is now a good while ago since her Majesty did grant him relief". The patent was made out by October. Of Hilliard's children, the first two, born in 1579 and 1580, were named Elizabeth and Frances respectively; but the three born after 1582 were all given names out of the family in Leicester House: Lettice, Penelope and Robert.* Hilliard painted several miniatures of

* Blakiston, *Burlington Magazine*, January, 1954.

Elizabeth, but there is no sign that Leicester possessed one of them; he had two or three pictures of the Queen by other hands at Kenilworth, and in the collection of portraits of crowned heads which it had pleased him to make at Wanstead. Here were King Henry VIII, Queen Elizabeth, her sister Queen Mary, two of "Mountseur", one of the Prince of Orange, of the Emperor Charles V, of Don John of Austria, of the Queen Mother of France. His books were superbly bound, with the bear and ragged staff deeply stamped in gold in the centre of their covers which were sometimes powdered with gold cinquefoils or oak-leaves. His wardrobe was extensive, full of velvet cloaks, furred gowns and satin doublets embroidered in gold. It contained one homely item; in the array of hats, velvet hats, taffeta hats, beaver hats, there was "one thrum hat", a woollen affair; perhaps he wore it for fishing.[1]

The Enterprise, which the Duke of Guise had been ready to man himself, and which the English Jesuits had insisted should be entrusted to the King of Spain, was delayed so long through Philip's habitual slowness that Walsingham uncovered the conspiracy before the invasion had time to get under way. In November, 1583, the discovery, through the arrest and examination under torture of Francis Throckmorton, of the plans of The Enterprise revealed that Mary Queen of Scots had been conversant with every detail of it; and that Mendoza, as his part in the affair, had undertaken to get into touch with every justice of the peace of Catholic sympathies and tell him to levy men, ostensibly for the Queen's defence, with a view to taking them over to the invader—a scheme that appeared to ignore what the feelings of the men themselves might be. These revelations had the immediate effect of intensifying the severity and cruelty with which the missionary priests were treated; seven of them were hanged and quartered, and the tale of their sufferings and courage was spread over Europe. But the person chiefly responsible for their fate was not Walsingham, or even Burleigh, but Dr. Allen, who was declaring in Paris that the English Catholics were at point to rise, so much so that Guise would be able to conquer the country with a mere four thousand men. When the Prince of Parma, who had taken over Alva's command in the Netherlands, discussed the number of men needed for the invasion of England as part of the Armada action, he said he had 23,000 at his disposal; he would need every one of them, and even then he did not guarantee success. Such was the opinion of a soldier. Dr. Allen's estimate was based on his assumption, which he boldly stated, that all the Catholics in the land were eager to welcome a foreign army whose object was to dethrone Queen Elizabeth.

Meantime the discovery of Mendoza's doings had decided the Privy Council that he must be dismissed. He left the shores of England saying haughtily that as he had not been able to satisfy the Queen in peace he would hope to do so in war, but he decamped as fast as he could, for since his share in the conspiracy had been made public he feared an outbreak of mob violence.

In March the Queen of Scots wrote to Mauvissière, exhorting him to explain to Queen Elizabeth the total unreliability of anything said by Lady Shrewsbury, for whom she now cherished a vindictive hatred. "I wish you could say to her privately, if possible, making her promise neither to commit it to anyone nor to make any further enquiries, that nothing has so alienated the Countess from me as the vain hope which she has conceived of placing the Crown of England on the head of her little granddaughter Arabella, and this by marrying her to a son of the Earl of Leicester." The children, Mary said, were being brought up in the expectation of their marriage, and their portraits had been sent to each other. "But for the notion of raising one of her family to the rank of Queen she would never have so turned away from me." The Ambassador replied with allegations about Lord Leicester. "Leicester," he said, "has told Elizabeth that I went about to try to gain her councillors, and everyone in the kingdom for you; but that *he* considered nothing but the service of his Queen. By this," said Mauvissière, "and all other means at his command, he has sought to regain her good will and is now in higher favour than he was four years ago. In a word, he cannot be much depended on." With unconscious irony, Mauvissière added: "Monsieur Bodin who is a learned man, an astrologer, wrote to me only two days ago, that you would soon see the end of your troubles." In three years, so far as this world was concerned, the Queen of Scots had seen the end of them.[1]

However outwardly decorous it might be, the position between the Earl of Leicester, the former lover, and Sir Edward Stafford, the present husband of Douglas Sheffield could never be comfortable, and a small provocation would produce a disproportionate degree of resentment. In May, 1584, Stafford wrote from Paris to Burleigh: "I have written to my Lord of Leicester but more because it was your advice than for anything else; for at my going away he sent for me and assured me he would be as good a friend to me as any I left behind me, and yet I have found the contrary. I am but a poor gentleman, but I love plain dealing."

In June Leicester decided to go to Buxton baths again. The Queen of Scots wanted to visit them also, and Mauvissière wrote to Lord Burleigh on her behalf, asking him to ask Queen Elizabeth if she might go there as soon as the Earl of Leicester should have left. He had departed by the third week in June and Mauvissière wrote again, this time to Walsingham, asking if the Queen of Scots might go now, "since the Earl of Leicester has gone away".

As Leicester came home, passing from Derby into Leicestershire, he took the opportunity to visit his sister Kate. It was said that "at his coming from the baths out of Derbyshire, the Earl of Leicester came to the town of Leicester on Thursday the eighteenth day of June and there lay at the Earl of Huntingdon's house at which time the Countess of Huntingdon his sister did receive him there." The Mayor and his brethren gave the Earl a hogshead of claret wine and two fat oxen, and he gave them largesse which was divided among the town's charities. He had been hunting by the way, for he left six bucks with Lady Huntingdon, asking her to give them to the corporation. "His honour stayed but one night in Leicester and was gone of the Friday morning by five of the clock",[1] a pleasant time for journeying in high summer.

It was said that the Queen refused to receive Lady Leicester, but a budget of news signed "R.F.", and sent to a friend abroad, makes out that Leicester's wife began her married life by having the entré at Court, and forfeited it through her arrogant and ostentatious conduct. The authority is not reliable, for, in giving a résumé of Lord Leicester's career, he places the death of Amy Dudley after the Rising in the North and the death of the Duke of Norfolk. However this may be, he says of Lady Leicester: "She now demeaned herself like a Princess, vied in her dress with the Queen till her Majesty after sundry admonitions, told her that as but one sun lightened the east, she would have but one queen in England, boxed her ears, and forbade her the Court." This statement, unsupported, is not convincing; but of some value is the visual description the writer gives next, of Lady Leicester driving about the streets of London: "She rides through Cheapside drawn by four milk-white steeds with four footmen in black velvet jackets and silver bears on their backs and breasts, two knights and thirty gentlemen before her, and coaches of gentlewomen, pages and servants behind her, so that it might be supposed to be the Queen or some foreign prince or ambassador."[2]

Some echoes of all this may sound in Leicester's letter to Burleigh of July, 1584. Leicester and his wife were journeying and they came, unannounced, to Theobalds. Though Lord and Lady Burleigh were not at home, in the tradition of hospitality at great houses the Earl and Countess of Leicester and their train were received at the house with every attention. Leicester wrote to tell Burleigh of their visit, and to thank him at the same time for having approached the Queen to try whether her rigour towards Lady Leicester might be softened. He thanked Burleigh "that it pleased you so friendly and honourably to deal in behalf of my poor wife. For truly, my Lord, in all reason, she is hardly dealt with; God only must help it with her Majesty," but Burleigh, he promised, should "find us most thankful, to the uttermost of our powers".*

On Sunday, July 19th, Leicester underwent a crushing misfortune. On this day, at Wanstead, little Lord Denbigh died. The only statement about his illness is in the unreliable source of *Leicester's Commonwealth*, which speaks of "such a strange calamity as the falling-sickness, in his infancy", which if true would mean that the child suffered from epilepsy, though there is no other mention of it. His little suit of armour, preserved at Warwick Castle, has one thigh-piece rather longer than the other, which shows that with legs of uneven length he must have had a slight limp, and this was the origin of the odious slander that his father had had him poisoned because he was a cripple. The heartbroken parents inscribed on his tomb that he was a child of great promise. Besides the natural pang, the calamity to Leicester was very heavy. His marriage had brought but one child in six years, and he had lost it; with it went his hopes of perpetuating his father's house, and undivulged ambitions, loftier and brighter.

Davison was now Ambassador at Holyrood, and Leicester wrote to him with a moving simplicity: "Cousin Davison, I have this 2nd of August received your letter of the 27th of July. It found me from the Court, whence I have been absent these fifteen days to comfort my sorrowful wife for the loss of my little only son, whom God has lately taken from us."[1] As the child died on July 19th, and Leicester said on August 2nd that he had been absent from the Court fifteen days, which meant that he left it on July 18th, it appears that he must have received a message calling him to Wanstead immediately. As the Court was at Nonsuch, in Surrey, he would have been in time to see the boy alive. Three days after the child's death he received a

* Conyers Read, *Lord Burleigh and Queen Elizabeth*.

letter from Hatton, written from the Court: "My singular good Lord," Hatton wrote, "your excellent good wisdom, made perfect in the school of our eternal God . . . will, I trust, subdue these . . . natural afflictions which now oppress your own loving heart." He went on to assure Leicester that his loss inspired sympathy in the hearts of "millions, who on my soul, do love you no less than children or brethren". However this might be, he then delivered a message of heartfelt sincerity. "I have told her Majesty of this unfortunate and untimely cause which constrained your sudden journey to London, whereof I assure your Lordship I find her very sorry, and wisheth your comfort even from the bottom of her heart." The Queen had said nothing further to him on the matter because she was going to write to Leicester herself.[1]

Robert Dudley, Baron of Denbigh, was buried in the Beauchamp Chapel at Warwick. The effigy on his tomb shows him lying on a bier edged with minute ragged staves and cinquefoils, wearing a long gown with a turned-down collar, a circlet round his head. The date of his birth is not given; as the date of his parents' marriage could be ascertained it would have emphasized how hard the one event followed upon the other; but full particulars of his family were inscribed: "Son of Robert Earl of Leicester, nephew and heir unto Ambrose Dudley Earl of Warwick, brethren both sons of the mighty Prince, John, late Duke of Northumberland, herein interred, a child of great parentage but far greater hope and towardness, taken from this transitory unto the everlasting life, in his tender age at Wanstead in Essex on Sunday, 19th of July, in the year of our Lord God 1584 . . . and in this place laid up among his noble ancestors, in assured hope of the general resurrection."

In July had come the news of the murder of William of Orange. This ghastly event following on the discovery that Mary Queen of Scots was in close touch with her uncle the Duke of Guise and his Enterprise, sharpened the apprehensions for Elizabeth's safety in everyone who regarded her continued existence as their only protection against the horrors of civil war. The Queen herself had never been in any doubt of her constant danger; in March of this year she had said in her speech at the closing of Parliament: "I know no creature that breathes whose life standeth hourly in more peril for religion than mine own." But she had impatiently refused the suggestion of an armed bodyguard, declaring she had sooner be dead than in such captivity. The strain had long been eating its way into her nervous system, making her more bitter, more tense, more suspicious; but her unconquerable instinct was to go freely about among the people; on horseback along the roads, in coach or litter through the streets, on foot in Richmond or St. James's or Greenwich parks. Frightened but brave, with her erect carriage of the head and piercing eyes, she daunted, without knowing it, more than one would-be assassin who had made his way into her presence: Parry said he would have done the deed but that she reminded him of Henry VIII. But the Privy Council now made up their minds that some decisive steps must be taken.

Camden said that Lord Leicester was the originator of the Bond of Association. Lord Burleigh, writing of the matter to Lord Cobham in Paris, said merely: "It was accorded in Council," This Bond, whoever drew it up, stated that, if the Queen were murdered, the signatories to the bond would not only pursue the murderer to the death, dispatching him out of hand; they would also put to death the person in whose interests the murder had been committed, and declare that person's heirs incapable of succession. Copies of the bond were carried over the shires, and signatures were made in such numbers, that when they were brought to Hampton Court to show the Queen they had to be crammed into a large trunk. The Bond was explained to the Queen of Scots by Sir Ralph Sadler, who had replaced Lord Shrewsbury as her guardian, and Mary replied with a superb gesture; she said that if he would produce a copy, she would sign it herself.

The next step was to get the Bond incorporated in an Act of Parliament. Elizabeth, with admirable statecraft, resisted its provisions in their present form. She was gratified by the passionate enthusiasm for her safety which they showed, but she objected to the summary execution without trial of any person merely for the act of someone else, and she did not in any circumstances want to see James made incapable of succession to the English throne. After considerable argument, the Bond was re-formed in accordance with Elizabeth's criticism, and made into a Bill which provided that the murderer was to be put on trial; and that the person in whose interests he had acted was to be put to death only if it could be proved that he or she had been a consenting party to the crime. The heir was not to be incapacitated, unless he too were proved to have a guilty knowledge.

If Leicester had not invented the oath himself, the fact that it was ascribed to him showed his reputation at this time for a gallant and fervent loyalty. This quality was recognized and appreciated by

Elizabeth, and she showed her feelings by undertaking his defence when a shattering attack was made upon him.

On September 29th, 1584, Sir Francis Walsingham wrote to the Earl: "My very good Lord: Yesterday I received from the Lord Mayor enclosed in a letter a printed libel against your Lordship, the most malicious-written thing that ever was penned since the beginning of the world." Walsingham states that the author "is Morgan the Queen of Scots' agent in France", and that he had been helped by some of the English Catholics in France, Lord Paget, Charles Arundel, and the man who regarded himself as Leicester's victim, William Tresham. Walsingham adds—a glimpse of his intelligence service— "About three years past I had notice given unto me in secret sort of such an intention, with a meaning to reach higher", which implies that another work was to have been written about the Queen herself. Walsingham says: "There is no good, no honest man (and though he were your Lordship's mortal enemy) that doth not condemn this treacherous manner of dealing." He asked Leicester what he would like him to say to the Queen about it, and "what order he thought meet to be taken with the bringer-over of the said books". The Lord Mayor had the latter under lock and key for the present, and Walsingham had sent for the volumes to ensure that nobody got a sight of them.*

The first edition of this work which Walsingham now had in his hands was entitled "The Copy of a Letter written by a Master of Art of Cambridge to his friend in London, concerning some talk passed of late between two worshipful and grave men about the present state, and some proceedings of the Earl of Leicester and his friends in England". When the book was reprinted in 1641, it was given the handier title of *Leicester's Commonwealth*. The first edition had a green cover, and the edges of the pages were stained green; as there was a considerable suspicion that the author was Campion's friend Parsons, the book was sometimes called Father Parsons' Greencoat. The determination of the authorities to ban it was so strong, and was countered by a determination to spread it of such strength, that more manuscript copies exist than copies of the printed first edition.

Despite its patent unreliability, the book is of extraordinary interest. It is a mine of contemporary gossip, so vivid and immediate that it conveys the effect of clair-audience. One of the reasons for its brilliant and long-lasting success, *succès de scandale* though it be, is the

* MSS., British Museum, Titus, B VII, f. 10.

vigour, bouyancy and raciness with which it is written. It is in the form of a three-cornered conversation between a "Gentleman", a "Lawyer" and a "Scholar". "Lawyer" is said to be a mild Papist. The fact that all three are sympathetic to the late Duke of Norfolk and in favour of the French match imparts a superficial air of Catholicism to the book, but the work carries quite as many evidences of Protestantism; indeed, it largely ignores sectarian interests, and concentrates upon a vindictive but very humorous satirical portrait of the Earl of Leicester. It is clearly written by someone who knew a great deal of inside gossip, and it conveys so strongly a sense of private information that to assess its worth as evidence in every detail would require almost more knowledge than could now be available. Its influence has been so great that, despite the lip-service paid to its unsoundness, statements about Leicester of which this book is the only source continue to be printed as matters of fact without reference to their origin. The chief of these are: that Dr. Bailey was asked to visit and prescribe for Lady Dudley, which he refused to do, fearing that his medicine would be used as a vehicle for poison; that Dr. Babington, in his oration at her funeral, made a slip of the tongue and called her "pitifully slain" instead of "pitifully dead"; that Leicester had Sir Nicholas Throckmorton poisoned with a salad while dining at Leicester House, out of long-nursed revenge because Throckmorton had reported the Queen of Scots' remark about the Queen of England's horse-keeper; that he had made three attempts to have Simier murdered; and that he first married Lady Essex privately at Kenilworth before the ceremony at Wanstead. The author is the first person to state in print, as a coherent narrative, that Lord Robert Dudley had his wife put to death, though the accusation had, of course, been very generally repeated by word of mouth. He, however, introduces for the first time the agency of Richard Verney into the story ("He, I say . . . can tell how she died"), and puts in the extremely interesting detail that the hood upon Lady Dudley's head was not disturbed although her neck was broken. These are the chief episodes to which the widest currency has been given, but the author also produced an array of pungent epigrams that are constantly quoted without acknowledgment, as that Leicester "was noble only in two descents, both stained with the block", and that Lady Sheffield and Lady Essex were known as "his Old and New Testaments".

The conversation recapitulates the treasons of the Duke of Northumberland, "wherein this fellow's hand was so far as, for his age, he could thrust the same". It describes the enormous power and wealth Leicester had acquired through "the gracious and sweet dispositions of her Majesty", and accuses him of attempting high treason in meaning to put Lord Huntingdon on the throne, and, again, of conspiring to obtain supreme power through supporting the claims of Arabella Stuart, and of private infamy as a murderer, a lecher and a covetous tyrant, and an atheist who exploited both Catholics and Protestants to serve his turn. He is accused of engrossing power by the adroit placing of his friends and dependents—this, indeed, repeated what Simier had heard the Queen say two years before. He had thwarted every noble match proposed to the Queen, taking envoys aside and telling them "that *he* (forsooth!) was contracted to her Majesty, and all other Princes must give over their suits for him", and when the Swedish envoy seemed, not unnaturally, to question this assertion, Leicester gave him "a most disloyal proof" of his intimacy with the Queen. This statement in itself indicates how unreliable the writer's charges are. The negotiations were being entertained not only because they amused the Queen, but as the basis of a network of alliances. If Leicester had dared seriously to interfere with them, even his career would not have survived it.

Then the Earl is accused of entering into a conspiracy with Lord Warwick to prevent the French match by force if necessary. "My Lord himself had given it out a little before at Kenilworth, that the matter would cost many broken heads before Michaelmas next, and my Lord of Warwick said openly at his table at Greenwich . . . that it was not to be suffered . . . which words (were) misliked by his own Lady then also present." In this gallimaufry of truth and falsehood Lady Warwick, as ever, shines out with a mild and steady light. "Such debasing" there was "of them that favoured the match." A marginal note adds: *Lord Burleigh, Lord Sussex and Sir James Croft*. Croft's name in this context is another instance of the enmity between Lord Leicester and him.

Immense knowledge of contemporary detail would be needed to sift the truth of all the author's assertions, but some are demonstrably false. He says Lady Dudley was "found murdered as all men said by the Crowner's inquest", but the verdict was accidental death. He says she was first buried in Cumnor Church and then disinterred and reburied in Oxford. The details of the funeral preparations show that this was not so. His charges against Lord Huntingdon of scheming for the crown are rebutted by everything known about Lord Huntingdon. The accusation that Leicester debased the University of Oxford by his Chancellorship because under him "all good order is disrupted and destroyed . . . the fervour of study extinguished, the public lectures abandoned . . . the apparel of students grown monstrous" shows a strange misunderstanding or misuse of actual information, because these were the very topics on which Leicester wrote to admonish the University in this identical year, 1584. No doubt there were many other flagrant inaccuracies and misrepresentations. The attraction of the book, however, is its quantity of personal details, which may or may not be true but have an irresistible interest. Speaking of the liaison with Lettice Knollys, the author explains how, in the time between the death of Lord Essex and the marriage with Lord Leicester, the matter was kept secret by "this man's hasty snatching up of the widow, whom he sent up and down the country from house to house, by privy ways, thereby to avoid the sight and knowledge of the Queen's Majesty. And albeit he had not only used her at his good liking before, for satisfying of his own lust, but also married and remarried her for contentation of her friends." The Queen's anger at the marriage was said to have infuriated Lady Leicester: "It did put the widow in such an open frenzy as she raged many months after at her Majesty and is not cold yet."

His surgeon, "come out of Italy", the famous Dr. Julio, was credited with skilful poisons of delayed action, which, by operating some time after they were administered (they "could make a man die in what manner or show of sickness you will"), shielded the poisoner from suspicion. The author says that Lady Essex, already pregnant by Leicester when Lord Essex was about to return from Ireland, was driven to an operation for abortion; if only she had known of Dr. Julio's powers in time, she might have employed them against her husband, and not needed "to have sitten so pensive at home and fearful of her husband's return . . . but might have spared the young child in her belly, which was she enforced to make away with, cruelly and unnaturally, for clearing the house against the good man's arrival". He accused Leicester of procuring the deaths by poison not only of Sir Nicholas Throckmorton but also of Lord Essex, Lady Lennox and Lord Sussex. He deals with the Earl's matrimonial and other arrangements by saying: "His Lordship changeth wives and minions, by killing the one, denying the other, using the third for a time and he fawning upon the fourth." If Lady Dudley, Lady Sheffield and Lady Essex are intended by the first, second and third, the Queen is probably the fourth. "And for this cause he hath his terms and pretences, I warrant you, of contracts, precontracts, postcontracts, protracts and retracts."

The question of Lady Sheffield's marriage to Leicester was brought up again. The writer says he resolved to make a retract of this post-contract, "though it were as surely done (as I have said) as bed and Bible could make the same, and to make a certain new protract (which is a continuation of using her for a time) with the widow of Essex . . . he was content to assign to the former a thousand pounds with other petty considerations (the pitifullest abused that ever was poor lady) and so betake his limbs to the latter, which latter, not withstanding, he so useth as we see, now confessing, now foreswearing, now dissembling the marriage". The writer was sure that the Earl could always yet keep "a void place for a new surcontract with any other when occasion shall require"; but he was mistaken there. The current Lady Leicester held the reins too firmly for that.

Allegations are made that Leicester was a lecher of omnivorous appetite whose failing powers were revived by Italian preparations—ointment, and a bottle at his bed-head of ten pounds the pint; and that, as a punishment for his way of life, he had developed what sound like abscesses on his stomach—"a broken belly on both sides of his bowels". The falling sickness of the child is mentioned as a consequence of the parents' sins; a marginal note gives a quotation from Proverbs: "The children of adulterers, shall be consumed and the seed of a wicked bed shall be rooted out." The note was probably added when news was heard of the child's death.

It is striking that throughout the book the Queen is absolved of any complicity with Leicester's tyranny, rapacity and persecution. She is shown as "of no strong or robustious constitution", harassed by Leicester, no rest night or day permitted her until she acceded to his demands however unreasonable, the victim of his unkindness and his remorseless greed, and in actual danger from his resentment because she had thwarted his ambition by refusing to marry him. The book concludes with "a heap of his enormities": theft, simony, embezzlement, treachery, treason of all kinds, private malice, covetousness, niggardliness, and an encouragement to all honest men to put him down, which might easily be done once the Queen's eyes were opened to his iniquities, for: "He hath nothing of his own, either from his ancestors or of himself, to stay upon in men's hearts or conceits; he hath not ancient nobility as others of our realm have, whereby men's affections are greatly moved." As for valour: "He hath as much as hath a mouse."

Sir Philip Sidney dashed off a passionate defence of his uncle which, however, was not printed in his own lifetime. The rebuttal of the charges is on general lines of probability and common sense. The author, he said, had been reckless indeed in "bringing persons yet alive to speak things which, they are ready to depose upon their salvation, never came into their thought". This sentence is very interesting, for it implies that Dr. Bailey, for instance, had been approached, and that denials would be forthcoming to support Leicester if he took any action. Sidney ridicules the notion of the writer's being able to collect such information as he pretends to: "Such a gentlewoman spoke of a matter, no less than treason, belike she whispered, yet he heard her! Such two knights spake together, of things not fit to call witness to, and yet this ass's ears were so long, that he heard them. And yet see his good nature all the while, that would never reveal them till now, for secrecy's sake, he puts them in print!" Sidney points out the inconsistencies of the portrait: "The same man, at the beginning of the book, so potent the Queen hath cause to fear him, the same man in the end thereof, so abject as any man might tread upon him." None of the accusations is answered, however, except the one to which Sidney devotes the greater part of the paper, that Leicester's father, Sidney's grandfather, John Duke of Northumberland, was of ignoble lineage. This roused Sidney beyond any charges of murder, treason, lechery, robbery, cruelty, greed and cowardice brought against his uncle. To say that the Duke of Northumberland was not a gentleman born! "In truth, if I should have studied with myself all points of false invective which a poisonous tongue could have spit out against that Duke, yet would it never have come into my head, of all other things, that any man would have objected want of gentry unto him." Much as he respected his father's family, Sidney said he reckoned it his chiefest honour that he could, through his mother, call himself a Dudley; and he entered into an exhaustive analysis of the Dudleys' noble connections. He admitted that as a family they had had their reverses; was it charitable to throw this in their teeth? "Our house received such an overthrow." He granted it. "And hath none else in England done so?" At least, the family of the quill driver must be exempt; he was "too low in the mire to be so thunderstricken".[1]

There was much in the "Copy of a Letter" that an impartial man found unjust, and still more that would rouse an affectionate nephew's indignation, and no one can find fault with Sidney for his defence of Leicester. It is his attitude to what was said about the Duke of Northumberland's treason that is extraordinary. His inability to understand why Northumberland had been hated at the time, and why his memory was still abhorred, throws an interesting light on the atmosphere of enclosed family affection and admiration in which Northumberland's children and grandchildren had been reared.

Why it should be thought necessary to defend Leicester against the work of an anonymous libeller is indicated by the importance attached to it by his enemies. Sir Francis Englefield was a Catholic who lived abroad, though he was allowed by the Queen to draw the income from his English property. He wrote to an unknown correspondent apropos the publication of the book: "Instead of the sword which we cannot obtain, we must fight with prayer and pen." Two other books against the Queen's government, "these, and Leicester's Life, have raised the building much. Let the same therefore be followed and backed up with some pamphlets of the like kind, fresh and fresh, from time to time." This, he thought, "ought to be to this Queen of England's annoyance . . . who I hope shall have a fall at last".*

A more effective defence than Sidney's unpublished one was put out by the Privy Council, in a statement which not only abused but ridiculed the work: "As though her Majesty should . . . want either good will, ability or courage (if she knew these enormities were true) to call any subject of hers whatsoever and to render sharp account of them, according to the force and effect of her laws!"

The Queen caused to be written a letter speaking of the book's slander, "of which most malicious and wicked imputations her Majesty in her own clear knowledge doth declare and testify his innocency to all the world". Copies of this, signed by her own hand, were distributed to the Lord Mayor, Sheriffs and Aldermen of London, and also in the northern counties; they were received by, among others, Lord Strange, the Bishop of Chester and the justices of the peace for Cheshire and Lancashire.

* C.S.P. Scottish.

XXV

ON NEW YEAR'S DAY, 1585, Leicester gave the Queen a sable wrap; it had a head and four feet of gold, studded with diamonds and rubies.

Two books were dedicated to the Earl in this year. He had given the University of Oxford a printing press, and the first book issued from it was naturally inscribed: *Illustrissimo viro domino Roberto Dudleio, Comiti Leycestriae, magistro equorum Reginae Elizabethae . . . et almae Oxoniensis Academiae Cancellario Dignissimo*. It was a work by John Case on the ethics of Aristotle. The other was of a very different character. The quarrelsome man of letters and gifted vagabond, Robert Greene, who worked on the original version of *Henry VI*, who alternated between the glowing splendour of success and extravagance and the freezing darkness of poverty, who wrote at last *A Groat's worth of Wit bought with a Million of Repentance*, and died worn out at thirty-two, now at twenty-three dedicated to Lord Leicester his *Planetomachia*, a semi-astrological work, in which the planets Saturn and Venus contest with each other. Its best passages are those describing the subjects of each. Those born under Saturn "prefer hate before love . . . hardly granting their right hand to any man . . . taking counsels in the night . . . they have their pulses slow and small, their sweat sour and heavy". They suffer from "terrible dreams, as of death, carcases, sepulchres, darkness, torments, devils and black things". The subject of Venus "delight in flowers and precious ointments, eating lettuce and stalking on their tiptoes, careful to increase their beauty, somewhat tickled with self-love". They have twinkling eyes and delicate hair. "They are very apt at begetting children and apply their minds to songs and sonnets." Greene's dedication indicates that Leicester was interested in such writers as himself, "which consideration of this your honour's rare and singular mind hath forced many to present the fruits of their labours to your Lordship", and he praises that courteous manner towards writers "that forced them to discover their skill for your Lordship's private pleasure". In this work, he says, he has mixed melancholy with music. He must have sung rarely for his supper at Leicester House.

Meanwhile "A Copy of a Letter", despite all efforts at suppressing it, was briskly going the rounds. It had reached Edinburgh, and on February 16th, 1585, King James issued a repudiation from Holyrood House of "a libel devised and set out by some seditious person of purpose to obscure with lewd lies the honour and reputation of our trusty cousin the Earl of Leicester".

On January 3rd Charles Paget had written from Paris to the Queen of Scots: "Leicester has lately told a friend that he will persecute you to the uttermost, for that he supposeth your Majesty to be privy to the setting-forth of the book against him."*

The annoyance of the Staffords was only less than that of Leicester himself. Sir Edward Stafford wrote to Walsingham in March that copies, translated into French, were expected to arrive any moment. "I am in a peck of troubles what to do in it, for to complain of it were to have the matter more divulged abroad ... because my nearest have a touch in it; which (though between God and my Lord of Leicester's conscience, and in the opinion of most Englishmen) her conscience be no further touched than an honest intent and a weak woman deceived, yet when it cometh to French heads ... who can neither speak nor think well of any, I doubt how they will interpret anything." While the French mulled it over, the position of the Ambassadress was going to be very uncomfortable. As Sir Edward said, "If by any device I could have it suppressed, I would do it, but their malice to my Lord of Leicester is such that it could not be done but by complaint, which is the worst way." He had not yet told his wife of the imminent appearance of the French translation. When she had read the English version, she had been very ill, largely owing to "the melancholy of the fear of misconception", and to what secret anguish, called up again? Stafford had been afraid at one point that she was going into a decline. He prayed God she would not relapse when she heard that the book was available to the ironical and uncharitable French.

Whatever came out, Lord Leicester maintained his position of *soupirant*. In April he wrote to the Queen of "the heart, bound to remain more desirous than able to serve you ... I take my leave," he said, "trusting shortly to attend at Court. From your old lodging in the Castle of Kenilworth, where you are daily prayed for and most often wished to be."[1] But no one can make an omelette without

* Murdin, ed., *State Papers.*

breaking the eggs; the Queen never went to Kenilworth again. In this year, however, she created Leicester Lord Steward of the Household. This was a post of very heavy organizing responsibility, and she proposed therefore, to bestow the office of Master of the Horse on someone else. But Leicester absolutely refused to give this up. It was one of the first appointments she had ever made; it had been bestowed on him at Hatfield in November of 1558. He was attached to it for sentimental reasons, and for its great practical advantages, for it meant constant attendance on her in all her movements. He would not endure to see it given to some other man. His objects were so vehement and so personal the Queen was moved by them, and she cancelled the arrangements she had meant to make.

Leicester was the more impelled to keep in his hands every means of access to her, not only to offset the disadvantage of his marriage, but because the Queen was now interested in another man. Walter Raleigh, dark, handsome, lively and extraordinarily intelligent, had made a powerful impression on her when he came over from Ireland in 1582, bringing despatches from Lord Grey de Wilton. His charm, his brilliance, his magnetism exercised at first an engrossing attraction for her. By 1585 he had been given grants and licences which made him able to indulge his taste for rich clothes, such as the Queen loved to see men wear. Though Elizabeth was always suceptible to a new attraction she did not shake off the old; but the last favourite but one always feared for his standing. Leicester had feared Hatton, Hatton had feared Oxford, they all united in a dislike of Raleigh. Then Leicester clipped Raleigh's wings by bringing forward his stepson the Earl of Essex, and once Essex had established himself in the Queen's affections, his jealousy and greed reached such heights of irrationality, he outdid all predecessors. In 1585 Raleigh was still called "the Queen's new favourite". Mendoza, now Ambassador at Paris, contrived to pick up a good deal of information about the English Court, and he said, on June 1st, that the Earl of Leicester was on very bad terms with Raleigh. Then Mendoza reverted to Stafford's troubles. "The ambassador here, Stafford, has by the Queen's orders, been bringing great pressure to bear on the King to prohibit the sale of certain books which have been translated into French about the lives of the Queen and the Earl of Leicester, and to order the arrest of the translator who is an Englishman."

Thomas Morgan, who Walsingham thought was the author of "A Copy of a Letter", wrote from Paris to the Queen of Scots in July, 1585. "Because Leicester is a great tyrant in the realm, where

Catholics are so plagued," he said, the family of Blount were all obliged, "to their great charges", to live as sycophants of Leicester's, hoping to buy themselves quiet thereby. Charles Paget, writing to her in the same month, told her of "the offer Mr. Christopher Blount makes to serve your Majesty. He is," said Paget, "a Gentleman of the Horse to the Earl of Leicester, and in very good place to do notable service to your Majesty if he will be faithful." Paget advised Mary to try him in some small matters first, "and upon sudden trial, to use greater". It was this young man, attached to Lord Leicester's entourage, who was to play a distinctive part in the latter's domestic circle, supplanting the Earl in his wife's affections.

Leicester had always done his best, at least after there was no more question of his being put forward as her husband, to keep a show of courteous and even kindly communication with the Queen of Scots. He was perhaps even more anxious to be on thoroughly good terms with James. In August, 1584, Davison, while he was ambassador at Holyrood, had written, warning Leicester of rumours that he, Leicester, had disparaged the awkward but intelligent young King. Leicester thanked Davison warmly, saying: "When you hear me misreported, I pray that you will give me knowledge of it." But for these particular accusations, he would not trouble to answer them; no man of his training and experience could be guilty of such offences. "My bringing-up has been too long about Princes to misuse anything towards them." He only wished the King would sift the matter himself, "not to condemn a poor nobleman who has enemies as others have". He had done the King many a good turn, "but let that pass", he said. "In these dangerous days, who can escape lewd or lying tongues? For my part, I trust the Lord will give me His grace to live in His fear, and to behave myself faithfully to my sovereign and honestly to the world. And so shall I pass over these calumniations."

He took pains, however, to entrench himself in the good opinion of the Scots Court. In July, 1585, he wrote, without occasion and though a total stranger, to the King's secretary, Sir John Maitland: "Sir, I do seldom use to seek acquaintance of strangers and yet, by some good inspiration, I suppose, I am moved to be thus bold with you, though altogether unknown to you, to show you my earnest desire that some such familiar office of friendship may pass between us, as men that do serve two Princes so near in blood and so dear in friendship as my mistress and your master be." ("That false Scots urchin!" the Queen had exclaimed when she heard of James' treachery to his guardian Morton. "Tell your King what good I have done for him, in holding the Crown on his head since he was born!" she shouted to the Scots envoys, in an access of exasperation at yet another instance of James' folly and ingratitude.) "And," continued Lord Leicester smoothly, "for my own part . . . I cannot like to live a stranger with such a person but to offer any kindness or acquaintance I may devise . . ."*

A more urgent matter than private relations with Scotland was now claiming paramount attention. The Spanish forces in the Netherlands were under the leadership of Parma, a general of consummate ability whose strategy was based on a minutely detailed study of the Netherlands terrain, which, partially submerged by tidal waters and intersected by dykes, had hitherto proved one of the best defences of the country. Parma's forces now threatened Antwerp, and the prospect of this city's fall made the English realize that helping the States was the only way to defend themselves. At the end of June a Commission from the Netherland States was received by Elizabeth. They begged her to accept the Sovereignty of the Provinces, and she positively refused to do so. Her utterances were often ambiguous, but nothing could be plainer than her words on this occasion. She told them outright that in no circumstances would she accept the role of governor of the United Provinces; to do so would be to declare war on Spain, and it must be clearly understood, once and for all, that she declined their proposal. She would, however, see what she could do towards their assistance, and the Commissioners were relegated to a series of meetings with the Privy Council, of which the chief members present were Burleigh, Leicester, Walsingham and Hatton.

The Dutch made at least two more efforts to persuade the Queen to change her mind. At last Lord Burleigh said to them: "We have told you, over and over again, that her Majesty will never think of accepting the sovereignty. She will assist you in money and men, but she must be repaid when the war is over, and as pledges of this she must hold one town in each province."†

Elizabeth agreed to accept the figures of men and money that the Council proposed, but she said she must provide this assistance secretly. The Council unanimously told her that to do this would be to deprive her aid of much of its effect. She must do it openly. While she was still shuddering on the brink of this appalling step, Antwerp's fall became certain. The Queen at once sanctioned the

---

* *Warrender Papers.*   † Motley, *History of the United Netherlands.*

despatch of two thousand troops, and four thousand more were to be shipped in a fortnight. It was agreed in return that she should hold the ports of Brill and Flushing.

It was now August, and Leicester, who this year had been created Chief Justice Itinerant of all the forests this side of Trent, had gone to Cornbury in Oxfordshire. Of the surrounding woodlands, he had bought those adjoining Langley when the Queen had given him the manor of Langley, and the Forest of Wychwood he held as assignee for one of his family connections. At Cornbury, of which he was Ranger, the Ranger's Lodge was set in five hundred acres of virgin forest. The Lodge was stone-built with mullioned windows; inside, a wooden staircase with a great wooden balustrade, the newel post topped with a wooden sphere the size of a human head, led to a panelled bedchamber, whose window looked out upon parkland scattered with trees that gradually thickened into deep woods. Into this lovely place he was pursued by a letter from Lord Burleigh, who, despite his own weighty preoccupations and the pressure of the time, had written him a letter of remonstrance because Burleigh's sister-in-law, Lady Russell, a vigorous, clamant and tiresome woman, in burdening the over-taxed Lord Treasurer with her affairs, had repeated to him some disobliging remarks which, she declared, Lord Leicester had made about him. Burleigh, whose great ascendancy and extraordinary powers of mind were strangely accompanied by a keen sensitiveness to personal attack, had written to protest against Leicester's attitude towards him. He ended a long letter by declaring: "Knowing in the sight of God mine own innocence of any unhonest action towards your Lordship . . . I will quiet my heart and arm myself against the wrong with patience. But," he said, "I am sure no man of my sort has abbiden more injuries this way, in hearing evil when I have done well . . . and if the place I hold might be bestowed by her Majesty upon another, without condemnation of mine honesty, I vow to Almighty God I would be most glad." Leicester seized his pen and wrote an answer rivalling Burleigh's letter in length. All he had to say, in effect, was that Lady Russell's remarks had not one word of truth in them. "Your own wisdom," he said, "will easily discharge me, being so well acquainted with the devices and prac- tices of these days, when men go about rather to sow all discord betwixt such as we are, than to do good offices." He showed an irritation and sensitiveness equal to Burleigh's own in the length of his expostulation; and he threw in at the close a reference to how much Lord Burleigh owed to the Duke of Northumberland, for making Burleigh his secretary, and promoting him to a seat on the Council of Edward VI. As he wrote of these endless jars, with the exquisite peace of Cornbury and its full-leaved August woods around him, he, a worn, dissipated, somewhat infirm, ageing man of fifty-two, may for the moment have meant what he said when he replied to Burleigh's statement in the same vein: "For my own part, I will answer faithfully and truthfully for myself, I do more desire my liberty, with her Majesty's favour, than any office in England."

But this was no time for anybody's resigning anything. In mid-August, Antwerp fell to Parma. Gilbert Talbot wrote to his father on August 26th: "Her Majesty was greatly troubled . . . and my Lord Treasurer who was at Theobalds, somewhat ill of the gout, was sent for, and so my Lord Leicester, to return to the Court. And it is thought that her Majesty shall be forced of very necessity to send some great person with great forces presently for the defence of Holland and Zeeland, or else they will, out of hand, follow Antwerp." It was said that the States themselves asked for the Earl of Leicester to command and Sir Philip Sidney to act as Governor of Flushing.

On August 28th, on his way up to London, Leicester wrote to Walsingham from Mr. Leigh's house, Stoneleigh, in Warwickshire. In his letter, Leicester declared his readiness to take the Netherlands command. He had had a fall from his horse and could not yet pull his boot on, but he wished he had a hundred thousand lives that he might spend them all in the Queen's service.

Elizabeth was now in the twenty-seventh year of her reign. By rigid economy and meticulous account keeping, as well as the unofficial levy of presents and hospitality to herself, she had up till now both kept within the limits of solvency and avoided asking parliament for heavy assistance. Her genius for ruling expressed itself in many ways, but peace, with its inseparable concomitant, economic stability, was the basis of her extraordinary success and the unique hold it gave her on the people's affection. The States now wanted her to cancel the policy of nearly thirty years, which had brought such great and growing rewards, and, by declaring war on Spain on their behalf, pour out men and treasure until she or Spain fell back exhausted and bled white. This she had sternly refused to do, rejecting the offer of the sovereignty of their country, and so showing herself a greater ruler than the Plantagenets, one of whom had fought a costly crusade in Palestine, while generations of the others had kept up the ruinous Hundred Years' War in France. Yet something drastic must be done. Alençon had died the same year as the Prince of

Orange, and Philip had immobilized France by a covenant with the French government known as the Holy Leage, which was to prevent the accession of the Huguenot Henry of Navarre. Freed from the fear of French interference, Spain was advancing, under Parma's generalship, to crush the United Provinces. It was no secret that England was to be the Spanish King's next object of attack, and the only obstacle to his invasion of the country was that he had not yet overcome the resistance of the Netherlands. Some help to them was absolutely necessary as a measure of English self-defence.

Even so, the danger of provoking a declaration of war from Spain was so great that it threw Elizabeth into almost unbearable agitation. Combined with the nervous distraction was the increased determination to use vigilance in all financial matters. She had agreed, on a basis of keeping Brill and Flushing in her hands as pledges for repayment, to keep four thousand foot and a thousand horse in the field, and to provide £125,000 a year to maintain them, a very large sum out of her annual income. Some great personage must be sent from England to command the expedition, and the choice could only fall on the Earl of Leicester. Burleigh and Walsingham agreed upon his suitability. He had had no military experience since he had fought for the King of Spain in 1557, but experienced military men such as Sir John Norris and Sir Roger Williams would be under him. His position and his personal grandeur carried the necessary weight, and he was prepared to lend and to spend freely out of his great wealth to provide for the expedition. Since the 1570's he had kept a close eye upon the Netherlands as a possible sphere of aggrandisement for himself, and at first he was delighted with the appointment. Walsingham was the minister who sympathized most keenly with his eagerness. Burleigh saw the necessity for the campaign, but like the Queen he regretted it, and was determined to keep the action within bounds. Walsingham regarded it as the opportunity he had always wanted for the country to take arms against the Catholic power of Spain.

Elizabeth had carried through the negotiations with shrewdness, caution and determination, but in the last week of September, when Leicester was actually making his preparations, the combined terrors of provoking Spain to a full-scale attack, of being sucked into a deadly whirlpool of financial ruin, and of the threat of possible injury and death to Leicester brought her, for the time being, to the verge of nervous collapse. A cross-current was set going which produced a different sort of displeasure. The trouble with Lady Leicester was, she either would not or could not travel quietly. Why, it might be asked, should she do so? She had not braved the hazards of becoming Countess of Leicester to creep about the streets as if she were nobody, and it was hardly possible for a great lady to travel without some stir. To this it might be answered that her own sister-in-law, Lady Warwick, wife though she was to the elder brother, found it possible to do so. No provoking éclat attended Lady Warwick's movements. People did not see her going by with a train of outriders, footmen and attendant coaches, and ask themselves what potentate could be visiting the Queen of England. Lady Leicester came from Kenilworth to Leicester House in her usual flamboyant state, and on September 25th Walsingham wrote to Davison, who was again in the Low Countries: "I see not her Majesty disposed to use the services of my Lord of Leicester. There is great offence taken at the conveying down of his lady."

Lady Leicester was at Leicester House, but the Earl himself was with the Queen at one of the palaces outside London. He wrote to Walsingham a letter which showed, as much as anything found in his writings, how much affection he had for Elizabeth: "Mr. Secretary, I find her Majesty very desirous to stay me. She makes the cause only the doubtfulness of her own self, by reason of her oft disease taking her of late and this last night worst of all. She used very pitiful words to me for her fear that she shall not live, and would not have me from her. You can consider what manner of persuasion this must be to me from her . . . I would not say much for any matter but did comfort her as well as I could, only I did let her know how far I had gone in preparation. I do think for all this that if she be well to-night, she will let me go, for she would not have me speak of it to the contrary to anybody . . . pray you send my wife word in the morning that I cannot come before Thursday to London."*

Six days later the position was hardly improved. He wrote to Walsingham: "I have this night at 1 o'clock received your letter which doth signify that her Majety's pleasure is that I should stay my preparations till I do speak with her." On her own order, he had despatched two hundred letters to friends and servants, to prepare themselves to go with him. "I am sure one hundred of them be already delivered, and the rest will be before I can revoke them." He had been to the Tower and taken up armour and steel saddles, and "two or three vessels to carry certain provisions". The States

* Bruce, ed., *Leicester Correspondence.*

envoys had been with him, imploring him to make haste: he ended: "Scribbled in my bed this Monday morning at almost 2 o'clock."*

This letter was for the eye of a secretary. It was accompanied by a note for Walsingham's own: "This is the strangest dealing in the world." The delay, if persisted in, would prove fatal. "For my part, I am weary of life and all. I pray you let me hear with speed. I will go this morning to Wanstead to see some horses I have there, and if the matter alter, I can have no heart to come at Court and look upon any man, for it will be thought some misliking in me doth stay the matter." Sir Philip Sidney was living with his wife in her parents' house at Barne Elms. "Send Philip to me," his uncle wrote, "and God keep you, and if possible, learn out the cause of this change." Later that same day, Walsingham sent to let him know that the Queen's objections were withdrawn, all was now to go forward, but Walsingham added the perennial warning: "If your Lordship's requests should minister matter of charges, it would be difficult."

Two young men had been appointed governors of the pledged towns: Sir Thomas Cecil, Burleigh's son by a first marriage, was governor of Brill, Sir Philip Sidney of Flushing. They sailed on November 16th. Leicester himself prepared to embark in the first week of December, 1585. Before he left England, he wrote a letter to Burleigh; the unnerving sense of the Queen's indecision after he himself was committed, and the lurking uneasiness of the man who puts himself at a disadvantage by leaving the seat of power, made him appeal to Burleigh's integrity, "albeit I have no mistrust, but in so great absence and such a service I might greatly rely upon your particular good will and regard of myself. But in this case I desire not respect nor regard of me but of the cause, which I beseech you my Lord I may at this farewell recommend to your Lordship's great wisdom and care." He hoped that, for the sake of all the lives and fortunes which were now adventured by the Queen's own command, "she will fortify and maintain her own actions to the full performance of that she hath agreed on. . . . In some haste this 5 December, on my way to the sea-side."

The Earl finally embarked on December 8th. He came with his train from Colchester to Manningtree, and thence dropped down the river to Harwich. The Admiral, William Burroughs, heard with surprise that he was determined to land at Brill. The harbour was unsuited to so large a fleet, and Burroughs had assumed that the

* Bruce, *op. cit.*

destination would be Flushing. He said so, but the Lieutenant General of the Queen's forces would not concede the point to a sailor who knew what he was talking about. Burroughs had but one pilot with him, whom he had engaged to take the Fleet into Flushing; if it were to enter Brill, many more would be needed. Leicester's unfitness for command was demonstrated even before he left Harwich; he showed himself greatly offended with the Admiral, who should, he declared, have had enough pilots ready to take the fleet "into whatever place it should please his Lordship to appoint to go unto". A hurried muster was made on shore of such pilots as could be found, who all confirmed the Admiral's opinion that Flushing was the appropriate harbour. Before noon Leicester had changed his mind and given orders to proceed to Flushing, but, as some of his ships laden with horses and provisions still stood in the Thames, he ordered Burroughs to send a pinnace to them with a message about the change of destination. Burroughs patiently explained that wind and tide were contrary; before a pinnace could reach them the ships would be out to sea. This small contingent was therefore left to make its own way to Brill.*

On December 10th Leicester, with near a hundred sail, landed at Flushing, where he was received by the governor, Sir Philip Sidney. The Netherlanders had prepared amazing scenes of welcome, bells, salutes of cannon, fireworks, triumphal arches, and allegorical displays, in the Hague, Rotterdam, Amsterdam and Delft.† Leicester's elation increased as city after city received and fêted him as a hero and a personage of the highest rank. At last he tasted his life's longing: *the sweet fruition of an earthly crown*. It was said that at Delft, in the intoxication of his triumph, he exclaimed that, in the persons of Lady Jane Grey and Lord Guildford Dudley, his family had been unjustly deprived of the crown of England. The Dutch themselves were staggered: it was but a moment's insanity. In his letter to Walsingham he wrote that there was so much noise in the streets of voices crying "God save Queen Elizabeth", it was as if the Queen herself were in Cheapside.

But these demonstrations were not of a kind to allay the Queen's anxiety; they were rather calculated to increase it. Elizabeth had recognized what self-preservation required England to do; but the step itself was so desperately dangerous, there might in the end be little to choose between it and the danger it was intended to avert. She had published a proclamation explaining the causes of

* Bruce, *op. cit.*   † Motley, *History of the United Netherlands.*

her intervention in the Netherlands: she was not, she declared, attempting to take away these territories from the King of Spain, their lawful sovereign; she was acting only to secure for them the degree of civil and religious freedom that was their inalienable right. When that was assured and their cities protected "against sack and desolation", she would withdraw her troops. She had come into the struggle only as "an aiding friend". She denied that she was doing anything that authorized the King of Spain to declare war on her. The comment of the King of Sweden was, that it was uncommonly brave of her to risk the crown on her head; no one else in Europe was going to do such a thing.

Leicester, meanwhile, established his headquarters and drew up ordinances. Strong emphasis was placed on the religious observance of the troops. The men were to attend divine service as soon as the trumpet summoned them; they were forbidden to blaspheme. Idle and vagrant women were not to be admitted for fear of disorders and "horrible abuses"; only wives, sick-nurses and laundresses were allowed in the garrison. One passage of the ordinances showed the Lieutenant General in an excellent light: No man, it said, was to lay violent hands upon any women with child or lying in childbed, old persons, widows, young virgins or babes. This was the more necessary as the campaign was expected to consist in retaking towns from Spanish hands.

A point in which Leicester took a great personal interest was that "no man shall ease himself or defile the camp or town of garrison save in such places as be appointed for the purpose, upon pain of imprisonment". He had brought with him great supplies of the strong perfumes made of musk and civet.

XXVI

BEFORE LEICESTER LEFT England, he had secured a Deed Poll of Incorporation for his Hospital at Warwick. The Act of Parliament permitting him to found this had been passed in 1572, and the terms of the Act had said the charity was founded "for the provision, sustentation and relief of needy, poor and impotent people". The premises he acquired for it consisted of the twelfth century chapel of St. John, built over the west gate of the town, and a collection of small timbered fifteenth and sixteenth century buildings that had once been the property of the town guilds. These included a hall, living quarters for the twelve inmates, and a Master's Lodge, forming the four sides of a courtyard.

Certain charities founded by the Beauchamps had been abrogated, and Leicester's gaining the establishment of his by Act of Parliament was not only important to the beneficiaries, but it reflected great credit and local prestige upon himself. It was, therefore, felt to be rather sharp practice that in 1585, by his Deed Poll of Incorporation, he changed what had been given parliamentary sanction as a public charity into a means of providing for his own retainers. The original Deed stated that the beneficiaries were to be twelve needy or impotent persons; foreseeing that after the Netherlands campaign he might have numerous wounded dependents upon his hands, Leicester framed the Deed of 1585 to say that they were to be "especially such as should be hereafter wounded, maimed or hurt in the wars, in the service of her Majesty, her heirs and successors"; and furthermore that places in the Hospital were open only to those born in the counties of Warwick or Gloucestershire, or living there four or five years at least. If no soldiers were seeking admission, then places might be given to "any poor and decayed by sickness or misfortune", but *not*, it was stated, those who were decayed "by their own wicked wastefulness and riotous consumption". Of those eligible for admission, preference was to be given to "the servants and tenants of us and our heirs", and entrants from the various towns were to be considered in this order: those from Warwick, Kenilworth, Stratford-on-Avon, Wootton-under-Edge and Erlingham: the last two being properties owned by Leicester in Gloucestershire. If there were no candidates from these places, then those from any other towns in Warwickshire might be considered. Since Leicester had provided the money for the charity in the first place, and since he proposed to admit only cases of genuine need, the arrangement no doubt seemed more justifiable to him than it could to anyone who considered it from a purely legal point of view. The community consisted of twelve poor brethren under the charge of a Master. The first Master was the Puritan Ralph Griffen. When he was appointed Dean of Lincoln in 1586 Leicester replaced him by the famous Dr. Thomas Cartwright, who had had a stirring career as a Puritan, and though now officially concerned only with the spiritual needs of twelve poor men, was reckoned so dangerous that his appointment was terminated four years later by his being put in gaol.

On New Year's Day, 1586, Leicester could not present his gift to the Queen in person since he was in the field. It was a pearl necklace "with one hundred and one jewels hanging thereat, a great table diamond in the midst and two rubies on each side of it". Lord and Lady Warwick gave her a folding table, "covered all over with plates of silver graven", and a square perfuming pan, also silver-plated, enclosing a copper pan for the glowing charcoal on which the scent was sprinkled.

This year George Whitney published his *Choice of Emblems*, dedicated to Lord Leicester, in which he compared him and his brother Lord Warwick to the two starry bears, Ursa Major and Ursa Minor, who have their light from the sun and bestow it to guide seafarers.

> And as these stars by Phoebus light are seen
> So both these Earls have honour, might and power
> From Phoebe bright, our most renownèd Queen
> Whose fame no might or envy can devour
> And under her, they show to others light
> And do rejoice ten thousand with their sight.

In the Netherlands, Leicester was doing little, but it had not been intended that he should do much; a vigorous offensive action was the last thing the Queen wanted to see, and she was already entertaining preliminary discussions with Parma on the possibility of making peace for the Netherlanders over their heads.

In these tentative approaches she let it be understood that, since the King of Spain was absolutely determined not to grant religious toleration, she herself might concede that point, with some qualification, if she could secure others which she thought would be to the States' advantage. Of the seventeen provinces in revolt against Philip, eleven were Catholic in any case, and it seemed to her that to reject a Settlement affecting the entire country for the sake of religious freedom for the six remaining provinces was unstatesmanlike. She had frequently expressed her disapproval of Philip's religious persecution; she had demanded impatiently of his ambassador why the King could not let his subjects go to the devil in their own way. Philip was persecuting from sheer fanaticism, with no reasons based on practical considerations, and she had not a particle of sympathy with his aims; but it therefore followed that she had none, either, with a fanatical opposition to them. "There is one faith and one Christ Jesus," she said, "the rest is a dispute about trifles." When it had been finally ascertained that Philip would not concede the point, and that, despite the economic consequences to himself, he was prepared to involve the Provinces in endless and illimitable devastation, she thought the least of many evils might be a treaty by which the civil and fiscal liberties of the States were guaranteed and the Spanish occupying army removed, though the minority were thereby obliged to accept Catholic observances. This was, of course, completely contrary to the intention of the Northern Provinces, whose inhabitants were prepared to die rather than concede their right to worship in the way they believed the only true one.

Elizabeth had not committed herself in any negotiations, but she was holding open the door. In this position of affairs Leicester now did something, in the circumstances so lunatic that it could only be explained as the irrepressible upsurge of instincts which he had been obliged to control for the greater part of his life, and were the stronger for being denied.

Since the murder of the Prince of Orange, the States had found their cause suffering from lack of cohesion. The sterling indomitable qualities of resistance were found in the citizens of the beleagured cities; the Stadtholders themselves were by no means heroically united. They knew the immense caution of the English Queen; they were determined to extract from her every penny she was good for, and to put their expenses on her account whenever they found a way to do it; and they thought they had hit upon a method both of gaining for themselves the centralizing authority of which their forces were in need, and of forcing the Queen of England's hand, committing her to the hilt by involving her in an unmistakable gesture of defiance against Spain, and thereby obliging her to throw in all her material resources behind them. A deputation waited on Lord Leicester on New Year's Day, 1586, and urged him to accept the position of Supreme Governor of the United Provinces.

There was nothing surprising in their doing this. The surprise lay in the fact that Leicester, whose boast it was that he knew the Queen better than any man alive, who was aware of the answers she had made over and over again when the sovereignty had been offered to herself—that Leicester should, after some consultation with his friends, have accepted this piece of gilded Dead Sea fruit; and having failed to establish himself as King Consort of England, father of a King Consort of England, or step-father of a wife to the King of Scots, he should now tour the northern provinces of Holland and Zealand in royal state, with the baldachin held over him which was the distinction reserved for crowned heads.

The installation took place on January 25th, in a burst of splendour, and it was now time to think of advising Elizabeth that her careful policy had been overturned. Davison was despatched to London with the information, and bad weather caused his journey to take ten days; but he was not sent till February 5th, more than a month after Leicester had received the States' invitation, and three weeks all but a day after he had accepted it. Needless to say, by the time Davison reached Greenwich the news had preceded him, and his task was a most unenviable one.

The Queen received him in the inner drawing room, and her anger, without rising or diminishing, remained at white heat throughout the interview. Davison made what explanations he could—the step had been expedient, it would assist the active prosecution of the war—but he could not slake her consuming indignation, since taking control of the Netherlands with a view to an aggressive campaign was the very thing for which she feared to be held responsible. What she had intended was very subtle, and Leicester had understood perfectly what it was. She now told Davison, in a steady stream of invective, what she thought of the Earl's treachery, his insolence, his self-seeking, his maddening idiocy. What he had done had been "against her express command, in contempt of her, and as if her consent had been of nothing worth or the thing no way concerning her". Although this interview took place on February 13th, Davison could effect so little by it that left unaltered the letter which she the Queen had written to Leicester three days before, and the only concession she would make was that Sir Thomas Heneage, who was to take over, though he must convey to Lord Leicester the matter of her displeasure, might use his discretion as to his manner of so doing.

When Elizabeth wished to convey a shade of meaning without committing herself, she wrote with a studied ambiguity; when she intended her meaning to be plain there was no possibility of mistaking it. The letter, dated February 10th, opened without any address. It said: "How contemptuously we conceive ourselves to have been used by you, you shall by this bearer understand. . . . We could never have imagined, had we not seen it fall out in experience, that a man raised up by ourself and extraordinarily favoured by us above any subject in this land, would have in so contemptible a sort broken our commandment, in a cause that so greatly toucheth our honour." The letter charged him on the duty of his allegiance—after which words any disobedience was high treason—that he should "obey and fulfil whatsoever the bearer hereof shall direct you to do in our name, whereof fail you not, as you will answer the contrary at your uttermost peril".

Walsingham, like Leicester himself, had wanted "a sharp war" in the Netherlands. Burleigh never had; but when he heard that the Queen's command, to be conveyed by Heneage, was that the Earl of Leicester should, upon the very spot where he had received the title, make a public renunciation of it, he felt that the effect would be so disastrous that, deplorable as Leicester's action had been in accepting the honour, he had better, as the lesser evil, be allowed to retain it. At first Elizabeth would not even listen to him, but when he made one of his very rare threats of resignation she, as always, showed herself ready to reconsider her own view as the first step towards accepting his.

While matters were in this precarious state, Lady Leicester added fuel to the flames. Any idea she may have had of joining her husband at his first going over had been put down by the Queen's strong disapproval. But now the glorious news had come to her that Lord Leicester was no longer in the Netherlands as the plenipotentiary of the English Queen; she herself was the wife of an independent sovereign, Supreme Governor of the United Netherlands, and it was told her Majesty that "my Lady was prepared (at once) to come over . . . with such a train of ladies and gentlewomen and such rich coaches, litters and side-saddles, as her Majesty had none such, and that there should be a court of ladies as should far surpass

her Majesty's court here". Leicester's correspondent told him that
the report was unfounded, and what a pity it was that it should have
got about. It did seem unfortunate, certainly, that a rumour so
eminently characteristic of Lady Leicester's manners and habits
should be spread abroad without there being one word of truth in it.
The Queen declared with heat that her Ladyship should stay where
she was; there should be no English courts except her own. Lady
Leicester's activity was checked for the time being, but she did not
immediately relinquish her scheme—as late as March 24th, Sir
Philip Sidney was writing apprehensively that he wished "some way
might be found to stay my Lady in England".

Heneage was at last sent off with the Queen's letter intact, but
with her verbal instructions modified by Lord Burleigh. The formal
resignation of the title had been waived, but the States were to be
told what the Queen's views were, and that their attempt to force
her hand were utterly repudiated.

Leicester's attitude towards the Queen at this crisis was one of
abject self-commiseration. All he asked now, he said, was to come
home and resume his duties as Master of the Queen's Horse. There
he could be of some use to her in rubbing her horses' heels; it was
all too plain that he could be of none where he was. To Davison,
however, he showed considerable venom. He made it clear that he
regarded his own acceptance of the title as largely Davison's fault,
and he wrote all this down in a very long minute dated March 10th,
1586. Against the more outrageous mis-statements, Davison wrote
his own comments: "*Denied*", or "*The contrary doth appear*". "It
hath not grieved me a little," wrote the Earl, "that by your means I
have fallen into her Majesty's so deep displeasure, but that you have
so carelessly discharged your part in the due declaration of all things
as they stood in truth. Knowing most assuredly that if you had
delivered to her Majesty indeed the truth of my dealings, her Highness
could never have conceived as I perceive she doth." It was only
Davison's undertaking to do this, Leicester said, that had caused
Leicester to yield to Davison's persuasions. "Therefore I conclude,
charging you with your conscience how you do deal now with me,
seeing you chiefly brought me into it. (*'Absolutely denied'*.) I did
very unwillingly come to the matter. (*'Herein let the world judge'*.)
Except your embassages have better success, I shall have no great
cause to commend them." This letter to Davison crossed one written
by the latter of the same date in which he gave news of Lady Leicester,
whom he had not seen for ten days: "Tomorrow," he said, "I hope

to do my duty towards her. I found her greatly troubled with the tempestuous news she received from court", but her dismay had abated, he said, "when she understood how I had proceeded with her Majesty."

Lord Warwick, however, who wrote on the same day, was highly alarmed. "Our mistress' extreme rage doth increase rather than diminish, and she gives out great threatening words towards yourself. Make the best assurance you can for yourself. Trust not her oath for her malice is great and unquenchable. . . . Have care for your safety, and if she will needs revoke you, to the overthrow of the cause, if I were you . . . I would go to the farthest part of Christendom rather than ever come into England again. Advise me what to do, for I mean to take such part as you do."

By the end of March, however, the Queen's feelings had calmed themselves in some degree. Prepared now to believe that, however mistakenly, he had at least thought he was acting for the best, on April 1st she wrote Leicester a remarkable letter. It showed firmness and a statesmanlike view of the Dutch situation, and, though her affection was evident throughout, it was written with considerable dignity:

"By the Queen: Right trusty and right well beloved cousin and Counsellor, we greet you well. It is always thought, in the opinion of the world, a hard bargain where both parties are losers, and so doth fall out the case betwixt us two. You, as we hear, are greatly grieved, in respect of the great displeasure you find we have conceived against you, and we no less grieved that a subject of ours, of that quality that you are, a creature of our own, and one that hath always received an extraordinary portion of our favour above all our subjects, even from the beginning of our reign, should deal so carelessly, we will not say contemptuously, as to give the world just cause to think that we are had in contempt by him . . . from whom we could never have looked to receive any such measure, which we do assure you, hath wrought as great grief in us as any one thing that ever happened to us." But, she went on, "for that your grieved and wounded mind hath more need of comfort than reproof, whom we are persuaded (though the act in respect of the contempt can no way be excused) had no other meaning and intent than to advance our service, we think meet to forbear to dwell upon a matter wherein we ourselves do find so little comfort"—and here was a veiled reference to Lady Leicester—"assuring you that whosoever professeth to love you best, taketh not more comfort of your well doing or discomfort of your evil doing, than ourself." Then she came to practical matters, to the harm he had done and how best it might be mitigated. He was to discuss the position fully with Sir Thomas Heneage and others competent to give advice, as to whether the States would yield him the authority carried by the title of Supreme Governor, if he relinquished the title itself and reverted to the one she had given him of Lieutenant General of her forces? It could best be decided on the spot, and if he found, upon advice, that the title could not be relinquished without fatally prejudicing the English power, "we can be content, if necessity shall so require, to tolerate the same for a time"; but as she did not mean his absolute government to continue indefinitely, she asked that the States should "devise some way how to satisfy us in the point of qualification". The letter showed true love, but it bore the conclusion of a formal document: "Given under our signet at our manor of Greenwich, the first day of April, in the twenty-eighth year of our reign."[1]

Burleigh and Walsingham now wished that, since the Queen would not be persuaded to prosecute the war with energy, she should treat openly for peace, and Walsingham wanted to see the peace negotiations in Leicester's hands. "I cannot but wish your Lordship to be a principal dealer therein, as well in respect for your own honour (as) I doubt, if it pass into other hands, it will not be so carefully dealt with." That he had gained Walsingham's good opinion was very much in Leicester's favour, and he cut a respectable figure in the eyes of the army. He went about inspecting fortifications and supervising works, and even Lord North, who was his friend, was surprised by his activity. North wrote to Walsingham in May: "My Lord of Leicester did so notably advise and direct the making of the trenches, a thing I did not look for, I confess, and to view the place he did put himself in danger of musket shot too much."*

Though Walsingham kept his eye upon everything, at home and abroad, in July, 1586, he was intensely occupied with a matter of his especial department, that of secret intelligence. This was the unravelling of the plot named after Antony Babington, a rich young man, an ardent Catholic and romantically devoted to the Queen of Scots, who was used by a group of conspirators far cleverer than himself, namely Thomas Morgan and his associates in Paris. The plot, which was to assassinate Queen Elizabeth, and then, with the help of Spanish troops landed by Parma at Newcastle, to overcome all resistance and place Mary Queen of Scots on the English throne, had come

* C. R. Markham, *The Fighting Veres.*

unexpectedly into Walsingham's net. Anxious to find out from the correspondence of the Queen of Scots what plans Philip was making for the invasion of England, he had caused Mary to be removed to Chartley, commandeering the house from young Lord Essex, who protested but in vain, and there arranged, by means of an *agent provocateur*, that she should entrust her correspondence to a channel which passed under his own eye. Looking for something quite different, Walsingham found letters exchanged between the Queen of Scots, Babington, Mendoza, who was now in Paris, Morgan, and his colleague Ballard. The whole scheme unrolled itself to Walsingham's gaze, and he found that, while the invasion by Parma was being negotiated from Paris, Babington had charged himself with procuring the murder of Elizabeth, which was to be accomplished by six gentlemen, all of whom had the entré to her presence. Walsingham had the information he needed to enable him to arrest all the conspirators—save one. He was waiting for a letter from the Queen of Scots showing that she approved of the proposed murder. This letter was written on July 19th; in it, Mary said: "When all is ready, the six gentlemen must be set at work, and you will provide that their design being accomplished, I may myself be rescued from this place and be in safe keeping till our friends arrive."* The letter was sent to reach Babington at Lichfield, but he was not there when he had promised to be, and it was desired to make sure that he had received it. Walsingham consulted Elizabeth, but no one else; he did not immediately tell even Burleigh, for he must have known that Burleigh would never allow him to use the Queen as live bait; but with her own consent he kept the trap open for eleven days. Babington did not come to Lichfield, where the letter awaited him, for over a week, and in that interval Elizabeth was nearly murdered by Barnewell, one of the six gentlemen, who came up to her while she was walking with a party of ladies and gentlemen, the latter all unarmed, in Richmond Park. As the would-be murderer approached, the Queen looked searchingly at him; his nerve failed, and he drew back. Meanwhile, the Queen of Scots had written to Mendoza of the delay in the plans for elevating her to the English throne. She did not mind it for herself, she said: "I feel the public misfortune more than my own."[1] The misfortune of having Elizabeth for a queen, however, was one which the public as a whole was very ready to endure.

By the second week in August the conspirators, fourteen in all, were rounded up. In the same month a raid was made on the Queen

* MSS., Mary Queen of Scots. Quoted by Froude, Vol. XII, p. 243.

of Scots' private papers at Chartley, and a vast mass of her correspondence with France and Spain, showing her participation in every
attempt at invasion and revolution which had been made since her
arrival in 1568, was discovered and carried up to London, with the
keys to sixty ciphers and a list of English noblemen who had made
advances to the Queen of Scots as the future Queen of England.
When this list was put into Elizabeth's hands, she first read it, then
burnt it, saying *Video et taceo*, I see and I say nothing.

Such was the climate of affairs at home, and that of affairs in the
Netherlands was increasingly dismaying. Elizabeth had agreed to
pay £160,000 a year, and large instalments of this sum had been sent
already, but no accounts had been received of how it had been spent,
only statements that further sums were urgently required. This
situation was driving Elizabeth almost to panic. For the first time in
twenty-eight years of her reign, she was unable to keep control of
expenditure which she was obliged to meet. She was committed
to paying a sum equal to half her normal expenses of government,
and even this, alarming as it was, was nothing like all that was
demanded of her. Leicester had early fallen foul of Sir John Norris,
one of the most capable officers of his staff, whose uncle was Treasurer-
at-War; from the very beginning, therefore, there was ill feeling
between the Lieutenant General and those charged with keeping
his accounts. Leicester began by increasing the pay of all officers,
including his own, which he raised from £6 a day to £10 13s. 4d.,
an annual increase of £1,715 in money of the time. The Treasurer
was obliged to tell Walsingham: "The disbursements are grown
great since his Excellency's coming, by extraordinaries crept in,
outside the rate which you gave at my coming away, so that a more
speedy supply is required."

Lord Burleigh wrote to Leicester on May 31st; "My Lord, until
the state of the Queen's army by musterbook and her monthly
charges may appear more clear, here will be no further means for
any more money." The confusion of the financial arrangements
was multitudinous in its origins and effects. Seven thousand English
troops were already in the Netherlands, in the pay of the States,
before Leicester and his contingent arrived. After the Treaty of
Greenwich, the States without a word transferred these men to the
payroll of the English crown. Elizabeth's money for her troops was
delivered to their captains; these drew the pay for a full muster even
if half their numbers had disappeared by desertion or death. Elizabeth
repeatedly ordered that payment should be made by poll, directly

to the men, and not by company to the Captain. To enforce such a measure, it was felt, would be difficult and unpopular, and it was decided to ignore the Queen's commands. The money she had sent disappeared without any account of how it had been spent, the men's pay was months in arrears, and the situation was made worse by her refusing to send more money till the last had been accounted for. The Treasurer did his best, but with such forces as were arrayed against him that was little. Sidney exclaimed that the garrisons in the pledged towns were on the verge of mutiny. The sufferings of the troops were dreadful; they wanted clothes to their backs, their officers cheated them of their food, and they were driven to prey on the inhabitants they were supposed to be delivering. Leicester wrote letters eloquent of the demoralized state to which the army was reduced. He spoke, too, of the deplorable manners and morals of the rising generation. It was a grief to his heart, he told Walsingham, "to see your youth in England, how clean they be marred and spoiled for ever being able to serve her Majesty or the realm. I am ashamed to think, much more to speak, of the young men that have come over. Believe me, you will all repent the (pampered) kind of bringing up at this day of young men." A high-minded critic of modern youth, what he did not do was to make a strenuous, single-minded effort to get reliable accounts sent in to the Queen, though she was perpetually asking for them.

The English army, however, though many of the troops were in bad case, was not considered negligible by Parma. Mattingley* has pointed out that in his estimation of the strength of fortified places Parma was accustomed to put down how many English they contained, a sign that he took their presence seriously. The sending of English forces into Holland and Zealand prevented his overrunning the northern provinces after his capture of Antwerp, while the English garrisoning of Brill and Flushing meant that he had no deep-water harbour, so that he could not use a fleet. The English forces had acted as a brake upon his advance, which was very much what Elizabeth had hoped to accomplish; the failure of the campaign was the utter wretchedness and destruction of large numbers of the soldiery, brought about at the same time that the Queen was pouring out money which, carefully hoarded through nearly thirty years, had been the life blood of her success.

The situation was one of the greatest complexity, for the internal dissensions of the Dutch were like their network of waterways, which

* Garrett Mattingley, *Defeat of the Spanish Armada.*

cut up the terrain and made it so difficult to take or defend; but one of the chief drawbacks on the English side was the character of Leicester. It was scarcely that he had not the ability the position required. Burleigh and Walsingham both thought he had; so did the Queen; the opinion of such a trio must have been well-grounded. But Leicester was incapable of following Elizabeth's own example. A great part of her ability showed itself in a capacity to recognize the ability of other people, and to co-operate with them on the score of it. Sir John Norris was not only a remarkably able soldier: he had fought for William of Orange, and therefore his experience should have made him invaluable. Leicester fell foul of him at once, and actually likened him to the Earl of Sussex, than which, in his view, there could hardly be greater condemnation. He told Walsingham that Norris might be Sussex' own son, "he will so dissemble, so crouch, so cunningly carry his doings as no man living would imagine there were half the malice or vindictive mind that doth plainly in his deeds prove to be"; however, a month later, having been warned that the Queen valued Norris' ability highly, Leicester wrote: "I will not write any more of Mr. John Norris' backwardness. He hath too good friends, and so hath all that like not me."[1]

Leicester maintained that the Queen, by publicly dissociating herself from responsibility in the matter of his holding the office of Supreme Governor, had "cracked his credit". His relations with the Commissioners of the States soon degenerated, and his letter to Walsingham showed how vindictively he regarded them. Paul Buis, the Deputy of Utrecht, aroused his especial ire. "If her Majesty mean to stand with this cause," he told Walsingham, "I will warrant him hanged, and one or two of his fellows; but you must not tell your shirt of this yet." "Mr. Paul Buis," he wrote again, "a most lewd man as ever lived . . . I have been fain to handle some of my masters somewhat plainly and roughly, too, for they thought I would droop; but I will rather be overthrown by her Majesty's doings, than overboarded by these churls and tinkers."

In June, 1586, Parma captured Grave; but in July Philip Sidney led an attack on Axel. At dead of night he swam the moat with forty men, scaled the wall, and opened the gates to his forces. The investing of this city gained the capitulation of four neighbouring cities, and by the breaching of the dykes the surrounding country was made impassable to the Spaniards. The speed and success of this action made people say that, if the English army were properly furnished and given its head, it could create such opposition as would engage Spain in a death-struggle.

On July 9th Walsingham told Leicester of the Queen: "She gathereth upon view of your Lordship's letter that the only salve to cure this sore is to make herself proprietory of that country and to put such an army into the same as may be able to make head to the enemy's. Those two things being so contrary to her Majesty's disposition, the one for that it breedeth a doubt of perpetual war, the other for that it requireth an increase of charges, doth marvellously distract her and make her repent that she ever entered into the action."

Leicester's quarrel with Sir John Norris extended to the latter's uncle, the Treasurer. The Queen continued her demands for accounts of how her money had been spent, and Leicester declared to Walsingham: "The treasurer delivers books one day and fetcheth them away another day, and till this day no perfect book given to the auditor." At the very mention of accounts he now became passionate. He rounded on the Queen herself. People criticized him, did they? He wrote to her on June 27th: "I pray God I may live to see you employ some of them that are thus careless of me, to see whether they will spend £20,000 of their own for you in seven months, but all is in mine own heart so little, though the greatest portion of all my land pay for it, so your Majesty do well accept of it." That he had spent so much was generous, loyal and very useful, but when he threw it in the Queen's face it did not seem to have crossed his mind where all his money had come from in the first place.

Nor did the Queen remind him of it. On July 19th she wrote him a letter in which, though she did not give way to his representations, she answered them mildly, and in a burst of tenderness thanked him warmly for what he had done. The wonderful contrast between the opening and closing sentences of this letter, and those of the one she had written the previous April, afford one of the clearest glimpses of the range and variety of her emotions:

"Rob: I am afraid you will suppose by my wandering writings that a midsummer moon hath taken large possession of my brains this month, but you must needs take things as they come in my head, though order be left behind me." She must defend Norris and his fellows, who had "many years won our nation honour and themselves fame; let them not be discouraged by any means". On the other hand, if they had been guilty of cheating the soldiers, he was to let her hear of it, and she would deal with them; for, she said, "it frets me not a little that the poor soldiers that hourly venture life, should want their due, that well deserve rather reward". If it should prove that the treasurer had been negligent or incompetent, he should be treated according to his deserts, "though," she added, "you know my old wont, that love not to discharge from office without deserts God forbid ○ ○ Now will I end, that do imagine I talk still with you, and therefore loth to say farewell . . . though ever I pray God bless you from all harm and save you from all foes, with my million and legion of thanks, for all your pains and cares. As you know, ever the same, E. R."

In September, 1586, occurred the most famous and calamitous episode of the campaign. Having captured Duisberg, the English regarded this as the preliminary to capturing Zutphen, the key city of Guelderland. On September 13th they encamped before the city and threw up entrenchments. On the 21st, a spy brought word that Parma would attempt to raise the siege by bringing a provision train into the city before dawn next day. Sir John Norris and Sir William Stanley, with five hundred men, were detailed to cut off the train, and they were accompanied by fifty volunteers, including Lord Essex and Sir Philip Sidney. The morning of September 22nd broke through a dense mist, and not until the baggage wagons were within ear-shot was it discovered, by a sudden lifting of the mist, that they were accompanied by three thousand Spanish troops. The English force performed wonders of bravery, one of which was the charge of the fifty heavily armed men with lances in rest, which proved how effective this tactic still was against a force much larger and armed with guns. The baggage train, however, entered the city, and the English attempt to arrest it was not only useless but worse than useless.

Philip Sidney was for some reason not wearing thigh-pieces; some said he had lent his to another man, others that he did not want to be more heavily armed than Sir William Pelham, who was without them. One horse was shot under him; he mounted another, and a musket ball entered his thigh. He would have disregarded the wound, but the horse bolted with him out of the field. Sidney rode a mile and a half, losing blood all the way, till he reached his uncle's camp. Exhausted, and desperately thirsty from loss of blood, he was just lifting to his mouth a bottle of water when he saw a foot soldier being carried past. The dying man gazed in hopeless longing at the flask, and Sidney, without putting it to his lips, handed it to the soldier, saying: "Thy necessity is yet greater than mine!"[1]

"Oh Philip!" exclaimed Leicester. "I am sorry for thy hurt!" He had Sidney put into his own barge and taken to his headquarters at

Arnhem. Here his wife, who was six months gone with child, came from Flushing to nurse him.

The wound itself was not a very serious one, and for the first fortnight it seemed that he had escaped the dread danger of blood poisoning. On October 2nd Leicester wrote to Walsingham: "He amends as well as is possible in this time . . . he sleeps and rests well and hath a good stomach to eat." Nevertheless, on September 30th he made his Will. Both his parents were dead, and after disposing of his property to pay his own and his father's debts and to provide for his wife, he spoke of Lord Leicester as the relative he most honoured, and left him one hundred pounds "as a token of my duteous service and great love which I have ever borne him in all duty". He left a hundred pounds with his love and duty to his uncle Warwick, "to my dear sister the Countess of Pembroke, my best jewel beset with diamonds, to my honoured good ladies the Countess of Huntingdon, the Countess of Warwick and the Countess of Leicester, every one of them a jewel, the best I have". On the morning of October 8th, sixteen days after he had received the wound, as he lifted up the bed-clothes he smelt the odour of putrefaction, and knew that gangrene had set in. It took nine days to kill him. On the morning of October 17th he had given his messages and farewells, and when he was silent those beside his bed were silent too, but he said: "I pray you, speak to me still." The last person whose words he could hear was his brother Robert Sidney. To him, the dying man spoke some sentences; one of them was: "Love my memory."

Leicester's grief was great, and the worse for having to impart the news to Walsingham and tell him of his daughter's plight. He wrote eight days after Philip Sidney's death: "The grief I have taken for the loss of my dear son and yours would not suffer me to write sooner of these ill news to you, of his good recovery. . . . For mine own part, I have lost, beside the comfort of my life, a most principal stay and help in my service here." He spoke with extreme kindness of young Lady Sidney. "Your sorrowful daughter and mine is here with me at Utrecht, till she may recover some strength, for she is wonderfully overthrown, through her long care since the beginning of her husband's hurt, and I am the more careful she should be in some strength ere she take her journey into England, for that she is with child, which I pray God send to be a son, if it be His will, but whether son or daughter they shall be my children too."[1]

Beside the campaign, with this tragic incident, there was another matter deeply engrossing Leicester's thoughts. The trial of the Queen of Scots, for the attempted murder of Queen Elizabeth by participation in the Babington conspiracy, had been held at Fotheringhay Castle, and she had been found guilty as "an imaginer and compasser of her Majesty's destruction". Leicester now heard from Walsingham that Elizabeth was refusing her consent to have sentence of death passed upon her.

Leicester, like others, had been anxious to conciliate Mary Queen of Scots in case she were to become Queen of England; but now that there was every reason for putting her to death, and nothing stood in the way but Elizabeth's shrinking from publishing sentence of death and signing a warrant for execution, Leicester determined with all his force that the Queen must be made to act. He wrote urgently to Walsingham: "It is most certain if you will have her Majesty safe, it must be done, for justice does crave it besides policy." He said: "I have written very earnestly both to her Majesty and my Lord Treasurer . . . and Mr. Vice-Chancellor, for the furtherance of justice on the Queen of Scots." He reminded Walsingham that after the Rising in the North, seventeen years before, "all the Council of England once dealt with her Majesty for justice to be done upon that person" for her complicity with the Earls of Northumberland and Westmoreland, and that so nearly had the Queen consented to her execution then that "the Great Seal of England was sent", but all was afterwards revoked. The Council should act decisively now, and not through their "temporizing solemnities" run the risk of Elizabeth's assassination. "God forbid!" he exclaimed. "Be you all stout and resolute for this speedy execution." On October 25th he wrote again: "My heart cannot rest for fear, since I heard that your matters are deferred." Had he been at the Council Meeting of which Walsingham told him, he believed he would have usurped the Queen's function, and ordered the execution himself, rather than have suffered "this dreadful mischief to be prolonged for her destruction".[1] So much alarmed was he by the inability of the Council to force Elizabeth's assent to Mary's execution that, Camden says, he advised "the sure but silent operation of poison and sent a divine privately to Walsingham to convince him it was lawful". Walsingham refused the suggestion.

But while Leicester's genuine loyalty and concern were directed over the Channel, the Queen for her part directed angry attention upon the affairs of the English army in the Northern Provinces. In spite of the personal tenderness which had dictated her letter of July 19th, she was still in a state of exasperation at the lack of information. In October she sent over £30,000 by Sir Thomas Wilkes, with peremptory instructions which read: "And whereas heretofore many letters have been written to our said Cousin the Earl of Leicester, as well from us as from our Privy Council and Secretary, requiring answer to many matters, concerning our service, whereof by reason of his manifold occupation (as we take it) there hath seldom been an answer returned, or mention of the receipt of the said letters," so, the instruction ran, "it is our will and pleasure that you shall from time to time, urge and procure answer to the said letters . . . (and) solicit our said cousin for answer to all and every the said letters and matters."[1]

But Leicester was now about to return to England. He was longing to do so. A summons had been issued for the opening of Parliament on October 29th; this session was to decide the affair of the Queen of Scots, and he told the States General he must leave them to take his place in it. The Queen had allowed of his return, and Lord Burleigh had written to Sir Edward Stafford that "the Earl of Leicester is like to be revoked with a pretence to give counsel to her Majesty". Stafford made a very secret reply: "If I might be bold to tell you what I think . . . if I had as much credit as your Lordship hath, and he born to do me no more good than he is, I would keep him where he is, and he should drink that which he has brewed. I would keep him there to undo himself, and sure enough from coming home to undo others." But nothing delayed the great Earl's return.

The Queen did not open Parliament herself, but on November 12th a deputation of Lord and Commons waited on her at Richmond. They said her person was in imminent danger of assassination, and they asked, they demanded the execution of the sentence already passed upon the Queen of Scots. The Queen's reply was of the greatest interest. She said that for the first time she had not opened Parliament, not because she was afraid that crowds might conceal a murderer, but because she shrank from hearing of the topic she knew they must debate. She thanked them for their love and care of her, and though she would not give them the assurance that they sought she said she would pray for inspiration to know what was best to do for "the safety of the Church, the preservation of your estates and the prosperity of the commonwealth under my charge". The most poignant passage of this speech, however, was uttered at its beginning. In it she spoke of the attempts that had been made to murder her, and, while admitting the natural fear which they aroused in her, told her listeners, simply and most movingly, that she had had to endure so much unhappiness, the mere fact of being deprived of life had now but few terrors for her. "As for me," she said, "I assure you, I find no great cause I should be fond to live . . . and yet I say not, but in the stroke coming, perhaps flesh and blood would be moved with it, and seek to shun it. I have had good experience and trial of this world. . . . I have found treason in trust, seen great benefits little regarded, and instead of gratefulness, courses of purpose to cross. These former remembrances, present feeling and future expectation of evils, I say, have made me think an evil is much the better, the less while it dureth, and so, them happiest that are soonest hence." If the murderers had succeeded, she said, "my pains should have been but small and short. Wherein, as I would be loth to die so bloody a death, so I doubt not but God would have given me grace to be prepared for such an event, which, when it shall chance, I refer to His good pleasure." Few could fail to know what was in her mind when she spoke of ingratitude for her benefits, and crossing of her purpose. The effect of such words on men who had the strongest possible self-interest in her continued safety, who recognized the deep emotion with which she spoke of their prosperity and well-being, who, if they thought her sufferings unreasonable, at least knew that they had been severe, was that of a most powerful appeal to their feelings. At the end of her speech the Queen assured them she knew as well as they did that delay was dangerous, and they should have her answer "with all conveniency". Whereupon, "they, most affectionately praying unto God for her long and happy reign over them, she for the same yielding great thanks thereof, departed".[1]

The heavy matter of the Queen of Scots, of having to put Mary to death by her own assent or stand the push of further attempts at the murder of herself, this, and the Netherlands war, disastrous in itself as a perpetual gaping wound through which her treasury, the life-blood of government, was bleeding away, and threatening imminent peril in case it should cause Spain to declare war on England, made a situation of oppressive gloom, except where it was lit, as by wildfire, by the doings of Sir Francis Drake. He had a secret understanding with the Queen, which perfectly satisfied him, that if he succeeded in his coup she would applaud him to the very echo, and if he fell into Spanish hands she could not intervene to save him. He had made a lightning raid, first on the west coast of Spain, sacking Vigo and burning shipping, then flying over the Atlantic to the West Indies, sacking the cities of San Domingo and Cartagena. His return, unscathed, from this tremendous demonstration of English sea-power thrilled the nation with confidence; it also made it impossible to convince the King of Spain that the Queen of England had no aggressive intentions towards him—but this, after all, would have been impossible in any case.

At the end of November Drake, with eight sail, went over to Holland to fetch home the Supreme Governor of the Netherlands. Leicester did not resign his title, nor did he give the Dutch any undertaking that he would return. They told him, for their part, that they would not confirm any treaty the Queen of England might make with Parma which denied them the freedom of their religion, and they wanted her contribution increased to ten thousand men and two thousand horse. No encouragement could be given that these demands would be met. Leicester made arrangements, meanwhile, to delegate his powers to the States General, and on November 23rd he set sail with Drake from Flushing. He did not depart without some demonstrations of friendliness and wishes expressed for his return. Madame de Brederode sent him a cutting of a rose he had asked for, and begged him to command anything in her garden.

Meanwhile Scots commissioners, sent by James, had arrived in London with a request that Elizabeth would spare his mother's life. Archibald Douglas wrote to the King that on November 23rd Parliament had told the Queen once again that the safety of her life was not compatible with the continued existence of the Queen of Scots, and had repeated their demands for the latter's execution. Elizabeth had replied that before she gave her answer she must take further advice. At ten o'clock that night the Earl of Leicester arrived at Court. All other considerations laid aside, the Queen was enchanted to see him. "Never since I was born did I receive a more gracious welcome",* was his own account. He immediately set about what he had come to do; he threw the weight of his influence into the demand for the execution. In the first week of December, Douglas reported to James: "I drove back from Court with my Lord of Leicester, who repeated to me that it was to your Majesty's interest that your Mother should suffer justice. I assured him your Majesty would receive that persuasion in no good part. He made many protestations of service to your Majesty for which I thanked him heartily as he doth govern the Court at this time at his pleasure."

Hardly a week in England as Leicester had been, the Queen's delight in his presence had created this impression. Douglas made an appointment with him for December 6th, "to discuss", as he wrote to

* Motley, *History of the United Netherlands.*

James, "your Majesty's affairs at greater length. It would be well to thank him in your next letter for his good offices."

The other commissioner, Sir William Keith, was somewhat of a bungler. James had written him a strongly worded letter which amounted to a threat against the Queen of England if she should presume to execute the Queen of Scots. Keith was received in audience by Elizabeth with this letter actually upon his person. He began to make some allusive remarks of a threatening tendency, and the Queen, with the keen-eyed rapacity of a hawk, divined instantly that their inspiration was in his pocket. She demanded peremptorily to see the letter. Keith was too startled to resist; he handed it over, and its contents threw the Queen into such a passion, he said, "it was a great deal of work to all of us, and to the Earl of Leicester, to appease her". Ten days later James wrote to Elizabeth, saying how sorry he was she had "misunderstood" his letter to Keith. "My only intention," he said, "was to inform you of the state of feeling in Scotland."[1]

The unhappy young widow of Philip Sidney had come home to her father's house at Barne Elms and there miscarried of a dead child. On December 22nd Leicester wrote to Walsingham: "I am heartily sorry for any further visitation to come to that house, for I must every way be partaker thereof." Next day he wrote again: "I cannot be quiet till I may know how my daughter doth amend; wishing her even as to my own child, which, God willing, I shall always esteem her to be." He would have liked to come to Barne Elms to see her, but the Queen required his presence at Court. "But my heart," he said, "is there with you and my prayers shall go to God for you and yours." Then he spoke of the letter the Queen of Scots had sent to Elizabeth. As ever, Mary treated accusations against herself by saying nothing about them. She did not now go into tedious arguments as to the rights or wrongs of her conviction for attempted murder; she merely stated that she was content to die as a martyr for the Catholic Church; but she gave detailed requests for the kind treatment of her servants after her death and for the disposal of her body. These lines made Elizabeth weep. Leicester said: "There is a letter come from the Queen of Scots which hath wrought tears, but I trust shall do no further harm, albeit the delay is so dangerous. From Greenwich, December 23rd, 1586."

The matter preyed upon Elizabeth increasingly. In this month a correspondent at Court wrote to Lord Rutland: "Her Majesty keepeth herself more private than she was wont."

XXVII

THE NETHERLANDS CAMPAIGN was telling so much upon the Queen's nerves and temper, Mendoza heard she had said that if she had done her duty as a Queen, she would have had Leicester and Walsingham hanged for having been the prime movers in it. The news from the theatre of war was now extremely grave. Sir William Stanley had done good service in Ireland, but he had not received any adequate reward. In the Netherlands campaign, Leicester had described him as "worth his weight in Pearl", and on Leicester's return to England in December, 1586, he left Stanley as Governor of Deventer, a key town of Guelderland, and Stanley's friend Rowland Yorke in charge of a small fortress or "sconce" outside Zutphen. To the horror and consternation of both Dutch and English, news came in February that Stanley and Yorke had opened their gates to Parma. Stanley said that he did it for religion's sake; he came of a Catholic family, and he could no longer act for a heretic Queen against the King of Spain. That Parma, with these strongholds in his grasp, did not immediately press on to final and complete victory was owing in part to the fact that he was already occupied with preparations for the invasion of England. The Queen continued her attempts at a negotiated peace, and Parma continued to hold her in play. The terms of peace, the Spaniard had decided, were going to be dictated to the English on English soil.

The first delight of Leicester's presence having subsided, the Queen again turned her attention to the accounts, and only second to her own interest in the matter was that of the Lord Treasurer of England. On February 7th Leicester wrote to Burleigh from Wanstead, declaring that it was an injury that he should be asked to account for what had been spent in the Low Countries; this was the province of an auditor or clerk, not of one in his position. He had given the Queen the fullest explanation in his power, and he resented the fact that Lord Burleigh had taken the Queen's part rather than his. Burleigh replied very patiently: "I never did say, nor mean to say, that your Lordship ought to be blamed for [the auditors'] imperfections in their accounts. I did say, and do still say, that their accounts are obscure, confused and without credit. . . . And I find, in truth, that they ought to have been commanded by your Lordship's authority to have reformed the same and made your Lordship more privy to their doings, for which not doing, I condemned them and not your Lordship." As for Leicester's accusation that Burleigh was hostile towards him, once again Burleigh asseverated that it was entirely groundless. He reminded Leicester of having heard the Queen, as he said, "tax me very sharply, that in not applauding her censures, I do commonly flatter . . . and hold opinions to please your Lordship and others". He was sick, he said, "of these ungrateful burdens of service".[1]

The previous November, the embalmed body of Philip Sidney had been brought in what was called the Black Pinnace, his own ship draped in black and with black sails, to Harwich. Amid crowds all wearing black or some sign of mourning, the coffin was landed at Tower Wharf and conveyed to a house in the Minories some distance from Walsingham's house in Seething Lane, where it lay for nearly three months, awaiting burial. The delay was owing to the fact that Sidney, through no fault of his own, had left, as Walsingham said, "a great number of poor creditors", and their claims must be met before the expenses of a costly funeral were undertaken. Sidney thought he had, by his Will, discharged his debts by arranging for the sale of some of his lands, but when Walsingham took legal advice the Will was found to be "imperfect". Walsingham himself paid £6,000 on his dead son-in-law's behalf, which, he told Leicester, "hath brought me into a most desperate and hard state", though that, he said, was as nothing compared with the loss of the young man "who was my chief wordly comfort". He said it cut him to the heart that a man of spotless reputation such as Philip Sidney, "who had so great cares to see all men satisfied, should be so exposed to the outcry of his creditors".

Leicester was in straits himself for ready money, but out of all the lands in his possession it is difficult not to think that he might have sold something, to share the financial burden with Walsingham. He neither did this, nor gave any other assistance towards raising the outstanding balance of the debts; and when Walsingham appealed to the Queen for some financial aid, Leicester refused to support his suit. It was left to Burleigh to secure him a substantial grant of land the following April, and the Chancellorship of the Duchy of

Lancaster, for which Leicester had put forward another candidate.[1] This gave a slightly disagreeable air to the exceptional warmth of the sympathy he expressed to Walsingham on the plight of young Lady Sidney, the widow brought to bed of a dead child, of whom Leicester had written to her father as "your sorrowful daughter and mine".

By February, however, Walsingham had, at whatever sacrifice to himself, made the necessary financial arrangements, and on February 16th, 1587, a funeral procession of almost unexampled splendour, comprising seven hundred persons, bore Philip Sidney to St. Paul's. The coffin was preceded by officers, pipers, drummers, and trumpeters of Sidney's regiment of horse, by his standard, and by a train of his friends walking in pairs, one of them being Sir Francis Drake. His war-horse, caparisoned in black and led by a black-clothed footman, was ridden by a little page who trailed a broken lance. Heralds bore his arms, his helmet, shield, tabard, spurs and gloves. The coffin, covered in black velvet, was slung between two poles, each supported by seven yeomen, robed and hooded in black. The chief mourner, his brother and heir Robert Sidney, walked alone after the coffin; then, riding on horseback two and two, came the Earl of Leicester and the Earl of Huntingdon, the Earl of Pembroke and the Earl of Warwick, Lord Willoughby and Lord North. Seven gentlemen of the Low Countries followed, representing the United Provinces. After these came the Lord Mayor and Aldermen, the Sherriffs and the Recorder of London. Four hundred citizens brought up the rear. The streets were so crowded that the long procession made its way with difficulty to the Cathedral. There, the funeral ceremony was preached from a text inscribed on the coffin: *Blessed are the dead who die in the Lord*. The burial was made in a vault in the Lady Chapel, and when, eighty years later, the Great Fire had destroyed St. Paul's, John Aubrey, visiting the gaping, blackened ruins, saw exposed the lead coffin of Sir Philip Sidney.

Just before Sidney's funeral, an event of wider significance and even more engrossing interest to the nation had taken place. On February 11th, 1587, after a grave warning from Lord Howard of Effingham that the people would not endure delay much longer, Elizabeth had signed at Greenwich the death warrant of Mary Queen of Scots. With the signed document in his hands at last, Lord Burleigh had convened a meeting of all the available Privy Councillors: Lord Leicester, Sir Francis Walsingham, Sir Christopher Hatton, Sir Francis Knollys, Lord Howard of Effingham, Lord Hunsdon, Lord

Cobham, Lord Derby, and Mr. Secretary Davison, to whom the Queen had given the warrant, telling him to carry it to the Lord Chancellor's office that it might be passed under the Great Seal.

Burleigh told them that the Queen had done her part in signing the warrant; they all knew how she shrank from the final act of ordering it to be used. The Act of Association had made it law that whoever after trial was found guilty of attempting the Queen's murder was to be put to death by her subjects as in duty bound. It was for them to act in accordance with the law. Let them send the warrant to Fotheringay and order the execution. There were ten of them present as he spoke. All would bear an equal responsibility, and their numbers would give them indemnity. The scheme was agreed upon and rapidly put into action: on the morning of February 17th, in the great hall of Fotheringhay, the awful deed was carried out.

The first intimation reached Elizabeth when she returned from riding in Greenwich Park and heard, borne down the serpentine windings of the river, the wild, exultant pealing of the London bells. She asked why they rang so, and was told, for joy that the Queen of Scots was beheaded.

The ensuing weeks were filled by Elizabeth's hysterical declarations that though she had signed the warrant she had not meant it to be used till she said so; that the councillors had wickedly deceived her, to enable them to commit the greatest crime of all, the usurpation of her power. The knowledge that the execution might expose her to retaliation from France, that France might combine with Scotland, or with Spain, and call up in revolt all the English Catholics who had hitherto been quiescent only, perhaps, because they looked forward to Mary Stuart as a Catholic successor—these were the practical considerations that tormented her. The theoretical one was of no less strength; the objection to teaching subjects that royal beings were not sacrosanct, that they could be brought to the bar, condemned and executed as common criminals. And beyond these lay the unnameable horror which had darkened her childhood, wrecked her nerves, disorganized her body and made her the de-natured creature that she was—that of cutting off the head of a Queen, a woman, a relation of her own. All these fears had been for the time being mastered when Lord Howard of Effingham had told her bluntly that she would refuse to sign the warrant at her peril. They were mastered because she was able to tell herself that signing was not the last step of all—it was the last but one. Beyond that, it remained still for her to give the order to put the warrant into effect. When she had been trapped into the last step before she had made up her mind to it, the fears rose again with annihilating force. Hours of hysterical weeping were succeeded by scenes of devastating violence. That if she had not in her inmost mind assented to the execution she would not have signed the warrant was obvious to everyone; but she evinced the symptom typical of hysteria, the self-deceiving denial of a responsibility too painful to face, and the Councillors could only bend to the storm and arm themselves to ride it out. Burleigh was banished from the Queen's presence, Hatton and the others were treated to reiterated denunciations, Davison was tried by the Court of Star Chamber, committed to the Tower, and visited with a heavy fine. His fine, however, was remitted, his conditions of imprisonment were of the easiest, and when he was released, though he was deprived of office, he continued to draw his secretary's salary for the rest of his life.

Slowly and painfully the situation healed. Lord Burleigh was recalled; no such political consequences as the Queen had feared showed themselves; but when Robert Carey visited Elizabeth as she was dying, he found her fetching great sighs, and he said he never remembered to have heard her sigh before—save when the Queen of Scots was executed. The most important result of Mary Stuart's death, however, was that, when faced with imminent invasion by Spain, the English Catholics had not to ask themselves whether they would prefer to keep Elizabeth on the throne or have the Queen of Scots put there by Spanish troops; they had only to consider whether they would prefer to remain as an independent and prosperous country, or be taken over by the King of Spain and ruled as a Spanish province on the lines of the martyred Netherlands. Confronted with this alternative, the majority of the English Catholics found no difficulty in making up their minds.

The stories about Elizabeth's having borne children to the Earl of Leicester were, of course, most frequent in the early years of her reign; but in 1587 a young man who declared that his name was Arthur Dudley presented himself in Madrid to the King of Spain's English secretary. He claimed to be the son of Elizabeth by Lord Robert Dudley. His story rested entirely on his own assertion, and the later part carried so little conviction that it was never, apparently, investigated; but the earlier part of it had been got up by somebody with considerable knowledge of the events and persons of twenty-five years before. Dudley was said to be twenty-five years old, and

1562 was the year in which Elizabeth had nearly died of smallpox; an illness of the Queen's was, therefore, established in the probable year of his birth. He said that Mrs. Ashley had given him at birth into the care of Robert Southern, a man who had been appointed Deputy Keeper of Enfield Chase in 1570, when Dudley would have been eight years old, and that Southern had brought him up there with his own children. He had run away at fifteen years old but been brought back from Milford Haven by warrant from the Privy Council, though afterwards allowed to join a Huguenot contingent fighting in the Netherlands. He was recalled to England by a message from the dying Southern, who confided to him that he was the son of Queen Elizabeth by Lord Leicester. He then appeared in France, and visited Sir Edward Stafford, to whom he told his story in an attempt to extort money. Stafford dismissed him as an imposter.

According to Dudley himself, the next events in his history were as follows. He returned to England and had an interview with Lord Leicester, who admitted with sighs and tears that Dudley was his child by the Queen, but said he must go abroad again, for he was like a frigate in full sail, "pretty but dangerous". To provide for his getting out of the country Leicester sent him, in charge of his secretary Mr. Fludd, to Walsingham's house, with a message asking for a passport as the young man was a special friend of the Earl's. Walsingham answered that he could not give this without interrogating the applicant. At this, Dudley said, he ran away; he got himself out of the country as a stowaway, and, his story now emerging into the light of day, Dudley spent some time in Germany and Italy, making contact wherever he could with enemies of England. When he heard of the execution of the Queen of Scots he came to Spain, told his story to the King's Council, and suggested that the King of Scots should be murdered and Scotland annexed to Catholic England. Dudley's own position should then be settled by consent of the neighbouring powers.

Robert Southern was dead, Mrs. Ashley was dead, and it must be admitted that not much would have been gained by interrogating the Earl of Leicester and his secretary; but Dudley had mentioned some people who could have been asked to substantiate his story, first and foremost Sir Francis Walsingham. No one, it would seem, thought it worth while to make any move in this direction, and the English secretary in Madrid gave it as his opinion that Dudley was probably a spy, working for either side indiscriminately.*

* A. Martin Hume, *Courtships of Queen Elizabeth*.

This story was afloat in the early summer of 1587. Leicester was preparing to return to the Netherlands in July, and before his departure another story was current about him, resting this time on more solid grounds.

The staunch Sir Robert Bulkeley, who had foiled the Earl in the latter's attempt to enlarge the boundaries of Snowden Forest, could not live as he did without creating some enemies. One of these, Mr. Woods of Rhosmore, came up from Wales to tell Lord Leicester, who, he knew, would hear it willingly, that one of the conspirators in the Babington plot, Thomas Salisbury, had been in Beaumaris, in long and close consultations with Sir Robert Bulkeley. Bulkeley was summoned to London, and in the presence of the Privy Council Leicester solemnly charged him with Woods' accusations. Bulkeley did not defend himself, but he routed the Earl completely. He said: "Your father was like to undo my father, telling him to proclaim Queen Jane, which he did. Had not my mother been one of Queen Mary's maids of honour, he had come to great trouble and danger." Leicester, as Lord Robert Dudley, had proclaimed Queen Jane himself, in the market place of King's Lynn. The audacity of such a reminder was enough to make the hearers blink. "Hearing these words, it was said, the Council rose and *hushed*."

Lord Leicester strode away to the Queen. He told her they had found Bulkeley to be a dangerous person, and saw cause to commit him to the Tower.

"What! Sir Richard Bulkeley!" exclaimed the Queen. "He never intended us any harm. We have brought him up from a boy and have had special trial of his fidelity. You shall not commit him." The Earl replied: "We who have the care of your Majesty's person see more and hear more of the man than you do. He is of an aspiring mind and lives in a remote place." The Queen darted to pick up a New Testament. Pressing it to her lips she exclaimed: "Before God, we will be sworn upon the Holy Evangelists, he never intended us any harm. You shall not commit him! We have brought him up from a boy."

Sir Robert, therefore, could not be put into the Tower, but presently a protégé of the Earl's named Green came to him and delivered him a challenge from Broomfield, one of the Gentlemen Pensioners. "Have you no other errand?" asked Sir Robert.

"No," said Green. Thereupon Sir Robert gave him a crack over the head and told him to take that back for the answer.

Bulkeley was to visit the Queen at Greenwich, and Green, Broomfield and some friends determined that when he was on the Thames they would collide with his boat and drown him. Bulkeley had the good fortune to have this news conveyed to him. Instead of taking boat with a waterman he hired the Lord Mayor's barge, and manned it with gunners, trumpeters and drummers. He was rowed downstream to Greenwich, where he landed with guns saluting, trumpets braying and the roll of drums. This extraordinary arrival beneath the palace windows attracted everyone's attention. Leicester said to the Queen that Bulkeley had come as if he wanted to start a rebellion; but it was a wry comment on the Earl's part; Sir Richard Bulkeley was the winner.

The Queen insisted that Lord Leicester should be friends with him, and Leicester, who knew "how to put his passion in his pocket", asked Bulkeley to dine with him in his lodging. Here, with a cordial candour, he told Sir Robert that the latter's interference in the matter of the boundaries had cost him ten thousand pounds. Then they sat down to dinner, but Sir Robert "*did eat nor drink anything but what he saw the Earl taste*".[1]

Elizabeth was still hoping, for it was Parma's intention to make her hope, that peace might be arranged with Spain on the basis of restoring the States' charters and withdrawing the Spanish troops. The prospect was illusory, for Philip had no intention of conceding anything in the Netherlands, and had at last got massive preparations in the making for the invasion of England. The Queen of Scots had bequeathed him the Crown of England, telling him at the same time that her son James had better be removed from Scotland and taken to Spain, there to be re-educated as a Catholic. It was a more tempting project to conquer England for himself than to put Mary Stuart on the throne, and Philip had decided that when he had taken the English crown he would give it to his daughter the Infanta Isabella. On April 14th he wrote to Parma apropos the negotiations for peace with England: "The peace commissioners may meet. But to you only I declare that my intention is that this shall never lead to any result, whatever conditions may be offered by them . . . this is done to cool them in their preparations for defence, by inducing them to believe that such preparations will not be necessary. You are well aware that the reverse of all this is the truth and that there is to be no slackness on our part but the greatest diligence in our efforts for the invasion of England, for which we have already made the most abundant provision."* But the most urgent reason for his now setting

* Motley, *History of the United Netherlands.*

about the conquest of England in earnest was the depredations the English were making upon Spanish shipping.

In April, 1587, Drake carried out another of his flying attacks. He was ready to sail at the beginning of April, and the Queen, elated but terrified by his success, tried at the last moment to restrain him by a message. But as he had written to Walsingham, "the wind commands me away, our ship is under sail", and he got out of Plymouth Sound before Elizabeth could stop him. With thirty-six vessels, six of which belonged to the Queen, the rest being found by London merchants, Drake sailed to Cadiz, where the great harbour was filled with store ships loaded with provisions for the use of the Armada. At the sight of Drake's squadron the crews abandoned them. Drake took off as many of the provisions as he had a mind to, set fire to the ships, and cut their cables. He then sailed for the mouth of the Tagus, meaning to go up to Lisbon, where the galleons for the invasion were being built, and burn everything in sight; but a pinnace bearing a message from the Queen overtook him, forbidding him to make this onslaught. The Queen was still hoping to negotiate a peace. Drake reluctantly obeyed; on the way home he found some consolation in capturing the *San Philip*, the largest treasure ship that had ever fallen into English hands.

Leicester's conduct of his Netherlands office had not been a distinguished success. Nevertheless, the multiplicity and division of authorities among the States was so great that the absence of the man in supreme command was now a very serious disadvantage. A commission was sent to the Queen asking for his return, and Burleigh and Walsingham both urged her strongly to send him back. Though he had shown no ability as an administrator or a soldier, and, what was much more serious, had quarrelled with instead of supporting the able men under his command, nevertheless Leicester's influence with the Queen was such, that Burleigh and Walsingham thought his presence in command of the forces was the best guarantee that Elizabeth would not suddenly withdraw from the campaign altogether. While the Earl was in England the Queen had sent over Thomas Sackville, now Lord Buckhurst, to make a report on the position, and what Buckhurst found he expressed in the comment that the command "had better been bestowed upon a meaner man of more skill". He told Walsingham that it was lamentable to see how Leicester had "abused her Majesty", making her name the means to justify and defend "his intolerable errors",* and declared

* Conyers Read, *Lord Burleigh and Queen Elizabeth*.

that neither Leicester's might, nor his malice, should prevent him from reporting truly on what he found. Leicester was so furious at Buckhurst's statements that he asserted Buckhurst was scheming to obtain the Netherlands command himself. He worked upon the Queen's belief in him to such an extent that he persuaded her to put Buckhurst under arrest. The latter was confined to his own house, and, though he could have had visits from his family and friends, he refused to receive any of them, declaring stoutly that he would abide by the letter of the Queen's command. This injurious treatment, totally undeserved as it was, was the only setback in Lord Buckhurst's career; the April following Lord Leicester's death he was given the Garter.

Despite his views of Leicester's conduct and capacity, however, Buckhurst had said that he ought to go back at once, as the absence of the one man who held a unifying command was disastrous to any scheme of defence. He should go, and take with him enough money to pay the English soldiers their arrears of wages.

Leicester himself declared that he was willing to go, but that he could not stir unless the Queen would lend him £10,000. This demand would have been unwelcome at any time and, in the state to which other people's incompetence and dishonesty had reduced her financial affairs, it was the last straw. So long as the conduct of her finances had rested in her own hands, principle, ability and the instinct for sheer self-preservation had made her keep them in scrupulous order. The nervous torment of seeing, without being able to check, *gâtisme* that was utterly ruinous to her, and being, for the first time in her life, deprived of effective control, caused in her a steadily mounting panic; in a burst of unreasoning fury she exclaimed that Leicester should not have the money. The Earl now felt that his constitution required him to take the waters, and this year he went to Bath. While he was there the Queen agreed to advance him the money, but on condition that it was repaid within the year. Leicester at first told Walsingham that this was more than he could do, if he were to keep up the state he felt his office required. He wrote: "Seeing I find her Majesty's hardness continue still to me as it doth, I pray you lend me your earnest and true furtherance for my abode at home and discharge, for my heart is more than half broke." However, the matter was adjusted, and on April 17th, Walsingham wrote to him that he thought affairs in the Netherlands were becoming so critical that he had asked the Queen to let him summon Leicester home. But the claims of his health were always paramount with Elizabeth, and she would not have him hurriedly recalled, because, Walsingham said: "After the use of the bath it would be dangerous for your Lordship to take any extraordinary travail. There is some doubt," he added, "that Ostend will be presently besieged."*

Parma, meanwhile, was advancing eastwards upon Ostend and Sluys, which were garrisoned by Dutch and English troops. The possession of these ports was essential to him if he were to launch an invasion upon the English coast. The report that he was besieging Sluys, and that the States, to whom the port was of little importance compared to the danger to England that it represented in Parma's hands, were refusing to risk men and ships for its relief, alarmed Elizabeth and the Council so much that Leicester's return was ordered at once. He left London on July 4th, but while he was still in England news reached him that his young Master of the Horse, Christopher Blount, had been wounded in an engagement, under some commander of whom Leicester's opinion was very low, and who may, therefore, very probably have been Sir John Norris. On June 7th, 1587, he wrote to Blount: "I am sorry, Mr. Kytt, for your hurt, yet glad you have escaped so well considering at whose direction you were, and whereof I was greatly afraid when I heard he had taken you with him. Well," he said, "I trust now to be with you very speedily . . . within fifteen days I trust to be in Flushing. There doth come with me 4,000 men which is the cause of my longer stay, but they are almost ready to come hither." He gave instructions to see that the arms and tents he had left were in order. "Commend me," he said, "to my old servant Mrs. Madleyn and bid her see all things handsome for me at the Hague against I come . . . Farewell, Kytt."†
Such a letter shows how charming Leicester must have been to Philip Sidney, to Lord Essex, to all the young men whom he attached to himself.

With four thousand men and another £30,000 of the Queen's money, Leicester set sail from Margate. As he passed the coast on his way into Flushing, he heard the terrific bombardment of Parma's batteries and those of the beleaguered in Sluys. Leicester planned to relieve the port by a combined sea and land operation. An English force was landed at Ostend and marched along the coast towards Sluys, but at Blankenburg a broken causeway prevented their further advance; and Prince Maurice of Nassau, who shared the command of the fleet with Leicester, refused to go into action unless the land

* Motley, *History of the United Netherlands.*
† H.M.C. Pepys.

army were co-operating. Leicester therefore signalled thàt the troops were to retire, take boat, and come up by sea. In the two days occupied by this manoeuvre, Parma moved so close that when he offered the garrison terms for their surrender they had no choice but to accept. The port therefore fell to Spanish hands, but Parma had been so much impressed by Sir Roger Williams' conduct of the defence that he approached Williams with a munificent and courtly offer, not to fight against his own country, but to enlist in the King of Spain's service against the Turks. Williams refused, but he may well have wondered whether the graciousness of a Spanish grandee and the professional appreciation of so great a soldier would not have made an agreeable change from his present situation. Leicester wrote to Walsingham: "I cannot for many respects, how well soever I think of Sir Roger Williams' valour and the other captains', give them countenance, or access to me, before they do give some good reason for the delivery of the town without sending to me first."

There was, however, one sphere in which Leicester never failed; in the circle of his immediate family he commanded unclouded loyalty and love. Walsingham had warned him: "The ill success of Sluys though your Lordship hath done your uttermost . . . hath wrought some alteration in her Majesty's favour towards you . . . I find there is some dealing underhand against your Lordship which proceedeth from the young sort of courtiers that take upon themselves to censure the greatest causes." Among the modern young men, none the less, Lord Leicester had an eager defender whom he had brought to Court to serve in just such a capacity. In 1587 Lord Essex, his stepson, was twenty-one years old. He had been to Cambridge, where he developed a passionate love of reading. This, and soldiering, he thought were to be the interests of his life; rapt in youthful self-absorption, he thought he wanted nothing from the world, and that he could live in perfect content at Lanfey, his small estate in the romantic, wild beauty of Pembrokeshire. For two years he did so, but then he was called to London to play a part which he found not only fitted him but dazzled and enthralled him. One of Leicester's attractive features was a knowledge of how to behave to young people. His father had gained the affection of the young Edward VI, Leicester himself was beloved by Philip Sidney, and it did not take him long to command his stepson's entire devotion. Leicester, in the words of a contemporary, "drew him into the fatal circle, from a retired privateness at his house at Lanfey in South Wales". The tall young man, who walked, head thrust forward, with a striding gait, with black eyes and auburn hair, whose passionate outbursts spoke his sincerity, whose rudeness and sullenness when thwarted were at other times offset by an extraordinary sweetness, who was inexperienced and ingenuous but had a touch of magic about him—he, Leicester hoped, would catch the fancy of the Queen and draw her interest, still magnetized by Walter Raleigh, back into the circle of Leicester House.

The device succeeded—for Essex it succeeded but too well. The excitement of gaining the Queen's favour made him reciprocate an over-strung metaphysical passion. Elizabeth in 1587 was fifty-four, but, unlike Leicester, she had kept a large measure of her looks; she was thin, active, elegant, high-spirited still, and the achievements of a reign of nearly thirty years had invested her with a super-normal attraction, enhanced by her stately appearance and epitomized in the living light of her jewels. Nicholas Breton, years after her death, exclaimed: "Old men will weep when they speak of her . . . how goodly a presence she carried even to her latter days . . . in the glass of light and in the grace of love." And Raleigh's apostrophe written at this era evokes the effect of her attractions at their best:

> O eyes that pierce our hearts without remorse,
> Oh hair, of right that wears a royal crown,
> O hands, that conquer more than Caesar's force,
> O wit, that turns huge kingdoms upside down,
>   Then Love be judge, what heart may these withstand,
>   Such eyes, such hair, such wit and such a hand?

One of Essex' letters to Elizabeth ran: "It is not in your power, great Queen as you are, to make me love you less," but the emotion never led him either to any unselfish affection, or, what was far more serious, to any real understanding of her genius. When his head had paid for his ignorance, the Queen explained the matter once for all. She said: "I had put up with but too much disrespect to my person, but I warned him he should not touch my sceptre."

This was fourteen years away. In July, 1587, Essex was a very young favourite, ardently attached to his stepfather's interests. The Queen was staying with Lord and Lady Burleigh at Theobalds, and Essex was of the party. While he was writing to Leicester, she was shut up with some of the Council discussing the loss of Sluys: "She hath been long since with her Council," he wrote. "What is decreed I know not . . . I desired her . . . if they laid any matter to your charge, that she would suspend her judgment till she heard yourself speak. I will watch with the best diligence I can, that your enemies may not take advantage of your absence . . . Your son, most ready to do you service, Essex."

Parma now having possession of Sluys, his preparations for the invasion of England went on apace. Leicester at last added his warnings to those already disregarded by the Queen, that this was the Spaniards' intention. He heard that Parma had provided saddles, bridles and spurs for three thousand horse, and seven thousand pairs of wading-boots.

It had been said that Leicester's return was to be for a period of three months, and the relations between him and many factions in the States were now so bad that, disappointed, resentful and vindictive, he was most anxious to go back to England. Lord Essex, eager and devoted, begged the Queen that his stepfather might be recalled immediately, and the charm the young man exercised upon the Queen is reflected in the letter he sent to Leicester: in talking to him Elizabeth had even referred, not unsympathetically, to his mother. "May it please your Lordship," Essex wrote, "I have divers times since the receipt of your letters, but most earnestly this afternoon, dealt with the Queen for your Lordship's return. After she had heard me awhile and the reasons I could allege, she said that there was not a lady in the land that should more desire the news of your return than herself . . . many good words she gave of you, expressing her desire to have you here. I doubt not but within short time I shall so labour her mind that I will effect this to your Lordship's contentment. Oatlands, this first of September, 1587. Your son, most ready to do you service—R. Essex."*

The Queen's affection for Leicester was undoubted, and her personal wish to have him near her once again; but no sentiment altered her anger and sense of injury at not being able to get from him a proper financial statement. She said she paid muster-masters and an auditor, and she still could not get the accounts brought up to date. "Though it be continually alleged that great sums are due," she said, "yet why such sums are due, or to whom they are due, and who are paid, and who are not paid . . . is never certified."†

She again refused further supplies until a satisfactory audit should be produced, but the soldiers, who came to the ground between the Queen's sometimes not paying the money and their captains' cheating them when she did, were in the direst straits. A crowd of them,

* Cott: Galba D 11, f. 139. (MSS., British Museum.)
† Neale, *English Historical Review*, 1930.

ragged and nearly starving, were in London, and thirty of them besieged the gates of Greenwich palace. Lord Burleigh, commanding that they should not be allowed to molest the Queen, opened a fund to be used in sending them back to their homes; but the Queen heard of their presence at the palace gates, and directed that two of them should be brought in to give information to the Privy Council. Word was sent to Leicester of what they had said, and the reply came from his headquarters that these men's captains had been paid in full. On December 16th, 1587, the Council sent a direction to the Lords Lieutenant of the counties, telling them to send to Court "all such soldiers as were sent and served in the Low Countries . . . and if they could duly claim and show manifest proof for any wages behind and unpaid for their service . . . they should upon their repair to the Court be fully satisfied thereof."*

At the end of November, Mendoza heard in Paris that the Earl of Leicester was expected in England with the first favourable wind. At the beginning of December, the Earl was at Flushing waiting to go on board. He was excessively offended because the States sent no representatives to take a ceremonious leave of him. He wrote to his secretary, Mr. Atye, who was coming home after him: "God send me shortly a wind to blow me from them all!" On December 19th he landed at Margate, and here, as he sat in a room of the lodging that had been prepared for him, he slapped his legs and declared: "These legs of mine shall never again go into Holland. Let the States get others to serve their mercenary turn. Me they shall not have."† Information from London told Mendoza that the Earl was well received by his mistress, but badly by the public.

It was now felt that, with what appeared to be so unsatisfactory a record behind him, Lord Leicester should submit to some investigation of his conduct by the Privy Council; and persons so interrogated were expected to kneel until they were told they might stand up. The mere imagination of himself kneeling before his colleagues Leicester found too painful to be borne. When the possibility of such an examination was mentioned to him, he sought the Queen privately; he fell at her feet, where, he said, he was happy to prostrate himself, but he implored her not to submit him to the degradation of kneeling before the Council.

He was the same age as Elizabeth, but no one looking at them now would be likely to think so; he was stout, he was red-faced, his hair

* Neale, *English Historical Review*, 1930.
† Motley, *History of the United Netherlands*.

and beard were white, and he was apt to call himself her poor old servant. Elizabeth had serious faults, but she invariably felt, to an unusual degree, the claim of a long-lived friendship. It was doubtful if she had ever had many illusions about her lover; if she had, they had been lost long since. But her affection did not rest upon illusion; she had always loved him for what he was and in spite of what he was; she did so still. When he humbled himself before her and begged her to be kind to him, her heart was wrung. She promised him that no abasement should be demanded of him.

So it happened that, when the Councillors assembled at their table, Lord Leicester, with an air of haughty calmness, took his seat among them. To their somewhat pressing questions, he would answer only that he had proceeded on secret instructions from the Queen, which he was not at liberty to disclose to them.*

His feelings found expression in a medal which he caused to be struck, celebrating his retirement from the Low Countries. Camden described it as "a piece of gold . . . on the one side his picture, on the other . . . some sheep and a dog, who, going, turned back his head to look upon them (as it were for pity) with the inscription: I forsake, to my grief". The States were moved to a retaliatory gesture; this was a medal with, on the one side, an ape strangling her young in her embrace, on the other, a man avoiding smoke and falling into the fire.

The Queen, against everything that Burleigh and Walsingham could urge, was still hoping and half believing that a way would be found to settle the war between the Spaniards and the Dutch by pacification, and to avoid one between the Spaniards and the English altogether. Burleigh and Walsingham assured her with all the force they could command that Philip was determined to crush the States without granting any concessions, and that, whereas he had originally meant this to be a prelude to his crushing England, he now determined that the latter project should be undertaken at once and the former one finished at his leisure. The accuracy of their views would have been strikingly confirmed if they could have read a letter from the King of Spain to Parma at the end of 1587, telling him that he need not wait for the Armada before carrying his men across to England; let him land there right away, the King had no doubt he would give a good account of himself, and the Armada should bring him reinforcements as soon as it could. As he received no immediate reply to this astonishing proposal, the King assumed that Parma was in England already. When words to this effect reached Parma, even

* Camden, *Annals*.

the Duke's polished courtesy was for once lost in sheer indignation. On December 21st, 1587, he gave the King an unvarnished account of the enormous difficulties to be overcome. He held Antwerp and Sluys, but the enemy's ships prevented him from getting out of either port, and he was having to dig a canal to the open sea. The Channel itself was swarming with English ships, while on land the English were already making preparations to repel an invasion. He had collected transport-vessels, flat-bottomed barges, and as soon as a convoy was provided he was ready to move his forces in them, but to land an army in England without the protection of the Armada was a literal impossibility. To soothe the King, however, he added a description of the saddles, accoutrements and crimson velvet suits of the light horse and arquebus companies with which he was going to make his state entry into London.

In preparation for the Spanish occupation of England, advices were sent to Spain on the condition of English affairs. A list of "the principal heretics" was supplied. These were: the Earl of Leicester, the Earl of Warwick his brother, the Earl of Huntingdon his brother-in-law, Lord Burleigh the Lord Treasurer, the Earl of Bedford, Lord Hunsdon, Sir Christopher Hatton, and the Secretary Walsingham. "These," the writer said, "are the principal devils that rule the Court and are the leaders of the Council." The writer went on to list "the enemies of his Majesty in the city of York"; then he enumerated the Catholics of Norfolk. Among these was an entry considerably out of date. Sir Henry Bedingfield, who had had charge of the Princess Elizabeth at Woodstock, had died in 1583, but he was here put down as ready to serve, a slander on his memory, among those on the reputations of others still living. There was no doubt that Sir Henry Bedingfield was the person meant, for the writer said he was formerly the guardian of the pretended Queen of England, during the whole time the Spanish King was in England. "I wish to God," exclaimed the writer, "that they had burnt her then, as she deserved, with the rest of the heretics, who were justly executed".*

* C.S.P. Spanish.

XXVIII

On march 20th, 1588, Philip wrote to Parma that the Armada, completely equipped, was on the verge of putting out to sea. It would carry twenty thousand troops. Out of these Parma was to select six thousand to join his invading army; the rest would remain to guard the subjugated provinces. Parma made it clear that these six thousand would be essential to the success of the invasion. He told the King: "When we talked of taking England by surprise, we never thought of less than 30,000. Now that she is alert and ready for us, and that it is certain we must fight by sea and land, 50,000 would be far too few." The only way, he said, to induce the English to abandon their defensive preparations was to continue to use the blind of the peace negotiations.

Few people in the English government attached any credence to these, but, of those few, the Queen was one. Even Lord Burleigh now thought that war against Spain was inevitable, and that to enter upon it boldly was the least of great evils. The Queen thought war itself so great an evil that, before she would adopt it as a means, she had to be convinced that the only alternative was annihilation. Burleigh and his colleagues were so convinced; Elizabeth still thought diplomacy might save at the eleventh hour. Two months before, in January, 1588, a commission to treat with Parma had crossed to Ostend; its members were Lord Derby, Lord Cobham, Dr. Dale and Sir James Croft.

Throughout Croft's long and devious career, he had managed always to retain a certain measure of the Queen's confidence. He thought, now, that he alone of the commissioners knew what she really wanted, and that if, secretly, he could get Parma's assent to his proposals, the Queen would confirm them. Breaking away from his colleagues, he met Parma at Bruges on April 17th, and put before him in the Queen's name the following scheme: Holland and Zealand should be returned to Philip, but the latter should withdraw from the Provinces all Spanish troops. He should grant such degree of religious toleration as "in honour" he might, and undertake not to set up the

Spanish Inquisition in the Low Countries. In return for these concessions, and on the understanding that Spain would relinquish all hostile preparations against England, the English would give up to him the garrisons in their hands, including the all-important ports of Brill, Flushing and Ostend.

The new of Croft's doings reached the Queen's ear, and it was immediately plain that he had made a serious miscalculation. He received a letter from her Majesty, demanding "to hear upon what ground or reason you presumed to wade so far into such matters or receive any answer thereto without having any warrant or direction from us for the same", and the other commissioners were instructed to disavow Croft's actions. By mid-June, however, Walsingham informed Croft that the Queen was now satisfied that he had meant no harm, and had overlooked the great impropriety of his conduct. As it turned out, it was most unfortunate that this assurance should have been given.

The Armada put out to sea at the end of May, but storms and mishaps drove it back to Lisbon; meanwhile, in England the shires were directed to muster men at arms, and the landowners provided and equipped contingents from their servants and tenants. Preparations were made for barricading roads and destroying bridges, and a great chain of beacons was established on headlands and on hills to carry the alarm when it should be received, from Land's End up to Cumberland with the speed of light.

Elizabeth had neglected and refused to do much in the way of proper provision for war, for her whole mind had been set on efforts to avoid it, but one thing she had done; from the earliest years of her reign she had developed her father's policy of ship-building. The sight of her shipyards at Chatham had astounded the Frenchmen in Alençon's train; as they saw the prospect of the dockyards in perspective, with the masts rising like groves, they had exclaimed; Well might she be called Queen of the Sea! Howard of Effingham, the Lord Admiral, wrote to Burleigh of these ships: "I do thank God they be in the state that they be in; there is never one of them that knows what a leak means."

The shore preparations lagged sorely behind those of the navy. On July 22nd the re-formed Armada came out to sea once more, and on that very day the Earl of Leicester was appointed head of the land forces—Lieutenant and Captain General of the Queen's Armies and Companies. He was personally to superintend the defence of the Thames estuary, where, it was said, it was Parma's intention to make his major landing attack. Seven or eight miles inland the river takes a sharp curve northward, and broadens steadily till it runs out to sea. At the last point where the water is still only half a mile across, Tilbury and Gravesend face each other on the northern and southern shores. The Romans had kept a fort at Tilbury, and here Leicester was to establish his camp and to throw a boom across the river to Gravesend, made of boats, spars, chains and ropes. From Gravesend he wrote to the Privy Council on July 24th, thanking them for his appointment.

He got to work with thorough energy and good will, full of his usual self-confidence and assertiveness, and, unhappily, with his usual inability to work smoothly with any officer of ability greater than his own. Twenty-three thousand men were to be in camp with him; twenty thousand more were to encamp above Dover; while twenty-three thousand under Lord Hunsdon's command, based at Windsor, were to form the protection of the Queen's person. Some additional spirit was infused into this duty by a report which one of Burleigh's spies had brought from Cardinal Allen's mace-bearer. The Cardinal said that the Armada's commander, the Duke of Medina Sidonia, had received instructions from the King of Spain that Queen Elizabeth was to be captured alive, for she was to be taken to Rome, "to the purpose that his Holiness the Pope should dispose thereof, in such sort as it should please him". The Pope, Sixtus V, had, it was true, re-published the Bull of Pius V against "the pretended Queen of England", but he appeared to have, none the less, a statesman's generous appreciation of a distinguished fellow-practitioner. "She is a great woman," he said, "and were she only a Catholic she would be without her match." The Pope made another comment, of much interest to English minds. "Sorry as we are to say it," he said, "we ourselves have no great opinion of that Armada."

The Pope's estimate was the true one; but had the venture succeeded, had Parma been able to get ashore twenty-three thousand of his veteran troops, no one can assert what the outcome would have been, how far mere courage could have withstood them, or, if their foothold had once been established, how long the miseries would have endured.

On July 29th the Armada was at last within sight of the coast of Cornwall. The towering, undulating crescent of ships, seven miles across, was descried from the Lizard, moving so slowly that its advance was imperceptible, yet hour by hour coming clearer and loftier; it approached as the embodied form of the terrors that had menaced England for the thirty years of Elizabeth's reign. As twilight veiled the summer evening, the beacon flames sprang up, each one giving birth to the next, from Land's End to Margate and from the Isle of Wight to the Scottish Border. While the light flew northwards, summoning the militia to their posts, and Lord Howard of Effingham directed that the sixty ships riding in Plymouth harbour should put out to sea, a defence of immemorial antiquity was brought into action. Above the cliffs of Padstowe and of Minehead, animals with a head like a horse and a long body composed of a train of men, covered by a fringe of streamers, performed incantations and ritual dances, invoking the might of strange powers to drive away the approaching evil from English shores. The moon was growing to the full, but her light was intermittent through a swift-sailing cloudy wrack that warned of storms.

A week after it had been sighted, the Armada had made its stately way up the Channel, followed by sharp-shooting attacks from the nimble English vessels, and after a heavy engagement in the Solent on August 4th had anchored, on August 6th, in Calais Roads. The superiority of the English ships in speed and mobility had been so overwhelmingly shown that Medina Sidonia had sent continual messages to Parma asking not only for ammunition and for pilots but for forty fly-boats, saying that his galleons could not manoeuvre quickly enough in a contest with the swift-moving English ships.

Leicester was now digging entrenchments in Tilbury. He kept in almost daily touch with Walsingham, to whom he described the site of the camp as "a most apt place", not far from the old Roman fort, on a hill called West Tilbury. The soil, which was sand and gravel, was firm and dry, the hill commanded a view up and down the river valley. On July 25th he rode over to Chelmsford to inspect four thousand Essex men, whose martial bearing delighted him; but his troubles began almost immediately, of which the gravest were indeed not of his own making. He was angered and alarmed by the slowness of the Council, which but reflected that of the Queen, in implementing the necessary measures to repel invasion. He wrote to Walsingham on August 3rd: "Let no man by hope or other abuse prevent your speedy provision of defence against the mighty enemy now knocking at our gate." The train bands to come from London were not ready, the arrangements for those already under arms were shockingly defective. When the four thousand men from Chelmsford marched into Tilbury they were, he told Walsingham, "as forward men and as willing to meet the enemy as any I ever saw", but "on their arrival they had not one barrel of beer nor one loaf of bread, enough after a twenty miles' march to have discouraged them and brought them to mutiny". Only their high spirit and great good will kept them from this, he said. He had ordered victuallers to come to the camp and bring provisions for ready money, "but there is not one victualler come in to this hour". Leicester sent out forage parties to provision the camp, and at the same time ordered a thousand men who were about to come down from London not to move till they could bring their provisions with them. He found everywhere "causes to increase my opinion of the dilatory wants you shall find upon all sudden hurley-burleys". The army had been raised, so far as musters went, yet "how hard a matter it will be to gather men together I find it now. If it will be five days to gather these country-men, judge what it will be to look in short space for those that dwell 40, 50 or 60 miles off!" He complained too that the great nobles were recruiting their contingents at the expense of the army he was attempting to put under arms. The spirit of the noblemen was epitomized in Lord Shrewsbury, whom Elizabeth called "my very good old man", He wrote to her: "Your quarrel makes me young again; tho' lame in body yet lusty in heart, to lend your greatest enemy one blow and to stand to your defence every way wherein your Highness shall employ me." It was noble, but five hundred soldiers recruiting themselves under Lord Shrewsbury or Lord Pembroke, though it brought the great advantage that the Earls provided their equipment and maintenance, meant that the Captain General of the Queen's Armies and Companies had the harder work to fill up his numbers.

These were the complaints of an energetic commander, but Leicester evinced, as he had in the Netherlands, an inability to get on with able subordinates, and a touchiness on the score of his own dignity, which revealed his essential lack of poise. Sir William Rogers was his Master of the Horse, Sir John Norris his Marshal of the Camp. After Leicester's treatment of them both in the Netherlands, it was not surprising, however regrettable it may have been, that they were not completely loyal to his wishes now. Hearing that the Armada was in the Channel they had flown off to Dover, with, it is true, the pretext of inspecting the camp there, but with so much the appearance of schoolboys on a lark as left the Captain General resentful and indignant. He told Walsingham on the day after their departure: "I assure you, I am angry with Sir John Norris and Sir Roger Williams. I am here cook, caterer and huntsman. I am left with no one to supply Sir John's place as Marshal, but for a day or two am willing to work the harder myself. I ordered them both to return this day early, which they faithfully promised. Yet on arrival this morning I hear nothing of either. . . . I am ill used. T'is now 4 o'clock, but here's not one of them. . . . Seeing her Majesty hath appointed me her Lieutenant General, I look that respect be used towards me such as is due to my place."

Leicester, for all his physical eminence, his height, stateliness, vigour and readiness, never achieved the effortless authority that is typical of men used to command. His dignity was so precarious that even an inadvertent omission of respect he at once regarded as a deliberate injury. Lord Hunsdon's commission was a grievance to him. He wanted clauses put into it, reserving the supreme authority to himself. "Either it must be so," he told Walsingham, "or I shall have wrong, if he absolutely command where my patent doth give me power." Later in that day Sir Roger Williams came into camp again, bringing a message that Sir John Norris would be back some time in the evening. It was natural that Leicester should have been displeased by the behaviour of both these gentlemen; but Sir John Smith, another able and experienced soldier, cut an even worse figure in Leicester's letters to Walsingham. "After the muster [he] entered into such strange cries for the mustering of men and for the fight with the weapon, as made me think he was not well. God forbid he should have charge of men, that knoweth so little as I dare pronounce he doth!"[1]

There was, however, one magnificently successful feature of this camp, for which Leicester deserved the credit. His close association with Elizabeth, which for thirty years had been envied and decried, now bore golden fruit. It was true that it had only recently been proved that his knowledge of her character was by no means complete, but one thing he thoroughly knew; that was, the magical effect she created by a personal appearance, and he arranged for her to come down to Tilbury and let the soldiers see her.

From a letter which he wrote to her on August 6th it is clear that the idea, under a different guise, had originated with her, and she had written to ask him what he thought of it, and also what he advised about the muster of armed bands in London, which, it seemed, were not yet even called together, let alone under training. She had suggested that she should come down to the coast and place herself at the head of the troops above Dover. Leicester grasped the possibilities of the situation at once. First, however, he gave his advice about the army: "My most dear and gracious Lady," he wrote, ". . . it doth much rejoice me to find by your letter your noble disposition, as well as in presently gathering your forces, as in employing your own person in this dangerous action. And because it pleases your Majesty to ask my advice touching your army, and to acquaint me with your secret determination touching your person, I will plainly and according to my poor knowledge deliver my opinion to you." She must, he said, assemble at London as many troops as she could raise, especially of horse, and put them under training at once, "every man to know his weapon". As Motley said, on August 6th, when this letter was written, the Armada was already lying in Calais Roads, hoping to cross to Dover the next morning; considering the reputation of Parma's enemy, it was indeed time that in the English forces every man should know his weapon.

As to the Queen's proposal of joining the army at Dover, Leicester said at once that she must not go near the coast: "I cannot, most dear Queen, consent to that." But he saw that, properly handled, the idea of her presence was nothing short of an inspiration. He roughed out a suitable scheme. Her visit should be to Tilbury, and he thought she might stay at Havering Bower, a house that stood fourteen miles away; then he changed his mind and decided that Ardern Hall, at present let to Mr. Rich, would be the best place for her. It was very near the camp; he had it inspected by her usher, and assured her that it was "a proper, sweet, cleanly house". Here, he said, her camp would be within a mile of her and her person to be as sure as at St. James's.

On the night of August 7th the Armada, warned by the Governor of Calais that the Roads were full of treacherous currents and liable to sudden squalls, were still riding at anchor, waiting impatiently for some sign that Parma was about to emerge with his troops in their fleet of flat-bottomed boats. That no sign of him appeared was because the ships belonging to the Provinces kept him blockaded; he could get out neither at Brill, Flushing nor Ostend. So defective were communications that Medina Sidonia had received no information of this, and the Spanish were waiting in rising impatience, anger and alarm.

Their hundred and fifty enormous ships, of a tonnage never seen in Europe before, the prows so lofty they were said to look like floating castles, presented an awe-inspiring sight as rank behind rank they rocked and trembled on the tides. A mile and a half away the English fleet was anchored, watching them.

What the Duke of Medina Sidonia did not know, Lord Howard of

Effingham did not know either. The former hoped, the latter feared to see Parma's fleet of barges appear at any moment. A meeting was held on the Admiral's flagship, and it was determined that the Spaniards must be dislodged before Parma could effect a junction with them. To accomplish this, the English decided to use fire-ships.

In the darkness six blazing craft, their light reflected in the waves, bearing down upon the anchored galleons, threw the Spaniards into a panic. They cut their cables, and, in the grip of the currents, drifted upon each other. When Monday morning came several abandoned wrecks were floating on the sea; the rest of the Armada was going before the wind towards the Flemish coast. On this Monday was fought the battle of Gravelines, when the slaughter of the Spanish soldiers, tightly packed in their ships, unable to return or to avoid the English fire, was so dreadful that, as one of the galleons keeled over, blood was seen pouring from the scuppers into the sea. The Armada made its way all through Monday night towards the north coast of Zealand; before they could reach it, on Tuesday August 9th the wind changed, and drove them into the North Sea, where the English pursued them, but could not have fired another shot to save their lives for their powder was all spent.

None of this was at present known in England. The peril of invasion was believed to be imminent, and the Council was by no means unanimous that the Queen ought to be allowed to go to Tilbury. Walsingham wrote to Leicester on August 16th of "what we like of the Queen's repair to the camp, and what doubts are made of misadventures that may fall". But it seemed that she was going to carry out her plan. Walsingham, acting on his own responsibility, without the knowledge even of Burleigh, had risked the Queen's death by assassination, by delaying the arrest of the conspirators in Babington's plot; but the matter had been more or less in his own hands. Like a great surgeon he had done, under extreme necessity, what less accomplished men would not be justified in attempting. That was a different matter from entrusting her person to an armed multitude, under cover of whose ranks some traitor or fanatic might achieve by a pistol-shot what the whole Armada had put to sea to do; for Cardinal Allen had told everyone, in his "Admonition to the Nobility and People of England", that they must welcome and support the Spanish invasion; no harm was intended to them by it; the Spaniards were coming only to remove Queen Elizabeth, who, Allen explained to the English, could not be tolerated any longer without the eternal infamy of their whole country. Walsingham was personally the least attached to Elizabeth of all the Ministers of State; but, as Naunton said, "he was a watchful servant over the safety of his mistress". He wrote to Leicester now: "I mean to steal to the camp when her Majesty shall be there."

Leicester, in the face of any possible disapproval on the part of the Council, was determined that the Queen should come. "Good, sweet Queen," he had written, "alter not your purpose if God give you health."

The Queen did not alter her purpose. The Court was at St. James's, and on August 18th she went from there the next way to Thames, which was probably Westminster Stairs. Besides her clothes and properties there was conveyed to Tilbury, by water or land, a white horse with hind quarters dappled iron grey, which Lord Burleigh's son Robert Cecil had given her. The Queen herself, accompanied by ladies, entered the Royal Barge; this was customarily rowed by forty men in their shirts; musicians played on board when the Queen travelled by water,* and among the furniture of the glassed-in, gilded cabin was a red velvet rug embroidered in gold.† She arrived at Tilbury Block House on the water's edge at midday. Leicester had always a sense of occasion, a talent for pageantry. His welcome of the Queen was inspiring; as the barge was brought to shore guns were discharged, fifes and drums sounded, and, as Elizabeth stepped on land, at a signal, in one movement, all over the camp, the companies' ensigns were raised in air.

The grass had been trodden away, and rows of huts had been erected, of poles twined with green branches, bearing their drying leaves. Inside these, the floors were spread with straw, and tables had been made from piles of turf. The Queen was brought into the middle of the camp in a coach which was painted "chequerwise" with an appearance of emeralds, diamonds and rubies; the stones were lustrous, for Aske who was present, spoke of the "sparkling rubies", and said the coach

> Cast such a glimpse, as if the heavenly car
> Of Phoebus were, by those his foaming steeds
> On four round wheels drawn all along that way.**

In the middle of the camp, Sir Roger Williams met the Queen with two thousand horse. Ordering one thousand to precede the coach and the other to follow it, he escorted her off the ground and away

* C.S.P. Venetian, January 23rd, 1559.
† Von Klarwill, *Queen Elizabeth and some Foreigners.*
** James Aske, *Elizabetha Triumphans.*

to Ardern Hall. Aske says very few soldiers on this occasion saw the
Queen herself; those who caught a sight of the strange brilliant coach
thought themselves fortunate. As it passed along, the ranks, who
could see nothing, kept up a continual shouting of "God save the
Queen!"

Next morning the Queen returned to the camp, for the function
she had come to perform. This was, to review the troops. For part of
the ceremony at least she was on foot, walking through the lines, for
Camden said she walked up and down, "sometimes like a woman,
sometimes with the countenance and pace of a soldier". But for the
celebrated episode of the day she rode on the white horse. The sleeves
and the great skirts of her dress were visible, but a polished steel
corselet covered her from neck to waist; and though she was bare-
headed a page carried on a cushion a helmet with a white plume.

She had been for months, amounting to years, in a state of neurotic
indecision, evasion, caution and sheer terror; but now that the time
had come the men who saw her on her white horse, in her silver-
shining breast-plate, saw only the firmness and brilliance of her
courage. Members of the Council (for she described them as "some
that are careful of our safety") had urged upon her that she ran a
considerable risk in appearing as she did. She not only disregarded
their advice, but she stripped herself even of the ordinary sovereign's
escort.

> Her ladies she did leave behind her
> And her guard which still did mind her.*

Lord Ormond walked in front of her carrying the sword of state.

> Then came the Queen on prancing steed
> Attirèd like an angel bright.

Lord Leicester walked bare-headed at her bridle; the page followed.
With this notably scant attendance the Queen rode up a little eminence, and said what she had to say. Even in her hard, high voice, the
words cannot have reached far; but the sense of them was communi-
cated throughout the army. She told them, first, of the warning she
had received, not to trust herself to armed multitudes for fear of
treachery, but, she assured them, "I do not desire to live, to distrust
my faithful and loving people". Tyrants might fear; she had always,
under God, regarded, as her chiefest strength and safeguard, the
loyal hearts and goodwill of her subjects. Therefore, she said: "I

* Deloney, *A Ballad on the Armada.*

am come to live or die amongst you all, to lay down for my God, and for my kingdom and for my people, my honour and my blood even in the dust." The straightforwardness and the glowing passion of the words gave them an electric force: they welded together her spirit of determination and that of the men to whom she spoke. "I know I have but the body of a weak, feeble woman, but I have the heart and stomach of a king—and a King of England, too—and think foul scorn that Parma, or Spain, or any Prince of Europe should dare to invade the borders of my realm."

After this tremendous climax, she commended to them her Lieutenant General, "than whom never Prince commanded a more noble or more worthy subject; not doubting", she said, "that by your obedience to my General, by your concord in the camp and your valour in the field, we shall shortly have a famous victory over these enemies of my God, my kingdom and my people". Her words and her presence, Camden said, "fortified the courage both of the captains and the soldiers beyond belief". It was the greatest public occasion of the reign. The thirty years' tale of genius and devotion behind it made it what it was, but some thanks were due to the man who had imagined the scene, encouraged the Queen in her intention, kept her to her undertaking, and arranged the details of the occasion with the loyalty and gallantry of a great courtier and the skill of an impresario.

It was later in the same day, August 19th, while the Queen and her company were dining in Leicester's tent, that the Earl of Cumberland came in with news of the week-old event, of the Armada driven by storms up the east coast of Scotland. Elizabeth's speech had brought in the name of Parma with overpowering effect; the terror of the great general's reputation and the nearness of his power had made his name, at the time, a more potent symbol than that of the King of Spain. The amazing relief and thankfulness brought by the news of the Armada's flight was tempered by the rest of Cumberland's budget; the rumour was abroad that Parma was none the less coming; with six thousand horse and fifty thousand foot, he would come out on the highest tide of the season. For some hours this was believed. Walsingham wrote to Burleigh after dinner of "a conceit her Majesty had that in honour she could not return to London, in case there were any likelihood that the enemy should attempt anything. Thus your Lordship seeth that this place breeds courage!"

With further news, however, of the destruction of the ships which should have conveyed him across the Channel, it became tolerably certain that Parma was held up indefinitely, and the Queen's return to London was decided. The weather for the past few days had been hot and bright; but as the Queen entered her barge at the Block House and the cannon fired a salute, even as their echoes filled the valley, the skies darkened and she departed up the river under heavy clouds, thunder and torrents of rain. Leicester remained to strike camp, and to see the return to store, as the Council ordered, of all anchors, cordages, ropes and planks which had formed the boom. While he was so employed he had a letter from Lord Shrewsbury, and it was so kind a one that, starving secretly for the affection, approval and respect which he had put it out of most people's power to feel for him, Leicester answered it with an overflowing heart: "My dear, good Lord, I cannot sufficiently imagine how to render you thanks enough for your loving and honourable care of me, but it doth me so much good to hear oft from you and specially in this so noble and kind manner as I can no way express it but only with so just and so assured good will as never to fail you while I live." He had been too busy to write before. "Our gracious Mistress hath been here with me to see her Camp and people, who so inflamed the hearts of her good subjects as I think the weakest person among them is able to match the proudest Spaniard that dares now land in England." Being now "full of business", he ended, "I will take leave and commit my dearest good Lord and friend to the Almighty".

At the Queen's return to London, the victory was celebrated with a series of tournaments and reviews. The sense of deliverance found vent in splendid public rejoicings. Their elation and thankfulness was matched by Elizabeth's own. She wanted, it seems, to make a gesture of trust and affection, honouring the man who had held out with her so long, and who had been at her side, supporting and admiring her, in one of the most keenly-lived hours of her existence. The story went that she meant to create the Earl of Leicester Lord Lieutenant of England and Ireland, a post of greater power and influence than had ever yet been conferred upon a subject; that Burleigh, Walsingham and Hatton, regarding the appointment as dangerous in itself and particularly so if bestowed on Leicester, entreated and at last persuaded her to relinquish the plan. The story is sometimes denied on the ground that it rests on no authority but Camden's. Camden, however, was a protégé of Lord Burleigh's, and allowed access to his papers; it is difficult to think whose authority could be greater, except that of one of the four persons directly concerned. It does, indeed, seem unlikely that Elizabeth, so jealous of any encroachment on her power, should have seriously considered placing so much authority in the hands of a subject. Perhaps she spoke merely of some such thing, and the three Councillors had no hard task to deflect her impulses back again into their usual current. At all events, the appointment was not made, and Camden said that as a result Leicester's mortification was furious and bitter.

But when the great Earl came back to London in the last week of August, to the eyes of the populace he must have seemed at the apex of such glory as neither cares nor disappointments could touch. A writer of "Advices" from London to the Spanish Embassy at Paris said he saw Lord Leicester coming up from Wanstead, and that he went "all through the city", as he would have to go; for, since he came in from Wanstead on the east of London, the city lay between him and Leicester House and the palaces beyond the city's western boundary. "He was accompanied," said the writer, "by as many gentlemen as if he were a king, and followed by his household and a troop of light horse. He was going from a country house of his to St. James's and was quite alone in his coach."

The days he spent in London marked a halcyon period in his relations with the Queen. The defeat of the Armada afforded, indeed, but a breathing space in the endless struggle, but it was a great and glorious gain; it created a brief pause when the past, with its shared memories of thirty years and more, threw a nimbus about the present's brilliant scene. Whatever anger he secretly nourished against others, his intercourse with the Queen was steeped in the tranquillity and the golden hues of an Indian summer:

> *The setting sun and music at its close*
> *As the last taste of sweets, is sweetest last.*

The same news-writer who had reported Leicester's triumphant progress through London heard it said that he dined every day with the Queen—a thing hitherto unheard of in connection with anybody. His malaria was taking him again, and the Queen, who was ailing herself, discussed his symptoms with him and suggested a specific. The writer had his last sight of the Earl in an appearance that was almost symbolic. Among the festivities with which the Court was celebrating the victory, the Earl of Essex held a review in the tilt yard at Whitehall. Stands for spectators lined three sides of this arena; the fourth side was occupied by the palace wall, in which, on the first floor, was a great window from which the Queen and her party could look down upon the spectacle. "The last time I saw him," said the writer, "was at the Earl of Essex' review, at the window with the Queen."

On August 27th the Earl left London for Buxton;* it was a couple of months later than his usual time for taking the waters, and he was already feverish and ill. His wife accompanied him, and their travelling equipage no doubt drew the eye of everyone in the streets, if not the enthusiastic homage. Leicester's unpopularity had always been great, and there was no sign that even the events of the last few weeks had removed the general distaste of him. In one place, at least, feeling against him amounted to a rage of hatred.

In a room in one of the prison quarters of the Tower, Sir James Croft was sitting. He had been assured by Walsingham before he came back from Ostend that the Queen had overlooked his dubious conduct; but on his return to London Lord Derby had had an interview with Lord Burleigh, and, as a result, Burleigh had committed Croft to the Tower. His quarters were comfortless and insanitary, and he ascribed the disappointing change in his fortunes to the powerful Earl who had long shown himself his ill-wisher. The old man himself, though bitter, was resigned. He trusted to the Queen's loyalty to an old servant to release him in the end, as in fact it did; but his son Edward Croft was wild with anger and burning for revenge. The villain who had persecuted his father appeared to be beyond the reach of retribution at the hands of human agents, and young Croft determined to invoke other forces.

Whether or not Lord Leicester had a hand in consigning Croft to prison, it was Lord Warwick's view that his brother would be able to get the prisoner released. Two days after Leicester's leaving London, Warwick wrote to him from St. James's: "My very good brother, I cannot but choose but even in very pity, among the rest, be a mean to your Lordship in the behalf of Mr. Comptroller, for your good favour to help towards his enlargement, or at least that he may be moved to some sweeter place. His age is great and his case lamentable, considering the course he hath run from his youth." Lord Warwick urged his brother to have consideration for the prisoner's "weak years". He said there could be no greater honour than "to forgive and help raise up such as are fallen so deeply, as of themselves they are in no hope to rise again". He was sure his brother

* It is sometimes said that his destination was Bath; but as he went to Rycote and Cornbury, and was understood to be making for Kenilworth, he was travelling north from London all the time.

would be "like himself" in this matter, "pitiful to them that yield themselves to mercy".*

Whether Lord Leicester would, on his return, have been moved by his brother's persuasion or no, when the letter was written he was two days' journey away from London. He was followed by another letter, eager and devoted, from Lord Essex, written the day after his departure. The Queen had invited Essex to occupy Leicester's lodging at St. James's, "which", the young man wrote, "I will forbear to do till I know your Lordship's pleasure, except the Queen force me to it. And so, offering to you my best service now or at any time else, I humbly take my leave. Your son, to do you service. R. Essex." Lord Warwick and Lord Essex were not the only ones who sent communications to the Earl while he was on his journey. The Queen sent a little present, "a token" to his stopping-place at Rycote. Here he had been given the rooms the Queen used to occupy. He wrote her an affectionate letter on the morning of August 29th, just before setting out on the next stage of his journey:

"At Rycote, August 29. I most humbly beseech your Majesty to pardon your poor old servant to be thus bold in sending to know how my gracious lady doth, and what ease of her late pain she finds, being the chiefest thing in this world I do pray for, for her to have good health and long life. For mine own poor case, I continue still your medicine, and find it amend much better than with any other thing that hath been given me. Thus, hoping to find perfect cure at the bath, with the continuance of my wonted prayer for your Majesty's most happy preservation, I humbly kiss your foot, from your old lodging at Rycote, this Thursday morning, ready to take on my journey. By your Majesty's most faithful, obedient servant, R. Leycester." There was a post-script: "Even as I had writ thus much I received your Majesty's token by young Tracey."

He went on to Cornbury, to the Ranger's Lodge in the midst of the timbered park, whose trees deepened all around into woods. Here he made a stay of nearly a week, for the journey from Rycote can scarcely have taken more than a day, and he had not left Cornbury on September 4th. He was perhaps feeling too ill on his arrival to go forward as soon as he had intended. It is a feature of malaria that if it is not checked the attacks increase in severity; this one proved the challenge that his constitution could not meet. "Of a continual burning fever, as 'twas said",† he died, in the dark panelled room

---

* Dudley MSS., Longleat, quoted by Tenison, *op. cit.*
† Camden, *Annals.*

overlooking the trees, on the morning of September 4th, 1588.

The story current about his death is worth repeating only to contradict it. Two editions of *Leicester's Commonwealth* were published in the reign of Charles I; the second had attached to it a set of doggerel verses called "Leicester's Ghost". Bliss, the early nineteenth century editor of Wood's *Athenae Oxonienses*, says that there came into his hands a manuscript copy of "Leicester's Ghost", to which had been attached a contemporary manuscript account of Leicester's death. The fragment was, apparently, undated and anonymous, but the writer states that he had the most important part of his information from Mr. William Haynes, once Lord Leicester's page, and his Gentleman of the Bedchamber at the time of the Earl's death. The story says that Leicester was jealous of Christopher Blount's intrigue with Lady Leicester before he himself had left the Netherlands, and that, while there, he had made an abortive attempt to have Blount assassinated. Lady Leicester and Blount together connived to revenge this attack. "The Earl," says the manuscript, "not patient of this great wrong of his wife's, purposed to carry her to Kenilworth and to leave her there until her death, by natural or by violent means, but rather by the last." Lady Leicester had secret intelligence of his scheme, and before setting out on the journey provided herself with a poison, which she had no opportunity to administer until they came to Cornbury. Here the Earl, "after his gluttonous manner, surfeiting with excess of eating and drinking, fell so ill that he was forced to stay there". William Haynes "protested" to the writer that while Leicester lay ill he, Haynes, "saw her give that fatal cup to the Earl which was his last draught, and an end of the plot against the Countess, and of his journey, and of himself".

The basis of fact in this story can fairly easily be separated from the growth of invention. Leicester went to Cornbury, he lay ill there. The marriage the following year of Lady Leicester with Christopher Blount appeared to confirm any rumours about them. This document is the only source of information; but, since the account it gives of Leicester's journey could have been readily disproved if not true, it is reasonable to believe that Lady Leicester was with him, and that, on leaving Cornbury, they intended to stop at Kenilworth on their way through Warwickshire, up into Derbyshire. If Lady Leicester were with her husband, on only outwardly decorous terms, then, while he lay ill in bed, suffering from a high fever, Mr. Haynes, as one on duty in the bedchamber, would almost certainly, unavoidably, have seen her give the patient something to drink. That Leicester had conceived such a sense of injury as to attempt to have Blount murdered seems completely disproved by the tone of his Will, which he wrote in August, 1587. It appears still more improbable that he intended any harm to his wife; Camden's comment upon his second marriage was, "much given to women, and finally, a good husband in excess". The unlikelihood of Lady Leicester's having poisoned him can be yet more plainly demonstrated. Had such a charge been brought home to her, it is not easy to say how surely she could have relied on the Queen's clemency to have the sentence commuted. The statutory penalty for women convicted of poisoning their husbands was burning alive.

The news was brought to Elizabeth, and she received it in the way that was characteristic of her. Though public, even to indiscretion, in her pleasures and enjoyments, all her life she made a private thing of grief. Only when she was old and weak, and had lost Burleigh, did the tears run down her cheeks when others named him; such mourning could not then be controlled; but usually she wept alone. Over this friend, hid in death's dateless night, her silence at last alarmed those about her. She retired into a chamber by herself; hours, a day, a night, another day passed, and she would let no one in. At last Lord Burleigh acted. Taking some of the Council with him, he ordered the door to be broken open.*

The Earl had always been a target for rumour and scandal, and the news of his death, so totally unexpected, caused a nine days' wonder. He who had been frequently accused of malpractices was naturally declared to have been a victim of something of the sort himself. Among the stories flying about, one at least received such credence that it was investigated by the Privy Council. Edward Croft and John Smith were interrogated, to test the accusation that they had conspired to procure the Earl's death by sorcery.

Croft's story was that, after his father was committed to gaol at Lord Leicester's instigation, he himself, at his house at Charing Cross, lamented his father's fate to some of his friends, including "Smith", and "Pilley's wife", Anne. Smith undertook to help Sir James Croft, but said he must have the names of the Privy Council, all of which Croft wrote down for him. Smith went out of the room with it, and "within a whistle" returned, saying the Earl of Leicester was the great enemy. Another list of names, on a more comprehensive scale, was prepared and sent to Smith's house by Anne Pilley; when she brought it back there were crosses against the names of all whom

* C.S.P. Spanish.

Smith said were Sir James' friends: the rest were his enemies. Another witness, George Lewis said: Mr. Croft came to Smith and said: "Now Leicester goes a journey into the country." Smith said: "He doth indeed, but he shall never return." Smith, examined, stated: "After the Earl was gone into the country I came into Mr. Croft's house and he said, that one of the Queen's physicians was come up from the Earl, who did report that he was sick." And Smith said: "Yea the Lord help him, for he is sick indeed. And now is the bear muzzled that was Mr. Croft's enemy." Pilley's wife said, the Earl was not dead. "No?" said this examinant. "Then I will be hanged." Then it seemed as if Smith could see the sands of the hour-glass running out; for he had said, "if he had £1,000, he could help the Earl, yet—and yet—and yet. Then he said, all the world could not help him. And the next news came, that the Earl was dead."

Sir James Croft was exonerated from any responsibility for these doings, and finally his son and Smith were let go. The latter appeared after all to have done nothing but give a remarkable demonstration of clairvoyance. A law had, it was true, been passed in 1563, for the suppression of soothsayers, necromancers, sodomites, coiners and perjurers; but this had not affected Dr. Dee's practice in court circles, and perhaps Smith profited by the same tolerance.

Within twelve days of the Earl's death, the Countess had secured probate of his Will. Like Philip Sidney's, this had been made without legal advice while the testator was in the Netherlands, and, like Sidney's, it was found in some respects imperfect, to the disadvantage of some of the legatees. The interest of the document is that, besides showing the extent of Leicester's great property, it is a personal expression of himself, or, as its overflowing graciousness may suggest, of the image of himself that he wished to present. He began it by saying: "First I take it to be the part of every true Christian to make a true testimony of his faith at all times and especially in such a case and such a time as this is." There follow some four hundred words of a statement of his beliefs as a Christian. The whole document[1] is, necessarily, very long, but although a few sentences here and there are incoherent the style is vigorous, colloquial and emotional.

He discusses first his own burial: "And for the place where my body should lie, that is hard to appoint, and I know not how convenient it is to desire it, but I have always wished as my dear wife doth know, and some of my friends, that it might be at Warwick, where sundry of my ancestors do lie."

As to his bequests: "They cannot be great . . . I have always lived above any living I had (for which I am heartily sorry), lest that through my many debts from time to time some men have taken loss by me."

He appointed Lady Leicester executrix, and Lord Howard of Effingham, Lord Warwick and Sir Christopher Hatton "to help, assist and comfort my dear and poor disconsolate wife", who, he said, "shall need this good favour and assurance of my good friends"; though he was loth to trouble them with his broken estate, "being I know not how many thousands above 20 in debt, and at this present not having the world £500 towards it".

He wrote some sentences of fervent gratitude to the Queen, for "advancing him to many honours" and "maintaining him many ways by her liberality". He had prepared an ornament to give her next time she came to Wanstead, but now he directed that it should be given to her on his death. It was a gift entirely suitable to the woman whose taste he had studied for thirty years: a pendant formed of three great emeralds, arranged, with diamonds, around a large table-diamond, and hung upon a rope of six hundred "fair white pearls".

"Next to her Majesty," he went on, "I will return to my dear wife, and set down for her that which cannot be so well as I would wish it but shall be as well as I am able to make it, having always found her a faithful and very loving and obedient careful wife, and so I do trust this Will of mine shall find her no less mindful of my being gone, than I was always of her, being alive."

Leicester then disposed, in detail and with much care for individual interests, of his great possessions. Though he was at a stand for ready money the tale of his lands, manors and leases made remarkable reading. The chief beneficiaries under the Will were Lady Leicester and Lord Warwick; his son Robert Dudley, who in every mention is called "my base son, Robert Dudley", was to inherit largely, but only after the death of the other two, or, in some cases, when he himself was twenty or twenty-one years old, till which time Lady Leicester was to hold property ultimately destined for him. In the year the Will was drawn, 1587, Robert Dudley was thirteen years old; there must have been provision made already for his support during the next eight years.

Lady Leicester was richly left. The chief items in her property were the house and manor of Drayton Basset in Staffordshire, the manors of Balsall and Long Itchington in Warwickshire, and Wanstead House, with all the lands "reserved purposely to be joined to the

Park at Wanstead" and all the lands and tenements Leicester owned in the wardship of Wanstead. All plate and jewels not otherwise bestowed were hers, and all the contents of Wanstead House and half the contents of Leicester House. The other half of the stuff here was to remain with the house, and the latter was to be hers for life, then to go to Robert Dudley, and, in default of heirs, to devolve on Lord Essex. Such lands as had come to Leicester from the long-disputed lawsuit with Lord Berkeley were to go to Lord Warwick, and as they had come "by descent" these were not, after Warwick's death, to go to the illegitimate son, but to the family's heir, Robert, the younger brother of Philip Sidney.

Robert Dudley was to have, at the age of twenty, the house and lands of Aldersbrooke that adjoined Wanstead Park, and Lady Leicester was asked to give him "the great Pond" before the door of Aldersbrooke House, as the pond was part of the manor of Wanstead.* At her death Dudley, as stated, was to have Leicester House; at Lord Warwick's death he was to have the castle and lands of Kenilworth, and the manors of Denbigh and Chirke. His father, though denying him legitimate birth, meant to provide for him according to his blood, and after the death of Lord Denbigh had perhaps transferred to the bastard the intentions he had once cherished for the lawful son. The year after Leicester's death, Charles Paget wrote to his agents in England to know, "what party Arabella and her friends adhere to, and how they mean to bestow her in marriage, seeing Leicester's intention to match her with his bastard is frustrate by his death?"

The Will was proved on September 16th; but by that time the Queen had collected herself. She had remained hidden while she endured the hours of anguish; now she came out into the world again, in possession of all her faculties.

The fact that faced her was that, of the £50,000 to which Leicester's debts amounted at his death, he owed the Crown £25,000. Camden said: "The Queen, who was flexible enough in all other things, was hardly even seen to remit anything due to her treasury." Besides this principle, she was possibly inspired by her hatred of Lady Leicester. She declared at once that the Earl's goods must be sold by public auction. It was for this purpose that the inventories were prepared of the contents of Leicester House, Wanstead and Kenilworth. It is difficult to say on what system the goods were chosen for sale.

* Reminders of Leicester's property remain in Wanstead in the names Aldersbrooke Road and the Lake House.

Presumably the Queen's command overrode any provisions of the Will; but the inventories do not cover all the contents of the houses, as is clear from a reading of them; and the jewels would appear not to have formed part of the auction, for a list remains called "A remembrance to show how my Lady hath been rid of her jewels",★ which shows how Blount sold some of them, in every year of his marriage to her. The sum raised by the auction was £29,000, and, though this would have repaid the Crown, the Queen was only one of the creditors. The "Remembrance" says that Lady Leicester had been obliged to pay £50,000 of her late husband's debts; of these she had paid the Crown £22,000 by the end of Elizabeth's reign; the outstanding £3,000 was remitted by James I.

The countess's fortunes, so far as they were injured, suffered not so much from the payment of the Earl's debts as from the extent to which her third husband havocked upon her property. The Remembrance, after noting that Sir Christopher Blount had sold many of her magnificent pieces of jewellery every year, "how he bestowed them, God knoweth", then shows the really serious injury he did to his wife's estate, and how rich this had been. Blount sold a lease in Kent of eight or ten thousand pounds, a lease of fifty years of Grafton pastures, worth £400 yearly above the rent, the lordship of Bennington, worth better than £300 a year, and the inheritance of Wanstead, better worth than £300 a year. However, Lady Leicester appeared fully contented with her bargain. In 1597 Sir Christopher Blount joined Lord Essex in the expedition to Fayal, and when the latter told his mother he was glad of Blount's assistance she replied, "You thank me for my best friend . . . nothing could get him from me, yourself excepted."†

Despite the picture of his poor disconsolate widow evoked by Leicester in his Will, his debts and the forced sale left her in no frame of mind to make any financial sacrifice to his wishes. In the Will, Leicester had dealt with the Hospital at Warwick: "I do think," he wrote, "I have fully accomplished the same, of £200 by the year, of sufficient land and rent, for the maintenance of the Master and poor men." If he had not, then Lord Warwick was to make up the deficit out of the manor of Hampton in Worcestershire. If it were not needed for this purpose, Warwick was to have the manor for himself, unless it were earmarked for part of Lady Leicester's jointure —writing extempore, the Earl could not recollect; but, if it were, he

★ Nichols, *Progresses of Queen Elizabeth.*
† Birch, *Reign of Queen Elizabeth.*

was sure she would not object to its being used to make up the revenue of the Hospital, so long as the amount of her jointure did not suffer. Then he said, he hoped she would feel moved to increase the charity and to add to it a provision "for some number of poor women", to match his for the poor men, "such as shall be not idle but to be set on work for making linen cloth or such like", and he hoped the scheme would not be the less acceptable to her in that it would join her name with his in finishing what he had begun. Leicester's flourishing pen had never run on to less purpose. So far from burdening herself with poor women, Lady Leicester even refused to disgorge £200 of ready money which the Earl had left the Hospital "for a stock to relieve their necessities". Two years after his death the Master, Thomas Cartwright, wrote to Lord Burleigh for assistance; the affairs of the Hospital were for the time being in dire straits, and Cartwright was having to advance money from his own resources, "considering," he said, "the Hospital cannot obtain of the Countess of Leicester any whit of the legacy of £200".*

In the same year, the Countess showed an audacious instance of rapacity. In 1590 Lord Warwick died, and the sixteen-year-old Robert Dudley became the owner of Kenilworth. Before the young man could take possession of his inheritance, Sir Christopher Blount made a forcible entry and occupied the castle; it required an order from the Privy Council to dislodge him. It had naturally been galling for the Countess that the fabulous castle, with its fields, waters and woods around it, and the brilliant riches within it, of which she had once been mistress, should go to the youth whose very existence the death of her own child had made hateful to her. Here, however, the law was on Robert Dudley's side, and the Countess was obliged to leave him in possession of what his father's Will had given him. In their next contest, the young man took the fall.

After Queen Elizabeth's death, in May, 1603, Robert Dudley began a process of attempting to prove that his father and mother had been legally married. The Court of Audiences at Canterbury gave him permission to interrogate witnesses at his father-in-law's house, Stoneleigh in Warwickshire. He then brought an action in the Consistory Court of Litchfield against one Buswell, for calling him a bastard. While he was making these approaches, news of his doings reached the Countess, who acted with formidable speed and competence. In February, 1604, she filed a bill in the Court of Star Chamber against Robert Dudley, his father-in-law, and his mother, Lady

* Strype, *Annals.*

Stafford, for conspiracy and defamation, since their object was to prove her not legally married to the Earl of Leicester. The following year the Court of Star Chamber decided that the means Robert Dudley had taken to establish his claim were illegal; Sir Thomas Drury, who had got up the action for him and collected the witnesses, was dead, but the three principal witnesses who claimed to have been present at the wedding, Henry Frodsham, Magdalen Salisbury and Owen Jones, were fined, and sentenced "for ever after to be held suspect in their testimonies", and all depositions and documents connected with the case were locked up, the Court ordering that they should never be produced again. The mass of documents* has been examined,** and no convincing proof ever extracted that a legal marriage took place; but it must be said that the legality of the marriage never came to trial: the Star Chamber proceedings were concerned only with the methods taken to prove it.

The ill-starred young man bore a strong likeness to the father who had injured him by begetting him. His countenance was a milder version of Leicester's, with very fair hair and beard. He had his father's height, and many of his father's qualities: "famous at the exercise of tilting, singularly skilled in all mathematical learning",† "above all, noted for riding the great horse . . . and for his being the first of all that taught a dog to sit in order to catch partridges".†† When the Star Chamber defended Lady Leicester's rights by locking up all evidence against them, Robert Dudley asked the King for a licence to travel for three years. It was granted, and, leaving his wife and several little daughters behind him, he went to Italy; his beautiful cousin Elizabeth Southwell, dressed as a boy, went with him, and they never returned. Dudley had a distinguished career as a navigator, explorer and naval architect, but separated both in place and time from the great country and the great era of his birth.

Lady Leicester flourished like the green bay tree. Sir Christopher Blount was beheaded at the same time as Lord Essex, for his part in the latter's rebellion in 1601. After this, the Countess felt it wiser to retire to the country altogether. She remained henceforward on her estate of Drayton Basset, and lived to become an active and highly thought of old lady, good to the poor and a brisk and benevolent grandmother to "the grandchildren of her grandchildren". She died, aged ninety-two, on Christmas Day in the morning.

She raised a soaring and resplendent monument to Lord Leicester

---

* Dudley MSS. at Longleat.   ** Warner, *Voyages of Robert Dudley*.
† Dugdale, *Antiquities of Warwickshire*.   †† Wood, *Athenae Oxonienses*.

and herself in the Beauchamp Chapel. Three grey marble pinnacles rise from its lofty apex, flanking and surmounting a massive entablature of the Garter bearing Leicester's motto, *Droit et loyal*, and crowned by a huge cinquefoil. Beneath is an alcove supported on two pairs of grey marble pillars, its lintel decorated with alternate ragged staves and cinquefoils in high relief. Within the alcove is an archway, its edge bordered with cinquefoils, and within this again a background of fluttering pennants and the rectangular tablet bearing the epitaph. The effigies of the Earl and Countess lie side by side, each with hands placed palm to palm. Leicester's figure is in armour, wearing the collar of the Order of St. Michael that he had received in that very church, and laid upon the furred lining of the Mantle of the Garter. The Earl's coronet has been wrenched away, leaving holes in the head with the beautifully engraved hair. On his left side the figure of the Countess lies in the coronet and mantle of a peeress.

The colours of the monument are those of the strong yet mild tones of natural marble, dark grey, silver grey and murrey; the background is a pale greyish blue, the border and the arc of cinquefoils a saffron clouded with pink. The figures themselves once displayed gilded coronets and scarlet-painted mantles.

The epitaph Lady Leicester caused to be inscribed states that she, "moeltissum uxor", the tenderest wife, out of her love and conjugal fidelity, caused the monument to be raised to the best and dearest of husbands. The erection of this elaborate and stately memorial could not possibly have been completed within a year of Leicester's death, that is to say until after her marriage with Sir Christopher Blount. The tablet, with its many superlatives, stands a few yards away from the tomb of Leicester's father, from whom he derived his ambitions, and a little further off from that of his child, in whom they ended. Spenser said in *The Ruins of Time:*

> He now is dead and all his glory gone
> And all his greatness vapourèd to nought,
> That as a glass upon the water shone
> Which vanished quite so soon as it was sought
> His name is worn already out of thought.

So it seemed to the poet, who was complaining that, three years after the Earl's death, none of all the writers who had lauded him as their patron had so much as written an elegy upon him. It was true that there was no public sign of mourning for Lord Leicester, but a memorial of him remains, more expressive of grief than the vast and towering structure in the Beauchamp Chapel. The letter he had written to Queen Elizabeth from Cornbury on August 29th was addressed on the outside: To the Queen's most excellent Majesty. Underneath this superscription appear these words, in the Queen's handwriting: *His last letter*.★

Camden said: "The Earl of Leicester . . . saw farther into the mind of Queen Elizabeth than any man": that he possessed more of her affection than any man, no one questioned. In their youth he had inspired her with a passion for himself, and he had kept it alive through thirty varying, tempestuous years; but at the height of even her youthful infatuation he had never held the first place in her mind and heart.

As a young Queen she had said: "I am already married to a husband, which is the people of England." As an old one she said the same thing. How, she one day asked John Harington's wife, did she keep her husband's love with such success? Lady Harington said, by behaving in such a way that he could not doubt *her* love for *him*. The Queen praised her good sense, then she went on to say: "After such sort do I keep the goodwill of all my husbands, my good people; for if they did not rest assured of some special love towards them, they would not readily yield me such good obedience."

The people were indeed assured of her special love. The faculty of communication was one of her most brilliant traits; and the ballad writers, with their infalliable instinct for popular feeling, showed again and again how the passion was recognized and returned. The *Song between the Queen's Majesty and England* of 1571, made her say: "*Here is my hand, my dear lover England. I am thine both with mind and heart*", and the theme was repeated in countless variations. In the Queen's latest years losses and griefs, of which Leicester's death was the first, came in a dread procession, the harder to bear because they came in age, when she turned her face away and cried at the mention of the dead Burleigh's name, and sat in the dark, wringing her hands, when Essex, a condemned traitor, was beheaded for high treason; but even the pains, in the last resort, did not mar the consolation of the great achievement. What she had wanted to be, most of all the world, was what she was: a great Queen whom the English people loved. Before this, all other desires faded; in the utter concentration upon this end, griefs were diminished and made endurable. The last time she addressed a parliamentary deputation, she spoke of her

★ Public Record Office, C.S.P. Domestic, 1581–90, Vol. CCXV, No. 65.

engrossing aim: "To content the subject, which is the duty that I owe", and of the great sheaf of praises laid at her feet, some of the simplest show best how the duty was fulfilled:

> *Elizabeth, Lord save!*
> *She is the jewel makes us glad,*
> *A greater good cannot be had,*
> *Whilst we have her, who can be sad?*
> *Elizabeth so brave!**

Who could be sad? they cried. The Queen herself was sad very often, with a heavy, despairing sadness; but in the realization of the heart's desire

> *All losses are restored, and sorrows end.*

* Furnivall, *Ballads from Manuscript Sources.*

BIBLIOGRAPHY

P.R.O.=Public Record Office.
H.M.C.=Historical Manuscripts Commission.
C.S.P.=Calendar of State Papers.

Adlard, G., *Amy Robsart and the Earl of Leicester*, London, 1870.
Aird, Ian, "The Death of Amy Robsart," *Eng. Hist. Review*, January 1956.
Ascham, Roger, *Letters and Works*, ed. J. A. Giles, London, 1865.
Aske, James, *Elizabetha Triumphans*.
Bell, H. N., *Huntingdon Peerage*, 2nd edn., London, 1821.
Birch, Thomas, *Memoirs of the Reign of Queen Elizabeth*, London, 1754.
Black, J. B., *The Reign of Elizabeth*, Oxford, 1959.
Blakiston, Noel, *Nicholas Hilliard*, Burlington Magazine, January 1954.
Bohum, Edmund, *Character of Queen Elizabeth*, London, 1693.
Bradford, C. A., *Helena, Marchioness of Northampton*, London, 1936.
Braybrooke, Richard, Lord, *History of Audley End*, London, 1836.
——*Diary and Correspondence of Samuel Pepys*, Vol. I, Appendix, 3rd ed., London, 1848.
Brookes, E. St. J., *Sir Christopher Hatton*, London, 1946.
Bruce, John, ed., *Correspondence of Robert Dudley, Earl of Leicester*, Camden Soc., 1844.
Cabala, Mysteries of State and Government.
Camden, William, *Annals of Elizabeth*.
Camm, Bede, *Lives of the English Martyrs*, Cambridge, 1929.
Chambers, E. K., *The Elizabethan Stage*, 1923.
Collins, A., *Sidney Papers*, London, 1746.
Collins' Peerage, London, 1812.
Copeman, W. S. C., *Doctors and Disease in Tudor Times*, London, 1960
D'Aubeuf, ed., *Ambassades Messieurs de Noailles en Angleterre*, Paris, 1763.
De la Ferrière, Artaud, *Projets de Mariage de la Reine Elizabeth*, 1882.
De la Mothe Fénélon, *Correspondance Diplomatique.*
Dictionary of National Biography.
Digges, Dudley, *Compleat Ambassador.*
Dillon, Viscount, *An Almain Armourer's Album*, London, 1905.
Dugdale, William, *Antiquities of Warwick and Warwick Castle*, Warwick, 1786.
Feuillerat, A., *Office of the Revels*, 1908.
Forbes, Patrick, *Public Transactions in the Reign of Elizabeth*, London, 1740.
Fox Bourne, H. R., *Sir Philip Sidney*, London, 1891.
Frere, H. T. Bartle, *Amy Robsart of Wymondham*, 1937.
Froude, J. A., *History of England*, London, 1870.
Furnivall, J. D., *Ballads from Manuscripts*, London, 1868.

Gairdner, James, "Bishop de Quadra's Letter and the Death of Amy Robsart," *Eng. Hist. Review*, 1898.

Goldsmid, E. M., *Letter from Leicester to Sussex*, Historical Tracts, 1884.

Greville, Fulke, *Life of the renowned Sir Philip Sidney*.

Halliwell, J. O., ed., *Diary of Dr. John Dee*.

Halpin, N. I., *Oberon's Vision*, Shakespeare Soc., 1843.

Hardwicke State Papers.

Harington, Sir John, *Metamorphosis of Ajax*.

——*Nugae Antiquae*.

Harrison, G. B., ed., *Letters of Queen Elizabeth*, London, 1935.

——*De Maisse, Journal*, London, 1931.

Harvey, Gabriel, *Letter Book*, 1573-1580, Camden Society.

Haynes, Samuel, ed., *Burleigh State Papers*, London, 1740.

Heutzner, Paul, *Travels in England*.

Hume, M. A. S., *Courtships of Queen Elizabeth*, London, 1904.

Hurstfield, Joel, *Elizabeth I and the Unity of England*, London, 1960.

Klarvill, V. von, *Queen Elizabeth and some Foreigners*, 1928.

Laneham, Robert, *Entertainment at Kenilworth* (*Nichols' Progresses of Queen Elizabeth*).

Leicester's Commonwealth.

Leland, John, *Collectanea*.

Lloyd, David, *State Worthies*, London, 1765.

Lodge, Edmund, *Illustrations of British History*, London, 1791.

Lysons, Daniel, *Environs of London*, London, 1792.

Lyte, H. C. Maxwell, *History of Eton College*, 1911.

Mattingley, Garreth, *The Defeat of the Spanish Armada*, London, 1959.

Morris, R. H., *Chester in Plantagenet and Tudor Reigns*, Chester, 1894.

Moss, W. E., *Bindings from the Library of Robert Dudley, Earl of Leicester*, privately printed, 1934.

Mounts, Charles E., "Spenser and the Countess of Leicester," *Journal of Eng. Lit. Hist.*, Baltimore, September 1953.

Motley, J. L., *Rise of the Dutch Republic*, London, 1855.

——*History of the United Netherlands*, London, 1867.

Mumby, F. A., *The Girlhood of Queen Elizabeth*, 1904.

——*Elizabeth and Mary Stuart*, 1914.

Murdin, William, ed., *Burleigh State Papers*, London, 1759.

Neale, Sir John, "Elizabeth and the Netherlands," *Eng. Hist. Review*, 1930.

——*Elizabeth and her Parliaments*, I, II, London, 1953, 1957.

Neustatter, W. Lindsay, *The Mind of the Murderer*, London, 1957.

Nichols, John, *Progresses of Queen Elizabeth*, London, 1823.

Nichols, J. G., ed., *Chronicle of Queen Jane*, Camden Soc., 1850.

Nicolas, N. H., *Life and Times of Sir Christopher Hatton*, London, 1847.

Ödberg, Fridolf, *Om Princessan Cecilia Wasa*, Stockholm, 1896.

Osborne, Francis, *Historical Memoirs on the Reigns of Queen Elizabeth and King James*.

Peck, Francis, *Desiderata Curiosa*, London, 1779.

Pennant, Thomas, *A Tour in Wales*, London, 1781.

Raumer, F. von, *Elizabeth and Mary Stuart*, London, 1836.

Read, Conyers, *Mr. Secretary Walsingham and the policy of Queen Elizabeth*, London, 1925.

——"A Letter from Robert Earl of Leicester to a Lady," *Huntington Library Bulletin*, April 1936.

——*Mr. Secretary Cecil and Queen Elizabeth*, London, 1955.

——*Lord Burleigh and Queen Elizabeth*, London, 1960.

Rosenberg, Eleanor, *Leicester, Patron of Letters*, New York, 1955.

Rowse, A. L., *The England of Elizabeth*, London, 1950.

——*The Expansion of Elizabethan England*, London, 1955.

Rye, W. B., *The Murder of Amy Robsart*, London, 1886.

Simpson, R., *The School of Shakespeare*, London, 1878.

Stevenson, J., *Selections from Unpublished Manuscripts*, Maitland Club, 1837.

Strickland, Agnes, *Lives of the Tudor and Stuart Princesses*, London, 1888.

——*Queen Elizabeth*, London, 1870.

Strype, John, *Works*, London, 1840.

Tenison, E. M., *Elizabethan England*, Leamington, 1951.

Tytler, P. F., *England under the Reigns of Edward VI and Mary*, London, 1839.

Wallace, M. W., *Life of Sir Philip Sidney*, Cambridge, 1915.

Warner, G. F., *Voyages of Sir Robert Dudley to the West Indies*, London, 1899.

Warrender Papers, ed., Cameron, Scot. Hist. Soc., 1931.

Wilts Archeological and Natural History Magazine, May 1877.

Wood, Anthony à, *History and Antiquities of the University of Oxford*, Oxford, 1792.

Wood, Thomas, *Puritan*, ed., Collinson, Letters, 1566–1577.

——Supp. No. 5, *Bulletin of the Institute of Hist. Res.*, November 1960.

Wright, Thomas, *Queen Elizabeth and her Times*, London, 1838.

REFERENCES

Page 19, 1.   Tytler, *England under the Reigns of Edward VI and Mary*.

26, 1.   *Chronicle of Queen Jane and Queen Mary*. Camden Society.

30, 1.   Tytler, *op. cit.*

33, 1.   *Leicester's Commonwealth*.

35, 1, 2.   *Ambassades en Angleterre de Messieurs de Noailles*.

36, 1.   C.S.P. Spanish.

40, 1.   C.S.P. Foreign.

40, 2.   Longleat MSS., *Wilts. Arch. and Nat. Hist. Magazine*, May, 1877.

44, 1.   P.R.O. Accounts Various, E.101/429/3.

48, 1.   Munby, *The Girlhood of Queen Elizabeth*.

53, 1.   *Wilts. Arch. and Natural Hist. Magazine*, May, 1877.

54, 1.   H. T. Bartle Frere, *Amy Robsart of Wymondham*.

59, 1.   *Wilts. Arch. and Natural Hist. Magazine*, May, 1877.

61, 1.   P.R.O. SP.12/24 ff., 104–107.

63, 1.   See Gairdner, *Eng. Hist. Review*, 1898.

65, 1.   *Leicester's Commonwealth*.

Page 66, 1.   Braybrooke, *Diary and Correspondence of S. Pepys*, Vol. 1. Appendix.

68, 1, 2. Braybrooke, *op. cit.*

69, 1.   Haynes, *Burleigh State Papers.*

69, 2.   *Wilts. Arch. and Nat. Hist. Magazine*, May, 1877.

69, 3.   Braybrooke, *op. cit.*

70, 1.   Bell, *Huntingdon Peerage*, 2nd ed.

71, 1.   *Wilts. Arch. and Nat. Hist. Magazine*, May, 1877.

71, 2.   C.S.P. Foreign.

73, 1.   Hardwicke State Papers.

74, 1.   C.S.P. Foreign.

76, 1.   Ödberg, *Om Princessan Cecilia Wasa.*

77, 1.   C.S.P. Foreign.

77, 2.   Strype, *Sir Thomas Smith.*

83, 1.   Strype, *Parker.*

83, 2.   Nichols, *Progresses of Queen Elizabeth.*

92, 1.   Forbes, *Public Transactions in the Reign of Elizabeth.*

95, 1.   C.S.P. Scottish, 1563–69, 233.

102, 1.   C.S.P. Foreign.

108, 1.   Nichols, *Progresses.*

108, 2.   Sir James Melville, *Memoirs.*

113, 1.   Wright, *Elizabeth and Her Times.*

144, 1.   Stevenson, *Selections from Unpublished Manuscripts.*

126, 1.   C.S.P. Spanish.

129, 1.   Von Raumer, *Elizabeth and Mary Stuart.*

135, 1.   Digges, *Compleat Ambassador.*

144, 1.   Nichols, *Progresses.*

146, 1.   P.R.O., LC9/62, f7.

146, 2.   Neale, *Elizabeth and her Parliaments*, Vol. II.

149, 1.   C.S.P. Foreign.

150, 1, 2. Stevenson, *Selections from Unpublished Manuscripts.*

162, 1.   MSS. British Museum. Harleian Roll, b35, I–XI.

163, 1.   Peck, *Desiderata Curiosa.*

164, 1.   H.M.C. Pepys.

168, 1.   Goldsmid, ed. Letter from Leicester to Sussex. Historical Tracts, 1884.

169, 1.   Goldsmid, *op. cit.*

171, 1.   C.S.P. Domestic, Addenda 1566–1579.

172, 1.   *Idem.*

175, 1.   *Idem.*

177, 1.   *Idem.*

178, 1.   à Wood, *History and Antiquities of the University of Oxford.*

184, 1.   Pennnant, *A Tour in Wales.*

185, 1.   Digges, *Compleat Ambassador.*

186, 1.   Nichols, *Progresses.*

191, 1.   Warner, *Voyages of Sir Robert Dudley.*

195, 1.   Murdin, *Burleigh State Papers.*

195, 2.   Chambers, *Elizabethan Stage.*

Page 201, 1.   Von Raumer, *Elizabeth and Mary Stuart.*
205, 1.   Nichols, *Leicestershire*, I.
205, 2.   H.M.C. Pepys.
221, 1.   H.M.C. Hatfield.
221, 2.   Lodge, *Illustrations of British History.*
222, 1.   C.S.P. Foreign.
222, 2.   *Idem.*
223, 1.   C.S.P. Foreign.
226, 1.   C.S.P. Foreign.
226, 2.   British Museum MSS. Harleian Roll, b35, I–XI.
230, 1.   C.S.P. Foreign.
230, 2.   Nichols, *Sir Christopher Hatton.*
233, 1.   C.S.P. Foreign.
233, 2.   Nichols, *Progresses.*
235, 1.   Tenison, *Elizabethan England.*
237, 1.   Morris, *Chester in Plantagenet and Tudor Reigns.*
242, 1.   Lodge, *Illustrations of British History.*
252, 1.   Harleian Roll, b35.
265, 1.   C.S.P. Domestic, Addenda, 1580–1625.
271, 1.   C.S.P. Spanish.
280, 1.   Von Raumer, *Elizabeth and Mary Stuart.*
281, 1.   *Idem.*
284, 1.   Harleian Roll, b36, I–XI.
285, 1.   Von Raumer, *op. cit.*
286, 1.   Nichols, *Leicestershire*, I.
286, 2.   C.S.P. Domestic.
287, 1.   C.S.P. Scottish.
288, 1.   Nicols, *Sir Christopher Hatton.*
295, 1.   Collins, *Sidney Papers.*
298, 1.   C.S.P. Domestic, Addenda, 1580–1625.
316, 1.   Bruce, ed., *Leicester Correspondence.*
317, 1.   Von Raumer, *op. cit.*
320, 1.   Bruce, *op. cit.*
322, 1.   Fulke Greville, *Sir Philip Sidney.*
232, 1.   Fox Bourne, *Sir Philip Sidney.*
324, 1.   Bruce, *op. cit.*
325, 1.   *Idem.*
326, 1.   Neale, *Elizabeth and Her Parliaments*, II.
328, 1.   *Warrender Papers.*
330, 1.   Conyers Read, *Lord Burleigh and Queen Elizabeth.*
331, 1.   *Idem.*
336, 1.   Pennant, *A Tour in Wales.*
351, 1.   Motley, *History of the United Netherlands.*
363, 1.   Collins, *Sidney Papers.*

INDEX